Chrysler
TorqueFlite
A-904 & A-727
TRANSMISSIONS

How to Rebuild

Tom Hand

CarTech®

CarTech®, Inc.
6118 Main Street
North Branch, MN 55056
Phone: 651-277-1200 or 800-551-4754
Fax: 651-277-1203
www.cartechbooks.com

Edit by Wes Eisenschenk
Layout by Monica Seiberlich

ISBN 978-1-61325-335-9
Item No. SA394

Library of Congress Cataloging-in-Publication Data
Names: Hand, Tom, author.
Title: Chrysler TorqueFlite A904 & A727 transmissions : how to rebuild / Tom Hand.
Other titles: Chrysler TorqueFlite A904 and A727 transmissions : how to rebuild
Description: Forest Lake, MN : CarTech, [2017]
Identifiers: LCCN 2016057962 | ISBN 9781613253359 (pbk.) | ISBN 9781613253559
Subjects: LCSH: Automobiles–Transmission devices, Automatic–Maintenance and repair–Handbooks, manuals, etc. | Chrysler automobile–Transmission devices, Automatic–Maintenance and repair–Handbooks, manuals, etc. | Chrysler automobile–Transmission devices, Automatic–Handbooks, manuals, etc. | LCGFT: Handbooks and manuals.
Classification: LCC TL263 .H37 2017 | DDC 629.2/4460288–dc23
LC record available at https://lccn.loc.gov/2016057962

Written, edited, and designed in the U.S.A.
Printed in China
10 9 8 7 6 5

Title Page:
The A-727 TorqueFlite is an engineering masterpiece that was used in some of the most powerful production muscle cars. Adding some of the best aftermarket components turns it into an almost indestructible transmission suitable for many applications!

Back Cover Photos

Top:
In an alternating fashion, knock each weight against the bolt head to free the pump. If no slide hammers are available, use a screwdriver or other prying device to wedge between the sun gear shell and the front clutch retainer or to tap on the rear side of the pump.

Middle Left:
The torque converter has an impeller integral in the housing, front cover, turbine, stator, ring gear, and, if it's a lock-up unit, a clutch and apply piston. This is a truck A-727 low-stall lock-up version.

Middle Right:
The low-reverse drum still inside the low-reverse band is splined to the inner race of the overrunning clutch. Slide the drum out; it may also pull the overrunning clutch inner race with it.

Bottom:
TorqueFlites were found in some of the best and most unique muscle cars. This 1970 AAR Cuda 340 6-barrel automatic (with TA Challenger engine notation decals) has only 34,000 miles on the original A-727.

DISTRIBUTION BY:

Europe
PGUK
63 Hatton Garden
London EC1N 8LE, England
Phone: 020 7061 1980 • Fax: 020 7242 3725
www.pguk.co.uk

Australia
Renniks Publications Ltd.
3/37-39 Green Street
Banksmeadow, NSW 2109, Australia
Phone: 2 9695 7055 • Fax: 2 9695 7355
www.renniks.com

Canada
Login Canada
300 Saulteaux Crescent
Winnipeg, MB, R3J 3T2 Canada
Phone: 800 665 1148 • Fax: 800 665 0103
www.lb.ca

CONTENTS

Preface 4
Acknowledgments 5
Introduction 7

**Chapter 1: History, Identification and Evolution of
the A-904 and A-727 TorqueFlite** 8
The Manufacturing Facility 9
Identification 9
Production Numbers and Transmission Identification 12
Evolution of the TorqueFlite A-904 and A-727 12

Chapter 2: TorqueFlite Components and Operation 15
The Components 15
The TorqueFlite in Operation 26

Chapter 3: Troubleshooting 33
Fluid Level 35
Shift Linkage 35
Throttle Pressure Linkage 35
Road Testing 38
Hydraulic Pressure Testing 39
Air Pressure Testing 44
Torque Converter Stall Testing 46
Noise Identification 46
Leaks 47
Summary 50

Chapter 4: Transmission Disassembly 51
General Safety 51
Tools, Chemicals and Miscellaneous Supplies 52
The Work Area 53
Cleaning for Disassembly and Inspection 54
Tearing It Down 58
Removing Subassemblies 59

Chapter 5: Component Preparation 73
Oil Pump 74
Front Clutch 79
Rear Clutch 85
Overrunning Clutch 90
Planetary Gear Assembly 92
Kickdown Servo and Band 94
Low-Reverse Servo and Band 95
Output Shaft, Governor and Parking Gear 96

Chapter 6: Control Valve Body Preparation 100
Pressure Control and Regulation Valves 100
Disassembly 101
Check Balls, Pressure Regulators, Transfer and
Separator Plate, Lock-Up Valve Assembly or
Stiffener and Filter 101
Shuttle Valve and Governor Plugs 104
Manual Lever and Throttle Pressure Lever 105
Shift Valves and Regulator Valve 109

Reassembly 109
Shift Valves and Regulator 109
Manual Lever and Throttle Pressure Lever 110
Shuttle Valve and Governor Plugs 111
Check Balls, Pressure Regulators, Transfer and
Separator Plate, Lock-Up Valve Assembly or
Stiffener and Filter 113

Chapter 7: Assembly 116
Subassembly Installation Tips and Pre-Assembly Tests .. 116
Air Checking Clutch Assemblies before Installation 117
Miscellaneous Component Preparation 117
Overrunning Clutch 120
Low-Reverse Servo 121
Low-Reverse Anchor, Band and Drum: A-904 122
Low-Reverse Anchor, Band and Drum: A-727 122
Planetary Gear Assemblies, Sun Gear and Sun Gear
Driving Shell 123
Kickdown Servo 127
Front and Rear Clutch Retainer 128
Kickdown Band 131
Oil Pump 132
Extension Housing 135
Air Checking Assemblies 137
Accumulator, Valve Body, Levers, Filter, Switch and Pan .. 138
Post-Install Procedure 141

Chapter 8: The Torque Converter 142
Torque Converter Basics 142
Details of a Continuous Cycle 146
Factors That Affect Converter Operation 148
Converter Issues 149
Factory Converters 150
Aftermarket Converters 153
Selecting a Converter 156

Chapter 9: Performance Modifications 158
Why Modify? 159
TorqueFlite Strengths 159
Modification Parts 161
Shift Modification Kits or Complete Valve Bodies 163
TorqueFlite Specialty Internal Part Upgrades 164
Friction Upgrades 170
Bands, Levers and Struts 173
Complete Overhaul Sets 175

Appendix A: TorqueFlite Transmission Numbers 184
**Appendix B: Troubleshooting Charts, Data and
Specifications** 195
**Appendix C: Performance Modifications and
Suggestions** 201

Source Guide 208

DEDICATION

Back in 1982, I wrote about the TorqueFlite and a young lady named Debbie typed it. She and I married and raised two wonderful daughters, Emma and Becky. In 2016, Debbie put off a lot of things while I again wrote about the TorqueFlite. I love her, our two daughters, and Matt and Brandon for having such patience.

PREFACE

I grew up in a family with three brothers and three sisters, a mom who was always home, and a dad who taught us how to work on things. I had a Kenner's Girder and Panel building set, a Gilbert Erector set, slot cars, model cars, model rockets, and progressed to bicycles, lawnmowers/go-karts, and cars. Dad was always a Pontiac guy, but in the late 1960s, he bought a 1969 Dodge Dart Swinger 340 automatic. I too bought a 340 Swinger, but mine was a 4-speed. His was quicker, but mine was faster. Of course, it was the TorqueFlite making his ET lower. Mark Poole and I took an automatic transmission class to learn about TorqueFlites.

Previously, I wrote three articles on the TorqueFlite for the Mopar Muscle Club International and the Walter P Chrysler Club. Around 1984, Kyle and his father, Dick Drake and I started the High Performance Auto Club for Chrysler products, which provided a source of Midwestern-based TorqueFlites for rebuilding and/or modifying. I was very fortunate to be able to rebuild some of the rarest ones ever made. In 1984, a trip to the Kokomo plant let me see how TorqueFlites were manufactured. And, a trip to Detroit provided time with Chrysler transmission engineers and one of the designers of the TorqueFlite, Mr. Bert Cartwright. Marriage in 1985 and family commitments took precedence, and time to wrench on transmissions diminished.

Fast forward to 2016. I was asked to consider putting together a book about the TorqueFlite and because I had some extra time, a wealth of publications, historical documents, training manuals, access to parts, and good friends to help, I agreed. I learned a lot (more) about this tremendous transmission and I hope you find this book to be interesting, educational, and beneficial.

Some friends leave lasting impressions because of their patience and generosity; Scott Thibault is one of them. Scott shared his transmission shop, tools, and his after-hours time to press bushings and teach me about transmissions. I owe him much.

Kyle Drake and I cruised the Kansas City streets; he was in his 1968 Roadrunner, I in my 1969 Dart. Kyle has always been one of my best Chrysler friends. He and his family trusted their Superbirds, Roadrunners, Little Red Express Truck, and other TorqueFlites with me. I am deeply indebted to Kyle and his late father and mother, Dick and Beverly Drake.

Bob Craighead, a terrific Service Trainer for Chrysler, shared information about A-904s, A-727s, and FWD A-404s/413s/470s and A-604s. Bob provided so much to me on his own time; I am honored to be able to use this book to share some of his wisdom.

Stuart Davis, one of my best Chrysler Corporation engineering friends, was instrumental in setting me on the right path with many of my projects; I thank him for the support on this one. John Donato, a "factory" TorqueFlite expert, provided valuable information and support years ago and again on this project. Thank you both.

Some books are boring without decent photographs and getting them requires skill. Brandon Waldrop suggested the hardware I should buy and he walked me though the basics of using it all. Dennis Hedberg took time to "dial me in." Paul Catlett and I worked together for years and when it comes to shooting inanimate objects with tough-to-see details, Paul is one of the best. I very much appreciate their help.

Being on the streets in some of the best years (late 1970s and early 1980s), people ended up in parking lots with owners of similar types of cars. Stuart Bays, Barry Spillman, Tom Palmer, Clark Riddle, and Mark Breeding were out and about in Mopars. When they needed transmission help, I was honored to have been allowed to "experiment" with theirs.

The FIRST (For Inspiration and Recognition of Science and Technology) organization exposes high school students to the technologies and skills needed in today's workplace. Designing, building, and testing 120-pound, 5-foot-tall robots in six-week build periods requires ultra-dedicated students. My daughters, Emma and Becky,

It is because of the generosity of my automotive friends over the last 37 years that I was able to amass all of the valuable references used for this book; thank you all.

were on their winning high school FIRST Team (#1987) and it was then (as a mentor) that I worked with the Team's CAD expert, Logan Smith. Because of his tremendous design and drafting skills, I asked Logan to help illustrate many sections of this book. Kenzie Settle, another FIRST Team #1987 member, was also responsible for the Team's CAD work, and she provided more of the illustrations. Logan and Kenzie, thank you.

One of the most honest repair shops (Steve's Auto Service) in the Kansas City area is run by the Hollo family: Steve Sr., Steve Jr., and his son, Joey. Since 1969, the shop has been known for its integrity and honesty. I married into the family and am forever grateful.

In the early 1980s, R. Michael Noe took the time to highlight a few parts I left out of an exploded view of an A-727. I wondered why he knew so much and learned that he was a final inspector at the Kokomo TorqueFlite Assembly plant. Michael arranged a tour of the Kokomo plant and he helped me throughout the years. I appreciate his help and friendship.

Mick Dobbins spent a lot of evenings in 1982 drawing the first diagrams that demonstrated what was on when the TorqueFlite was operating. His work was invaluable then and I appreciate even more now the time he spent with that drafting pencil.

Jerry McLain is a Chrysler parts expert and I asked him to help me complete the list of TorqueFlite numbers. Having collections of parts manuals on Microfiche, I knew he would help, and for the ones he lacked, he had a guy who helped fill in the blanks, Brent Piburn. Brent opened his machine shop and library so I could review and copy parts books and training publications. For newer numbers, I turned to a current parts manager, Mike Gibbons. These three (and Bob Craighead) helped me compile part numbers of TorqueFlites.

When you do anything with TorqueFlites, converters soon enter the conversation. I met Kris Abrahamson of Continental Torque Converters in the late 1980s. He was known for his ability to build converters that work amazingly at the strip but act like stock converters on the street. Kris always took time to talk converters with me and before his recent retirement, he spent a lot of time doing so again. I owe much to Kris Abrahamson.

Rob Hall is "the guy you all knew back then" who had the cool Mopar stuff. Rob has evolved into a premier Hemi collector and he gladly loaned me Hemi TorqueFlite parts. Rob is one of the most organized and knowledgeable Hemi guys I have ever met, and I am thankful I met.

Tyler and Tim Schloss provided the measuring equipment, a lot of the supplies used in the photography backgrounds, and water-jet and machined parts. Their support is much appreciated.

There are many performance parts for TorqueFlites and one way to share information and pictures was to borrow them from suppliers. Rick Allison from A&A Transmission, Roy Baker from Alto Products Corporation, and John Sackevich and Gregg Nader from Sonnax Industries Inc. took time to read my original requests and trust me with thousands of dollars' worth of their parts. Their help was very important and appreciated.

I want to thank a few Mopar enthusiasts. Rob Merritt provided names and contacts; Al Vasquez offered suggestions, comments, and questions; David Zatz put CarTech and me in touch; and Rodney Byrd, Tracy Lambeth, Rick Allison, and Lon Kopaska took time to provide input to the Modifications chapter.

A&Reds Transmission Parts in Wichita, Kansas, has been my choice of suppliers from the beginning. Leon Autry, president, and his wonderful and efficient wife, Pam, have been so kind and helpful from the first time I met them in the early 1980s. Their Kansas City, Missouri, store, operated by Gale and Valetta Autry and Bob Belzer kept me supplied with the transmission parts I needed. (Over the last 35 years, if I accidentally ordered incorrect parts, Pam was always happy to take them back.) I thank the entire A&Reds organization for all they have done.

The late Gil Younger, Mr. Shift from TransGo, always took time to answer my questions and offer words of wisdom regarding TorqueFlites and life in general. He used to tell me, "his printed materials were worthless unless they were ragged and worn out from usage." Gil, you would be proud to know that I have almost destroyed some of the pages of the books you sent me so long ago. I thank you sincerely.

Finally, I want to express thanks and appreciation to my dad, Jim Hand, one of the smartest Pontiac guys around. Dad worked with CarTech in 2003 to write one of its first Pontiac performance books, which is now, unfortunately, out of print. Dad spent so much time making sure his book was accurate and useful to the reader and I hope I have done the same with this one.

The 3-speed TorqueFlite was produced from around 1960 until 2003. The basic design of the transmission covers two families: the smaller, lighter-duty A-904, and the heavier, stronger A-727.

The original goal for this book was to cover just the rebuilding and modification of the TorqueFlite transmission but experience in the engineering field taught me that it's important to understand what's inside and how and why things work before trying to repair them. Therefore, I expanded the book's scope. Chapter 1 briefly covers the history and evolution. Chapter 2 details the parts inside and how and why they interact. Chapter 3 covers troubleshooting. Chapter 4 provides step-by-step disassembly procedures. Chapter 5 addresses subassemblies and their reuse or replacement. Because of its importance, the valve body is covered in Chapter 6. Chapter 7 details the reassembly along with air checking and adjustment. The torque converter is covered in Chapter 8. Chapter 9 is dedicated to parts and processes to add strength and provide shift improvements.

The scope for Chapter 9 was to discuss street and mild strip/semi-heavy-duty applications and not get into "extreme" TorqueFlites. I did this for a good reason: to build SAFE and severe-duty transmissions requires the right combination of parts and technologies. I strongly suggest talking with reputable builders and the ones I listed (along with many others) know what to do to TorqueFlites to prevent catastrophic failure. Please be safe and use their expertise.

Appendix A is a relatively comprehensive list of TorqueFlite transmission numbers from beginning to end. All numbers came from Chrysler sources but while assembling it, I found variations and omissions. (Numbers of remanufactured TorqueFlite were omitted.) I ask that if you have updates, additions, or corrections, please contact me through CarTech so the changes can be made.

Appendix B lists specifications for assembly and adjustment. Troubleshooting charts are provided along with torque converter specifications.

Appendix C has modification suggestions from industry-leading TorqueFlite experts, experienced transmission mechanics, and Mopar enthusiasts. The Source Guide has contact information for companies and several prominent individuals in the world of TorqueFlites. (There are many others in this field and no ill will is intended by their omission.)

In today's age of rapidly advancing technology, Internet sources are often used exclusively, which may cause books to be overlooked. I hope that after reading this CarTech offering on TorqueFlites, you refer to it often for general and specific information on this amazing transmission.

This 1962 Dodge has a 1965 A-727 case and geartrain, performance-lined rigid kickdown band, 1971 pump and clutch retainers, and a TransGo TF-3 valve body.

HISTORY, IDENTIFICATION AND EVOLUTION OF THE A-904 AND A-727 TORQUEFLITE

The TorqueFlite transmission, introduced in the mid-1950s, was a simple, yet advanced, engineering masterpiece. Compared to its contemporaries it was exceptionally well designed, functional, robust, lightweight, and adaptable to different torque levels. In 1956, the relative of the A-904 and A-727, the A-466, was an option in Chrysler Imperials. The A-466 had a cast-iron body, aluminum converter housing, and aluminum tail shaft housing. The forward-gear ratios were 2.45:1 (low), 1.45:1 (second), and 1.00:1 (direct); reverse was 2.21:1. The A-466 Torque-Flite transmission was offered in 1957 Imperials and other Chryslers. Prominent ads and reviews heralded the A-466 as "the best automatic in the world." This TorqueFlite, like later versions, had a three-element torque converter coupled to an automatically shifted 3-speed Simpson gear set operated by two bands, two multi-disc clutch assemblies, and a one-way clutch. The aluminum case A-904 TorqueFlite was introduced in 1960 and the A-727 in 1962. With its torque converter, the A-727 weighed about 160 pounds.

Around 1965, the bolt-on driveshaft yoke changed to a slip yoke and the push-button shifter changed to a traditional column or console shift. In addition, because Chrysler products had become so reliable, the necessity for a push-starting system disappeared, eliminating the need for the output shaft-rotated rear oil pump.

After these major design changes occurred, the TorqueFlite stayed fairly consistent; it enjoyed a long run and

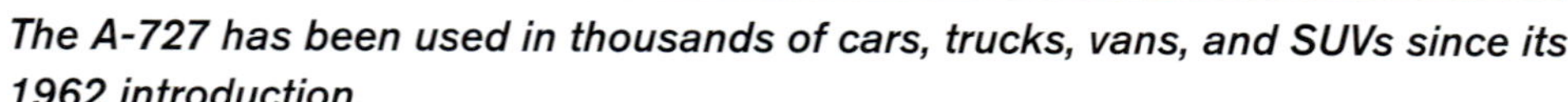

The A-727 has been used in thousands of cars, trucks, vans, and SUVs since its 1962 introduction.

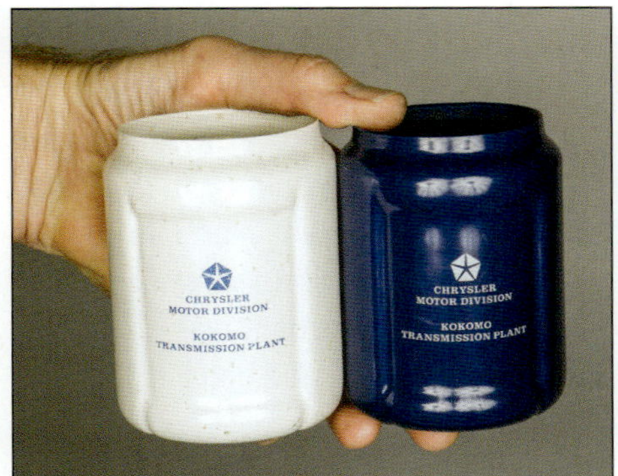

A tour of the Kokomo plant provided memories and these drink holders.

Many think this 1962 Dart (with a Polara grille) is out of the ordinary; with a big-block, 4-barrel, and new-for-1962 A-727, it was.

the A-904 family lived until 2003. Anyone who inspects the first and last one can see that they are essentially the same transmission. A 43-year run for any car part is unheard of, but because of the great design by Bert Cartwright, Erv Miller, and Teno Iavelli, the TorqueFlite experienced it.

The TorqueFlite used in some trucks was called a LoadFlite and those in AMC vehicles were called Torque Commands; for consistency in this book, TorqueFlites will normally be referred to as A-904s and A-727s.

The Manufacturing Facility

The first cast-iron TorqueFlites were built at the Kokomo Transmission plant in Kokomo, Indiana. After a run of cast-iron units, production of the first aluminum A-904s began around 1959 and in 1962, the aluminum A-727 went into full production. Around 1977, the Kokomo plant began the lock-up converter-equipped TorqueFlites and the front-wheel-drive TorqueFlites went into production.

Identification

Most A-904s and A-727s have a number stamped on the pan rail above the oil pan on the driver's side.

This historically significant A-727 transmission case (PK1942275) was cast in 1961.

Late TorqueFlites had eight-digit part numbers. This lock-up (PK52118017) had a high-stall converter and was used in a 3.9-liter-powered 1994–1996 truck.

The last three part number digits were stamped on some converters. This is a 1977 high-stall, non-lock-up converter.

Along with a three-digit number, some converters had a four-digit date code. This 6093 possibly came from a late 1977 production run.

This transmission assembly number usually had a "PK" followed by seven digits. The seven-digit number (used until around 1990) was sometimes followed by an alpha-betical plant code, a warranty date code, and a four-digit daily production number based on a 10,000-day calendar. Reported data indicates the 10,000-Day Date Correlation

The Pushbutton and Cable-Shift Mechanism

The early TorqueFlites were shifted by an ingenious push-button mechanism. Each button moved a lever/plate that controlled a cable connected to the valve body. The reverse plate had a tab to trigger and activate a reverse light switch. When used, a Park lever reset the other buttons and pulled the park pawl into the parking gear to lock the output shaft. Around 1964–1965, the push-button shifter changed to a traditional column or console shift. A reason given is a mid-1960s Federal Government mandate that all drivers were to have available a standardized way of selecting gears. Because the pushbutton arrangement was so unique among automakers, Chrysler "stood out" and had to change. ■

A push-button shift module controlled early TorqueFlites. This 1962 Dart has a manual valve body and its buttons get pushed a lot!

The module controls the valve body/park mechanism through the gearshift control cable and a parking lock cable.

These small cables transfer driver signals to the valve body.

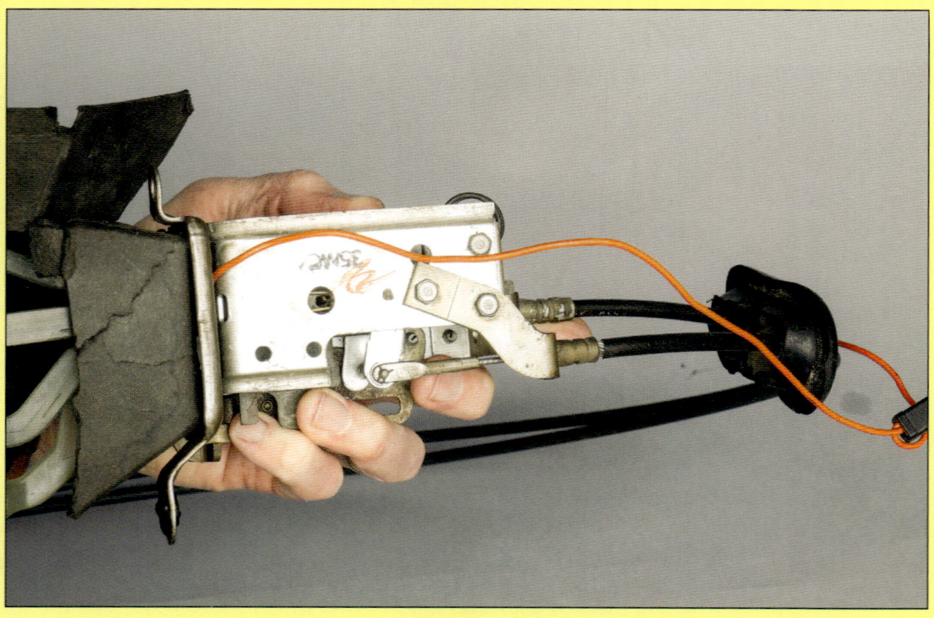

The mechanism consists of plates, levers, and springs that advance or retract the gearshift control cable. A separately activated Park lever "cancels" all gears and moves the parking lock cable.

A tab on the reverse plate actuates the reverse switch. When the tab pushes forward, it moves the "V"-shaped linkage to hit the switch and turn on the reverse lights.

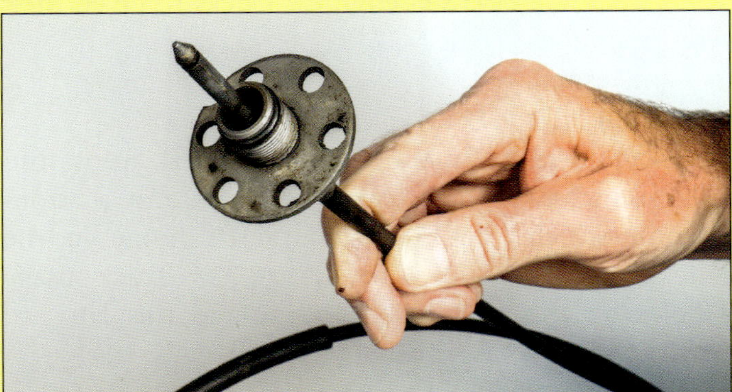

This end of the cable fits in the case. The large ring (control cable adjusting wheel) rotates on the threaded ferrule to pull/push the gearshift control cable.

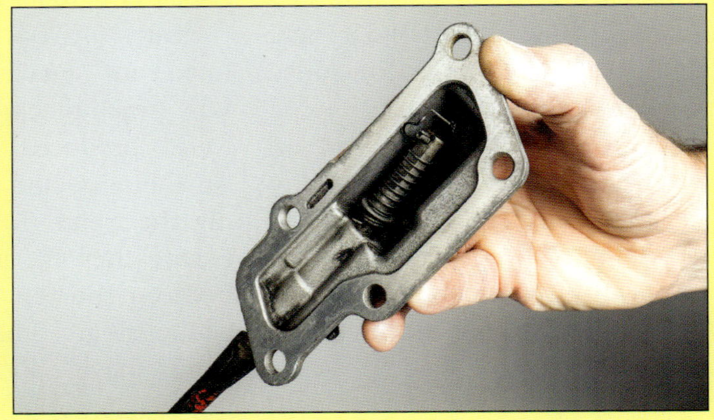

In the park cable housing, an adapter hooks on the park lever to pull it on or off.

TorqueFlites with small-block engines have 7.75 inches between these top two holes.

A-727s for big-blocks and HEMIs have about 6.25 inches between the holes.

Production Numbers and Transmission Identification

Appendix A lists the available production numbers and usage information for A-904s and A-727s.

Evolution of the TorqueFlite A-904 and A-727

All of the 3-speed TorqueFlites are very similar and incremental changes occurred yearly to make them stronger, smoother, and more efficient. It would take a very large chapter to detail all of the changes made, so a very abbreviated list of key, year-to-year engineering and production changes is provided.

1960

Production of the A-904 for Slant-6 engines in lightweight cars occurs.

1961

The A-904 was modified for the torque of the 225-ci Slant-6.

1962

The A-727s for V-8 applications were manufactured and strong versions were used with the powerful 413-ci engines. Trucks received their first A-727s.

1963

A heavy-duty A-904 went into Police cars and Taxis and a stronger A-727 found its home in the 300J Chrysler. A-727 Truck usage expanded to include the Forward Control A-100.

1964

Minor updates were made to the A-904 and the 413-ci, the 426-ci Wedge, and the 426 Hemi received

numbers started in 1962. For example, January 1, 1972, is a 3812 and January 1, 1982, is 7462. The first 10,000-day date calendar concluded in the late 1980s.

Beginning in 1969, a pad on the bellhousing in front of the dipstick tube was stamped with an abbreviated version of the Vehicle Identification Number (VIN): eight numbers match the last eight on the VIN.

Some torque converters are identified by a stamped four-digit date code and the last three digits of its part number; these are located on the crowned surface of the converter close to the weld seam.

Early A-904s were manufactured for 6-cylinders and small V-8 (small-block) engines. A-727s were produced for 6-cylinders, small-blocks, and big-blocks including the Hemi. To determine which engine they fit, measure the space between the top two holes on the bellhousing. Small-block Torque-Flites have about 7.75 inches between the bolts, big-blocks have about 6.25 inches, and 6-cylinder TorqueFlites have the starter high on the bellhousing.

robust A-727s. Six-cylinder versions went into trucks.

1965

The A-904 was strengthened and a high-performance version with a higher-shifting governor went into 273 4-barrel A-bodies. High-performance big blocks and Street Hemis got a beefed-up A-727. The bolt-on yoke changed to a sliding yoke.

1966

The rear pump was eliminated from A-904s and A-727s and both got rod-operated shift linkage, eliminating use of shift cables. A more positive Park lock mechanism was introduced.

1967

A part-throttle kickdown circuit was used in 6-cylinder A-904s. The rear servo piston changed and a "stiff spring-integral cushion" went into A-904s and A-727s. The A-727 got an enlarged input shaft; and 440s and Hemis got high-strength output shafts and input shafts identified with a yellow paint stripe and a groove. Four-pinion planetaries were used in high-performance A-727s.

1968

The A-904 was strengthened for the new 318 by incorporating a larger input shaft and other changes. The output shaft front spline diameter increased and a one-hole filter was adopted for the A-904 and A-727.

1969

The single terminal neutral start switch picked up two more terminals to control reverse lights. Valve bodies were modified for the new switch and they received a "reverse pressure" relief ball. A VIN pad was added to

the case and the bolt-on oil fill tube was changed to a push-in design.

1970

A-904s and A-727s for new E-bodies received a shift control linkage boss on the left side. The 1–2 shift valve governor plug was changed to speed up the manual 1–2 shift. The A-727 for 440 6-barrel cars received the 426 Hemi TorqueFlite internals. An A-727 was released for the 413 truck engine.

1971

A-904s were modified for economical 1.6- and 1.8-liter Simcas. Part throttle downshift circuits were introduced for A-904s and A-727s. The A-727 had a running change/introduction of the wide bushing front clutch retainer, a reaction shaft support with new sealing rings, and the front clutch retainer shorter lip seals.

1972

The A-904 received short lip seals in the front clutch retainer. The A-727 rear clutch spacer ring changed from steel to nylon. A heavy-duty extension for truck A-727 was added. AMC and International Harvester adopted TorqueFlites. A-727 extensions on Imperials were fitted with dampener weights.

1973

Valve bodies received revised throttle and line-pressure adjusting brackets, enabling "computerized" pressure adjustments during assembly. The oil filter was enlarged by 50 percent. Part-throttle kickdown circuits went into trucks. The flexible A-727 (flex) kickdown band arrived.

1974

Neutral-to-Drive and Neutral-to-Reverse shift quality improvements

were made by adding valve body restrictions and check balls. The A-727 rear clutch assembly received a stronger Belleville spring washer. A governor filter was added and A-904s got their first stamped-steel planetaries. The A-999 heavy-duty "mini-Hemi" version of the A-904 was built for 360-ci engines. The A-998 for 318s was released with the A-999-type front clutch retainer components.

1975

Some trucks featured rear timing holes in the bellhousings. Valve bodies were changed to reduced part throttle downshift sensitivity.

1976

A new valve body filter prevented regulator valve sticking. The A-727 output shaft front planetary spline angle changed from 45 degrees to 37.5 degrees. The A-904 thrust washer between input and output shaft changed to steel-backed bronze; all A-904s had a Teflon seal ring on the input shaft. The A-727s received tin-nickel-plated front clutch seal rings, the rear servo piston lip seal changed to Viton, and front clutch inner and outer seals changed from lathe cut to molded. Use of redesigned converters began.

1977

An A-904 was released for Colts and Arrows and a 1978 transmission design "built out" 1977 compact trucks.

1978

Lock-up converter-equipped A-904s and A-727s received new pumps, reaction shaft supports, input shafts, and valve bodies. The A-727 was equipped with a tabbed thrust washer between input and output shaft, the neutral start switch was shortened, and magnets were placed in oil pans. A-998s and A-999s received controlled-load kickdown servos.

1979

The A-904 received a controlled-load kickdown servo and a thin, polished-steel thrust plate for the third thrust washer. The A-727 case was modified to accept lock-up valve bodies and they were changed to improve converter lock-up. The A-998s and A-999s had check balls added in the transfer plate and other changes to eliminate "reverse squawk."

1980

Wide-ratio gear sets for the A-904 family and flexible kickdown bands for standard and wide front clutch retainers were introduced. An AMC four-wheel-drive A-904 version was used and truck extension housings were strengthened. The governor weight body diameter was increased by .070 inch to allow common tooling. A-998 and A-999 valve bodies had 1–2 and Neutral-to-Drive quality improvements. Six cylinder applications had revised lock-up springs.

1981

The A-904 and A-727 cases were changed for shift quality improvements.

1982

The AMC and MMC A-904s featured wide-ratio gear sets. Minor case changes occurred and a Viton rear servo piston seal was introduced for fleet A-904s.

1983

The A-999 had the lock-up speed increased in vehicles with 2.2:1 rear axles. Slant-6, non-lock-up A-727s were released for California. All A-904s had Viton rear servo piston seals.

1984

A non-lock-up A-999 was released for high-altitude (car) use. The A-727 truck transmissions for 318 and 360 with high-stall converters received four-pinion front planetaries, four-disc front clutch retainers, and a special Borg Warner kickdown bands. A new A-904 case went into production for postal trucks.

1985

A-904s for AMC diesels were released. Vans and wagons had standard, long A-727 extension housings instead of the heavy-duty truck version.

1986

Part throttle converter unlock was used across the board for all 318 (A-999) and 225 (A-904) lock-up transmissions. A threaded hole was added for the lock-up solenoid connector on the A-904 case along with other changes to the valve body due to the solenoid. A-999s and A-904s received heavy-duty extensions for long wheelbase trucks.

1987

Some truck A-727 transmissions were released with a stronger rear bearing. The Dakota's A-998 received new exhaust support mounting locations; a new four-wheel-drive transmission was produced. Reverse bands for A-904s and A-727s were changed to a (non-asbestos) Kevlar material. Mitsubishi 1.6-liter vehicles received an A-904.

1988

The overrunning clutch changed from a 10-roller to a 12-roller design in the A-904 family.

1989

The A-727 reaction shaft was modified to increase oil flow to the number-3 thrust washer, and the reaction shaft support was heat treated and polished. The A-727 non-lock-up transmissions were modified for Cummins diesels.

1990–1993

The Park sprag was widened and the number-3 thrust washer was made more durable. Material was removed from all input shafts and A-727 output shafts. The A-727 reverse band anchor strut and link assembly were modified to accommodate reinforced band lugs. The A-999 sun gear shell thickness was increased by .035 inch and the thrust plate's thickness was decreased. A-998s and A-999s were used in 3.9- and 5.2-liter trucks. A-998 and A-999 front clutch retainers added a rear bushing. The A-904 family oil pumps switched from tabs to flats on inner gear rotors. Some 1991 and later A-727s had 14-roller-overrunning clutches.

1994–1996

The A-904 was renamed to the 30RH; the A-998 was 31RH; A-999 was 32RH and A-727s were known as a 36RH in 5.2-liter trucks. Rear planetaries received five pinions on some A-727s and steel front planetaries with five pinions went into some HD trucks.

1997–1999

The 36RH continued use in the AB-van. The speedometer gear was replaced with a vehicle speed sensor.

2000–2003

In 2001, the 32RH replaced the last 36RH for AB-vans until production of the 3-speed TorqueFlite ended (2003).

TorqueFlite Components and Operation

It is easier troubleshooting, repairing, or modifying any assembly when you know how it works; TorqueFlites are no different. Unlike some of the other common 3-speed transmissions, a TorqueFlite shifts from a one-way roller clutch to a band, releases the band, and adds another clutch. This band-to-clutch shifting requires critical timing. This method makes TorqueFlites lighter, easier to work on, and often cheaper to repair.

To become familiar with the TorqueFlite's parts, Chrysler's part names are used throughout, and the part's purpose, location, and relationship to others is explained in this chapter to make the disassembly and reassembly logical and understandable. And, even though most know the positions identified on the push-button display, steering column, or console as "1, 2, 3" or "First, Second, Third," or maybe "Low, Second, Drive," the Chrysler names of "Drive Breakaway, Drive Second, and Drive Direct" are commonly used.

Please note that when the A-904 is discussed, the A-998 and A-999 (and the later numerical-alphabetical codes) are often being referenced. The A-727 and its later alphanumeric coded versions are usually discussed together as well.

The Components

The A-904 and A-727 have about the same amount and style of components. The only real difference is their size and credit goes to the designers for reducing the size rather than altering their great design.

Torque Converter

A manual transmission–equipped vehicle depends on a clutch and flywheel to transfer engine power to the transmission. However, in an automatic transmission–equipped car or truck, there is

TorqueFlites were used in some unique muscle cars. This 34,000-mile 1970 AAR Cuda 340 6-barrel has an automatic and TA Challenger engine decals.

Most A-904s and many A-727s have 10.75-inch-diameter converters; on A-727s, these are described as having wide-ring gears. The A-727 11.75-inch converters are known as narrow-ring-gear units. The converter diameter changes but the ring gear diameter stays the same. This is a late-1970s high-stall, non-lock-up unit.

A-727 lock-ups have a friction lining bonded to the front cover. A piston between the turbine and cover forces a pressure plate into the friction material, locking the turbine to the cover to directly couple the engine and transmission.

The torque converter has an impeller integral in the housing, front cover, turbine, stator, ring gear, and, if a lock-up unit, a clutch and apply piston. This is a truck A-727 low-stall, lock-up version.

no "true" flywheel and clutch assembly, so there must be another way to transfer motion; that way is through the torque converter.

The torque converter multiplies torque and couples the engine to the drivetrain, hydraulically through fluid transfer or mechanically through a lock-up clutch. By multiplying engine torque, it makes an automatic vehicle more drivable, enables it to run lower numerical gears, and with a lock-up converter, the fuel economy is almost equal to manual transmission–equipped vehicles.

A non-lock-up torque converter has three active elements: an impeller, stator, and turbine. The lock-up torque converter has another key element: the clutch assembly.

The impeller is integral to the rear half of the converter, and because of its vane curvature and its rotation with the engine, it throws fluid into the turbine, creating a fluid coupling. A finned stator is added between the impeller and turbine to give direction to fluid thrown between the two. By redirecting the fluid, the stator's fins make the turbine's fluid hit the impeller's fins harder adding torque to the input shaft.

The torque converter has a hub to drive the transmission's oil pump via slots or flats that engage the inner rotor of the pump.

In summary, the torque converter:

1. Couples (hydraulically/mechanically) the engine and transmission.
2. Drives the oil pump.
3. Multiplies engine torque.
4. Often provides a ring gear for starting. The torque converter will be discussed in Chapter 8.

Disassembled TorqueFlite

The disassembled A-727 TorqueFlite (PK4039537) used for photographs came out of a 1977 318- to 360-ci truck. It was functional, had not been modified, but it had a few issues.

Here is an "exploded" A-727.

All of the internal parts are displayed roughly in the order they come apart.

TorqueFlite Case Assembly

The parts have to be contained inside a housing, which is the case. This one is for the small-block Chrysler engine. Like most two-wheel-drive trucks and cars, it has a long extension housing (but not the heavy-duty truck version).

Along with other external features, this case contains the neutral starting switch that performs a couple of functions: it allows the engine to start only in Park or Neutral and it passes electrical current to the reverse lights when it is in Reverse. This style of switch was used after 1968; earlier models had reverse lights controlled from another switch by the steering column, in the push-button module, or the console shifter.

To support the output shaft, there is an output shaft support that bolts to the case. The support also provides a bearing surface for the low-reverse drum, enables the governor-output shaft assembly to rotate inside it, supports the governor, and directs fluid to and from its weights and valves to control shift points.

Inside the extension housing is a lever that locks the output shaft in place in Park. A bushing at the housing's end supports the driveshaft yoke, and its extension housing seal contacts the yoke to contain the fluid.

An oil pan, (the main sump for the hydraulic system) helps cool the fluid

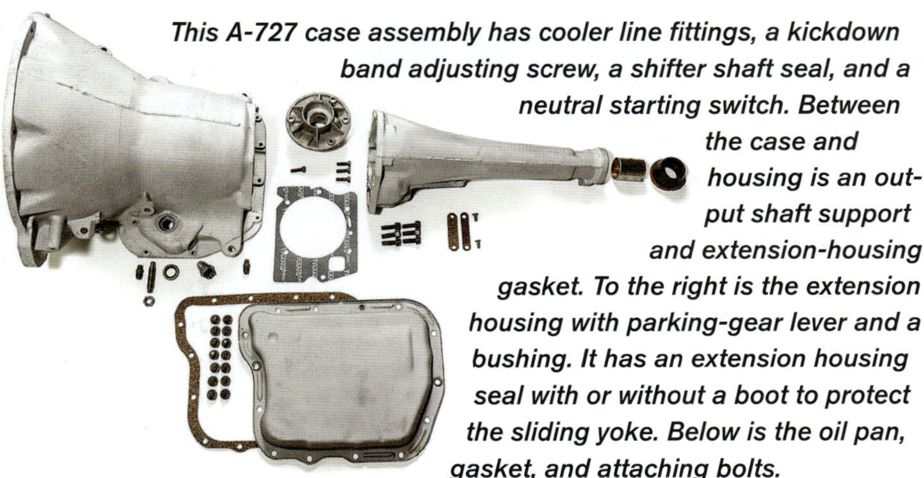

This A-727 case assembly has cooler line fittings, a kickdown band adjusting screw, a shifter shaft seal, and a neutral starting switch. Between the case and housing is an output shaft support and extension-housing gasket. To the right is the extension housing with parking-gear lever and a bushing. It has an extension housing seal with or without a boot to protect the sliding yoke. Below is the oil pan, gasket, and attaching bolts.

Short Extension Housings for Trucks and Four-Wheel-Drive Vehicles

Some early compact trucks and four-wheel-drive vehicles have a short output shaft and extension housing. The transmission case and internals are the same, but the output shaft is short to enable a transfer case or shorter extension housing to fit. The speedometer gear is then usually found in the transfer case. The four-wheel-drive extension housing is roughly 1/3 as long as the standard housing.

The A-904 case is similar to the A-727 except that it is smaller. An easy way to identify them is to look at the oil pan or pan rail. An A-727 has an extra section on the passenger side for the kickdown servo but the A-904 has a "straight" rail.

Chrysler built A-727 cases to fit small-blocks, big-blocks, diesels, Slant-6s, and some International Harvesters, AMCs, Jeeps, and other foreign engines.

The A-904 fit Chrysler small-block and Slant-6s, some AMCs, U.S. Postal Service trucks, other makes, and Chrysler 2.2/2.5 4-cylinders in 1980s small trucks.

Four-wheel-drive trucks (and some AMC cars with A-904s) have a short output shaft and extension housing with a flange for the transfer case.

A-727 cases (left) have a "kicked-out" section and corresponding pan to accommodate the (larger) kickdown servo. The A-904 (right) has a relatively square pan and rail.

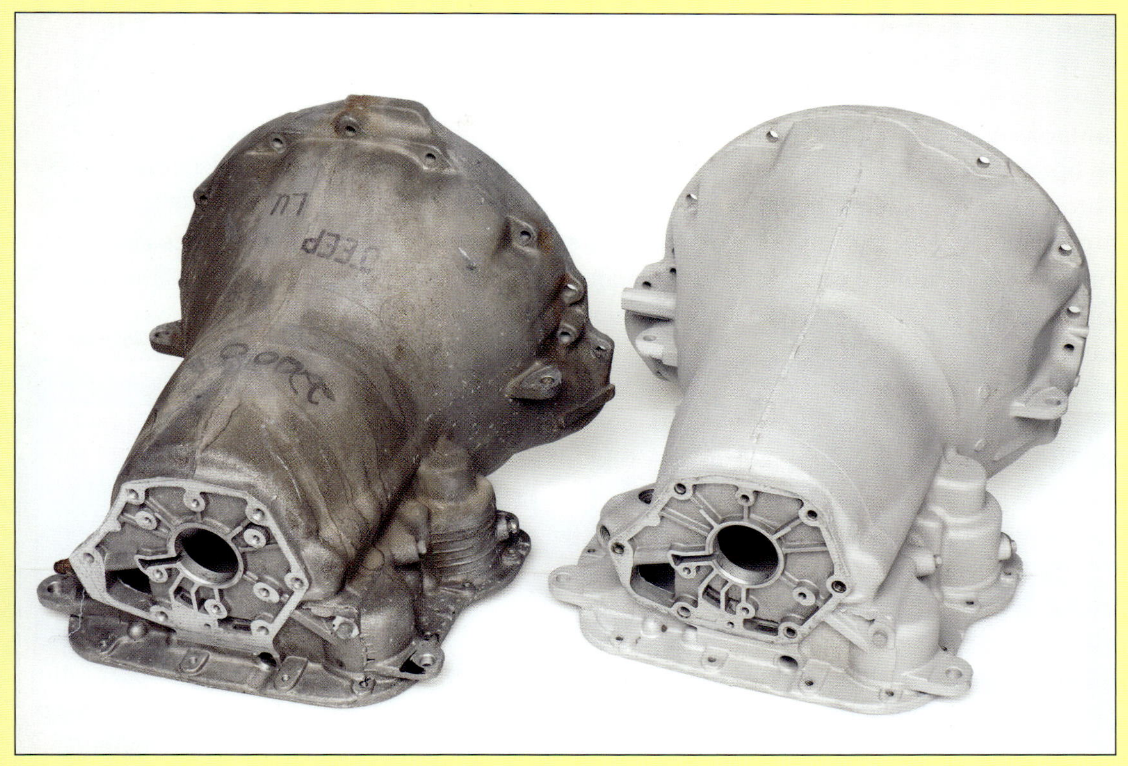

The Jeep case (left) has a different attaching bolt pattern than a typical Chrysler A-727 (right) and an A-904.

A radically different 1969 HD Slant-6 A-727 (left) case contrasts with an early 1962 cable-shifted big-block case (right).

and bolts on the case. A tube with a dipstick (not shown) that enables the transmission to be filled and the fluid level checked pushes or bolts on.

Oil Pump Assembly

The oil pumps are all similar and provide hydraulic pressure to operate and lubricate the TorqueFlite. The A-727 internal rotor has 14 external teeth and the external rotor has 15 internal teeth. The torque converter's hub locks into the pump's inner rotor that meshes with the outer rotor in just a few locations. A gap is formed and when the rotors are spun, fluid is pulled into the gap and is squeezed out into a cavity close to the meshing teeth. This pressurized fluid travels through the pump body passageways, leading into the case and valve body, where it is regulated and directed to subsequent hydraulic components.

The pump's reaction shaft fits into the torque converter to hold the stator's hub stationary. The reaction shaft supports the input shaft internally and the front clutch retainer externally. The front clutch retainer "seals" to the support by two rings that rotate to direct oil from the pump to "apply" the front clutch piston.

The oil pump body contains an internal bushing to support the torque converter's hub and a seal to prevent fluid leakage around it. The reaction shaft support has an internal bushing to support the input shaft/rear clutch retainer assembly. On the A-727, various-thickness fiber thrust washers prevent the front clutch retainer from wearing the reaction shaft's journal and they set endplay. The A-904 has a small-thickness thrust washer between the pump and retainer because its endplay is adjusted by various-thickness thrust washers between the input and output shaft.

A-727 Pump and Input Shaft Differences

There have been a few A-727 pump and input shaft changes. The 1962 to 1966 versions had 1.125-inch-diameter input shafts with 19 turbine splines, whereas the 1967 through 1970 versions had 1.175-inch-diameter shafts with 24 turbine splines. Both had reaction shaft supports for narrow front clutch retainer bushings. In 1971 through 1977, the input shafts stayed 1.175-inch diameter, but the front clutch retainer bushings widened. From 1978 to 1997, the shaft and retainer bushings stayed the same, but an additional sealing ring/groove was added to the input shaft. To prevent interchange, 1978-later lock-up A-727s had only 23 turbine splines on the input shaft. ∎

The oil pump has a pump body, two rotors, and a reaction shaft support with bushings, sealing rings, and seal. There are differences between non-lock-up and lock-up converter-equipped oil pumps and they can't be interchanged.

The A-727, A-904 and Lock-Up/Non-Lock-Up Pumps

The A-904 oil pump is smaller, but the main difference between it and the A-727 is that each of its pump body and reaction shaft supports makes up one half of the assembly. When dealing with lock-up versus non-lock up pumps, the lock-up reaction shaft has three passages sealed with steel balls and the non-lock-up support has only two passages sealed with the balls. ∎

The A-727 oil pump (top) uses a larger body and smaller reaction shaft support, whereas the A-904 pump (bottom) splits into two relatively equal halves.

Front Clutch Assembly

The front clutch assembly has several purposes; it holds the clutch pack to provide Drive Direct and Reverse, and the kickdown band clamps its outer surface to create Second. The clutch pack's friction discs are lined with organic-based or paper-based material and they may have radial or waffle patterns cut or pressed into them or they may be smooth with a slight wavy shape.

The retainer's outer tabs interlock with the sun gear shell to transfer torque to the planetary assemblies.

The most common A-727 front clutch retainer holds three or four friction discs and those in Hemi and 440 6-barrel cars held five.

To operate the front clutch, pressurized fluid is directed between the two sealing rings on the reaction shaft support. Oil is fed through the hole in the reaction shaft support, through the rings, and into the holes or slots in the ID of the retainer. This pressurized fluid in the retainer forces two lip seals against their sealing surface to create a closed hydraulic system. When this fluid pressure overcomes the spring force of the clutch release springs, the apply piston moves away from the rear of the retainer to "clamp" the friction (driving) discs and clutch (driven) plates together. The inner lugs of the driving discs hold the front clutch hub of the rear clutch retainer assembly. The locked discs and plates enable torque to transmit through the rotating input shaft to the clamped

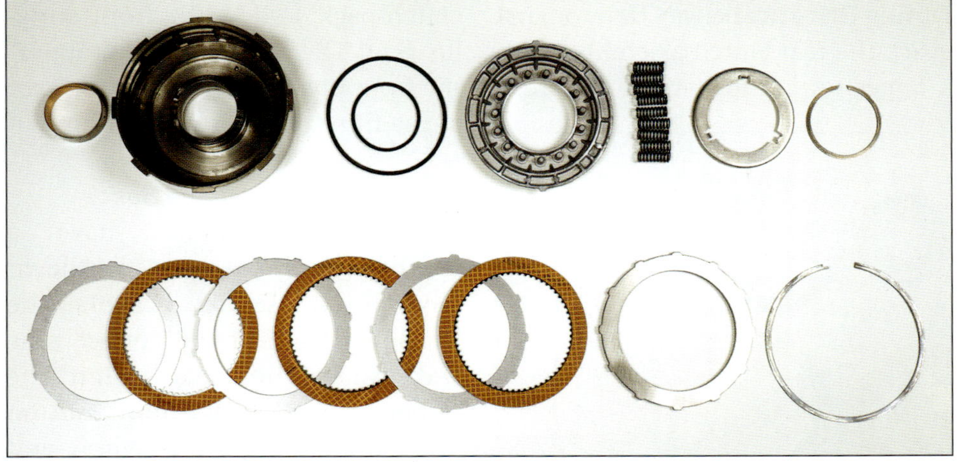

This A-727 front clutch assembly has a bushing, a clutch retainer, two synthetic rubber lip seals, an aluminum piston, release springs, a spring retainer, a snap ring, a clutch "pack" consisting of alternating driving (friction) discs, driven (steel) plates, a thick pressure plate, and one of four different-size snap rings.

Certain heavy-duty A-727s use a four or five friction-disc front clutch retainer; others, such as this right one, hold three friction discs.

Front Clutch Retainer A-727 and A-904

The A-904 front clutch assembly is smaller and has only one large release spring; the theory of operation is the same as the multiple-spring A-727. A-904s, like A-727s, use various types and quantities of friction plates and different sizes of snap rings to set clutch pack clearances. And, like the A-727, depending upon vehicle and engine usage, the A-904 has two widths of retainers to hold friction plates and driving discs. Shift qualities change by using different types and quantities of discs and plates; by varying the strength of release spring(s); by changing the clutch pack clearance, and by controlling the timing of the kickdown band release. ■

A-727s (top) use application-dependent quantities of piston return springs. A-904s (bottom) use one large spring.

clutch pack assembly and, therefore, through the front clutch retainer assembly. When the fluid pressure is removed, the retainer's release springs force the apply piston back and release the friction discs from the driven plates.

Rear Clutch Assembly

One of the "busiest" assemblies in all TorqueFlites is the rear clutch; it is applied in all forward gears. The rear clutch pack is similar to the front and, in fact, the steel-driven plates are identical. However, the rear friction (driving) discs are lined with a thinner and smooth material that has only a few grooves.

The operation of the rear clutch assembly mirrors the front. Pressurized fluid is directed through sealing rings on the input shaft, through the channel in the input shaft, and into the retainer. This pressurized fluid forces the lip seals against their sealing surfaces and the piston pushes away from the retainer to drive the Belleville piston spring-pressure plate assembly and clamp the clutch pack. During Drive Breakaway (Low or First gear), the rear clutch assembly holds a larger torque load than the front clutch; the Belleville piston spring is a lever that multiplies the apply force from the apply piston to adequately clamp the friction discs and drive plates. The Belleville piston spring also holds the apply piston in place when the clutch is non-operational during Park, Reverse, or Neutral.

Once the driving plates and friction discs are clamped in the rear clutch assembly, power transmits from the torque converter turbine, through the input shaft, to the locked clutch-pack, and to the front annulus gear. The annulus gear "rotates" the front planet carrier, which is part of the front planetary assembly.

Servos, Accumulator and Bands

Most late A-727s have a controlled-load servo kickdown servo piston assembly. It applies the kickdown band at the correct time and cushions the 3–2 downshift. The earlier basic servo assembly uses no internal spring/piston assembly and was found in pre-1971 transmissions

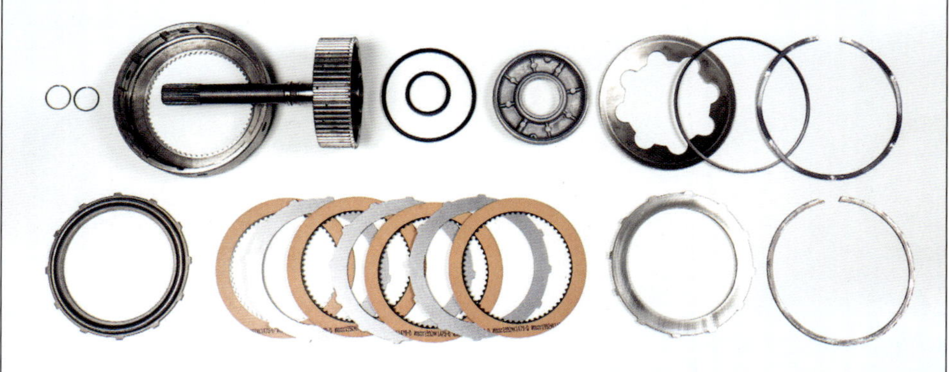

The A-727 rear clutch assembly consists of sealing rings, a clutch retainer, an input shaft-front clutch hub assembly, two synthetic rubber lip seals, a cast-aluminum apply piston, a Belleville piston spring washer, a spacer ring, and a waved spring (snap ring). It also has an apply pressure plate, alternating driving discs and driven plates, an outer pressure plate, and one of four snap rings.

This retainer is light and easy to assemble but higher tooling costs may have prevented production.

This is a never-released stamped A-727 rear clutch retainer and input shaft.

A Very Important Steel Ball

A steel check ball is used in the rear clutch apply piston and front clutch retainer. When the retainers are spinning but not hydraulically operating, residual fluid can force the apply piston against the pressure plate in the front clutch or the Belleville piston spring in the rear. This fluid may force the friction plates and driving discs together creating "clutch drag." The steel ball acts as a check valve and lets fluid (under pressure due to the clutch assembly spinning) out of the retainer before the piston inadvertently clamps clutches together. ■

A-727 and A-904 Rear Clutch

The A-904 rear clutch assembly is smaller but operates like the A-727. A difference is that the A-727 assembly easily separates into two pieces. ■

Similar in operation, the A-727 (top) and A-904 (bottom) rear clutch retainers differ in size.

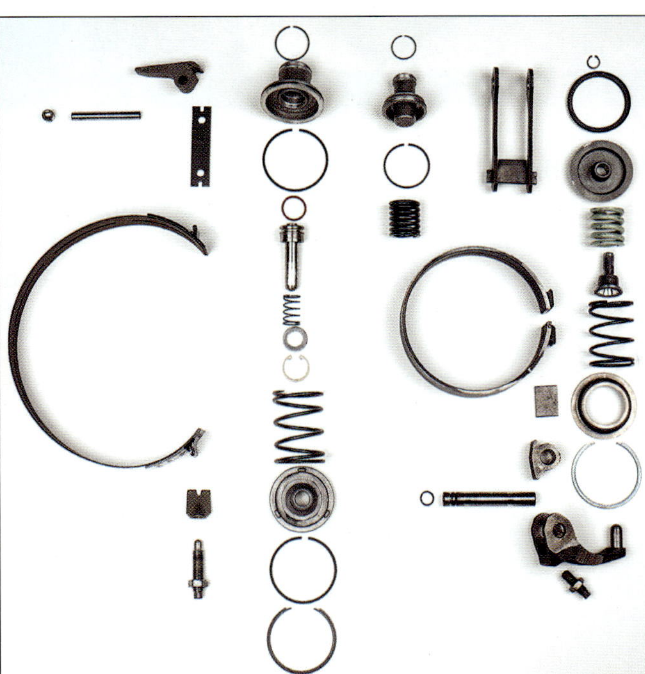

These are A-727 servos, bands, accumulators, and associated springs and levers. The kickdown band apply lever, above the C-shaped flexible kickdown band, comes in different ratios, depending on transmission usage. The low-reverse band and its hardware are on the right.

shape. These are known as "Flex" bands and most late TorqueFlites had them.

The Hemi and 440 6-barrel TorqueFlites had wider kickdown bands to stop the heavier and wider five-friction disc front clutch retainer during the 1–2 shift. The bands fit the five-friction disc A-727 retainers but are too wide for the standard retainers. With equal line pressure, the wider kickdown band, with the 5.0:1 ratio apply lever, produced greater holding power than the standard-width stock cast or flex kickdown band combination.

The accumulator piston and spring combination cushions the application of the kickdown band during the 1–2 upshift *and* the application of the rear clutch when the gearshift is placed in any forward driving range. When placed in a forward gear, the application of the rear clutch is not completed until the accumulator seats against the valve body's transfer plate. The 1–2 upshift is not completed until the accumulator piston has moved its maximum distance in the opposite direction. This is why the type of spring (or lack of it) in the accumulator circuit affects rear clutch engagement *and* 1–2 upshift quality.

The low-reverse band and servo are similar between the two families of TorqueFlites, but the A-727 has only one width of low-reverse band. It applies to clamp the low-reverse drum in Reverse and in Manual Low; the low-reverse band works with the overrunning clutch to hold the low-reverse drum stationary. The A-904 and A-727 depend on the low-reverse band's additional holding power to prevent breakage of the overrunning clutch race during hard acceleration.

and some later applications where soft down shifts at higher torque loads would be detrimental. The A-904s also uses the two styles of servo piston assemblies.

Higher-performance transmissions used apply levers with 3.8:1, 4.2:1, or a 5.0:1 ratios. The higher ratio levers multiply the apply force more

to tighten the kickdown band harder around the front clutch retainer but may take longer to do so, creating timing issues if used incorrectly.

Throughout its production, A-727s had different styles of kickdown bands. Some were cast and maintained their circular shape; others are flexible and don't retain their

Kickdown and Low-Reverse Bands

The TorqueFlite uses different widths and styles of kickdown bands to stop the front clutch retainer's rotation. The A-904 kickdown band is smaller than the A-727's. Most A-904s are the same width, but some A-998 and A-999s have a five-friction disc front clutch retainer and use a wider kickdown band. The A-904 started with cast, round bands but later switched to "flex" bands.

The low-reverse bands are similar but the A-904 uses two different types of bands. One is a double wrap band, used to give greater low-reverse drum holding capability for V-8 vehicles. The other is a single wrap band, which has less torque-holding capability for use with 4- and 6-cylinder engines.

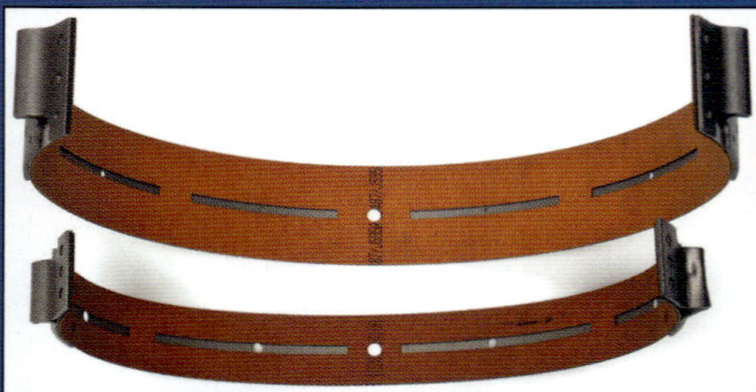

Later 1970s TorqueFlites had flexible or "flex" kickdown bands. The larger A-727 band is above; the A-904 band is below.

The A-727 (left) uses a single-wrap low-reverse band; the A-904 (right) uses a double-wrap band for V-8 applications.

Planetaries, Output Shaft and Governor

Three separate assemblies, the planetary gear assemblies (planetaries), the output shaft and governor, and the output shaft support bearing transfer and time torque changes. The planetaries and sun gear provide gear reduction and rotation reversal to create three forward gears and Reverse. The output shaft transfers engine torque from transmission to driveshaft. The governor controls the shifts and a bearing supports the shaft.

The front annulus gear splines to the rear clutch retainer friction discs, and the gear surrounds and drives the front planet carrier. Depending on which gear the transmission is in, the sun gear–driving shell assembly is driven by the front or rear clutch packs and may transmit torque to the rear planetary assembly. Thrust washers prevent wear between the various rotating parts and control the overall endplay.

The output shaft has a thrust washer between it and the input shaft that is fiber or bronze, depending on the transmission. Later model A-727s and A-904s have a hardened steel washer between a bronze washer and the output shaft. The output shaft has four sets of splines; small ones fit in the front planet carrier, a second set holds the rear annulus gear, a third holds the governor-park assembly, and the longest set is for the drive shaft yoke. The shaft also has worm gear teeth to drive the speedometer gear.

The governor assembly and output shaft support bearing are held

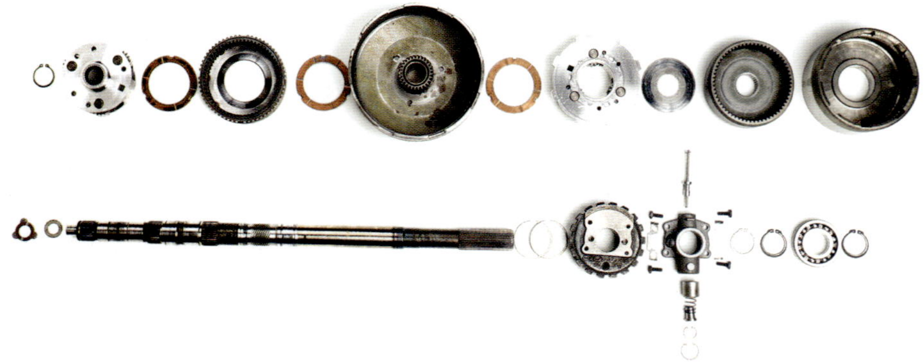

On the front of A-727 planetary assemblies (from left to right), a snap ring holds the planetaries on, a front planetary gear, thrust washer, front annulus gear, thrust washer, sun gear-driving shell assembly, thrust washer, rear planetary gear, thin steel thrust washer, and rear annulus gear. The last three parts are contained "inside" the low-reverse drum. The govenor and bearing also mount on the shell.

A Planetary Assembly and Output Shaft Comparison

Like other internal parts, A-904 planetaries, its output shaft, and governor assembly are smaller than those in A-727s. Depending on engine size and application, the A-904 and A-727 use three or four (and some five) planet pinion gears in the planet carrier assembly. The four- and five-pinion setups are usually found in higher-performance units. ■

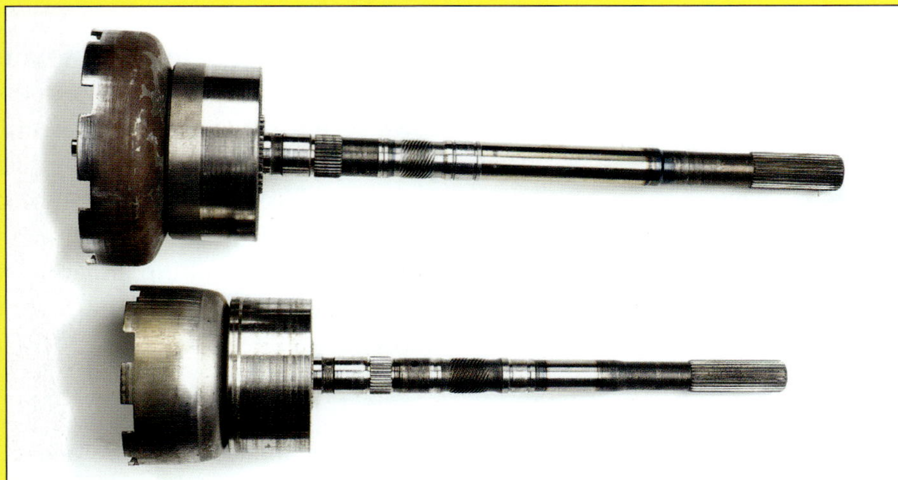

A-727s and A-904s use the same type of parts to achieve low and intermediate gear ratios. A-904s have smaller components, but later versions have a wider ratio gear set to work with steeper rear axle ratios.

on the output shaft by snap rings. The governor creates a hydraulic signal, which works with the throttle pressure circuit to control shift points according to the vehicle speed and torque requirements. Two sealing rings, the governor body-park pawl assembly, and the governor valve-weight-spring assembly create and deliver the governor signal to the valve body. A thin snap ring holds the governor body-park pawl assembly to the output shaft. The output shaft bearing supports the shaft and internal components and is held on by one (A-904) or two (A-727) thick snap rings.

Control Valve Body and Filter

The control valve body is the "brain" of the transmission. It uses hydraulic signals from the governor, the throttle pressure rod or cable, and the manual shift valve, and combines them with fluid pressure from the oil pump to time and control all transmission functions. The valve body plates, fluid passages and restrictions, springs, and valves modulate the fluid pressure and control the timing and firmness of band and clutch application. Lock-up transmissions have a small, separate valve body that controls converter clutch lock-up. To provide the necessary clean fluid, most TorqueFlites have a large square Dacron filter but early ones were smaller, and up until 1966, they had an additional hole for the rear pump.

The control valve body consists of a filter, separator plate, transfer plate, and upper valve body with associated valves, springs, balls, and end plates. Lock-up converters required an additional small valve body and tube. Later versions had electronic solenoids.

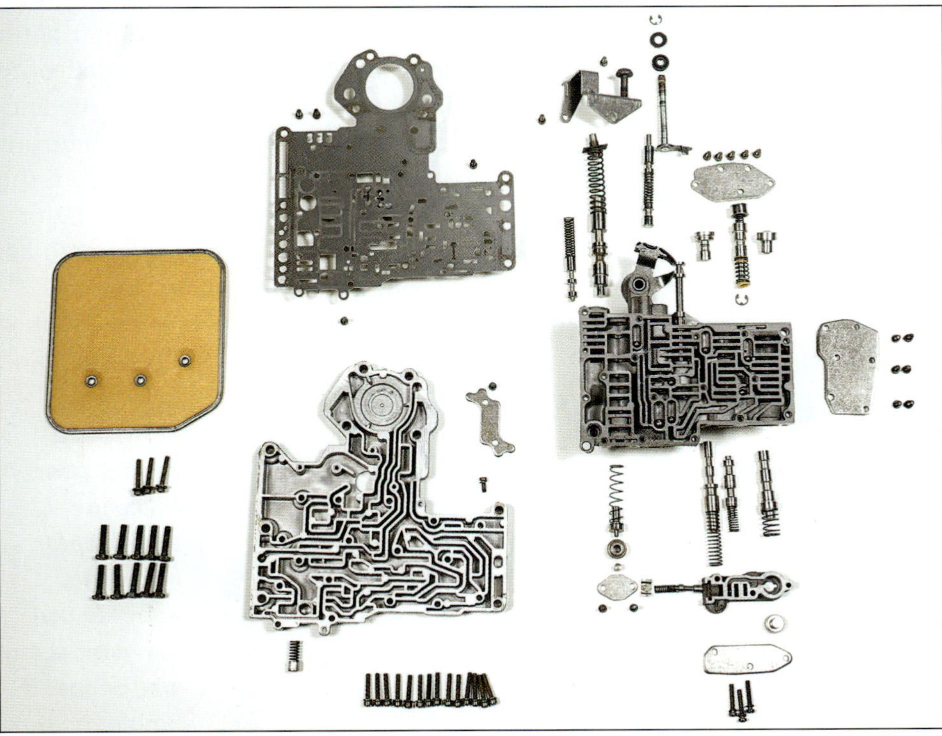

Control Valve Bodies Interchangeability

The A-904 valve body interchanges with similar year A-727s if one hole in the transfer plate is elongated. They may have different valves, springs, and orifice sizes but operation is similar although shift quality and timing may not be adequate for the application without some modifications. ∎

As alternatives, the aftermarket offers more porous, tightly woven stainless steel or brass screens.

Overrunning Clutch

The TorqueFlite's overrunning clutch serves a critical function in Drive Breakaway. It is a one-way clutch assembly consisting of an inner race (hub), springs, rollers, and the outer race (cam). In the A-727, the outer race is pressed into the case; in the A-904, the race rivets in.

When accelerating in Drive Breakaway or Manual Low, the inner race tries to roll in the opposite direction because of the force on the low-reverse drum by the rear planetary. The rollers are pushed by their springs so they wedge between the inner and outer race, locking the assembly to stop the rotation of the inner race. When the transmission is not in Breakaway or Manual Low, the clutch freewheels because the rollers move away from the outer race's (cam) pinch points, letting the inner race spin.

The vehicle absolutely depends on the overrunning clutch's 10 or 12 rollers "wedging" in the outer race and locking the low-reverse rear drum to gain the planetary gear advantage. A low gear ratio moves the vehicle easily from a dead stop or a slow roll. If the TorqueFlite is "slammed" into Drive from Park or Neutral, or if the transmission has been modified so it has no accumulator cushioning during Drive Breakaway application with the throttle on hard, the overrunning clutch's outer race may be damaged. And, if not all 10 or 12 rollers touch at the same time, the force per area of those touching is increased. Anything that dramatically shocks the inner and outer race can potentially cause an overrunning clutch explosion

Speedometer Assembly

The speedometer gear has different quantities of teeth, depending on the rear axle ratio and tire size. The output shaft drives the speedometer gear, which is held in a rotatable/ adaptable housing that accommodates all of the different gears. The adapter housing uses an O-ring on its outer diameter and a lip seal in its inner diameter.

The TorqueFlite in Operation

Now that the TorqueFlite components' locations and purposes have been covered, the transmission can be discussed as a complete hydraulic-mechanical unit. A block diagram of the transmission in each gear shows its operation and a power flow diagram highlights the parts to show how clutches and bands transfer power.

Block Diagram: Neutral and Park

Neutral and Park are similar; neither have applied or functional hydraulic units. With no clutches or bands applied, the spinning input shaft (as part of the front clutch hub/ retainer assembly) and its rear clutch pack do nothing. Because the friction discs and these steel driven plates are not hydraulically clamped, the friction discs (which spline to the front annulus gear) freely spin, and the annulus gear just "idles." Therefore, power from the engine does not pass through any clutch assembly.

However, there is a mechanical difference between Neutral and Park.

The overrunning clutch provides a way to achieve Drive Breakaway and then it just "freewheels." The rollers are wedged into the smaller section of the outer race (cam) by the springs, locking it.

This speedometer gear housing and adapter rotates to adapt to contain almost any size of speedometer gear.

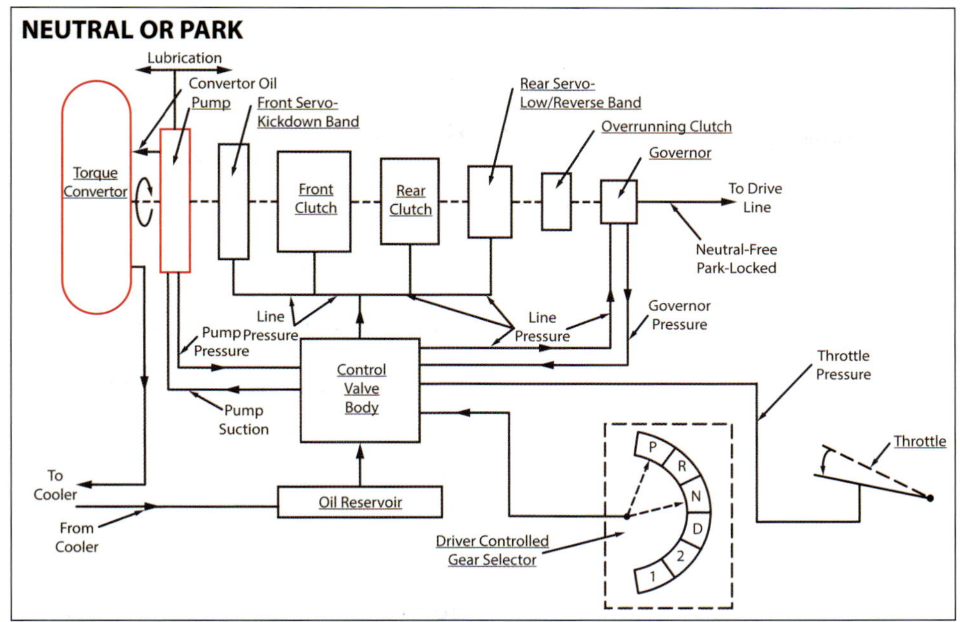

The converter and pump are shown in red to indicate that they are the only units "operating." The pump is pumping and the converter is spinning, but not much else is happening because in Neutral or Park, no clutches or bands are applied.

To lock the output shaft in Park, a piece of linkage is pushed into the parking gear lever by a cam/ball on the parking linkage (non-cable shift). Therefore, the parking gear-governor assembly (splined to the output shaft) can't rotate and neither can the output shaft.

There is also a hydraulic difference between Neutral and Park: "intentionally" reduced line pressure. When the shift lever or button is in Park, the "park" location of the manual valve (inside the valve body) allows fluid to leak by one land, causing a line pressure drop. Lower pressure in Park keeps the converter from filling completely and loading the engine unnecessarily. When the transmission is in Neutral however, the converter fills because there are no "controlled leaks" in the valve body. This is why the TorqueFlites' fluid level is checked in Neutral. If the level is checked in Park, it appears higher because the converter is not filled. Checking in any other gear is also incorrect because fluid will be use by hydraulic units.

Block Diagram: Drive Breakaway

When the shift lever or push button is put in Drive, the rear clutch pack clamps together applies). The rear clutch's friction plates, now locked to the driven plates, rotate the front annulus gear, which rotates the pinions, and spins the sun gear in a reverse direction. The sun gear rotates the pinion gears of the rear planetary in the same direction as the engine, providing gear reduction.

The converter, pump, rear clutch, overrunning clutch, and governor are all highlighted in red to indicate their use in Drive Breakaway. The rear clutch is applied and the overrunning clutch is locked.

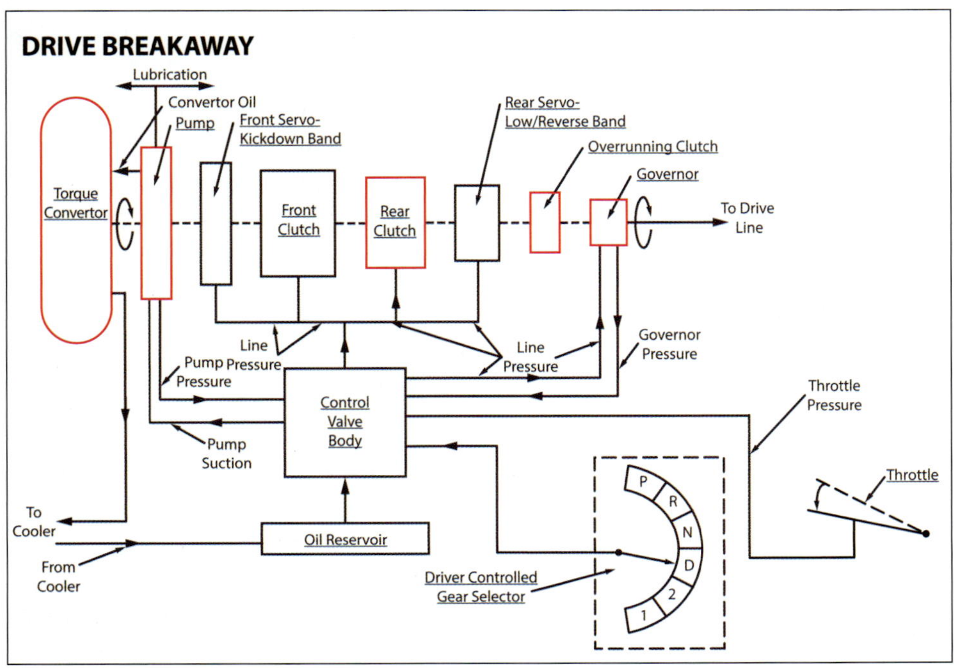

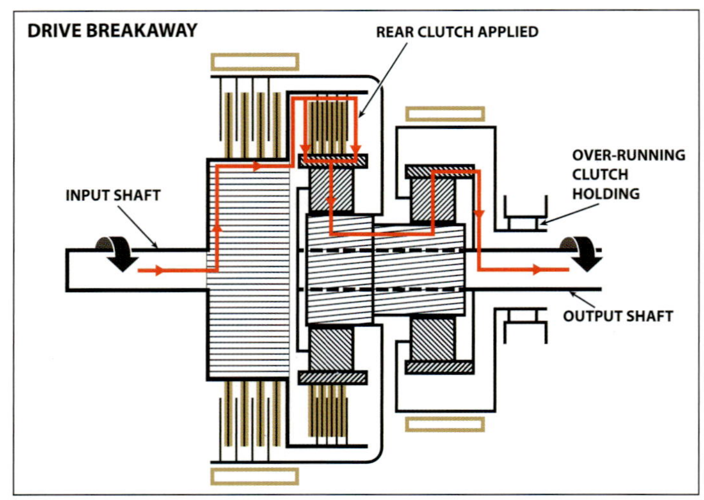

In Drive Breakaway, power is transferred through both planetary assemblies, providing the gear reduction to move the vehicle from a standstill or slow roll.

While in Drive/Breakaway, line pressure is directed to various valves in the valve body and to the governor. Once the vehicle is moving and the governor is spinning, the pressure signal is modulated and returned to the valve body to prepare for the 1–2 shift.

Power Flow: Drive Breakaway

The rear clutch friction and driven plates are clamped holding the annulus gear, driving the front planet carrier and rotating the inner sun gear to transfer power to the rear planetary, the rear annulus gear, and the output shaft. The overrunning clutch holds but the low-reverse band is not clamped on the low-reverse drum. With both planetaries now working, a Low gear of 2.45:1 or 2.67:1 is provided.

Block Diagram: Manual Low

When the selector lever or push button is placed in Low or "1,"

another assembly gets active. Placing the selector in Manual Low usually slows the vehicle if in Drive Second or Drive Direct. A driver may also want to hold the transmission in Low longer than the governor and throttle pressure circuit normally allow. Engine braking (the slowing of the vehicle) is accomplished when the low-reverse band stops the low-reverse drum (once out of Low, the drum normally freewheels). Remember, Low is a combination of the front and rear planetary sets, and the low-reverse drum has to be stationary to hold the rear planet carrier (to provide gear reduction). When the vehicle moves from a stop while the transmission is in Low, the overrunning clutch holds the drum, but once out of Low, the drum can only be stopped by the low-reverse band.

Power Flow: Manual Low

As in Drive Breakaway, during Manual Low, the rear clutch friction and driven plates are clamped and they drive the front planet carrier

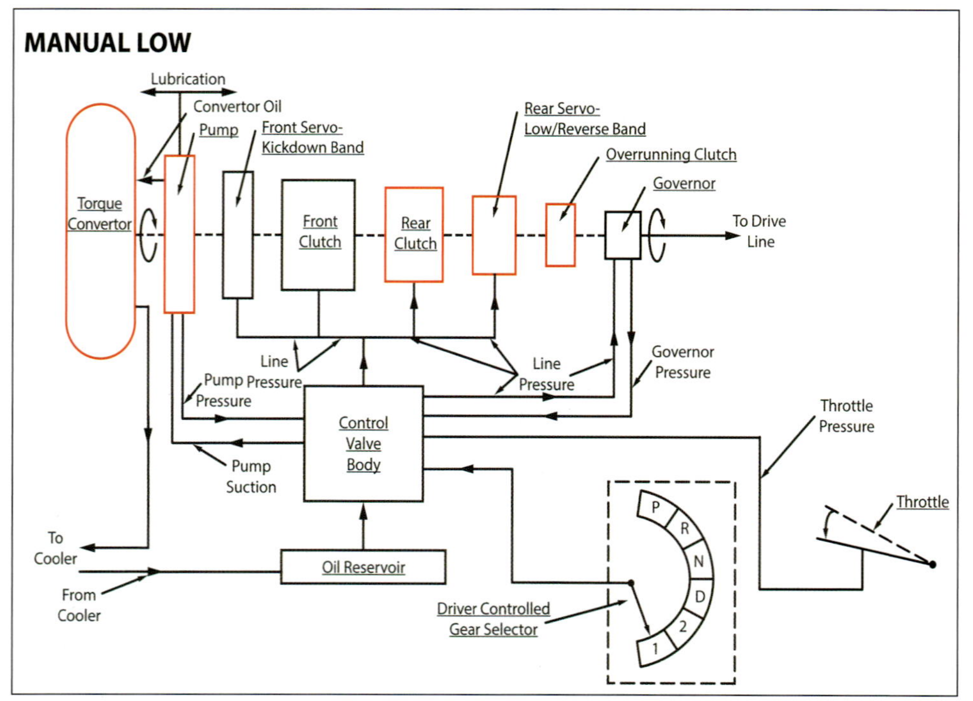

Note that Manual Low is basically Drive Breakaway with the addition of the low-reverse servo-band clamping the low-reverse drum; the governor signal to the 1–2 shift valve is blocked to prevent it from moving and allowing an upshift. ■

Along with the same parts in use for Drive Breakaway, this diagram also has the rear servo/low-reverse band in red to show it is functioning in Manual Low. The rear clutch and the low-reverse band are applied with the overrunning clutch.

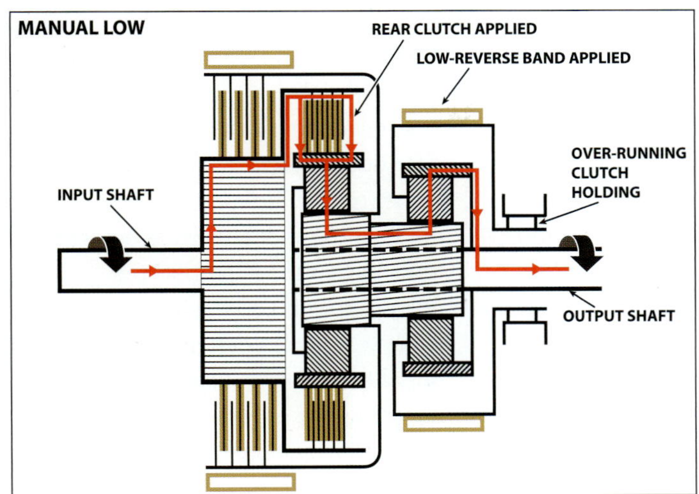

Manual Low uses the rear clutch and low-reverse band to hold the correct planetary components to provide a low gear of approximately 2.67:1 (wide ratio) or 2.54:1 input/output shaft speed. Manual Low also supplies engine breaking.

to rotate the inner sun gear, transferring power back to the rear planetary, the rear annulus gear, and into the output shaft providing a (Low) gear ratio of 2.45:1 or 2.67:1. The overrunning clutch is locked and the low-reverse band is also clamped on the low-reverse drum, providing engine braking not available in Drive Breakaway.

Block Diagram: Drive Second or Manual Second

With the selector or push button in Drive, the TorqueFlite shifts automatically into Second after the governor's modulated fluid moves the 1–2 shift valve allowing line pressure to be directed to the front servo-kickdown band assembly and accumulator. (The governor signal is generated by the output shaft's rotation, which throws the governor weights outward, working against spring pressure.) The governor pressure signal is also directed to the 2–3 valve in preparation for that shift. Along with the rear clutch (in operation) the fluid pushes the kickdown servo, actuating the apply lever to clamp the kickdown band on the front clutch retainer and stop it.

If the shift lever or push button is placed in (Manual) Second, it is the same as Drive Second with a hydraulic difference. With the lever in Second, the vehicle starts in Low and shifts to Second but the manual valve works with the line pressure to block the 2–3 shift valve preventing a 2–3 upshift. Governor pressure can't overcome line pressure on the 2–3 valve until the shifter is placed into Drive. When manually downshifting from Drive Direct to Second, the same Manual Second circuits function preventing an upshift back to Direct while the 2–3 shift valve is blocked by line pressure.

Power Flow: Drive Second

In Drive Second, the rear clutch plates are (still) clamped and transferring power into the front planetary's annulus gear and the front servo is now clamping the kickdown band. The band stops the front clutch retainer, which is locked into the sun gear driving shell that contains the sun gear. Because the kickdown band is holding the sun gear stationary via the sun gear shell, the applied rear clutch plates drive the front planetary annulus gear, forces

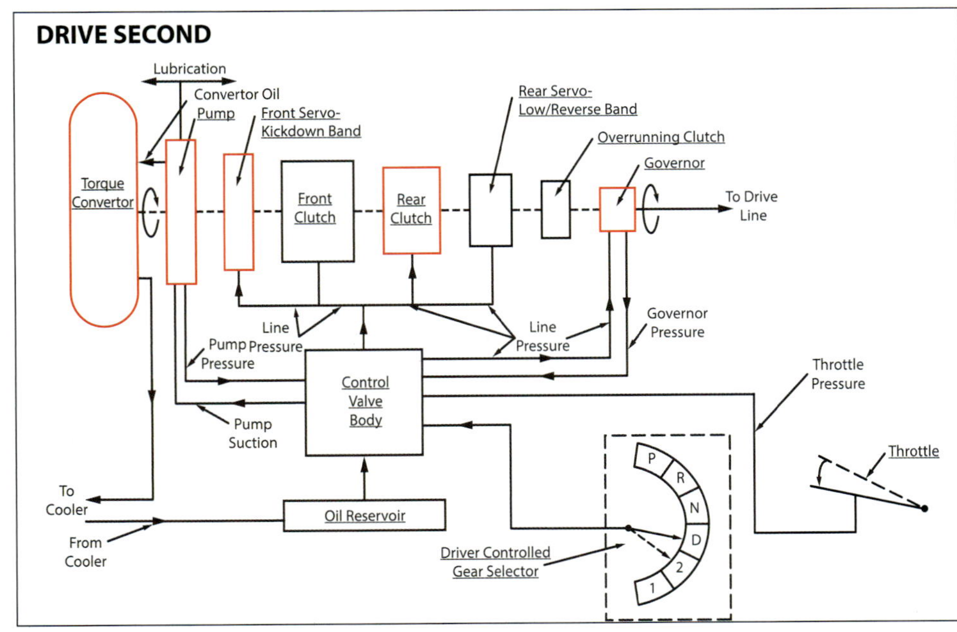

The converter, pump, front servo/kickdown band, rear clutch, and governor are highlighted in red to show that they function in Drive Second. The overrunning clutch is black, even though it was required in Drive Breakaway during acceleration. Once out of Low gear/Drive Breakaway, though, the overrunning clutch freewheels. Drive Second and Manual Second depend upon the application of the rear clutch and the kickdown band.

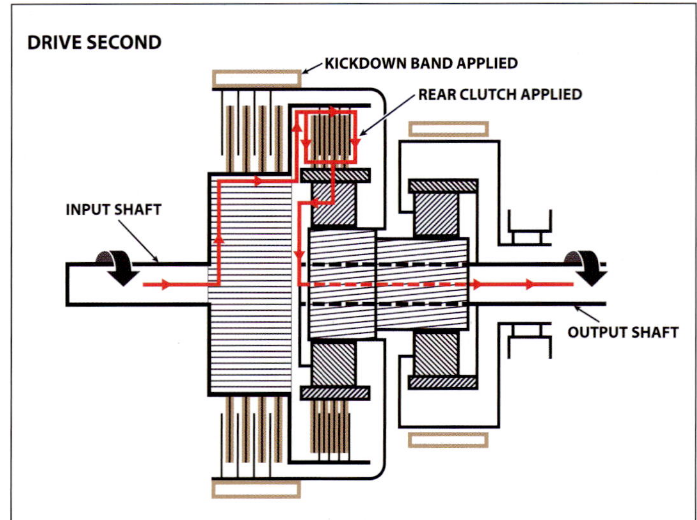

In Drive Second, the rear clutch clamps onto and rotates one part of the front planetary; the kickdown band/sun gear shell hold the other, causing the front planet carrier to rotate the output shaft at approximately 1.54:1 (wide ratio) or 1.45:1 input/output shaft speed ratio.

Front Planetary Assembly

The power flow transfer in Second gear occurs exclusively in the front planet carrier. Tight converters combined with high-torque engines feeding power to TorqueFlites equipped with aggressive shift kits in heavy vehicles can rip the splines out of the aluminum carriers. Some combinations may require steel or modified aluminum planet carriers. ∎

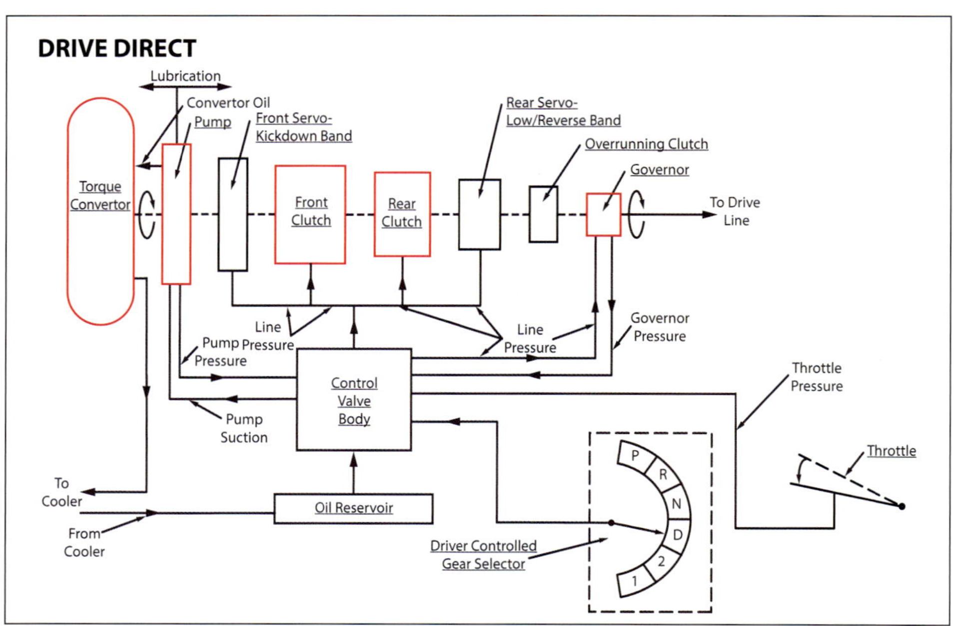

Shown in red are the assemblies that hydraulically function in Drive Direct: converter, pump, front clutch, rear clutch, and governor. To create Drive Direct requires the rear clutch and the Front/Direct clutch is added as the kickdown band drops off.

the front planet carrier to rotate in engine direction at a reduced speed. Moreover, because the front planet carrier's annulus gear is splined directly to the output shaft, the shaft now rotates at the reduced speed of roughly 1.45:1 or 1.52:1 (input speed to output speed). The overrunning clutch stays locked until the 1–2 shift completes.

Block Diagram: Drive Direct

With the selector or push button in Drive, and while the transmission is in Second, governor pressure is present on the 2–3 shift valve, the front clutch retainer has been stopped by the kickdown band, and the rear clutch is applied and rotating the front planetary and the output shaft.

When the signal is allowed to push the 2–3 shift valve in the valve body, fluid is directed to the release side of the front servo, releasing the kickdown band. Fluid is also directed into the front clutch retainer and pushes the piston clamping the friction discs and driven plates together. Because the kickdown band releases quickly, the front clutch retainer spins up almost immediately to create Direct Drive.

Power Flow: Drive Direct

With the valve body and governor now creating the signal, the rear clutch plates stay applied, the kickdown band releases the front clutch retainer allowing it to spin, and its clutch plates clamp together, locking the front clutch retainer to the rear clutch hub and the sun gear driving shell. The front clutch retainer is now spinning at engine speed and in the same direction, so the sun gear shell does the same. The rear clutch plates are still driving the annulus gear of the front planetary assembly, which is splined to the output shaft, and it also is at engine speed and rotating in the same direction. Because there are now two parts of the same planetary gear set running at the same speed

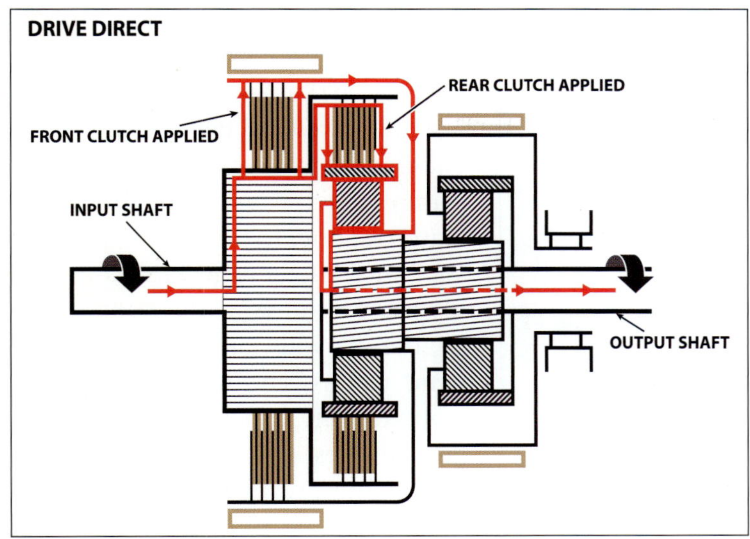

In Drive Direct, the rear clutch holds the front planetary annulus gear and the front clutch holds the sun gear shell/sun gear. Because two parts of the same planetary assembly are rotating at the same speed (engine speed), the planetary that is splined to the output shaft is rotating at that speed to provide Direct Drive or a 1:1 input/output shaft ratio.

in the same direction, the planetary assembly is essentially one solid unit. When this occurs, the planetary transfers the same power out of it as that put into it, in other words, it spins at engine speed. Because it is splined to the output shaft via the rear annulus gear, the output shaft is driven at engine speed. Drive Direct gets its name because engine speed is transferred "directly in a 1:1 ratio" through the transmission.

Block Diagram: Reverse Gear

When the TorqueFlite shift selector is placed into Reverse, the rear clutch assembly, used in all Forward gears, gets no fluid so the friction discs and driven plates are not clamped/applied. However, the front clutch now has fluid pressure directed to it, clamping the friction plates to the steel discs locking the front clutch assembly to the front clutch hub-input shaft assembly. Along with application of the front clutch, fluid is also directed to the low-reverse servo, clamping the low-reverse band around the low-reverse drum/rear planet carrier assembly.

Hydraulically, there are exciting things happening in Reverse. Governor pressure is ignored and line pressure can be from about 160 to 270 psi (normal line pressure is 55 to 90 psi). It may not be obvious why Reverse requires such high line pressure until

the mechanism of the front and rear clutch assembly is compared. The rear clutch pack is clamped in all Forward gears and it uses a Belleville spring washer to multiply piston apply force to transmit engine torque through the clutch pack. Unfortunately, the front clutch has no "force multiplying device" other than a slightly larger surface area of the apply piston. Because Direct Drive is the only other time the front clutch assembly is applied and the vehicle is already in motion, no extraordinary holding power is needed to lock the front clutch friction discs to the steel-driven plates. However, with the selector in Reverse, the vehicle is likely stationary and greater torque has to be transmitted through the applied front clutch plates. Therefore, through a couple of hydraulic changes, line pressure is almost tripled to provide the clamping force the front clutch assembly needs to transfer the power.

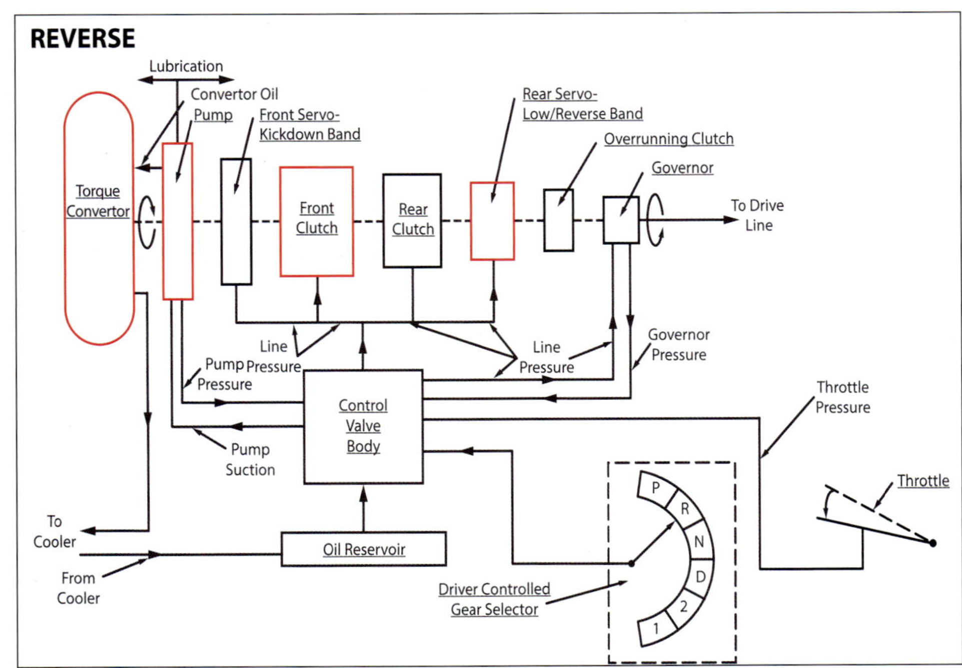

The assemblies in red that work to provide Reverse are the converter, pump, front clutch, and rear servo/low reverse band. No governor signal is needed. Reverse gives the rear clutch a break, but the low-reverse band and front clutch are now applied.

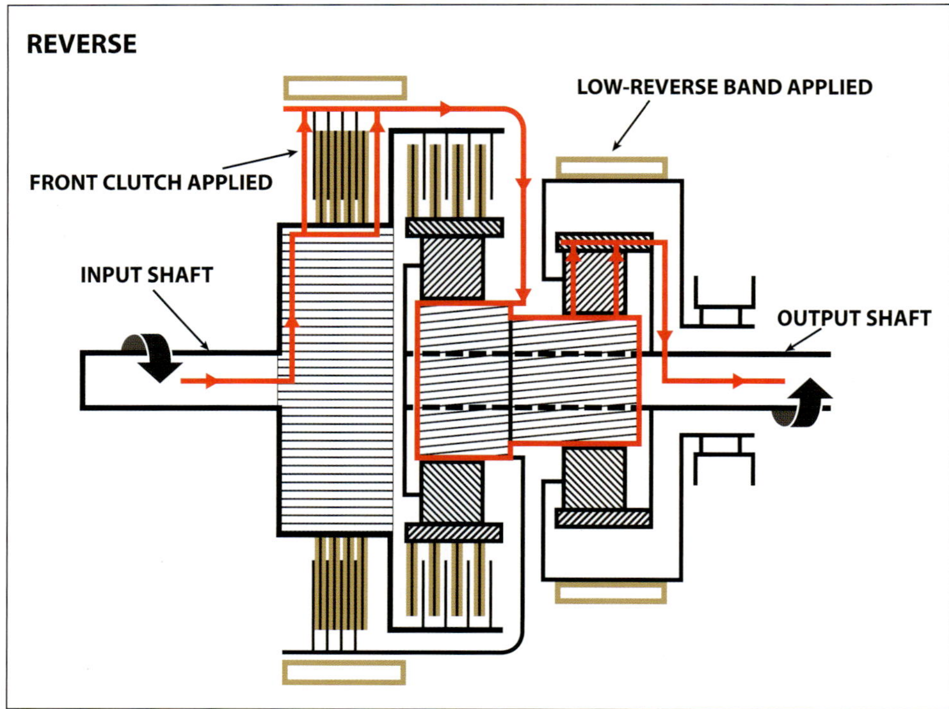

For Reverse, the front clutch holds the sun gear to transfer power into the rear planet carrier. However, the low-reverse band holds the planet carrier via the low-reverse drum. With the planetary held and the sun gear rotating, all that can happen is the annulus gear rotates at a 2.2:1 input/output shaft speed ratio. The annulus gear reverses direction, and it is splined to the output shaft so it also reverses, providing a way to back up the vehicle.

CLUTCH AND BAND APPLICATION CHART

LOW (D) (Breakaway) 2.45:1 2.67:1*	LOW (1) (Manual) 2.45:1 2.67:1*	SECOND 1.45:1 1.52:1*	DIRECT 1.00:1 1.00:1*	REVERSE 2.21:1 2.21:1*
REAR CLUTCH DRIVES FRONT ANNULUS GEAR	REAR CLUTCH DRIVES FRONT ANNULUS GEAR	REAR CLUTCH DRIVES FRONT ANNULUS GEAR	REAR CLUTCH DRIVES FRONT ANNULUS GEAR	FRONT CLUTCH DRIVES SUN GEAR
OVERRUNNING CLUTCH HOLDS REAR PLANET CARRIER	LOW AND REVERSE BAND HOLDS REAR PLANET CARRIER	KICKDOWN BAND HOLDS SUN GEAR	FRONT CLUTCH DRIVES SUN GEAR	LOW AND REVERSE BAND HOLDS REAR PLANET CARRIER

*Wide ratio used in A-998 and A-999

This summary chart helps you remember "What's on When."

Power Flow: Reverse

Unlike in forward gears, with the selector in Reverse, the rear clutch is not applied. In Reverse, the front clutch friction and driven plates clamp together, which locks the clutch retainer to the sun gear driving shell and the sun gear. This assembly rotates the same direction as the engine. In addition, the low-reverse band clamps the low-reverse drum stopping it. Therefore, the sun gear rotates with the engine, the rear planet carrier is held by the low-reverse drum/low-reverse band, and the annulus gear has to rotate, but in this case, it reverses direction. The engine torque transfers from the rear planet's pinion gears to the rear annulus gear splined to the output shaft. The output shaft now rotates in the opposite direction as the engine, and at a ratio of ~2.20:1 (input-to-output shaft speed). Engine torque transfers through the transmission and with the output shaft rotating in the reverse direction, the vehicle backs up.

Clutch and Band Application

As a reminder of how the Torque-Flite components combine to create various gear ratios and rotations, see the simple clutch and band application chart.

TROUBLESHOOTING

Troubleshooting is simply finding and fixing a problem. With the TorqueFlite, identifying the problem and knowing where to look for its solution is sometimes tough. This chapter helps focus attention on the internal assemblies and exterior parts that often create common issues.

Like any device designed and assembled by humans, TorqueFlites are not infallible. Over time and with use, their elastomeric materials change due to fluid exposure and heat. Friction materials wear out. Springs change tension. Wear particles from gears and friction materials end up in the wrong places. Driver abuse and neglect take a toll. Eventually, several things combine to cause operational and shifting issues, noises, leaks, and worst case, catastrophic failures.

Troubleshooting is a bit more difficult now compared to when the TorqueFlites were new because, over time, owners have made "improvements," swapped parts, enlarged transfer plate holes, and changed springs in the valve body. Many TorqueFlites degrade due to storage. Fixing them when they were newer was relatively straightforward; you made sure their parts met the original specifications and you adjusted everything according to factory specifications and engineering changes. Unfortunately, as time passes, original parts are replaced, and original engines and carburetors and the matching throttle pressure linkage, manifolds, and levers are long separated.

Combine several changes and it becomes apparent why it is much more difficult to predict and explain what could be wrong and why it may be tough to find and fix every problem. Unfortunately, (or fortunately, if you have fun doing it) TorqueFlites may simply need to be removed for repair. It is not uncommon to buy a vehicle that has what seems like a simple transmission issue, but that turns into something much more difficult. Often, you just have to return it to its original condition. Knowing the history of the transmission is very important, but many times, it may not be possible to get all the information needed.

In this chapter, information from factory and aftermarket literature is combined with input from experienced mechanics to highlight TorqueFlite operational issues, what could cause them, and what steps can be taken to correct them.

In 1970, Superbirds stood out because of their long nose and big wing. This brilliant white one retains its original A-727, which was rebuilt in the early 1980s.

Fortunately, because A-904s and A-727s are closely related, troubleshooting is similar.

There are three "Trouble" charts provided in Appendix B: one that deals with troubles that can be diagnosed and fixed with the transmission in the vehicle, a second that requires removal of the transmission/converter for repair, and a third that is exclusively for lock-up converter-equipped problems. Noises and fluid leaks are discussed.

There is a logical and ordered sequence that should be followed when troubleshooting a transmission. By doing it in this way, simple things can be identified and corrected first. One manufacturer states it most eloquently: "The logical and proper procedure is diagnosis before disassembly." In other words, identify the problems and use your knowledge of how the TorqueFlite works before automatically jumping in and tearing it down.

Fortunately, there are a few basic things that cause most of the trouble.

- The fluid level is too high or too low.
- The throttle pressure is wrong.
- The engine is not running right.
- The shift linkage is not correct.
- The band(s) is out of adjustment.

And if correcting these easy things doesn't fix the problem, there are always more complex things to look at.

- Hydraulic pressures are out of specification.
- Internal hydraulic issues are present.
- Mechanical failures have occurred.
- Mismatched parts and technology are combined.

Chapter 2 offered insight as to how the TorqueFlite actually works so one can understand what the transmission is doing in each gear. Diagnosing in the proper sequence helps the problem be identified quicker.

- The basic things should always be checked and corrected early.
- To gather additional operational data, a diagnostic road test can be taken (if drivable).
- After road testing is complete, you may be able to decide what is wrong. If not, hydraulic pressure tests can be made to provide more internal information.
- If after pressure testing, the problem is still not apparent, removal of the valve body lets an air-pressure test be made of the transmission to determine the condition of the hydraulic sections.
- Torque converter issues may be part of or even the whole problem; the "nerve-racking" converter stall test can be performed.

Rough Steels

One of the things done to increase torque capacity is to increase the quantity of friction discs and steel plates in the front clutch retainer. This requires a larger, deeper retainer, thinner steels, thinner frictions, or a modified piston (along with extra return springs) or any combination thereof. For an A-727 behind a worked-over 340, I thinned some front steel plates by getting them ground and then smoothed them out with a light sand blast, followed by a lot of sanding. I then added thinner rear clutch friction discs and was able to install seven (I believe). It worked pretty well with a nice firm shift at wide-open throttle. After a few days, I needed to make a minor kickdown band adjustment to eliminate the spin-up that started during light throttle 2–3 shifts. I knew everything was right so it must have been just the kickdown band wearing in. A few more days and another band adjustment was needed. A few more days and another minor readjustment did not take care of it.

I knew the pressure was right and the fluid level was correct. The fluid looked a little darker, but that was expected. The throttle pressure was reset, but it was close enough. No way could it be my modifications. I suspected the kickdown band was failing so out the transmission came. The pump and the front clutch retainer, along with the kickdown band and kickdown servo, were removed. The band and servo were perfect. The front friction discs, unfortunately, were devoid of almost all friction material. Those custom steel plates that I just knew would smooth out and be polished by the "sort of rough" friction discs looked the same as when they were installed.

Would any additional tests have identified this issue? In this case, the history of the transmission needed to be understood. Testing the transmission may have provided some answers, but questioning the transmission mechanic's background in physics would have told the story. (Always remember, steel plates have to be smooth and almost polished to avoid damage to the less durable paper-based material they interleave with. Rough metal almost always wins against paper.)

By combining (1) the information gathered from the tests, (2) data in the three troubleshooting charts, and (3) any known history of the TorqueFlite in question, you should be able to determine the problem and identify the fix needed.

Fortunately, some of the simplest things to check cause the highest percentage of problems. Pulling the dipstick to check the fluid level, verifying that the shift linkage is close, and checking the throttle pressure linkage can all be performed rapidly and without any tools.

Fluid Level

Start by checking the fluid level. With the engine at a general idle speed and the fluid warm to hot, the fluid level in Neutral should be between the "full" and "add one pint" level. If it is too low, the pump, via the filter, can suck in air causing all types of hydraulic issues. It the level is too high, the gears and spinning parts can whip the fluid into a foam or froth, which also causes similar issues.

While checking the level, look at the fluid to be sure it is red or light brown; it should never be black, burnt smelling, or have flakes or tiny metal particulates in it. Newer fluids

This filter did its job; the size of metal particles and friction material flakes it caught range from microscopic to 1/16 inch in diameter.

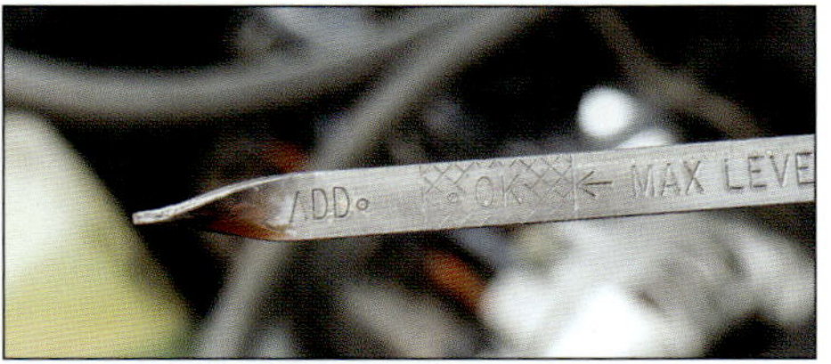

Your first step should be to check the fluid level. This one is down a pint, probably due to a pan gasket leak.

Adding type 7176 Mopar fluid brings the level to the lower part of the range.

tend to smell more burnt so you may have to put a few drops on a white cloth to see if it is blackish or dark brown. If there is metal in the fluid or pieces of things floating around in it, it is likely too late.

Shift Linkage

With the fluid level verified, check the shift linkage, whatever kind yours has. Assuming the neutral starting switch is functional, move the shifter to "Park" or "P," and if the starter spins over when you turn the key, it is good (so far). Move the selector to "N" and hit the key again. If it spins over in "N," the linkage is probably pretty close. If it just misses each position by a little bit, look at the linkage to see if the pins are worn out, or the holes are elongated, or the plastic bushings are shot.

If you have an aftermarket shifter, you may have to slowly "feel it" through all the detent positions to be sure it is even close. At one extreme it has to be in "L" or "1" and

at the other it has to be in "P." Often, the levers that may have been put on your transmission may be the wrong length and you may have "P" or "L" ("1") but not both.

As difficult as it is to drill holes or modify expensive aftermarket parts, levers may need drilling so "P" and "L" are correctly located and that in "N" and "P," the starter spins over. Many times it is as simple as changing to the correct lever on the transmission manual valve shaft but it may be hard finding the right one. The total distance the shifter lever moves at the cable attaching point has to match the distance the cable attaching point of the manual lever moves.

Throttle Pressure Linkage

This is by far the most important signal the stock TorqueFlite needs to work properly. The throttle pressure signal tells the valve body where the carburetor or throttle body lever is at any given point in time. Is the engine idling or under load? Is the throttle wide open or did the driver just lift off the gas? The linkage transmits the signal that tells the transmission how hard to shift, when to shift, when to downshift, and when to ease up or increase pressures. If the

An intake and carburetor change usually requires a change in the length of the throttle pressure link. As a temporary fix, a 1/4-20 bolt and nut was added to make up the gap.

This longer throttle pressure link corrects the differences caused by a swap.

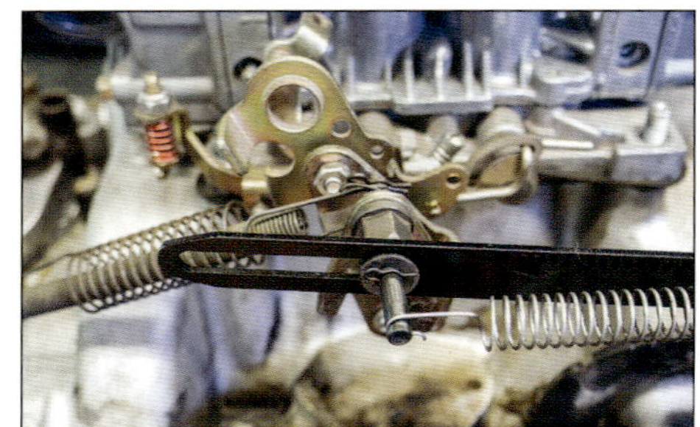

With the new link on, the rear of the slot is at the throttle linkage pin allowing pressure to be set correctly.

The shift linkage on this 1987 truck uses two plastic bushings to support the horizontal shaft. Always check these for looseness if you experience starting or manual shifting issues.

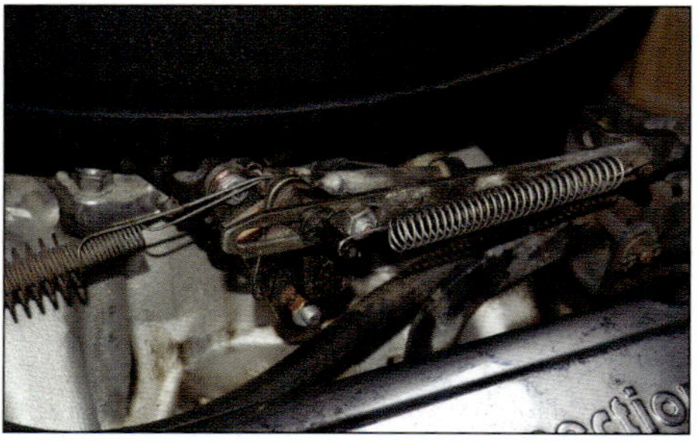

This truck has a 500-cfm Edelbrock AVS carburetor and an owner-modified throttle pressure link. With the nut and bolt, the rear of the link touched the pin, although it was not the right way to solve the mismatch.

This bushing is under the driver's left foot; often overlooked, it is critical to proper gear selection.

This bushing is on the transmission side bracket. The lever on the shaft uses another molded bushing into which the linkage snaps. Older Torque-Flites have pins in holes held with clips and cotter pins. The bushings or holes and pins can wear making linkage feel sloppy and cause starting issues.

At wide-open throttle, the link pushes the throttle valve in the valve body correctly.

throttle pressure linkage is wrong, most everything about the shift is wrong. It must be correct.

Unfortunately, even though the "top side" of the engine's linkage can be correct, the lever on the transmission may be wrong. The 2- and 4-barrel engines often had different linkage lengths and shapes, so it may be as easy as switching to a shorter lever or one with the different angle if your linkage is still off. As long as the throttle pressure linkage follows the carburetor or throttle body pin and ends up close to full detent when the carburetor or throttle body is wide open and it goes back when at idle, you can get by without damage. Leaving it off because you do not need "kickdown" is never, ever acceptable unless the lever on the transmission is tied to keep pressure on the internal throttle valve. Even then it is truly only correct at one position unless it is a manual valve body and the pressure is maxed out.

There is another way to take care of mismatched throttle pressure linkage. Bouchillon Performance Engineering and Lokar Performance Products sell cable-operated throttle pressure kits that replace the OEM mechanical rods and linkage. The parts they come with help you adapt to most any combination, and their instructions detail how to set the pressure correctly at idle and wide-open-throttle conditions. If you have changes that render the rod-type linkage too difficult to use, either of these should help.

"Adapting" to Change

If you have a non-stock carburetor or throttle body, adapters from Edelbrock and Holley help get the linkage adjustments back within stock specifications. The key thing is the throttle valve inside the valve body needs to move in unison with the throttle pin on the carburetor or throttle body. For this to happen, the linkage from the manual shaft on the valve body to the throttle body or carburetor needs to be right and have similar geometry. In other words, the total movement of the carburetor or throttle body pin needs to match the total movement of the lever at the transmission.

Here's an example. On a 1968 Barracuda with an A-904, the throttle pressure rod's connection on the transmission to the upper bell crank is adjusted according to factory specs, and it moves roughly 1⅝ inches from baseline (closed) throttle pressure to maximum (wide-open) throttle pressure. Therefore, for the transmission to receive the correct signal, the item that actuates or pushes the bell crank also has to move a total distance of 1⅝ inches. Fortunately, a 4611 Carter AVS (a 1969 340-ci V-8 original carburetor) pin that the throttle cable and throttle pressure link attaches to moves 1⅝ inches from dead closed to wide-open throttle. However, if you toss on a typical Holley carburetor "out of the box" and have to move the pivot pin to the only hole on the Holley that it fits in, which is farther away from the throttle blade's shaft, the total movement from closed to wide-open throttle is 2¼ inches. If you hook the throttle pressure linkage to it, you find it is out of alignment side-to-side and the length is way off. If you are crafty, you make it fit, but it still may not work. The carburetor can be at idle with the throttle pressure link adjusted so the back of its groove hits the pin on the carburetor lever.

A test drive reveals that something is wrong; with the pedal to the floor, it doesn't seem to have as much power as it used to. The transmission shifts fine at wide-open throttle, but the vehicle feels doggy. You look into the carburetor or throttle body with the pedal to the floor but the secondary is not wide open. Easy enough to fix you figure: reset the throttle pressure linkage so that at wide-open throttle, the linkage aligns with the maxed-out throttle pressure lever on the transmission or at the bell crank. Now you can achieve maximum power because the throttle body or carburetor can go wide open. It runs hard and shifts great at wide-open throttle, but it shifts terrible at light throttle. It slips and shifts way too soft and soon. Why is this? The transmission lever needs only 1⅝ inches total movement for everything to work correctly. Unfortunately, this carburetor pin moves 2¼ inches with it in the wrong hole (which

A Holley 670 Avenger without a throttle pressure adapter bracket and with the throttle linkage pin in the only hole it fits, has a drastic linkage misalignment in length and angle. In this situation, many may say "forget it" and leave the linkage off. You should never do this.

is the only one t fit). And here is the most terrible thing done so frequently to the TorqueFlite: "Oh well, no need for kickdown, I'll just leave the 'kickdown' linkage off."

Here's how to fix this. Edelbrock and Holley offer an adapter (the Edelbrock version is PN 8021; Holley's is PN 20-7) for their respective carburetors for Chrysler applications that holds the pin the right distance from the throttle shaft so that the linkage moves the 1⅝ inches from closed to wide-open throttle. You may have to make a longer throttle pressure link or raise the throttle cable bracket (or both if you use taller intake) to get it correct if yours was a 2-barrel vehicle. By using these adapters, the transmission always receives the throttle pressure signal it needs. ■

Almost anytime a carburetor is replaced on a Torque-Flite vehicle, you need one of these adapters to reposition the throttle linkage pin to the correct location.

"Adapting" to Change *CONTINUED*

With the adapter installed, the movement of the throttle linkage pin is correct and the linkage pushes relatively straight back.

Sometimes, if you use a taller intake or if a carburetor spacer is used, this bracket may have to be raised so that the cable pulls horizontally.

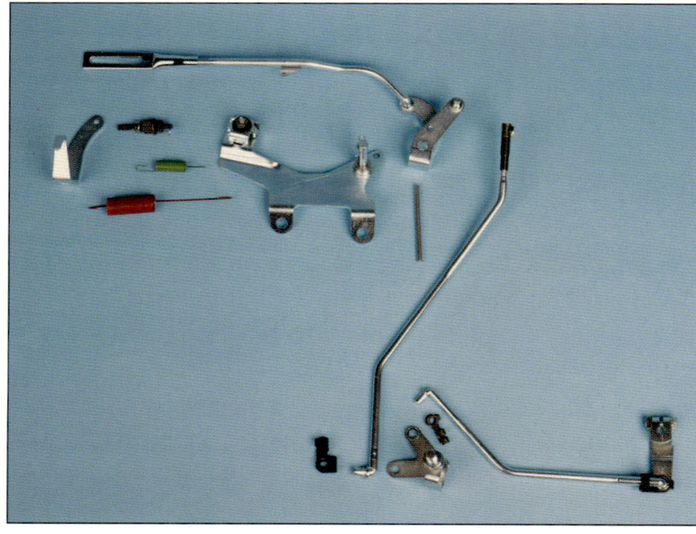

When starting with nothing or fighting a mix of parts, a good way to go is to get an entire throttle pressure linkage kit. This A&A setup is for a 1969–1970 340-ci engine having an AVS carburetor.

If after the three most basic things (fluid level, manual linkage, and throttle pressure linkage) have been checked and set correctly, you still have an issue, a road test may let you determine what other things are happening inside the TorqueFlite.

Road Testing

If it moves, drive the car or truck in each gear position and feel for any slippage or incorrect shifts. Pay attention to see if shifts are late and hard or early and soft. Notice if the engine "winds way up" in first and then skips Second and goes straight to Direct, or if it's mushy in a certain gear position.

Read the "What's on When" chart (end of Chapter 2) before and after the road test to help identify the issues. Here are a couple of examples.

1. In all Forward gears, the rear clutch assembly is active. If the vehicle moves okay until it shifts into "D" Direct and then it slips, it could be the rear clutch dropping out, but more than likely the front clutch assembly is slipping. Because you know the TorqueFlite also uses the front clutch for Reverse, place the shifter in Reverse. If the transmission also slips in Reverse, suspect the front clutch because the rear clutch is not used in Reverse.

2. If you have Low and Direct but Second gear feels funny or takes a long time to "engage" fully, suspect something in the kickdown band assembly. Why? You know it can't be the rear or front clutch assemblies because Low and Direct work. When it shifts into Second, the kickdown band is added into the equation. Using the knowledge of how the TorqueFlite works helps narrow down the problem(s).

If you still don't know what is wrong, the next troubleshooting step can be hydraulic pressure testing to learn what is going on inside.

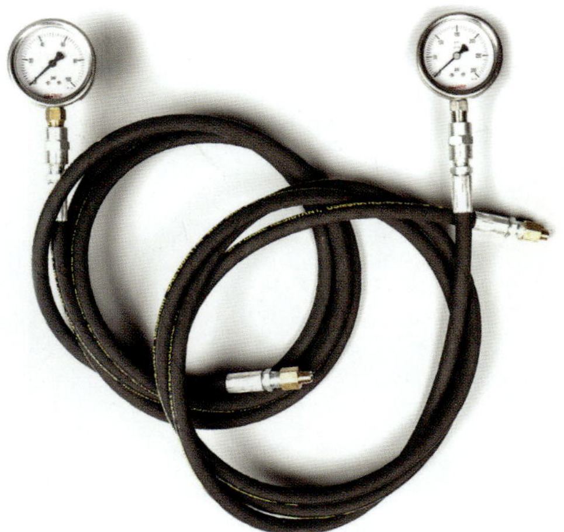

To perform hydraulic pressure tests, you need a pressure-rated hose, 100- and 300-psi gauges, and adapters to fit 1/8-inch NPT ports in the transmission. I used two assemblies to get data twice as fast.

If a shift modification kit is installed, or the main line pressure was adjusted higher than stock, your pressure values may be higher than the ones shown.

Hydraulic Pressure Testing

Pressure testing various sections of the TorqueFlite is possible because of the 1/8-inch NPT (National Pipe Taper) pressure ports strategically located on the exterior of the transmission. To test it, I used two pressure-rated hoses with easy-to-read and accurate gauges along with straight and 90-degree 1/8-inch NPT male pipe fittings. A 300-psi gauge is required for Reverse pressure but a 100-psi gauge works for everything else. With a long hose, you can locate the gauge well away from the transmission, eliminating the need to be underneath the vehicle while testing it.

The four 1/8-inch NPT ports enable measurement of line pressure, rear servo apply pressure, front servo release pressure, and governor pressure. By adding a "tee" into the cooler line circuit at the transmission rear cooler line fitting or at the radiator, the lubrication pressure can be checked. These five pressures allow diagnosis of most any stock-type internal failure. As an added bonus, it's fun to watch the gauges during operation.

Again, be sure the simple things (fluid level, linkage adjustments, etc.) have been checked and corrected before pressure testing. Along with gauges and hoses, a tachometer and a safe way to raise and support the vehicle (preferably a lift) are

On the side is the line pressure and front servo release pressure port.

On the rear is a governor pressure and rear servo apply pressure port. All are 1/8-inch female NPT.

required. I never recommend doing this on cheap and flimsy jack stands, nor do I suggest lying underneath a car or truck on jack stands while manually shifting the transmission and/or moving the throttle pressure lever. No transmission test is worth your life. Locate the gauges away from underneath and operate the linkages from above. For another level of safety, the rear wheels and tires can be removed.

Pressure in Manual "1" or "L"

This tests the pump, pressure regulation, and the rear clutch and rear servo assemblies.

Connect two 100-psi pressure gauges: one to the line pressure port and the other to the rear servo port. With the engine speed held at approximately 1,000 rpm and the transmission shifted to "1" or "L," release the brakes so the wheels turn and observe the pressures. Slowly push the throttle pressure linkage from its idle (front) location to its farthest rear location and watch the gauges. The line pressure should start around 54 to 60 psi and increase to 90 to 96 psi, and the rear servo pressure should follow line pressure within about 3 psi. Apply the brakes to stop the wheels before putting the transmission back in "P."

Pressure in Manual "2"

This tests the pump, pressure regulation, the rear clutch, and the lubrication pressure.

Connect two 100-psi pressure gauges: one to the line pressure port and one to the rear cooler line. You can tee the 0- to 100-psi gauge into the cooler line at the radiator or at the cooler return line on the rear of the driver's side of the case. With the engine speed held at approximately 1,000 rpm and the transmission shifted to "2," release the brakes so the wheels can turn and observe/record the pressure after it shifts into Second gear. Slowly push the throttle pressure linkage from the minimum (front) to the maximum (rear). The line pressure should increase from 54 to 60 psi up to 90 to 96 psi, and the lubrication pressure should increase

At slightly above idle, approximately 1,000 rpm, in Manual Low, with the throttle pressure at minimum, line pressure should be close to 60 psi (left gauge). The rear servo apply pressure should be within 3 psi of it because in Manual Low, the rear servo uses line pressure to push the band lever to clamp the low-reverse drum. The pressure (right gauge) is close to 60 psi.

Pushing the throttle pressure linkage to its maximum, the line pressure (left) and the rear servo apply pressure (right) and climb to about 90 psi. These two tests show that the pump, pressure regulation, rear servo, and rear clutch assemblies are working.

Checking lubrication pressure via the cooler line, with the engine running at 1,000 rpm, throttle pressure at its minimum, and the transmission in Manual Second, the line pressure should be around 60 psi and lubrication pressure at about 15 psi when shifted into Second.

Pushing the throttle pressure linkage to its maximum, line pressure increases to 90 psi and lubrication pressure doubles to around 30 psi. These two tests prove that the pump and pressure regulation is correct, and lubrication pressure is great.

from 5 to 15 psi at idle to 10 to 30 psi. Apply the brakes to stop the wheels before putting the transmission back in "P." Even though lubrication pressure should not cause shifting or driving issues, it is the lifeblood of the TorqueFlite, and it is important to see how it acts when the transmission is operating.

Pressure in "D"

This tests the pump, pressure regulation, and the front and rear clutch, along with the lock-up converter circuit (if so equipped).

Connect two 100-psi pressure gauges: one to the line pressure port and one to the front servo release port. Hold the engine speed to about 1,600 rpm and place the selector lever in D, release the brakes so the wheels can turn, and observe the pressure after the wheels rotate and the transmission shifts into Direct. Slowly push the throttle pressure linkage from the front to the maximum rearward travel. The line pressure should have started around 54 to 60 psi and increased from there as the throttle pressure linkage moves rearward. The front servo pressure should read the same as the line pressure (within about 3 psi), up to the point that detent downshift occurs and the transmission kicks down to Second. At this point, the pressure drops to basically 0 psi. Apply the brakes to stop the wheels before putting the transmission back in "P."

Pressure in "R"

This tests the rear servo assembly. Connect the 300-psi gauge to the rear servo apply port. Place the selector lever in "R," hold the engine speed to about 1,600 rpm, release the brakes so the wheels can turn, and observe the pressure gauge. The rear servo apply pressure should read anywhere from 160 to 270 psi. Apply the brakes and after the wheels have stopped, move the selector lever to "D" to verify that the rear servo apply pressure drops back to 0 psi.

The 300-psi gauge attaches to the rear servo apply port to monitor Reverse pressure. With the throttle pressure at minimum, and while holding the brake on, put it in Reverse and raise the engine speed to 1,600 rpm. Older TorqueFlites have around 270 psi, but the late-1980s A-727s are around 160 psi.

For the next two tests, one gauge monitors line pressure and the other measures front servo release pressure. The throttle pressure is at idle condition and the transmission is in Drive Direct with the engine held to around 1,600 rpm. The gauges show that line pressure is about 60 psi and the front servo release pressure is within a few psi of 60. This makes sense; for the transmission to be in Drive Direct, the kickdown band has to be off (released) because the release side of the servo has 60 psi applied to it.

While still in Reverse, the throttle is returned to idle, the brakes are applied, and the shifter is placed in Drive Direct. The rear servo apply pressure should drop to zero because the servo is not applied in Drive Direct (it is on only in Reverse and Manual Low). The 172 psi noted in the previous test and the current 0 psi shows that there is no significant leakage in the rear servo apply side. No extraneous fluid pressure is leaking into the servo during Drive Direct.

With the gauges still showing line pressure and front servo release pressure, at 1,600 rpm in Drive Direct, the throttle pressure linkage is pushed all the way rearward. When this occurs, the valve body goes into kickdown mode and the transmission comes out of Drive Direct and drops back into Second. The kickdown band is applied and the servo release pressure falls off to about 0 psi. The line pressure is around 90 psi and servo release pressure should be close to 0 psi; this shows that the pump and pressure regulation system are good and the front and rear clutch circuits are functioning and relatively leak-free.

Governor Pressure

This test is usually only needed if the transmission shifts at abnormal speeds, even though the throttle pressure is correctly set. The values given are typical for a vehicle equipped with a 2.71 to 3.23 final drive ratio with the throttle pressure linkage hooked up and functioning correctly.

Connect the 100-psi gauge to the governor pressure port on the rear of the case. Place the transmission in "D," release the brakes so the wheels can turn and the transmission shifts into Direct, and watch the pressure gauge with the speedometer showing 21 to 24 mph. The governor pressure should be around 15 psi. Increase the speed up to 50 to 65 mph and the

To verify that the governor is working, the pressure gauge is attached to the governor port. On this truck with a 3.21 rear axle ratio, the speed was increased from 0 to about 25 mph. The governor pressure smoothly rose to 20 psi.

Still monitoring governor pressure, the speed was increased to about 80 to 85 mph; the governor pressure should rise to around 60 psi, which it did.

Lifting off the gas and applying the brakes to stop the rear wheels should cause the governor pressure to fall to 0 psi. This enables an almost unnoticeable downshift into Breakaway or Low gear. The gauge showed that the governor was working.

Results from Pressure Testing

- If you recorded and/or observed the listed line pressures when the throttle pressure linkage is moved from its forward to its rearward positions, the pump and regulation system are functioning correctly.
- If you observed low pressure readings in "D," "1," and "2" but proper pressure in "R," it means there is a leak in the rear clutch circuit.
- If there were low-pressure readings in "R" and "1" but correct pressures in "2," it means there is leakage in the rear servo assembly.
- If you observed correct pressure in "1" but low pressures in "D" and "R," there is likely leakage in the front clutch circuit.
- If you observed low line pressure in every position, it may indicate a clogged oil filter, low fluid, a bad oil pump, or a stuck pressure regulator valve in the valve body.
- If the values observed during the governor tests do not match the suggested values at the correct speeds, there may be a sticking valve or weight in the governor body. The pressures should increase smoothly and proportionately to changes in throttle and speed. With the wheels completely stopped but the transmission still in the "D" position, the governor pressure should not be much above 1.5 psi or it may not downshift correctly. If the throttle pressure linkage is set wrong and it is being pushed rearward even though the engine is idling, it can cause high governor pressure making the transmission stay in a higher gear.

From this sequence of tests, one thing should be very apparent: the transmission absolutely depends upon the throttle pressure linkage for almost anything it does. The throttle pressure linkage has to be right, but if it's not, the pressures are wrong and things happen at the wrong time and with the wrong force. If there is a gap between the pin of the throttle and the linkage, it can cause runaway or flaring upshifts at light throttle, way too early and too soft upshifts, and possibly no or incorrectly timed downshifts at wide-open throttle. If the linkage is set too far the other way, in other words, it is being pushed, even though the throttle is still closed and the engine is at idle speed, there may be late and harsh upshifts and slamming in gear when the transmission is shifted into Forward or Reverse gears from Park or Neutral. ■

No Need for Throttle Pressure Linkage?

One thing that becomes obvious when working on hot-rodded vehicles with TorqueFlites is how often people ignore the transmission's need for correct throttle pressure signals. Because it is such a common occurrence, I believe it was the cause for the failure of the transmission discussed here. The transmission is an A-999 and the oil and filter had recently been changed; it was obvious because of the new gasket. However, the filter was plugged with flakes and metal particles. The transmission had a deep pan, a filter extension, and it had been converted to cable shift. It had mismatched pan bolts and had the line pressure cranked up. The oil pump clearances were perfect. The endplay was fine and all the hard parts looked good. The rear clutch assembly was totally burnt, the kickdown band was discolored and had been hot, and the front clutch friction discs were burnt and the steel plates had hot spots. Clearly, everything had been slipping.

Based on seeing this many times, here is my analysis. The transmission was in a car and the owner put in a floor shifter, a deep pan, and a filter extension. He or she added a new 4-barrel intake and carburetor. The throttle pressure did not fit the new carburetor as it did the old 2-barrel and "because it is only for kickdown," he or she tossed it. The car shifted soft and started to slip so he or she dropped the pan, cranked up the line pressure, and swapped on a new filter (at least once). He or she continued to drive and hot rod it, but it kept getting worse and slipping more. Likely as not, he or she dropped the pan again and changed the filter one last time, but it was getting filled with black friction flakes and metal particles. The last straw was after the fluid change; it acted the same and would not pull itself. Out came the transmission and it ended up going to the transmission parts supplier as a core.

The small shiny particles (metallic particles) and the collection of black and dark-brown particles and flakes (friction material) show that the filter was doing its job. Clearly, though, something was wrong with this transmission.

Note how dirty the filter really is; this is after it had been changed at least once.

After stripping the transmission, it is easy to see where the black/brown and metallic particles originated. The friction materials used for the forward gears were damaged; most were burnt and/or ruined.

The rear clutch assembly friction discs were destroyed. Most of the material is removed and, in this case, there was metal-to-metal interaction. However, the rubber seals and steel and Teflon sealing rings were fine.

No Need for Throttle Pressure Linkage? *CONTINUED*

Would the testing provided in this chapter have identified the problem? Absolutely. Step one is to check the most basic things. The fluid check would have shown that it was getting hot and was filled with particulate contamination. The shifter adjustment was likely okay. However, when the throttle pressure linkage was checked, the answer would have been obvious. ■

The kickdown band was slipping and had become hot. In fact, the band's friction material was burnt and flaking off. The front clutch retainer, onto which the band clamps, was shiny.

If this vehicle's transmission made it to Drive Direct, it was low on line pressure. The hotspots on the steel plates tell the tale of weak clamping force. All signs indicated reduced line pressure, likely caused by lack of, or incorrectly adjusted, throttle linkage pressure.

governor pressure should be around 40 psi. Increase the speed to about 85 mph and the governor pressure should rise to about 60 psi. Apply the brakes to stop the wheels, but leave the transmission in "D." The governor pressure should drop to zero (at least no higher than 1.5 psi). Place the transmission back in "P."

Air Pressure Testing

The previous hydraulic pressure tests provide data to verify the pump is working correctly, that the governor and lubrication circuits are functional, and that they show the integrity of the hydraulic sections. They may not indicate that clutch frictions and steels are completely worn out, that bands are too loose, or that something was put together incorrectly. They do provide valuable information without tearing into the transmission. However, applying air instead of fluid to some sections and using your ears can offer even more clues. Fortunately, some of the key internal hydraulic components can be air tested. Similar to tests after a rebuild, air can be directed into different ports to actuate circuits. The pan and the valve body need to be dropped, but valuable information is provided from the tests.

Where do you begin? Let the vehicle cool before removing oil pan bolts to drain the fluid. The valve body stays hot for a long time; don't be in a hurry. Remove the filter; while more fluid drains, loosen the pinch bolts holding the shift and throttle pressure levers on the manual lever shaft and remove them. Loosen the 10 valve body (7/16-inch headed) bolts and drop it enough to let fluid drain; it will do so for a long time. When it slows to a drip, remove the 10 bolts and the E-clip from the park rod. Preferably, pull the whole park rod out of the transmission with the valve body by rotating the driveshaft until the rod breaks free from the park pawl assembly. Set the valve body aside in a clean pan.

Front Clutch Test

Use 30 to 40 psi air from a rubber-tipped blowgun and apply it to the front clutch passage (located next to the front valve body bolt hole and the small rectangular pump pressure output port. If everything is okay, you'll hear a dull thud. If not and there is a lot of air hissing, something is wrong in the front clutch assembly. Likely as not, Drive Direct and Reverse felt odd.

Rear Clutch Test

The rear clutch apply port is next to the front clutch apply port; apply 30 to 40 psi of air to it and listen for a thud; it should not hiss or burble, which indicates an excessive leak. An air leak or no thud may indicate the rear clutch assembly was slipping. In this case, all forward gears may have had problems.

Not having a transmission in a vehicle to test, the air pressure test procedures are being demonstrated on a lock-up A-904 out of the car. Applying 30- to 40-psi air pressure to the front clutch apply circuit reveals the integrity of sealing rings and the lip seals in the front clutch retainer.

Putting 30- to 40-psi air pressure to the rear clutch apply circuit determines if it is in good condition or leaking "hydraulically." A dull "thud" or "thump" is a good outcome and a lot of air leakage shows that something is likely wrong.

Low-Reverse Servo Test

This port is between the accumulator piston and the rear servo bore, and air will pressurize the servo. Direct 30 to 40 psi air into it and the servo piston should push out and clamp the band around the low-reverse drum. If it doesn't work, you likely had issues with Reverse gear or Manual Low felt "funny."

Kickdown Servo Test

This port is between the accumulator piston and the front servo. Direct 30 to 40 psi air into it and the servo piston should push out, clamping the band around the retainer. If it does not work correctly, you had issues with Second gear.

Air Pressure Test Results

If all air tests indicate the hydraulic portions of the TorqueFlite are correct, and the previous tests did not indicate any malfunctions, something may have gone bad in the converter or the valve body. If the servos pushed out but did not clamp hard on the retainers, recheck band adjustments.

If the history of the transmission is unknown because you just bought it (or the car or truck it was in) and/or it just never felt quite right, maybe it was put together incorrectly or incompatible modifications were performed. It could be that mismatched parts were used somewhere. Before removing it, there is still one more test that can be made.

Directing 30 to 40 psi of air into the rear servo apply port reveals if the low-reverse band is functional. If it applies, the servo piston lip seal is in good condition and the piston should clamp the adjusted band correctly. No air leakage is good; no piston movement indicates a problem.

To test the kickdown band circuit, pressurize the kickdown band apply port and watch the piston push out to clamp the kickdown band. If a transmission is having Second-gear issues, this may not be working correctly.

Torque Converter Stall Testing

When most rear-wheel-drive vehicles were new, and the parking and service brakes worked correctly, the converter stall test was "relatively" safe. However, after all these years and after brake changes have been made, it may not be as safe. With engine output up to a level higher than ever before, you must be very careful doing this test. Do it only in a safe location with nothing in front; the parking and service brakes have to work correctly. I think it is a mentally difficult test to do unless you have a lot of nerve, great brakes, (and it's not your vehicle being tested).

This is an "exciting" test and the brakes are held on hard, the tires are blocked, and the throttle is held wide open until the engine reaches a point that it can't rev any higher. This is where the torque converter "stalls" and it should be done no longer than about 5 seconds. In this test, maximum engine speed is limited by the restriction of the oil flow inside the converter as it is forced through the locked-in-place stator. The test puts engine power (via the spinning converter and its integral impeller) against the stalled turbine, stator, and the transmission that is (hopefully) locked by the brakes holding the rear wheels. As you can imagine, working the oil over with this much sheering force creates a lot of heat, and for this reason, the test should only last a few seconds and be followed by cool-down time in Neutral with the engine at idle.

TorqueFlites have low-stall converters, high-stall converters, and everything in between. Hemis and 340s act one way under stall testing due to their looser, higher-stall con-verters and 383 2-barrel cars with low-stall converters act another way. Much of this difference is due to the diameter of the converter and the parts inside of it, but the engine torque also affects it. This is why the engine has to be running correctly before testing. Regardless of the engine/vehicle/converter combination, stall testing enables mechanics and owners to verify that the torque converter is still functioning according to the design engineer's recommendations.

Let's look at possible outcomes. If the stall speed is above the stated stall RPM, the converter may be incorrect, or the transmission is slipping. However, if the engine can't reach the factory-stated stall RPM, but the brakes are holding, the converter may be incorrectly matched to the engine, the engine may be running poorly, or the stator's overrunning clutch inside the converter is slipping or broken completely. If so, the vehicle will feel sluggish at low speeds, almost as if it is in Drive Direct all the time. If, on the other hand, the vehicle accelerates correctly at lower speeds, but at highway speeds the throttle has to be pushed hard, the stator assembly may be locked up. In both cases, the converter has to be replaced.

A sample of the factory-stated stall speeds of many engine and transmission combinations is given in Appendix B.

Noise Identification

Unlike manual transmissions, noises from automatics are less prevalent and a little tougher to figure out.

Internal Buzzing

A light buzz that sounds as if it is coming from the center of the trans-mission is often a check ball vibrating in the valve body or a governor valve buzzing. Dad's 1969 340 Dart Swinger used to buzz, but engineering changes to the valve body eliminated the problem. Many shift modification kits also address this noise.

Front Section Noise

A louder whine from the front of the transmission is commonly converter-related. There may be something rubbing on the inspection cover/plate that can be fixed by bending the plate and/or tightening loose bolts. The later-year converters may have a needle roller bearing that fails. Lock-up converters can fail and the apply plate may be close to the friction material at the wrong time causing a hiss or slipping sound. The only fix for internal converter issues is replacement.

Knocking noises can occur and, like other issues on older transmissions, they may be caused by someone not following recommended torque specifications. In some cases, the use of different bolts can create interference. Often, wear in the crankshaft's main thrust bearing can let the crank move front to rear with engine speed and load. The most common knock is where a converter bolt starts to back out, hitting the thin steel inspection cover first and eventually, the back of the block. As the crank moves, the knock may come and go. If the crank bearing has a bit more clearance, the knock may be louder, and if the bolt eventually backs out farther, the knock can be really loud.

A cracked or broken flexplate can create a loud and terrible knocking that sounds as if a rod is about to fly out of the block. In both cases, remove the inspection cover and check the converter bolts and the flexplate.

Gear Sounds

Damaged teeth in the planetaries can cause gear noises that sound like loud grinding or knocking. This is very serious, and the vehicle should not be driven because metal particles will get into the entire lubrication, governor, valve body, and torque converter circuits. Fortunately, few TorqueFlites damage planetary gears in typical street, mild off-road, or mild strip usage.

Vibration in Floor

A whining/vibration felt and heard is often caused by a bad output shaft bearing. I have seen this most often in truck transmissions, and it gets louder and its pitch increases with road speed. Fortunately, extension housings can be removed and the bearing changed without pulling the transmission.

Knocking in/on the Floor

With oil leaks and age-related wear, rear transmission mounts can fail. When it happens, there may be a banging and knocking noise under the seat or on the floor when shifting from Forward to Reverse or when hitting bumps. The mount can be changed without removing the transmission.

Leaks

Leaks seem easy but often they turn out to be more complicated. In the bellhousing area, there are many sources of potential leaks and, unfortunately, most of them require you to remove the transmission.

If dealing with a leak, clean the underside of the vehicle at a car wash to pinpoint the source. Pressure wash the lower portion of the engine as well as the floorpan surrounding the transmission. Wash around the rear seal and the floor surrounding it to learn if fluid is being spun out by the U-joint. With dual exhausts and headers, this job is sometimes tough on cars and 4WD trucks, but to get an accurate determination requires things be clean enough that leaking fluid can be detected.

An Important Tool to Make

Shop manuals show fabrication of a curved bracket that bolts to the bellhousing and its purpose is to help mechanics decide if oil is thrown off the converter or if it is running out of the pump seals. When dealing with a bellhousing area leak, this tool is invaluable and very easy to make. Fabricate it from a scrap of thin (22-gauge) aluminum, 6 inches long and 1.5 inches wide; a 1/4-inch hole is drilled into it for its attaching bolt.

With the tool on, start the engine, put the transmission in "N" (Neutral), and hold the speed to 2,200 to 2,600 rpm for a couple of minutes. If the tool shows fluid is being spun off the converter, it may be cracked or leaking, or the front seal is spraying fluid on the hub and converter body, which throws all over the inside of the bellhousing. If the gasket between the pump, the pump bolt seals, or the kickdown servo pin plug are leaking, there will be fluid inside the bottom of the bellhousing, but it is not spun off the converter hitting the tool. If the leak is bad enough, it runs out the lower portion of the housing. A cracked case, although not common, can act like a leaky pump gasket and servo plug seal because the fluid runs out, but it is not sprayed on the converter and thrown everywhere. Use of this leak tool helps identify the source. ■

A rumbling sound under the floor that becomes louder and changes pitch with vehicle speed is almost always a rough and/or worn-out output shaft bearing.

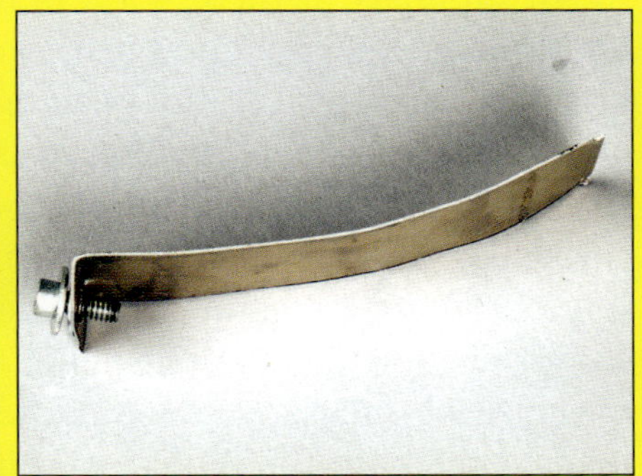

If fighting a leak in the bellhousing area, cut a 6 x 1.5–inch strip of thin metal and bend it to match the bellhousing's curvature. Drill a 1/4-inch hole in it so it can be bolted on.

With the curved bracket installed, run the engine a few minutes, in gear if possible. A leaking weld on the converter throws fluid onto the tool.

An Overlooked Weld

I installed an A-727 in one of my cars that had different friction plate quantities and styles, a shift kit, and a different kickdown band. After pulling it a few times to "optimize all my tricks," it finally felt good. After a few days, I noticed a small leak in the bellhousing area. The starter and the inspection cover/dust shield were removed to reveal most fluid was getting thrown from the converter body. Easy enough; yank it out and change the obviously leaking front seal (after making sure the hub was good and not scarred).

Everything looked fine so in went another new seal. After a day of sitting, it was fine, no leaks. I took it for an easy drive and although not too bad, it still leaked. I decided it must be from the front seal area, so it came out, the pump was yanked, and a new converter hub bushing and seal were installed. It worked well sitting for another day, so I tested it idling in Park. No leaks.

Another test drive and the leak started again. I figured it must be a porous pump so in went another one because pumps were cheap and easy to get. Same thing. After pulling it for the seventh time, it was time to think and read. The shop manual had many suggestions regarding sealing the case and blowing air into it, as well as sealing the converter and doing the same. It showed a simple tool to make to determine where a leak was coming from but I chose to ignore it. I never considered that maybe the converter builder had missed something. Looking over his welds, they looked fine. The drain plug was dry so I decided to air check it, even though I knew it had to be fine. I poked a hole in the protective polyethylene plastic cap that comes on the hub and pressurized the converter. Sure enough, there was an almost invisible leak in one of the welds. Darn it.

I now know that when the converter was filled and under pressure, it spit fluid out. Under high load, in gear, it was far worse. In idle, it never seemed to do much, but remember, idling in Park does not tell you much because the converter is not charged the same as it is in Neutral or any Forward or Reverse gear. Had I been able to lie underneath it and watch it under stall conditions, it would have been spitting a lot more fluid out. Had I made that recommended tool immediately, I would have negated the need to yank it so many times. Welding the pinhole shut took the local converter builder a few seconds. ■

If there is a converter leak identified by the tool, look very closely at the weld between both halves of the converter. If a hole is not visible, it may require sealing the hub with a plastic cap, poking a hole in it, and pressurizing it. Even a microscopic leak should show small bubbles around the hole.

Bellhousing/Converter Area

After everything is as clean as possible, verify that the fluid level is correct; an overfull condition can force whipped-up fluid out of the pump vent and then onto the converter. If you have an older TorqueFlite with the small inspection cover/dust shield that unbolts to allow access to converter bolts, remove it and look or feel inside the bellhousing with the engine off. The starter can be removed to get the complete inspection cover off so the leak's origin can be found. If there is lot of fluid in the bellhousing that was not removed, wipe or rinse it out.

In summary, if there is a leak in the front area, it could be a bad converter, oil pump seal and/or bushing, oil pump gasket, oil pump bolt seals, kickdown servo lever shaft plug, a cracked or porous case, or fluid being spit out of the breather. An older converter may have a drain plug; it too must be snug and sealed. Other than correcting the fluid overfull condition, all of these require pulling the transmission to repair.

Dipstick

You may be lucky and have only a bad O-ring on the dipstick. Older

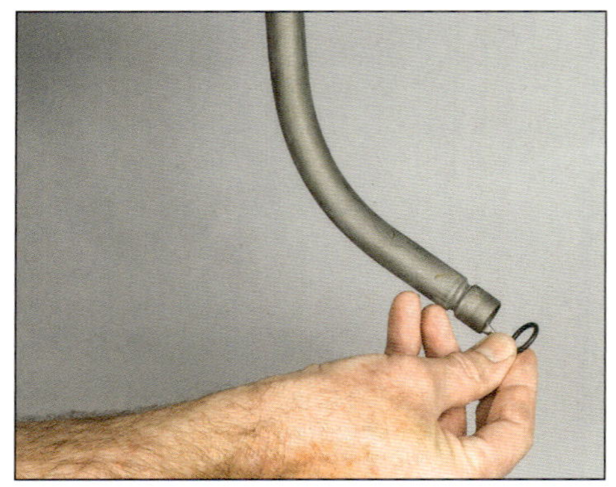

If the O-ring seal is hard and brittle, replace it, and lubricate the new one before reinstallation. Some use an RTV-silicone seal for insurance, but if everything is correct, no sealer should be needed.

Over time, cork pan gaskets become saturated with fluid and may swell like this one. Overtightening it may crush it and cause it to break and leak. If a simple "snug" does not stop a leak, replace the gasket. It's time to replace this one.

As with some premium valvecover gaskets, engineers created this reusable metal-core A-727 pan gasket. A close-up reveals the embossed ridges located in strategic areas. Dealerships, A&A Transmission, and others offer them.

TorqueFlite dipsticks (pre-1969), bolt on by the pan area, but later ones were held on with one of the transmission-to-engine bolts. Remove the dipstick, replace the O-ring, grease, and reinstall it.

Pan Gasket

A large potential leak is from the pan gasket. There are many varieties, but most common are cork gaskets. A paper-based gasket is included in some filter and overhaul sets, and these seem a bit more difficult to keep sealed. I have torn many transmissions apart that had an excessive amount of RTV-type silicone on the

A Way to Fix the Seal

To access the seal, the throttle pressure and shift selector levers need to come off so the valve body can be dropped. With a four-wheel-drive truck or car with headers, it will be tough to get to the levers. Once the valve body is out, drive the old seal out with a flat screwdriver or punch. Buy a couple of seals (one for a spare) and get two flat washers that are larger than the seal. You will use a 3/8-16-inch nut and a 1.5- to 2.0-inch-long, 3/8-16-inch bolt to sandwich the seal between the washers and the case. Put some RTV-type silicone sealer around the circumference of the seal and then place it on top of the case opening. Place a bolt through the top of the washer, through the seal, and the case. From the bottom, install another washer and nut. Tighten the nut (while holding the bolt) a small amount at a time to pull the seal into place. Stop if it does not pull straight in. Retry it. Use the spare if you bent the first one. After it is in nice and flat, grease it, and reinstall the valve body and levers.

To replace a leaky shifter shaft seal, use a special tool or a nut, bolt, and three washers.

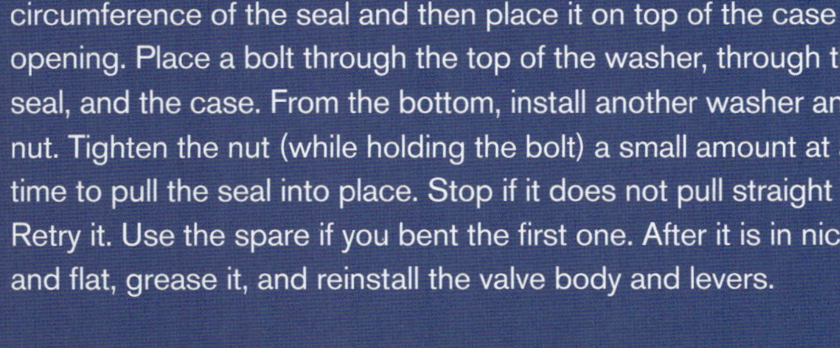

Place the bolt and washer on top. Put a thin coat of an RTV-type silicone sealant around the new seal and place it in position.

Thread the nut against a washer on the bottom and tighten it slowly to pull in the seal. Be sure the seal is flat; continue slowly tightening the nut.

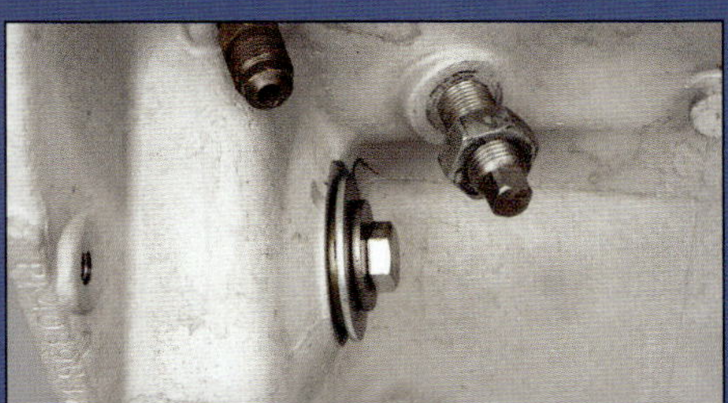

Tighten until the nut and bolt are snug, remove them, and make sure the seal is flat, flush, and not damaged or distorted. If it's not perfect, knock it out and redo it.

pan bolts and gasket, and worst of all, it was inside the pan and on the filter. If the pan is flat and came with a gasket, there is never a reason to use this type of sealer (later transmissions often used no gasket and required sealer). For TorqueFlites that require gaskets, a high-quality cork gasket torqued to factory specifications (150 in-lbs) will work well for several years. The bolts may require a tweak after driving the vehicle, but they should stay leak-free for a long time.

There were some cork gaskets with metal cores that lasted a long time and could be reused, but they have disappeared. The Chrysler dealers and aftermarket suppliers now offer replacement plastic or metal cored composite gaskets with a silicone or urethane rubber seal pattern (imprinted on both sides) that work very well.

Shifter Shaft Seal

A leaking shifter shaft seal is a bit tougher to replace, but it can be done in the vehicle. This leak seems to occur more often when the car or truck sits for long periods of time. This makes sense because the fluid accumulates in the pan when the pump is not sending it everywhere during operational conditions. With the area clean around the top of the shifter shaft, the leak can be identified quickly.

Speedometer Adapter O-Ring and Internal Seal

If the speedometer cable is removed from the adapter and fluid runs out the end of the cable and adapter housing, chances are high that the internal lip seal is bad. If fluid is leaking around the body of the adapter, the O-ring may be shot. Either way, it is easy to pull the adapter and replace both. Make a note of the orientation of the adapter in the extension housing. Put the lip seal back in the adapter with the lip facing the inside, grease the gear shaft, put the new O-ring around the outside, and grease it before putting it back in the extension housing.

Rear Band Anchor Pin

This one, if leaking, is more difficult and requires a lot of work to fix. Go to the appropriate section in Chapter 5 and Chapter 8 for specifics, but a summary is that the extension housing has to be removed, the valve body pulled out, the low-reverse band loosened, and the pin pulled out from the rear so the O-ring can be replaced. I have seen somewhat successful repairs where the leaky area is cleaned with solvent and then a large amount of silicone sealer is put on the pin and the case surrounding it. It looks bad, but it often works for a while.

Extension Housing, Bolts and Bearing Snap-Ring Cover Plate Gasket

The extension housing gasket could be leaking, but I have never had a bad one. If yours is, remove the housing and replace the gasket, and while you are there, replace the bearing snap ring plate's cork or paper gasket. You should replace the rear seal too. Sometimes, bolts holding on the extension housing may seep. If yours looks damp, put a bit of RTV-type silicone on them before reinstallation.

Rear Seal

This can be replaced with the extension housing on the transmission, but look closely at the rear bushing and driveshaft yoke because they could be damaged enough to wear the bushing and take out the seal. Push up and down on the driveshaft with it in the transmission and see how much slop there is. New ones have very little but if yours wobbles a lot, the bushing is likely worn and needs to be replaced. There is a tool to do it with the housing in place. If the bushing is worn out, remove the housing and visit your local transmission shop if you don't have the bushing driver. Install a new seal with a bit of RTV-silicone sealer around its circumference. Often, time and miles just wear out rear seals and this may be the only thing wrong with it. New types of elastomeric materials are better than they used to be, so it's not unusual to have an original-type seal that seeps or leaks a little now and then.

Summary

Diagnosing new, unspoiled, and unmodified TorqueFlites must have been a bit more straightforward back then. No doubt, unexpected engineering changes and technical service bulletins caused complications, as they do today. Now, with the passing of years and changes made by several owners, figuring out what makes TorqueFlites underperform or fail can be a mystery. If performing all of the tests in this chapter offers no concrete solutions, you may just have to remove it, go through it, and put it back like it used to be.

This booted rear seal is doing its job. No oil is dripping or seeping and the U-joint is throwing none around.

TRANSMISSION DISASSEMBLY

To have the clearest photos of the transmission, it was previously disassembled, meticulously cleaned, and wear and abnormalities were documented. The outside of the case and extension housing was lightly sandblasted and cleaned again. It was reassembled using original parts and everything was reused except for the pump gasket, pan gasket, two pump bolt washer-seals, and the extension-housing gasket. I did this so the condition of the parts would be visible during teardown photographs. Fluid on parts sometimes hides scratches, burns, and wear. Clean parts provide better photos.

General Safety

Since the introduction of OSHA in the early 1970s, many things have changed for the better and the science of health safety has evolved. The potential impact of many accidents has been reduced because personal protective equipment is better. Solvent and chemical resistant gloves, polycarbonate safety glasses and side shields, and better training make us aware of, and more immune to, potential safety incidents that can occur in disassembly, repair, and reassembly operations. Working on TorqueFlites, although seemingly mild, has "opportunities" for injuries.

Suggestions

Wear safety glasses anytime things are struck with a hammer. Chips of metal can come from the hammer, a punch or chisel, or the parts being hit. Take care of punches and chisels by grinding off loose and mushroomed ends. These slivers or chips can end up in or under your skin or worse, in your eyes. Getting them removed at an emergency room is not fun.

Use solvent-resistant gloves if your hands are in transmission fluid or cleaning chemicals for a long time. You can buy boxes of gloves for a fair price from local parts suppliers; the better ones designed for mechanical work are adequate. Your skin can dry, split, and bleed without wearing gloves.

Most consumer-accessible non-chlorinated cleaning solvents are flammable or combustible. Flash points below 100 degrees F, by National Fire Protection Association standards, are considered

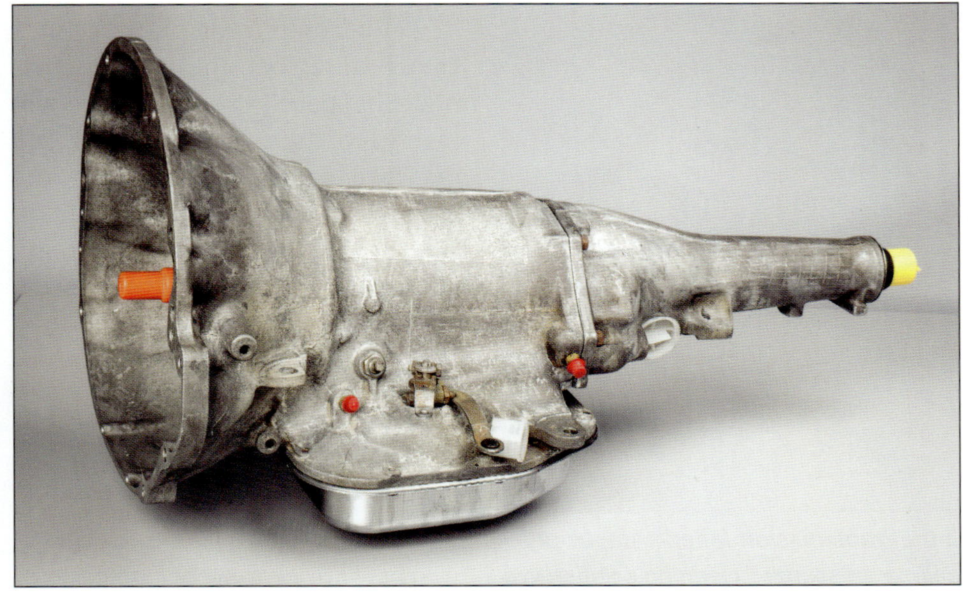

This A-904 awaits a future teardown and overhaul.

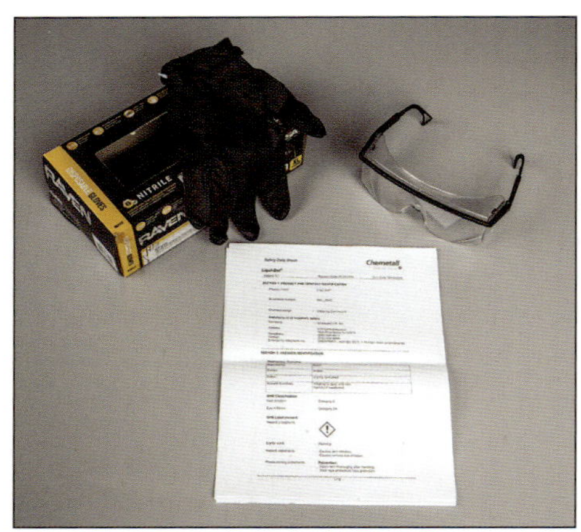

These are good things to have: safety glasses, solvent- and oil-resistant gloves, and a Safety Data Sheet (SDS) for chemicals.

Several detergents are handy during transmission work. They vary from a highly alkaline degreaser to a rust-removing chelating agent to a neutral industrial detergent blend.

flammable and those above 100 degrees F are combustible. Unfortunately, faster evaporating solvents often have low flash points. Traditional solvents in solvent-based parts washers have flash points in the range of 140 degrees F or higher, and these are safer to use for most applications. Because of flammability or combustibility, always take care around heat sources or open flames. It's always best to read the Material Safety Data Sheet (MSDS) or the Safety Data Sheet (SDS) for details.

Some chlorinated solvents are typically used in brake cleaners. These are often formulated with perchloroethylene and should never be used around open flames (like in garages with gas furnaces). The reaction byproducts will corrode aluminum and oxidize steels. Pay attention to the MSDS and SDS.

When dealing with alkaline or neutral and, for sure, acidic-based detergents, keep them out of eyes and off the skin. Not only can they dry out skin and hands, they can cause permanent eye damage and/or a lot of intense burning (until they are rinsed out). Always, read the MSDS or the SDS to learn about the chemical(s) you have.

When disposing of cleaning chemicals, put solvents (without chlorine) in a container with oils and hydraulic fluids and most auto parts stores will accept them. Alkaline, acidic, or neutral solutions can be treated like strong detergents commonly used, but never dump concentrated materials in sewers, creeks, or ponds. The safest way is to read the directions about the chemicals

If the transmission failed catastrophically, a pressurized cleaning solution is a great way to flush out the cooler circuit.

and dispose of them in the way the manufacturer suggests.

A safe solution to flush the transmission cooler lines is important, although it is not often used directly during the overhaul procedure. If there was a catastrophic transmission failure, residue may be trapped in the lines or small openings in the cooler; a pressurized solution attached to the cooler lines will force cleaner through the system. Be mindful of safety precautions with these too.

Be aware that some TorqueFlite assemblies have stiff springs and sharp edges so take care during spring removal and always use proper tools to compress them.

Before pulling or pushing on a wrench or ratchet, think about what might happen if it slips. Where will fingers, wrists, hands, or arms end up? Take care and make sure the scraping blade you use doesn't slip. Don't let hands, fingers, eyes, or any body parts be injured because of an avoidable accident. A little time spent planning can prevent a lot of time in the urgent care facility.

Tools, Chemicals and Miscellaneous Supplies

There are a couple of categories of tools for TorqueFlite repair and they

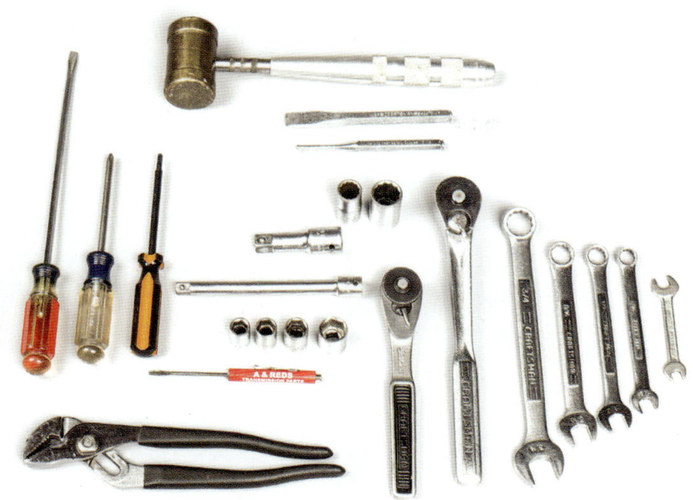

These are the basic tools to disassemble a TorqueFlite.

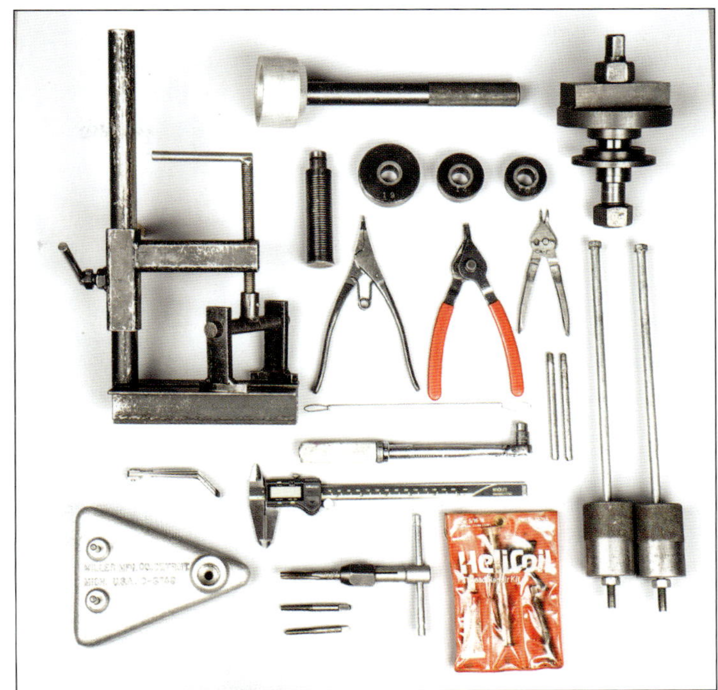

Specialized tools, including clutch spring compressors, thread repair sets, and slide hammers, make transmission work much easier.

can be divided into "basic tools" that are required and "specialized tools" that are nice to have.

Basic Tools

You need a good set of sockets and wrenches, a small and large flat-bladed screwdriver, and a good Phillips screwdriver. You may need Torx drivers for later valve bodies. You can't get by without a hammer and a punch or blunt flat screwdriver to use as a light-duty "punch." Some big C-clamps will compress the clutch retainer springs. Snap ring pliers that are suitable for internal and external snap rings are required. Good Allen wrenches come in handy.

Specialized Tools

It's great to have a support stand or a way to hold the transmission on a bench or floor. It's good to have a 5/16-inch eight-point socket for band adjustment and an inch-pound and foot-pound torque wrenches. Calipers and a dial indicator provide accurate measurements of end-

A compressed-air tank enables air checking various assemblies during troubleshooting and final assembly.

play and part thicknesses. A gasket scraper or a single-sided razor blade to remove broken gasket material is helpful. A clutch-spring compressor is a safer way to remove and reinstall clutch springs. A lip seal tool is good to have and many overhaul kits come with a disc to do the same thing. Slide hammers to pull the pump and pins to locate the pump as it goes back on are handy. Bushing drivers and a tool for rear seal installation are great to

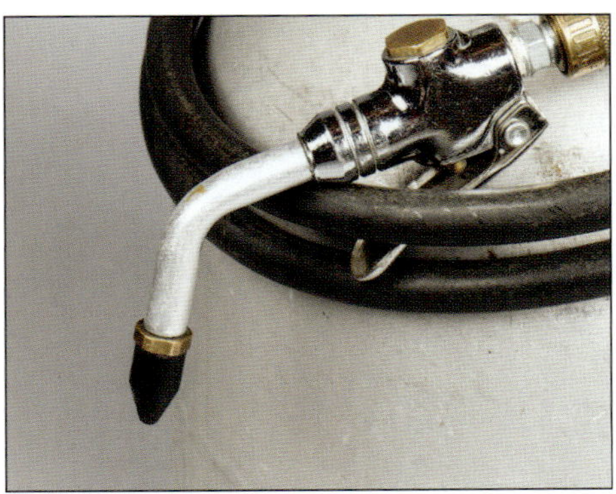

The rubber-tipped blowgun seals the air to the passageways when actuating servos and clutch assemblies.

have. A thread repair set and a good tap and die set are nice for damaged threads. A compressed air source and rubber-tipped blowgun enable air checking.

The Work Area

It's important to prepare a work area before taking anything apart. Preparation includes:

- Finding a large, well lit, and clean location.

Tools of Compression

Two large C-clamps compress the front clutch retainer return springs; using them is not the easiest, but they work.

A Miller tool, called out in Chrysler-based repair manuals, works for either an A-904 or an A-727, but not both. The tool is not convenient because the snap ring is difficult to access when the spring retainer is compressed. However, a bonus with the A-727 version is that it also presses the overrunning clutch cam in the case avoiding the use of a hammer and long punches.

Another option is the universal clutch spring compressor. These look a bit crude but work well, are easy to use, and fit almost any automatic transmission. It is simple to adjust and snap rings are accessible.

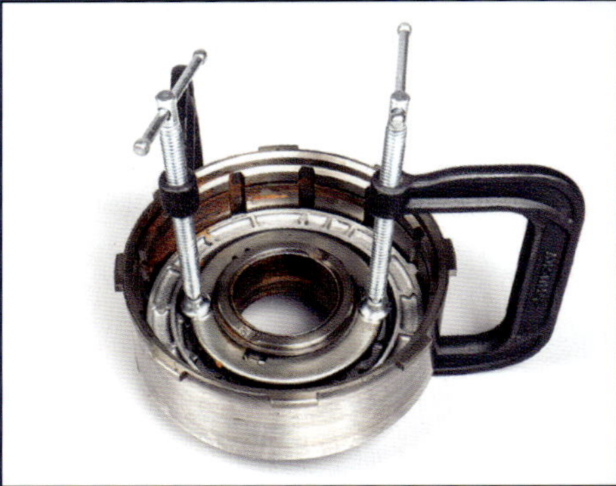

C-clamps compress the front clutch spring retainer providing access to the snap ring.

The Miller SP-3583 clutch spring tool compresses the spring retainer, but access to the snap ring is partially blocked.

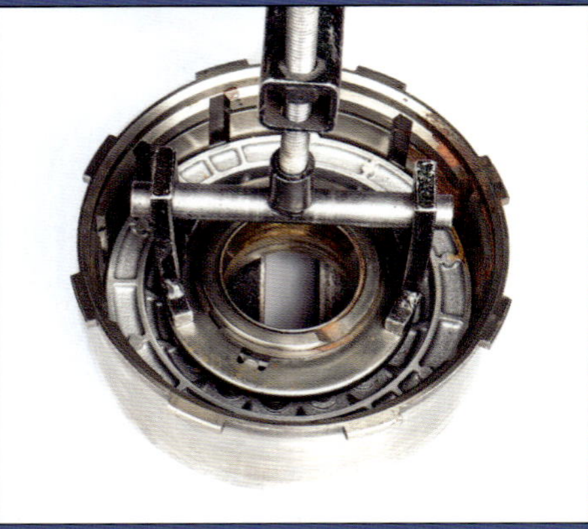

A universal clutch spring compressor works for all types of transmissions.

A large plastic pail and common kitchen containers can hold most internal parts and some cleaning solvents/solutions.

If this is your first time tearing into a transmission and like to keep parts segregated, you can use small kitchen containers and sandwich bags.

- Getting tools out and accessible.
- Locating containers for loose parts.
- Verifying floors and work surfaces can handle transmission fluid.
- Being sure that anything needed is easily reached.

I usually have toolboxes out and open, a large aluminum commercial baking tray available, and two or three 5-gallon plastic pails.

The pails and small containers hold bolts, levers, and subassemblies as they are removed. If this is the first time you've torn a TorqueFlite apart, you might want to have several small plastic boxes, plastic food containers, or write-on food bags for bolts and related items.

Cleaning for Disassembly and Inspection

It's tough to completely seal a transmission for high-pressure washing, but if it is terribly dirty, it's worth trying to do so. Plug cooler line fittings, the dipstick hole, and the extension housing to prevent a significant portion of water from entering. Realistically, it will be torn apart so do it soon after washing to minimize rusting.

If you use a car wash, cleaning can be done several ways depending upon the transmission's weight, the time of year, the vehicle available to carry things, your strength, and willingness to get wet. I used to take transmissions to a car wash as one unit. The dipstick was left in and the transmission was sprayed with hot, soapy water followed by several high-pressure rinses. This works very well because the high-pressure soapy water and rinses remove the loose material. It is a dirty operation; have layers of clothes that can be removed, safety glasses, and towels to dry yourself and protect your vehicle's interior.

Often, it's too much work for one person to load a full transmission into a car or truck for the car wash trip. If this is the case, bear with the grease, dirt, and grime; disassemble it and then take the case, extension housing, and pan to the car wash.

If you have a buddy at a transmission or machine shop, ask if they would use their specialized pressure washers to clean the case parts. Most washers use water-based cleaning solutions compatible with aluminum parts. These washers operate hotter and use cleaners with more detergents instead of depending upon high alkalinity to cut grease.

High-pressure, hot soapy water strips off dirt, grease, and road residue.

After detergent washing, high-pressure water rinses get rid of the loosened residue and most of the remaining soap.

If you are lucky, the car wash has a deionized water rinse to let the TorqueFlite dry spot-free.

Almost every transmission shop is equipped with an industrial, heated detergent washer. They are like a hot "hurricane in a box" that cleans cases and external parts wonderfully. The parts rotate in front of, underneath, and on top of nozzles or precision holes that spray detergent solution.

For cleaning valve bodies and other internal parts, nothing beats a traditional solvent parts washer and brush.

Most solvent parts washers, such as this one, recirculate a combustible hydrocarbon solvent that, over time, becomes saturated with the dissolved oil and grease. These minimize evaporation and are usually equipped with a lid that closes during a fire.

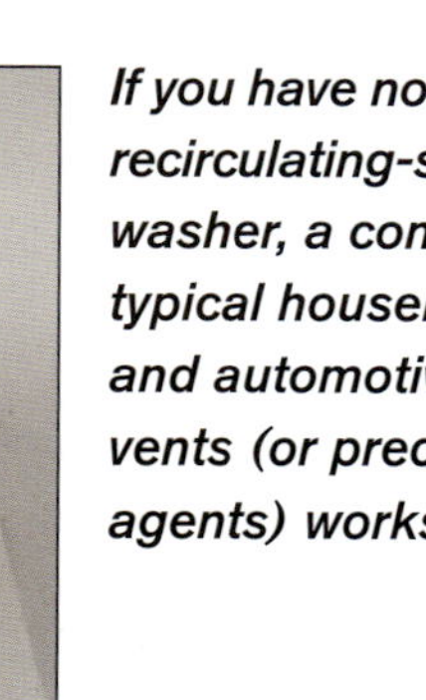

If you have no access to a recirculating-solvent parts washer, a combination of typical household solvents and automotive spray solvents (or precision cleaning agents) works fine.

Most parts washers spray from underneath, the sides, and from the top while parts rotate in front of spray nozzles or tubes. Be absolutely sure that the washer can clean aluminum parts and that it does not use a highly-alkaline solution. Higher-alkalinity solutions without inhibitors are for cast-iron or steel parts and they will damage the case, extension housing, and any aluminum parts.

As the transmission is disassembled, individual parts can be placed in a solvent-based parts washer or in containers of safe, high flash-point solvents, such as those based on mineral spirits. Natural products such as d-limonene or soybean-based solvents will also dissolve transmission fluid and greasy residue.

Kerosene or diesel fuel is used to clean, but experience has shown that it is difficult to eliminate the diesel smell. Whatever you use, make sure it's not a low-flash-point solvent such as gasoline, methanol, ethanol, isopropyl alcohol, or acetone unless you are outside and away from fire, sparks, and household ventilation systems. Mineral spirits, similar to paint thinner, is a relatively safe solvent and it cleans almost anything in a TorqueFlite transmission. There are specialized cleaners that also work well and they range from "simple"

Natural Solvents

If a natural solvent such as d-limonene, pine turpentine, or a soybean-based solvent is used, do not store solvent-soaked cloths, rags, or paper towels in a container in the garage or house because they can ignite. Let the rags evaporate outside in the sun and/or breeze before disposing of them or using them again. ◼

A small compressor blows off residual solvent and water from cleaned parts.

Various specialty lubricants and sealing chemicals are often needed during a rebuild.

Transmission Condition

One of the important things to check before tearing it down is the endplay (input shaft). This tells the condition of the thrust washers and mating surfaces or it shows if the correct-thickness snap rings and thrust washers were used. A dial indicator held magnetically or bolted on the pump provides an accurate measurement.

The goal is to see how far the input shaft can be pushed in and pulled out. (After many years working on transmissions, seasoned mechanics have a good feel as to how much is too much.) On this A-727, a dial indicator was attached magnetically to the pump and the input shaft was pushed in and the indicator was zeroed.

The input shaft was pulled out as far as it would go and the dial indicator was read. A-727s should be between .036 and .084 inch, and the A-904 should be between .023 and .090 inch. Write down or remember the value, and if it is within range, thrust washers can probably be reused if they look good.

A dial indicator and stand mounted to the oil pump provides an accurate method of measuring endplay.

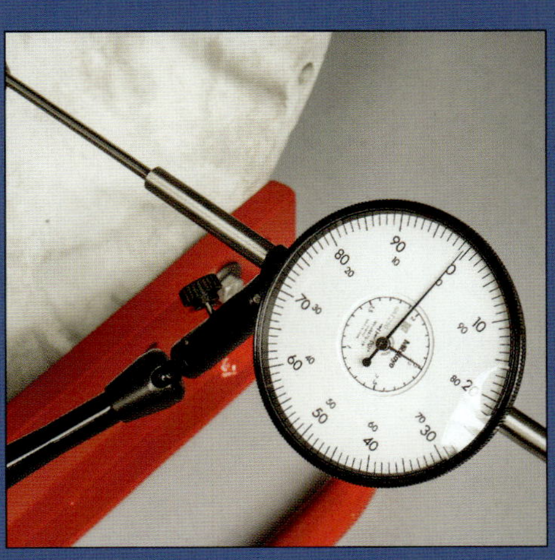

Push the input shaft in as hard as possible, hold it, and zero the indicator.

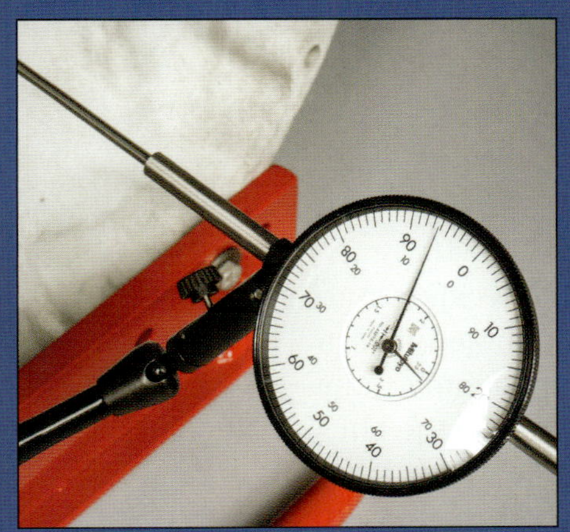

Pull the input shaft out as far as possible and read the indicator. This overall endplay is about .093 to .095 inch. The A-727 limit is .084 inch, so this one needs a thicker pump selective thrust washer, at a minimum.

aerosol brake cleaners to solvents created for cleaning critical communication and weapons electronics. Some current solvents are natural-based blends, and although they may be "green," they have other issues to be aware of.

Transmission parts need to stay clean through the assembly process so after they are rinsed well, air dry or blow them off with compressed air. Avoid wiping parts with rags or paper towels because fuzz and lint are generated that end up in the Dacron filter or could pass through a brass screen. Keep fuzz and lint out; avoid linty rags and cloths.

Lubricants and Sealers

During assembly, it's good to have transmission-specific lubricants and automotive chemicals at hand. For example, special assembly greases will melt at low temperatures and blend with transmission fluids. They are thick enough to hold things together which really helps during assembly.

For valve body and governor lubrication, several lubricants work. One common one looks and acts like transmission fluid but contains special additives to provide good break-in.

Like many automotive tasks where fluids are involved, the proper RTV-type silicone sealer comes in handy for many seals.

Tearing It Down

After the outside of the transmission is clean, or if you decide not to clean it until it is disassembled, loosen the clamp bolts and remove the throttle pressure lever and the shift selector lever from the valve body manual shaft and throttle pressure shaft. It requires a 7/16-inch wrench or a 7/16-inch socket but if they've been on a long time, a flat screwdriver helps pry them off.

Getting It Fixtured

Because I do not have a metal-topped workbench, I use the Miller Tool stand to hold Torque-Flites. It installs easily; flip it upside down, lay it on top of the transmission, and bolt it through the bellhousing bolt holes. Flip it right side up and it is ready. The transmission and stand can be stood up to drain fluid from the rear seal.

The stand allows you to work on the transmission on a basement or garage floor. I set mine in a large aluminum pan (an old commercial bread baking tray) and once the pump is out, residual fluid can drain out. With the transmission upside down, other areas containing fluid can be controllably drained.

Most have no need for a stand, but another way is to lay the transmission on its side and keep it upside down on the floor or on a bench. At some shops, professional mechanics use a bench or a table-mounted holder that bolts onto the tabs on the case/bellhousing. With this arrangement, the transmission

An old commercial aluminum baking sheet makes a perfect drain pan to catch residual fluid. Thin-gauge steel drip trays also work well.

Neutral Starting Switches

The later and more common neutral starting switch has three pins; the outside two pins connect to the reverse lamps to provide a complete circuit when in Reverse. Up to 1969, the screw-in switch had only a center terminal. The center terminal makes contact through the valve body to provide a starter motor-relay ground for Park or Neutral. This is how and why TorqueFlite-equipped cars and trucks start only in these two positions. ■

The single-terminal neutral-start switch is rare; it was used only until 1969 and then it gained two pins for reverse light actuation.

can be flipped in every direction. Some transmissions are simply disassembled on a workbench equipped with a drain to capture fluid. No matter how you choose to do it, as long as the transmission is comfortable to work on, things are good.

Removing Subassemblies

Rather than strip each subassembly into pieces upon removal, they will be removed as units and placed aside for later disassembly. This allows better diagnosis and makes verification and inspection easier.

Oil Pan, Filter, Neutral Starting Switch

With the transmission on a stand, the floor, or a bench, unscrew and remove the neutral starting switch to prevent it from getting damaged if the case is rolled over on its side.

Remove the pan bolts and gasket and check all bolt holes to be sure the threads are good. If not, they will be fixed later using thread inserts.

With the pan off, you see the filter, valve body, and low-reverse and kickdown servo. Use the appropriate tool (flat/Phillips screwdriver/TORX driver) and remove the filter. Inspect it for debris and particulate and let it drain before tossing it. If your transmission has a reusable brass or stainless steel filter you can save it.

Neutral Starting Switch, Oil Pan, Filter, Removal

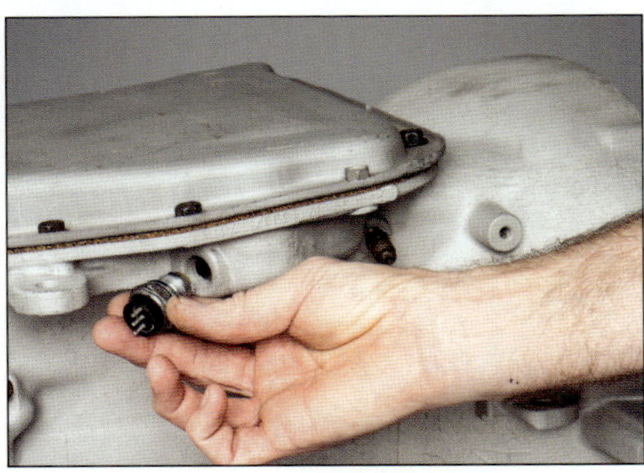

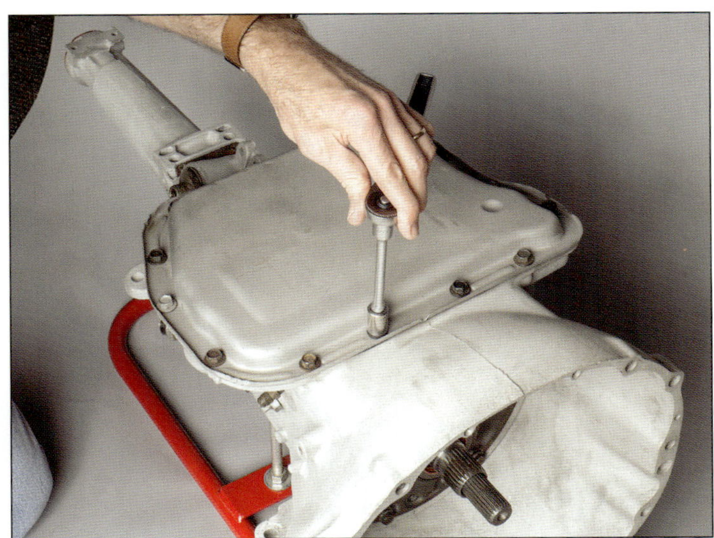

1 *Unscrew the neutral starting switch to protect its pins from accidental damage.*

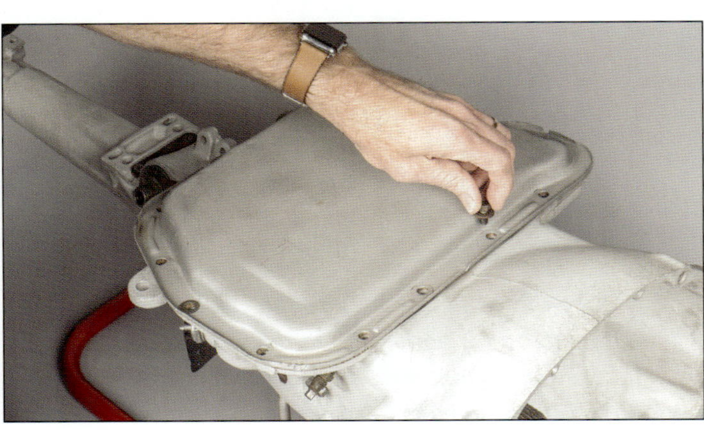

2 *Loosen and remove pan bolts. A TorqueFlite has 5/16-18 bolts with an integral but loose washer.*

3 *Keep pan bolts separate and once they are removed, pull the pan, inspect it for residue, and verify that the bolt holes are not stripped or damaged.*

4 Loosen and remove the three slotted, Phillips, or Torx screws and remove the filter. Inspect it for residue to provide hints about the internal condition.

Valve Body

After filter removal, loosen and then remove the 10 7/16-inch-headed valve body bolts. A small ratchet or wrench works fine.

TorqueFlites built after 1965 have the park lock rod attached to the valve body selector; once the 10 bolts are out, rotate the output shaft to let the park lock rod clear the mechanism in the extension housing and then pull the valve body out and away from the case. If this does not work, remove the E-clip holding the park lock rod to the valve body manual lever. The E-clip may be hard to get to, so reattach the valve body with a bolt, reattach the manual lever (outside the case) and shift to a different gear to reveal the E-clip. Remove it, the outside lever, the valve body bolt, and lift the valve body off the case.

With the valve body out of the way, grab the loose park control rod and pull it toward the pump. If it still doesn't come out, rotate the output shaft while tugging on the rod. (I leave the rod on the valve body, pull the assembly up, rotate the output shaft, and pull the whole thing together.)

Valve Body Removal

1 Remove the 10 valve body bolts; loosen them in a staggered pattern.

2 Once the bolts are out and the valve body is pulled up and off far enough to remove the shifter shaft from its case bore, pull the assembly to the front so the parking lock rod releases.

Accumulator and Spring

With the valve body off, the accumulator piston, approximately 2 inches in diameter, usually has a spring on it but some trucks may have a spring under it. Remove the spring, grab the piston, and pull it out of the case. If there is a spring or rod under it, pull it out.

If the accumulator had no spring on the piston, and there was a rod under it, a previous owner modified it.

Accumulator and Spring Removal

1 An accumulator spring should be on the accumulator piston; pull it off.

2 Grab and remove the accumulator piston.

Extension Housing Seal, Speedometer Assembly and Extension Housing

It is good to remove the rear seal from the extension housing while it is bolted on the case. Use a sharp punch or an old, cheap flat screwdriver to get between the flange and extension housing to pry and drive the seal out. This is easier now than trying to remove the seal from the loose housing later.

Remove the 1/2-inch-head bolt and bracket that holds the speedometer housing-adapter to the extension housing. With the bolt and bracket off, grab the threaded portion and pull the adapter out of the extension housing. If it is snug, wrap the threaded portion of the housing with a rag, grab it lightly with pliers, and pull. The O-ring that holds it may have swelled. The bolt holding the speedometer clamp is longer than a pan bolt so keep it separate or just remember that its washer is smaller and its length is longer.

Look at the housing where the transmission mount attached; there are two Phillips screws holding on a plate. On a car transmission, the plate is on the "bottom" of the housing; on many trucks it is on the side. A good Phillips screwdriver and some strength are needed to break these loose. (This plate and gasket covers a snap ring that releases the extension housing from the output shaft bearing.) If you have trouble loosening the screws, use a hammer and "smack" the screwdriver handle to jar them. If this is unsuccessful, use a small manual impact driver to break them loose.

Whatever it takes, the plate has to be off to access the snap ring.

Looking toward the case, six 9/16-inch-headed bolts hold the extension housing on. These are typically tight (around 25 ft-lbs) so use a 1/2-inch-drive ratchet, break them loose, and remove them. One or two of them may hold on a bracket that holds in the neutral start switch or lock-up converter wiring, or catalytic converter support brackets; take photos or remember where they went.

With the two Phillips screws and the six 9/16-inch-headed bolts removed, use wide-jaw snap-ring pliers and spread the bearing snap ring. Tap the extension housing with a mallet, rubber hammer, or the side of your fist to break it loose and pull it off.

Extension Housing Seal, Speedometer Assembly and Extension Housing Removal

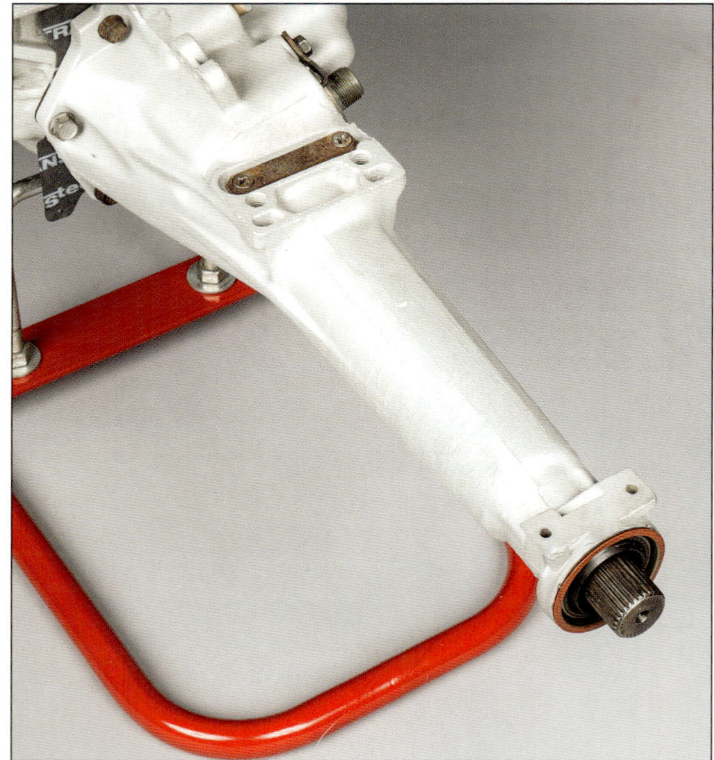

1 *If it is a two-wheel-drive vehicle, it has a rear seal on the extension housing. It is easier to remove it now.*

2 *Use a hammer and chisel or flat blunt screwdriver to drive out the seal. It may require hits around the perimeter to free it.*

3 Loosen and remove the speedometer adapter clamp bolt.

4 Pull out the speedometer adapter and remove the speedometer gear from the adapter. Take note of the tooth quantity and determine, based on speedometer accuracy, if it needs to be changed.

5 Remove these two Phillips screws to gain access to the snap ring holding the extension housing onto the output shaft bearing. Often, they are tight, but a small handheld impact driver helps.

6 With the screws out, remove the plate and gasket.

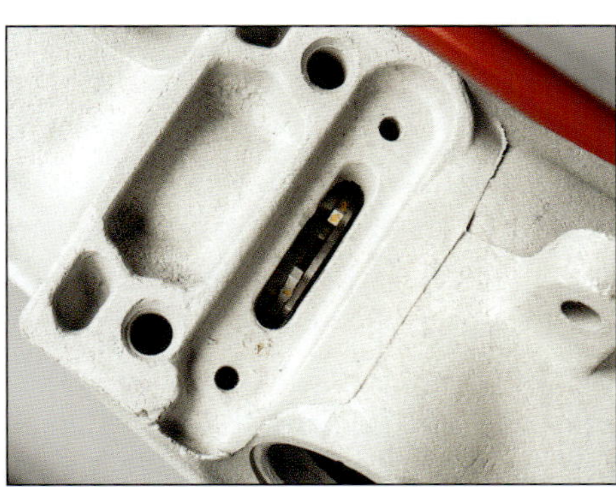

7 After plate and gasket have been removed, the snap ring's tangs are visible.

8 Use a large ratchet and 9/16-inch socket to loosen and remove the six extension housing bolts.

9 *Expand the snap ring with wide-bladed snap-ring pliers to free the housing from the bearing so it can be removed.*

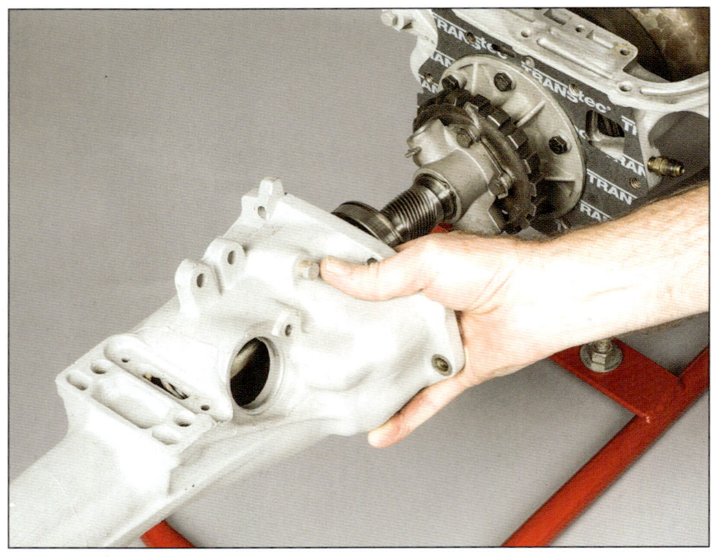

10 *You can thump the housing to break it loose if the gasket sticks; pull it straight back.*

11 *The groove in the bearing is now visible; remove the gasket if it is stuck.*

Oil Pump

Before removing the pump, snug the front band to hold both clutch retainers in position. Use a ratchet and 3/4-inch socket or a 3/4-inch wrench and loosen the kickdown band adjustment lock nut, and then snug the 5/16-inch square-head screw until it stops.

With the band adjustment screw snug, unscrew and remove the seven 1/2-inch-headed bolts (A-727) or six 1/2-inch-headed bolts (A-904 family) holding the pump on.

Now, locate the two threaded holes (3/8-16 inch) in the pump housing and screw slide hammers into the holes. On the A-727, the threaded holes are roughly at the three and nine o'clock locations. On the A-904 series, the holes are approximately at six and eleven o'clock.

After the slide hammers are screwed in, tap the weights evenly against the head of the bolts until the pump pulls loose from the case. Pull the pump carefully over the input shaft and set it so remaining fluid can drain. Unscrew both slide hammers.

If you do not have slide hammers, use something else to tap the pump from behind and drive it loose (there is not much room). Alternatively, a long screwdriver or pry bar can be wedged between the sun gear slots and the front and rear clutch pump.

Oil Pump Removal

1 *Loosen the 3/4-inch lock nut and screw in the kickdown band adjusting screw.*

2 *Loosen and remove the pump bolts. Don't forget to unscrew, pry, or cut the sealing washers off the housing and bolts.*

3 *Screw slide hammers into the threaded holes at approximately the 3 o'clock and 9 o'clock positions.*

4 *In an alternating fashion, knock each weight against the bolt head to free the pump. If you do not have a slide hammer, use a screwdriver or other prying device to wedge between the sun gear shell and the front clutch retainer.*

5 *Remove the slide hammers and set the pump in a drain pan.*

Input Shaft, Kickdown Band, Clutch Retainers and Thrust Washer

With the pump removed, loosen the kickdown band adjustment screw and back it out. This will allow the band struts and anchor (A-727) to drop, leaving the band floating freely around the front clutch retainer. Remove the band carefully to protect its friction material.

With the band out of the way, grab the input shaft and pull both retainers out. If it acts as if something is stuck, the rear clutches may have failed and are distorted and bound to the front clutch hub or the annulus gear of the front planetary. Use a big screwdriver and carefully pry to remove things.

Between the input and output shaft are one or two small thrust washers. One of them may stick to the output shaft or the end of the input shaft. Some TorqueFlites may have a fiber (Phenolic) or a bronze composite washer and some may also have a polished steel washer that stays on the output shaft. Pull them off and put it (them) into a container.

Kickdown Band, Input Shaft, Clutch Retainers and Thrust Washer Removal

1 *Unscrew and remove the kickdown band adjusting screw and release the band from the front clutch retainer.*

2 *With the adjusting screw removed, the band floats freely.*

3 *Pinch together the band's anchors and pull it out between the pump bolt holes.*

4 *Remove the heavy input shaft and front and rear clutch retainers. If rear frictions and/or steels are damaged, the retainers may stick on the front planetary annulus gear. Prying between the sun gear shell and rear clutch retainer should free them.*

5 *Mid-1970s and later TorqueFlites have a polished, hardened steel and a bronze composite thrust washer; earlier versions use only one. Remove them.*

The Planetary Assemblies, Sun Gear Shell and Thrust Washers

With clutch retainers out, use snap-ring pliers to remove the snap ring holding the planetaries on. On the A-727, remove the front planetary gear, thrust washer, annulus gear, another thrust washer, sun gear driving shell, another thrust washer, rear planetary gear assembly, rear annulus gear, and the steel thrust washer inside it. The A-904 front planetary is an assembly and its thrust washer is inside.

Planetary Assemblies, Sun Gear Shell and Thrust Washer Removal

1 This snap ring holds the planetary assemblies on and adjusts the output shaft's endplay.

2 Use snap-ring pliers (or adapt needle-nose pliers) to expand the ring and remove it.

3 On the A-727, the front planetary comes off first, then a thrust washer followed by the annulus gear. Burrs may cause the planetary to stick; you can tap the output shaft with a block of wood to break it loose.

4 With the front planetary assembly off, rotate and remove the sun gear shell/sun gear assembly.

5 Remove the thrust washer on the rear planetary.

6 *Reach in and pull out the rear planetary from its annulus gear.*

7 *The annulus gear splines to the output shaft; slide it forward to remove it and its steel thrust washer.*

Low-Reverse Drum, Low-Reverse Band and Associated Parts

Resting on the governor support or, more accurately, positioned inside the overrunning clutch inner race is the low-reverse drum. The low-reverse band is around it. Rotate and pull the low-reverse drum out and away from the overrunning clutch inner race and the band. The inner race of the overrunning clutch may come out with the drum and springs and rollers will fall out. No need to worry. After removing the A-727 drum, loosen the lock nut holding the rear band adjuster, unscrew it until the strut falls out, and remove the band. The A-904 requires the adjusting screw to be backed out before removal of the band; it has no separate strut. Pull the band out.

Grab the output shaft, pull it out of the output shaft support, and carefully set it aside.

On the A-727, with the low-reverse drum out of the way, note the low-reverse band link and lever. From the rear, pull the pin out (or push from the front), releasing the link so it can be removed. Note the very important O-ring(s) on this pin. Your freshly overhauled transmission will likely leak if this O-ring is left as is or left off. Do not forget to install a new O-ring.

The A-904 also has a pin that is used as an anchor point for the double wrap band with V-8s; do not forget to replace any O-ring on it.

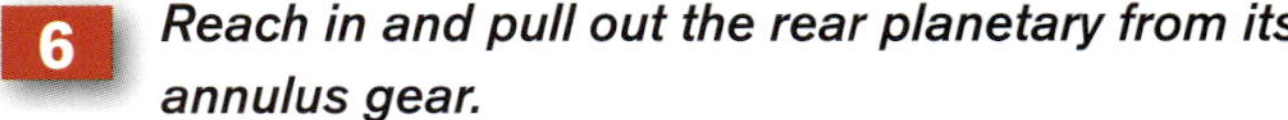

Low-Reverse Drum, Low-Reverse Band and Associated Parts Removal

1 *The low-reverse drum, still inside the low-reverse band, splines to the overrunning clutch inner race. Slide out the drum; it may pull the overrunning clutch race with it.*

2 *Loosen the low-reverse band adjusting screw and remove the rectangular strut (A-727).*

3 *Rotate the low-reverse band a few degrees counter-clockwise to pull it off the link and out of the case.*

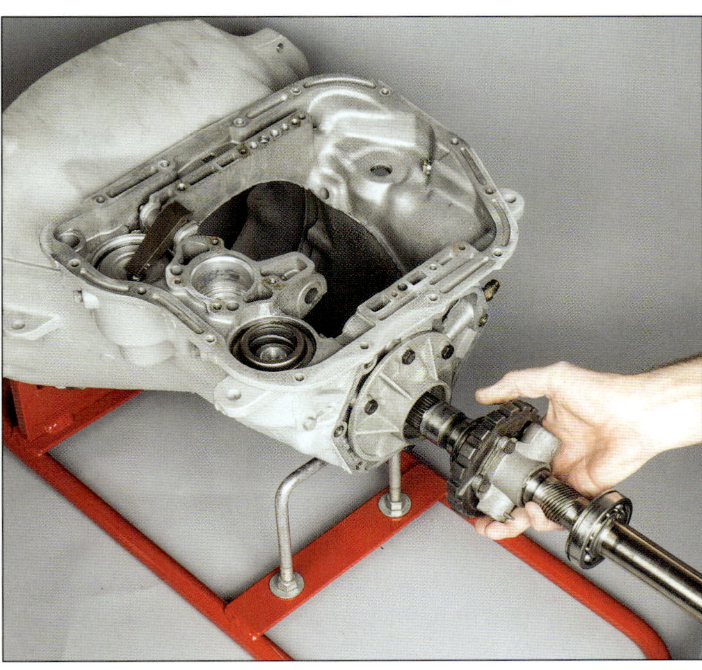

4 *With the geartrain removed, slide the output shaft and governor assembly out of the support.*

5 *The low-reverse band anchor link pin is held in with an O-ring-sealed pin; tap it out from the front of the case area with a long skinny screwdriver or a rod.*

6 *With the pin removed, the low-reverse band anchor link and levers fall out.*

Overrunning Clutch Assembly and Output Shaft

Unless it pulled out with the low-reverse drum, the overrunning clutch assembly (rollers, springs, and inner race) should still be in the case. Note the spring position and orientation and rotate the inner race verifying that it rotates one direction only. Grab the inner race or use a screwdriver to rotate it out. Let the rollers and springs fall; there should be the same number of springs and rollers as there are tabs in the overrunning clutch spring retainer.

Overrunning Clutch Assembly and Output Shaft Removal

1 *The case is almost empty, with the exception of the overrunning clutch. If it is still intact, note how the springs wedge the rollers into the small area of the outer race.*

2 *Rotate while pulling the inner race clockwise and it slides out.*

3 *With the inner race removed, springs and rollers tumble out.*

4 *Count the springs and rollers to make sure there are the same number as spring tabs.*

Kickdown Servo, Low-Reverse Servo, Shifter Shaft Seal and Output Shaft Support

All that remains in the case are the kickdown and low-reverse servo. To remove the kickdown servo, push on the top servo rod guide (the "piston") and get a flat-bladed screwdriver behind the snap ring to pry it out. Be careful; the springs under the guide are strong. You can compress the spring by pushing it with your fingers, but a special tool (A&A's servo tool) or a valvespring compressor will help. Often, when the snap ring is out, the guide "pops" out, but thumping it with a screw-driver handle will help. Be ready for it to fly out and spray fluid all over. When the snap ring and the guide are out, pull the spring, and with the non-controlled-load servo, remove the rod and the servo. To pull the non-controlled piston out, use snap ring pliers and expand them inside the piston. If the servo is a controlled-load type, grab the rod by hand and pull it. If it's difficult, wrap the rod with a rag and use pliers.

To remove the low-reverse servo, compress the low-reverse servo piston spring retainer to get behind and remove its snap ring. This one is easier than the front servo (unless it has a spring from a shift modification kit, which is stronger). With the snap ring out, pull out the spring retainer, the spring, and the servo piston.

From the inside, use a hammer and blunt chisel or worn-out flat blade screwdriver and knock the shifter shaft seal out. Do not damage the case bore.

Bolted to the rear of the case with four 1/2-inch-headed bolts is the output shaft support. Loosen and remove the bolts and lightly tap it with a wooden or rubber mallet. Critical governor and lube areas can be cleaned and inspected.

Kickdown Servo, Low-Reverse Servo, Shifter Shaft Seal and Output Shaft Support Removal

1 In the valve body area, use a screwdriver to pry out the kickdown servo snap ring. Depending on the spring(s) under it, the servo guide piston may have to be pushed in pretty hard.

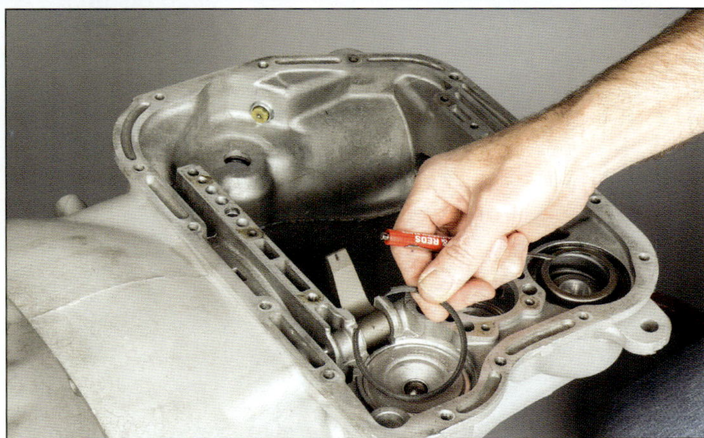

2 If you're lucky, the snap ring lifts out, leaving the servo guide piston stuck in the case.

3 If the servo guide piston is stuck in the case, thump it with a plastic screwdriver handle and prepare for it to fly out, spraying fluid everywhere.

4 The controlled-load servo's pin can be grabbed and the whole assembly pulled out; there will be some fluid under it. If it has a non-controlled-load servo, pull out the spring and the servo pin, and use expanding pliers to pull out the piston.

5 Use a screwdriver to remove the low-reverse servo's snap ring.

6 The servo spring retainer and spring lifts out, leaving the servo piston in the bore.

7 *Remove the low-reverse servo piston.*

8 *Use a hammer and flat chisel or old flat screwdriver to knock out the shifter shaft seal.*

9 *The output shaft support is held with four 5/16-18 bolts. Remove them and tap out the support with a rubber, plastic, or wooden mallet.*

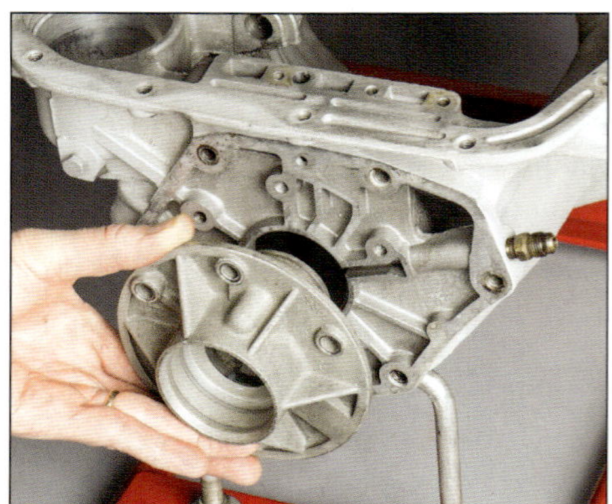

10 *Some supports pull off without any persuasion (such as this one).*

The Kickdown Servo Lever Shaft

In the pump area is a 1/4-inch square plug holding in the kickdown servo lever pivot pin. Remove it with a 1/4-inch-drive extension because the plug needs to be resealed.

At this point, the transmission should be free of any internal or external parts other than pressure test port plugs. The extension housing should also be free of removable parts. If a stand was used, remove it and set the case aside for draining and subsequent cleaning. If headed to the car wash, remove the pressure port plugs so the case can be washed, rinsed, and dried.

Kickdown Servo Lever Shaft Removal

1 *Use a 1/4-inch extension on a small ratchet to remove the plug holding the kickdown servo lever pin.*

2 *Remove the pin with a small magnet or pry the pin from the open side of the case, moving it a bit at a time until it can be grabbed. Pull it and grab the servo lever. You are finished!*

COMPONENT PREPARATION

Now that internal subassemblies are out, it's time to decide what parts to reuse, replace, rebuild, or exchange. Many steps are required to verify the quality of the parts and involve measurement and/or the use of special tools. What you will note is that overhaul parts for Torque-Flites are often inexpensive enough that it may not be cost effective to rework "wear" items (thrust washers, for example). You spend a lot of time taking it out, rebuilding and reinstalling it so is a part that is almost out of specification worth reusing if a new one is inexpensive?

Buying a complete overhaul kit makes sense because reputable suppliers' deluxe kits have high-quality materials, most wear items, and include needed selective thrust washers.

Torque values, clearance specifications, thrust washer thicknesses, and "typical" quantities of front clutch friction discs versus return springs are provided in Appendix B.

Part Replacement Suggestions

1. Sealing rings: Don't reuse them if you have new ones.
2. External seals: The front seal, rear seal, shifter shaft seal, speedometer seal, and low-reverse band anchor pin O-ring should always be replaced.
3. Thrust washers: Consider replacing them if they have any visible wear; new ones are not expensive.
4. Kickdown band: Unless the band is relatively new and looks pristine, I replace it. A thorough inspection for any damage helps decide what to do.
5. Friction plates: Unless their history is known and has been good, I replace them.
6. Steel (driven) plates: Some mechanics reuse steel plates to save the consumer money; I always replace them. ■

After tearing down the A-727, subassemblies await teardown, inspection, measurement, and part replacement.

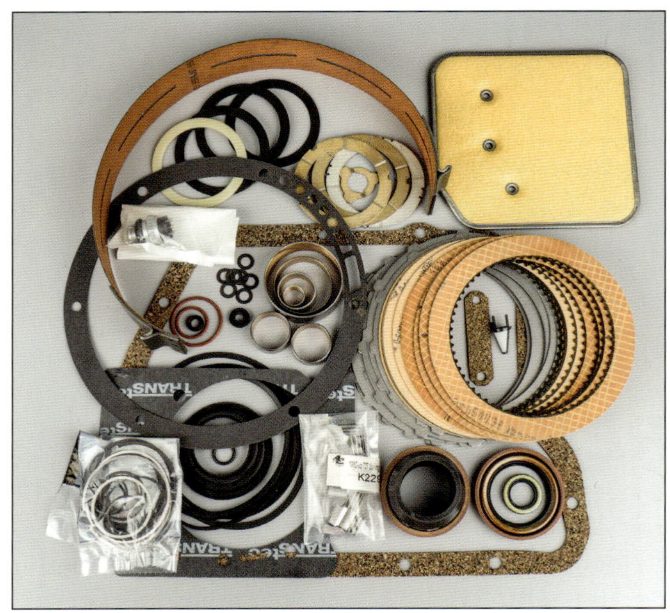

Typical, high-quality Deluxe or Master overhaul kits include most wear items.

Steel Plates: Rework or Replace?

The steel driven plates should never be reused if scored, scratched, warped, or heat-tint damaged (bluing). If reused, they can ruin new friction discs. To save them may be difficult and time-consuming compared to the cost of new ones. If you aggressively sand the steels to remove flaws and leave radial scratches on them, the shift feel and life of the friction material is affected. Experts suggest that steel clutch plates need a certain finish so they "break in" with the friction discs. Unfortunately, this finish is usually only provided by immersion in a vibratory tumbler with appropriate media. Raybestos suggests that shiny used ones will work with new frictions; however, it is suggested that you maximize clutch performance and minimize wear by using new steel plates with new friction clutches. Never waste time saving questionable used ones. ■

Oil Pump

A-904 pumps are similar but smaller than A-727s. The teardown, verification, and reassembly are essentially the same for both so they are covered together.

Teardown

Remove two sealing rings from the reaction shaft support and the bolts from the rear of the reaction shaft support to separate it from the main pump body.

Pull the square-cut O-ring off the perimeter of the pump body. Remove the pump gears from the pump body cavity. Drive the front seal out from the rear using a blunt screwdriver or a punch. Clean all parts and blow them dry with compressed air or let them air dry.

Oil Pump Teardown

1 *Remove the bolts holding the reaction shaft support to the oil pump body.*

2 *Separate the support from the body.*

Verification

Look for excessive wear in the reaction shaft support grooves where the interlocking sealing rings spin. The rings should have had interlocking ends unless they are Teflon, badly worn, or damaged. Feel the sides of the rings and if sharp, the reaction shaft support grooves may be damaged. This could have been caused by excessive input shaft endplay that allowed the front clutch retainer to wobble on the support. Excessive oil pressure can also cause this wear, but it's not common. If the grooves are badly worn, replace the support.

Remove the front thrust washer, and if reusing it because input shaft endplay was acceptable, make sure it is not broken or damaged. Check its thickness; an A-904 pump thrust washer should measure between .061 and .063 inch; A-727 washers are available in four different sizes (.043, .061 to .063, .084 to .086, and .102 to .104 inch). The different sizes provide a way to set the A-727 input shaft endplay between .036 and .084 inch. Look at the support surface where the thrust washer rides and remove nicks or scratches. Replace the washer if it looks damaged.

Inspect both oil pump rotors and be sure there's no scarring, scratching, nicking, or denting. Look at the pump body where the rotors live and verify that there are no scratches, grooves, or wear. If there is any damage to the pump's rotors, there is probably pump damage.

To measure for wear, place both clean rotors in the pump and place a straightedge across the housing. Measure the clearance between the rotors and the straightedge; it should be .0025 inch or less. If it is more, replace the rotors (and pump body if it is damaged).

Inspect the converter bushing in the pump and the corresponding wear surface on the torque converter's hub (if available). If there is wear or deep scratches on either surface, replace the pump bushing and smooth the hub. If the hub has a groove as wide as the bushing, replace the converter or have it rebuilt.

To remove the bushing, a set of bushing drivers really helps. However, without access to a bushing driver, use a flat or blunt-nosed chisel to drive it out. It distorts and can be pushed out pretty easily. Smooth any rough edges in the pump using a small file, crocus cloth, sandpaper, or a burnishing tool before putting in a new bushing. To avoid damaging the new bushing, use a bushing driver or a round, flat object with a larger diameter than the bushing. Press or drive it in from the gear rotor side.

Once the bushing is in, use a blunt punch and create two indentations in the corresponding slots in the pump. After staking, use a knife to remove high points.

Bushings are inside the reaction shaft support; they seldom require replacement. That's not to say that you can ignore yours, but Torque-Flites' input shafts seem to be easy on these bushings. To remove these may require special tools, so visit your local transmission shop and have them do it. Another option is to get a replacement reaction shaft support. If the input shaft journals look fine, the internal bushings in the reaction shaft support are likely fine. Conversely, if the journals are torn up, scratched, or burned, you should change the shaft and the reaction shaft support/bushings.

Take a look inside the support where the input shaft sealing rings seal; there should not be deep grooves; replace if there are.

Oil Pump Verification

1 Remove the sealing rings by pinching them where they hook to let one pop above the other. Remove them carefully feeling their sides for excessive wear and sharp edges.

2 Inspect the sealing ring grooves and the front clutch retainer surface. This one is fine.

3 *Measure the thrust washer. All A-904 reaction shaft support washers and this (selective) A-727 one are between .061 and .063 inch thick. A-727 can also have other thicknesses.*

4 *Look at gears, rotors, and the reaction shaft support for scratches, gouges, and excessive wear. They should always look relatively untouched.*

5 *If the rotors are damaged in any way, more than likely the pump cavity is also damaged.*

6 *The pump gears-to-pump body clearance should be between .001 and .003 inch. This .0015-inch feeler gauge barely fits.*

7 *This bushing supports the torque converter hub and it should be smooth and free of gouges, nicks, and damage. This one has bad sections.*

8 *Use a driver, chisel, or punch to drive out the bushing from the pump body side. Remove any burrs.*

9 *Drive the new bushing flush with the edge of the pump cavity.*

10 Use a punch to stake the bushing in two places and use a knife to remove flared-up areas.

11 Look past the bushing into the reaction shaft support to verify that the input shaft sealing rings did not cause wear grooves.

Reassembly

Lightly spread RTV silicone-type sealer (suitable for ATF) around the circumference of the front seal and use a large flat object (a large-diameter bushing driver) to drive it in flush. A hammer can be used to carefully tap around the seal until it is flush. Turn the pump body over and verify that the spring is still inside the seal.

Put a little assembly grease in the pump cavity and on the inner and outer rotor before installing them. Rotate them so the bushing opening and the inner rotor ID align. This enables the converter hub to mesh with the rotor. Doing this now is easier than trying it with the transmission together.

Holding the oil pump body so the gear cavity is facing up, place the reaction shaft support over it and screw the six bolts into their respective holes. On the A-904 pump, it's a good idea to make a large-diameter clamp that surrounds the circumference of the pump. Hook a series of small gear-type clamps together until long enough and then tighten it around the oil pump body and

reaction shaft to align them. Snug the bolts and then torque them in an alternating pattern to 160 in-lbs. For the A-727, place the reaction shaft support in place and torque the six bolts in an alternating pattern to 160 in-lbs.

Carefully stretch a greased new O-ring around the outside of the pump and drop it into the slot. Correct any twists.

Place assembly grease on the thrust washer, and put it on the reaction shaft support. Put a very small amount of assembly grease in the ring grooves and lock the new, lightly greased sealing rings in. Rotate them so that the lock of one is 180 degrees opposed to the lock of the other.

Once more, grease the sealing rings, thrust washer, O-ring around the pump, the lip of the front seal, and inside the reaction shaft support where the input shaft fits.

Set the completed oil pump aside in a clean location.

Oil Pump Reassembly

1 Lightly apply an RTV-type silicone sealer to the circumference of the pump seal.

2 *Tap in the seal flatly with a hammer or large-diameter bushing driver.*

3 *Grease the inside of the pump seal and converter bushing and then load the lightly greased pump rotors into the cavity. Rotate the inner rotor so the converter slots or flats can align with the pump tabs or slots when it is installed.*

4 *Screw the six bolts back in, torqueing them in a cross pattern to 160 in-lbs.*

5 *Stretch the new square-cut O-ring seal around the pump body and drop it in the slot, being sure that it does not twist.*

6 *Lightly grease the new sealing rings, install them, and lock them on the reaction shaft support. Rotate the rings' end hooks 180 degrees apart. Grease the thrust washer, the inside diameter of the support, the front clutch retainer journal, and the perimeter O-ring seal. Set it aside in a clean, safe area.*

Front Clutch

The following applies to the A-904 and the A-727. The main difference is the A-904 retainer uses one large piston return spring, whereas the A-727 uses a number of smaller springs.

Teardown

Use a flat-blade screwdriver to pry behind and remove the large snap ring. Once out, remove the pressure plate, friction (driving) discs, and steel (driven) clutch plates. Set them aside in order for inspection.

Use a compressing tool to compress the spring retainer far enough to remove the snap ring. After removing the ring, relax the compressor's tension and remove the spring retainer and spring(s) from the hub (if using C-clamps, be careful and alternately tighten or loosen them).

Grab the aluminum piston, wiggle it a bit, and pull it out. If it doesn't come out, turn the retainer upside down and thump its open face against a wooden block or non-scratching material. Once the piston is out, remove the outer lip seal and the inner seal using a small hook or screwdriver.

Front Clutch Teardown

1 Use a flat-bladed screwdriver to pry and remove the snap ring that holds the clutch pack. Remove the plates and discs.

2 Use C-clamps or a clutch spring compressor to force the retainer down to gain access to the snap ring. Remove the snap ring, the spring retainer, and the tool.

3 This A-727 retainer has nine evenly spaced return springs. The A-904 uses one large spring.

4 Pull the apply piston out and remove the outer seal, checking it for any damage. These friction plates were in good condition; the seals were functioning.

5 *Use a hook tool or small screwdriver to dig out the inner seal.*

Verification

Inspect the clutch retainer where the reaction shaft support rings fit inside it. Make sure there are no grooves or gouges because they may cause leakage and/or break the new rings during reassembly and/or operation. Serious wear or grooves require replacement of the retainer and possibly the reaction shaft support. If the damaged area is sanded or machined enough to remove the grooves, it may be so large that the rings do not seal. Don't try to save money by using worn-out parts.

If planning to reuse the friction discs and/or the steel clutch plates, inspect them closely to verify that they are not burned, scratched, damaged, and have no flaking or distortion.

Inspect the bore of the clutch retainer where the piston fits and if you see or feel anything that could damage rubber lip seals, remove it with crocus cloth or very fine sandpaper.

Be sure that the check ball in the retainer is free (it rattles when shaken).

Make sure the spring retainer is flat; over time or with worn friction material and/or high line pressure, it may have distorted.

If the front clutch retainer bushing looks worn or damaged, replace it. Make a note of how far it sits in the bore. The safe way to remove and replace it is to use a bushing driver.

TECH TIP

Excessive Endplay = Worn Retainer?

If there is significant wear in the reaction shaft support sealing ring area or inside the clutch retainer, the transmission likely had excessive endplay. In the case of the transmission used for photographs, this is true. Having too much endplay, you may find (a) one or more thrust washers worn out, (b) worn and loose bushings, (c) broken sealing rings, or (d) other damage throughout the transmission. Looking at the wear pattern created by the sealing rings inside of the front clutch retainer, the wide wear pattern is obvious. This indicates that the front clutch retainer was moving back and forth on the support and over time, it wears out the rings, breaking their locking ends, and creates numerous failures. In this retainer, the "back and forth" play had not progressed enough to do more than light burnishing. ∎

Inspect the inner diameter of the retainer where the reaction shaft support sealing rings fit against it; note the wide wear patterns. The marks measure around .150 inch wide but the rings are only .092 inch wide. This transmission had excessive endplay and the retainer was moving fore and aft. The wear is not too severe.

Lay the clutch retainer, with the open end facing down, on a clean and smooth non-marking surface and use a bushing driver and press or knock the bushing out. If using a punch, alternate locations until the bushing is free. After the bushing is out, clean the inside surface and eliminate any scratches or nicks. Lay the clutch retainer on a non-damaging surface with the open end up; use a bushing driver (or whatever tool you chose) to drive the new bushing in to the same depth as the original.

There are a couple of bushings for 1971 and later A-727 front clutch retainers: a smooth one and a grooved one.

Front Clutch Verification

1 *The overhaul kit came with a front clutch retainer bushing and even though the existing bushing is good, the new one is going to be installed. Take a second to check its depth before knocking it out.*

2 *Drive in the new bushing from the open side to the proper depth.*

3 *When the bushing is installed correctly, it sits slightly below flush. This bushing has grooves for better lubrication.*

Reassembly

Lubricate the new lip seals using transmission assembly grease, a door wax, or specialized lubricant and install them. Make sure the open part of the lip faces the rear of the retainer.

Getting the piston in the retainer is tough because the piston has to "slide" into the clutch retainer without damaging its seal. Factory manuals suggest using a wax lubricant to bind the outer edge of the seals to the piston. It helps to rotate the piston in your hand while pinching the outer seal but doing this too much makes the seal more flexible and it flares back out. When it's ready, drop it in and grab the spring alignment pins or inside the piston recess and twist it back and forth while lightly pushing. If it is ready, it drops right in. If it doesn't, pull it out and compress the lip seal some more and try again. It will eventually drop in, and when it does, you can tell. This is one of those "completely right" or "completely wrong" things, and if you are careful, a light push will not hurt it.

Once the piston is in, place the spring(s) on the piston in the correctly spaced orientation (A-727) and set the spring/retainer and snap ring on the springs. Safely compress the spring/retainer with a special tool or C-clamps. When it compresses far enough, roll the snap ring in and drop it into the groove. Remove the tool(s).

Before installation, soak new friction discs in transmission fluid. Place one steel clutch plate in the retainer on top of the piston. Then, before dropping the frictions in, squeegee off transmission fluid by pinching and rotating them between your thumb and forefinger. Alternate friction discs with steel plates until the right amount is in.

Place the pressure plate in and put a snap ring in place. To get the correct clearance, some later A-904s and A-727s use a waved snap ring or one of four sizes of flat snap rings. Measure, using the feeler gauge, between the pressure plate and the snap ring, and refer to the specification chart in Appendix B for the clearance required. Use the proper snap ring to achieve it. Be aware that a front clutch that uses a wavy ring has a different clearance specification and measurement technique: measure the largest clearance between the ring and the pressure plate. A wavy snap ring helps eliminate harsh Reverse engagement, but the clearance has to be right.

Front Clutch Reassembly

1 *After installing the outer seal on the apply piston, grease it and rotate the piston while compressing the seal.*

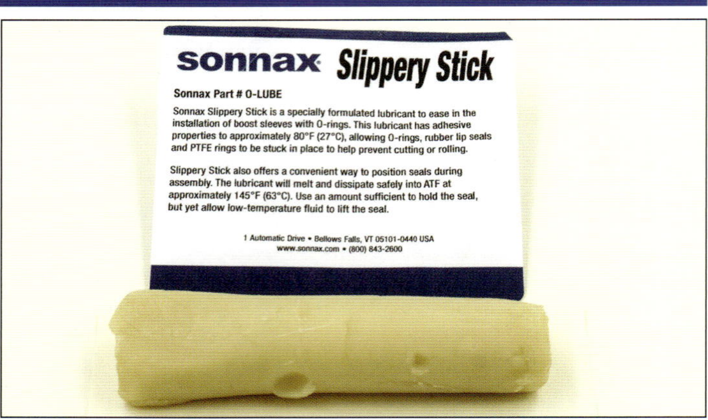

2 *This specialty lube from Sonnax is similar to a low-melting, sticky wax; it keeps seals in position so the pistons fit in the retainers more easily.*

3 *Install the inner seal, lightly lube it, and place the piston in the retainer. Grab the spring support pins (on the A-727) and rotate the piston back and forth while lightly pushing it down. It drops once the seals compress. Remove and recompress the outer seal as needed.*

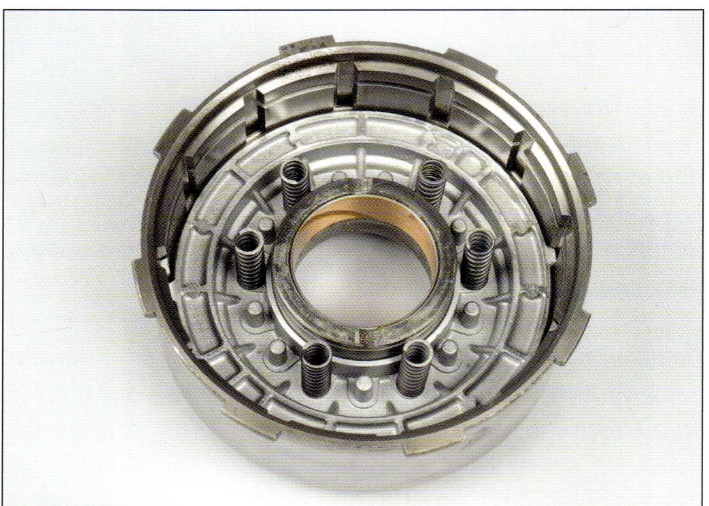

4 *A-727s use different quantities of return springs. For example, if equipped with six, this is how they are arranged.*

5 *Eight return springs are organized like this.*

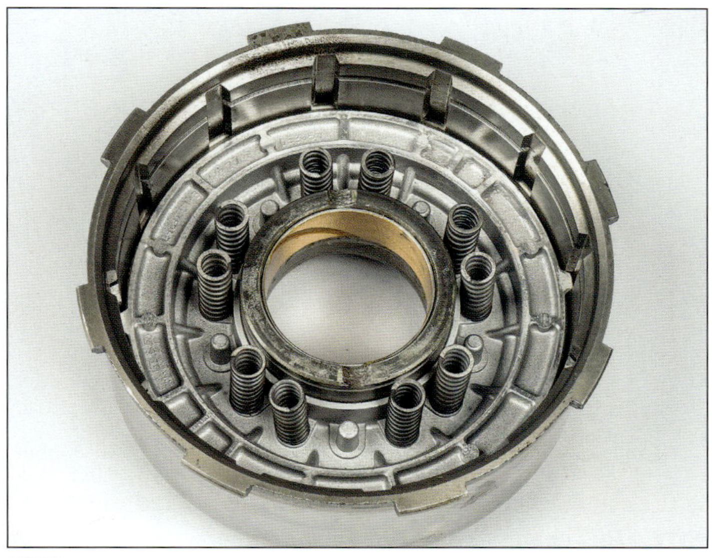

6 *If you have 10 springs, they are organized like this.*

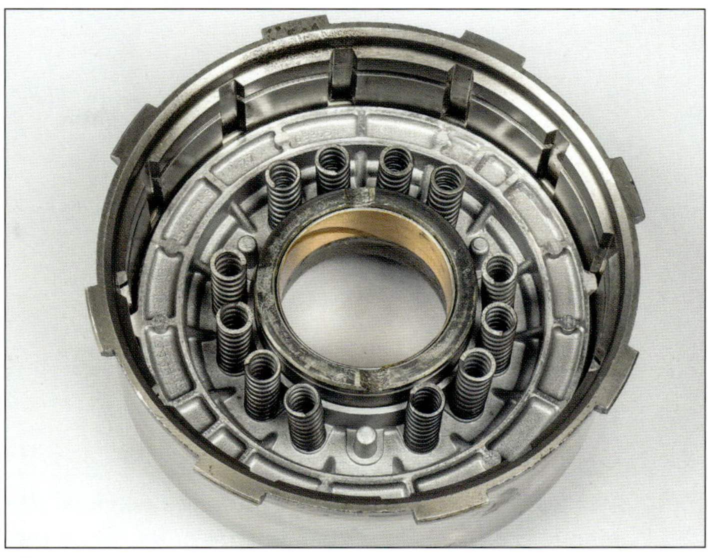

7 *Twelve springs are placed in this manner. An odd number of springs are arranged similarly.*

8 *Before installing new friction discs (or bands), presoak them in transmission fluid for at least 15 minutes.*

9 *Start with a steel driven plate and then add a friction disc; alternate until you have the correct quantity. This one has three each.*

10 *Install the pressure plate then the snap ring (waved, if it had one) and check the clearance.*

11 *With wavy rings, place the feeler gauge between the snap ring's waves and the pressure plate; measure its widest gap.*

12 *This example has .083 inch of clearance, which is in the correct range for a three-disc retainer.*

Too Little Clearance

Teardown of this transmission revealed a few incorrect things, one being the front clutch clearance. This likely happened because the wrong year specification was used and/or there was a misunderstanding of clearance measurement technique using the waved snap ring. A-727s without waved steel snap rings have different clearances than those with the waved ring. The builder must have used the wrong specification and the clearance must have seemed "excessively loose." In actuality, it was correct because of the presence of the waved snap ring.

Take a look at the pattern on the pressure plate and the extra steel plate. To reduce excessive clearance, an extra steel plate was inserted against the pressure plate. This left only about .045-inch clearance, when it should have a minimum of .082-inch clearance. Because of this, the friction discs and steel plates were too tight; I believe the only thing that prevented front clutch failure is that it had enough clearance to barely slip.

Because TorqueFlites are in Direct (Drive) a lot of the time they were clamped anyway. Probably one of the issues the owner would have noticed is the car/truck would have tried to drive in Neutral after overhaul and the 2–3 shift would have felt "funny." ∎

1 *Notice the odd wear marks on this pressure plate and steel driven plate? They should not have been assembled against each other.*

Non-Stock Variations

In the TorqueFlite, the clearance in the front clutch retainer, the ratio of the kickdown band apply lever, the amount of return springs, the amount of friction discs, the friction material used on the kickdown band and the friction discs, and the kickdown band adjustment will determine the kind of 2–3 shift achieved. Charts are provided in Appendix B that show some of the variations in return spring quantity versus the quantity of friction discs used in A-727s and changes in clutch plate clearance for different versions of A-904s and A-727s. Be aware that if building the transmission for performance or non-stock applications, the clearance may vary from the stock specifications. ∎

Rear Clutch

The rear clutch is the "work horse" in the hierarchy of transmission internal components. It is on virtually all the time the vehicle is in motion. We'll look at the A-904 and A-727 separately.

Teardown: A-904

Unhook and remove the sealing rings from the input shaft. Inspect them and verify that the input shaft's grooves are not worn from spinning rings.

Using a flat-blade screwdriver, pry the large snap ring out and remove the pressure plate, the friction (driving) discs, and the steel

2 *Removal of the friction discs and steel plates revealed that there is one too many steels.*

3 *After noting the wear pattern on the steel plate and pressure plate, clutches were reinstalled so a clearance measurement could be taken.*

4 *The friction discs could hardly be rotated in the retainer so the clearance was suspect. The assembly had only .049-inch clearance at the widest point in the waved ring. This would be close for an A-727 three-friction-disc front clutch equipped with a flat snap ring, but it's wrong for a waved ring.*

(driven) clutch plates. For inspection, set them aside in the order they were removed.

With a thin-tipped but strong flat-blade screwdriver, carefully pry one end of the wavy snap ring ("spring") out of its groove and remove it, the Belleville spring, and clutch piston. Remove both lip seals from the piston, noting which direction the open lips face.

Verification: A-904

Look at the friction discs for burned, pitted, or flaking material. If they're going to be replaced, this is mainly for your diagnostic curiosity. Inspect the steel plates for heat discoloration, scoring, or damage, especially if the friction discs were worn. I always replace them but if you choose not to, be sure that they're in great shape and look virtually brand new.

Look at the pressure plates, lower and upper, to verify that they are not scratched, burnt, distorted, or damaged in any way. If they are, replace them. The outer pressure plate can be flipped over and reused if it is flat.

Shake the piston and make sure the check ball rattles. Inspect the groove for nicks or scratches where the lip seals fit.

Inspect the input shaft and its sealing ring grooves. The metal rings have locking hooks, and if they were broken, look for excessive endplay or worn-out bushings.

The thrust washer that separates the rear and front clutch may be temporarily stuck to the rear clutch retainer; remove it, check it for damage, and measure its thickness. Usable ones will be .061 to .063 inch thick. If your overhaul kit includes a washer kit, it should have a new one, but if you did not get one, use the original if it meets specification.

Reassembly: A-904

Use transmission assembly grease, a special wax, or lubricant to lubricate the seals and install them on the piston; the open lip faces the body of the clutch retainer.

Carefully set the piston assembly in the retainer and lightly push on it while rotating it. If it does not drop right in, which most will not, use a lip seal tool (made from piano wire and aluminum tubing), or the round plastic disc that (hopefully) came with the overhaul kit, or a thin feeler gauge to compress the inner seal. Once this occurs, the piston will slightly drop in.

Insert the lip seal tool or roll the round disc around the circumference of the piston to compress the outer seal. Do not force it. If it does not go in, try it again; the piston will eventually fall in.

Place the Belleville spring on top of the piston and install the waved spring in its groove. Start one end and then feed the spring into the groove until fully seated. When correct, there will be little to no clearance between the piston and the Belleville spring.

Install the inner pressure plate by aligning the external lugs into the clutch retainer's grooves and set it on the Belleville spring.

Soak the new friction discs in transmission fluid and use your fingers to squeegee off the excess fluid before setting one of the discs into the clutch retainer. Alternate with the steel plates and end with a friction disc, making sure to use the correct quantity.

Install the outer pressure plate and snap ring. Push firmly against the pressure plate while using the feeler gauge to measure the clearance between the plate and the snap ring. Use one of three snap rings (.060, .068, or .076 inch) to achieve the proper clearance.

Install a lightly greased thrust washer, grease the sealing rings, and put them on the input shaft. Lock the rings and rotate them so the gaps are 180 degrees opposed. Put a bit more grease on the rings and washer before setting the assembly aside.

Teardown: A-727

Remove the sealing rings from the input shaft and check the rings and grooves for damage or wear.

Pry the large snap ring out using a flat-blade screwdriver and remove the pressure plate, the friction discs, and steel clutch plates. For inspection, set them aside in the order they came out.

Use a long, thin, strong flat-bladed screwdriver to pry one end of the waved snap ring spring out of its groove. Remove it, the spacer, the Belleville spring, and the piston. For ease of access, slide the outer retainer off the hub/piston retainer.

Remove both lip seals from the piston, noting which direction the lips face. Check them closely to see if they were worn out, stiff from old age, or cut. In any of these situations, the transmission may have had slow engagement into Forward (Drive) positions. If this was the case, there may be friction discs and steel plates with damage.

Rear Clutch Teardown

1 *Unhook and remove the input shaft sealing rings and inspect their grooves for damage. If there was excessive endplay, they might be worn and/or broken.*

2 *Don't forget to remove the large-diameter ring sometimes found on A-727s and A-904s.*

3 Use a large, flat-bladed screwdriver to access behind it to pry out the snap ring.

4 *After removal from the rear clutch retainer, inspect the frictions and steels. These have an odd wear pattern that may have happened when they fit against a warped steel/pressure plate; they may have been extremely loaded.*

5 Use a long screwdriver or sharp tool to pry out the wavy snap-ring spring below the apply pressure plate.

6 On an A-727, remove the plastic or steel spacer and safely store it. A-904s don't have one.

Verification: A-727

Look at the friction discs to see if they were burned, pitted, or have any material flaking from them. If they're going to be replaced, this inspection will show you more about the transmission's condition. Inspect the steel plates for burning, scoring, or metal damage. I replace them all, but if you decide to reuse them, make sure they are acceptable. Check both pressure plates to verify that they are not scratched, burnt, or warped; if they are, replace them. The outer pressure plate can be reversed if it's flat.

Shake the piston, making sure the check ball rattles. Check the lip seal grooves in the piston and make sure there are no nicks, scratches, or gouges.

Inspect the input shaft sealing ring grooves closely to verify that they are not worn. If new rings fit sloppily, the input shaft or assembly needs to be replaced.

Unlike the A-904, there is a small bushing in the A-727 input shaft. If it is damaged, there is a special puller to remove it. I've used a Dremel tool with a small ball mill bit to cut grooves in it before chiseling it out. If you do this, be sure there are no sharp edges or gouges left, and clean it. Lightly tap in a new bushing with a bushing driver or a flat object of the right diameter. Test fit it on the output shaft.

Check the thrust washer that separates the front and rear retainers for damage and measure it; it should be .061- to .063-inch thick. A new thrust washer kit will have this one, but if you do not have new ones and the old one is fine, reuse it.

Rear Clutch Verification

1 *Remove the apply piston and shake it to be sure the check ball is loose. Pull off the inner and outer lip seals noting their direction.*

2 *Slide the clutch retainer (A-727) off the hub. The sealing ring grooves should be smooth and undamaged.*

3 *Remove the remaining thrust washer and check it for damage. Obviously, this one fails.*

4 *Measurement shows that it was still in the correct thickness range.*

Reassembly: A-727

Using the appropriate grease, lubricate and install the inner and the outer seals on the clutch piston so the open section of the seals face the body of the clutch retainer. Run your fingers around the piston to compress the lip of the seal. Carefully set the piston assembly in the clutch retainer and lightly rotate and/or wobble it back and forth until it seats. If it does not want to drop in, do not force it. Pull it out, recompress the lip seal, and try again. Use a piano wire lip seal tool or the round disc that comes with some overhaul kits, and slip the disc or the lip seal tool in the outer diameter of the piston and roll/slide it around, compressing the lip seal. The piston will drop in.

Slide the piston retainer/hub back into the clutch retainer (if you removed it).

Place the Belleville (washer) piston spring on the piston and then place the steel or Nylon spacer ring on it. Install the wavy snap ring in the groove by starting one end and then feeding and rolling the rest of the spring in the groove. If needed, lightly tap it in until it's fully seated. When correct, there is virtually no gap between the spacer and the spring.

Install the inner pressure plate into the clutch retainer with its narrow section sitting on the Belleville piston spring.

Remove the friction discs from the transmission fluid (where they have soaked for a while) and use your fingers to squeegee off excess fluid. Set one of them into the retainer and alternate with steel plates, ending with the friction disc. Use the right quantity.

Install the outer pressure plate and snap ring. Push firmly against the pressure plate while inserting the feeler gauge between the plate and the snap ring. Set the clearance to the proper range for your transmission using one of four thickness snap rings (.060, .074, .088, or .106 inch). Put assembly grease on the sealing rings, install them, and install the thrust washer, grease it, and set the rear clutch aside in a clean area.

1 *Grease the inner and outer lip seals and install them on the piston. Rotate the piston and compress the outer and inner seals using your fingers.*

2 *Place the piston in the retainer and lightly push while rotating it. Usually, this requires a tool; you can use a piano wire tool or the plastic disc from the gasket set. Rotate and push against the seals to compress them, allowing the piston to drop in. Reinstall the Belleville spring, spacer (A-727), and wavy snap-ring spring, followed by the inner pressure plate.*

3 *After the presoak, rotate the frictions between your fingers to squeegee off excess fluid.*

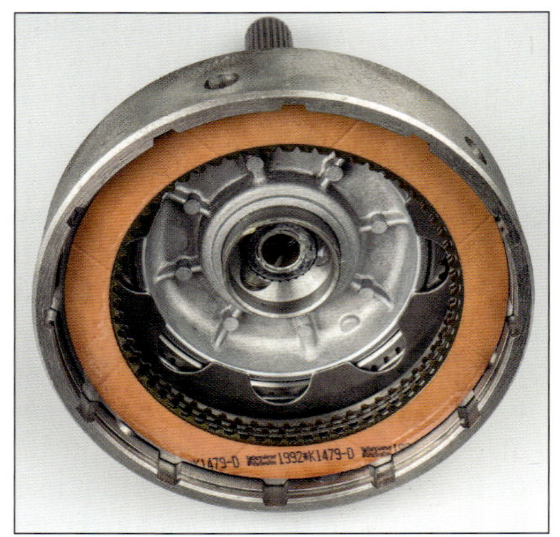

4 *Alternate friction discs and steel driven plates, ending with a friction disc.*

5 *Measure the clearance with a feeler gauge placed between the outer pressure plate and snap ring. The rear clutch (most A-727s) should have between .025- and .045-inch clearance.*

6 *The new frictions and steel plates with the original snap ring provide an acceptable clearance of .035 inch.*

Overrunning Clutch

The overrunning clutch, although not hydraulically actuated like the rear clutch, has to function in Drive Breakaway for the vehicle to pull away from a dead stop.

Teardown

The overrunning clutch's individual parts were already removed but look closely at the outer race to be sure it is not cracked or loose in the case.

Verification

If you plan to reuse the clutch rollers, be sure they are smooth and round. Look for damage such as flat spots, chips, or "brinelling" (a surface condition where permanent indentions are noted). Look for damage or wear in the contact areas of the cam and race.

Inspect the roller springs for distortion, wear, excessive compression, or other damage. Fortunately, a new spring and roller kit is cheap enough that it makes sense to replace it all.

Verify that the A-904 cam is tight in the case and that the rivets have not come loose. Any looseness is a good indication that it should be replaced.

Check the setscrew that holds the cam in the A-727 case and if it is loose, check the cam and the spring retainer under the cam, as both may be loose. If so, back out the screw and lightly hammer or use a tool and press the cam back in. Re-stake the case on the front side using a blunt chisel to indent it on the existing factory marks. Tighten the screw and re-stake the case around the screw.

Overrunning Clutch Verification

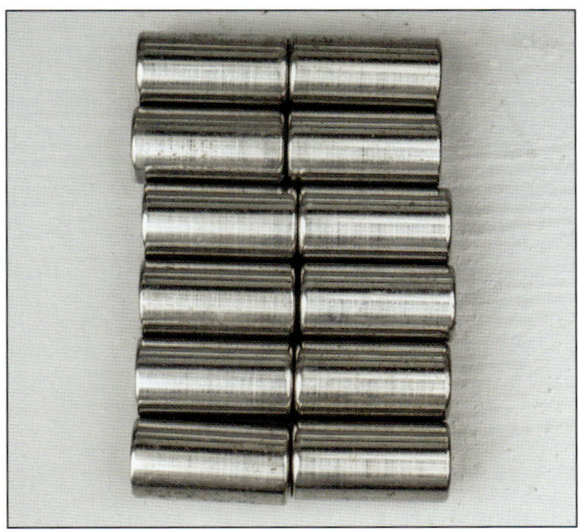

1 *Overrunning clutch rollers need to be round, undamaged, and free of wear. Other than being lightly rusted (from cleaning without adequate drying), these are okay but will be replaced with the springs.*

2 *The inner race must be smooth and free of gouges or nicks; this one passes the test.*

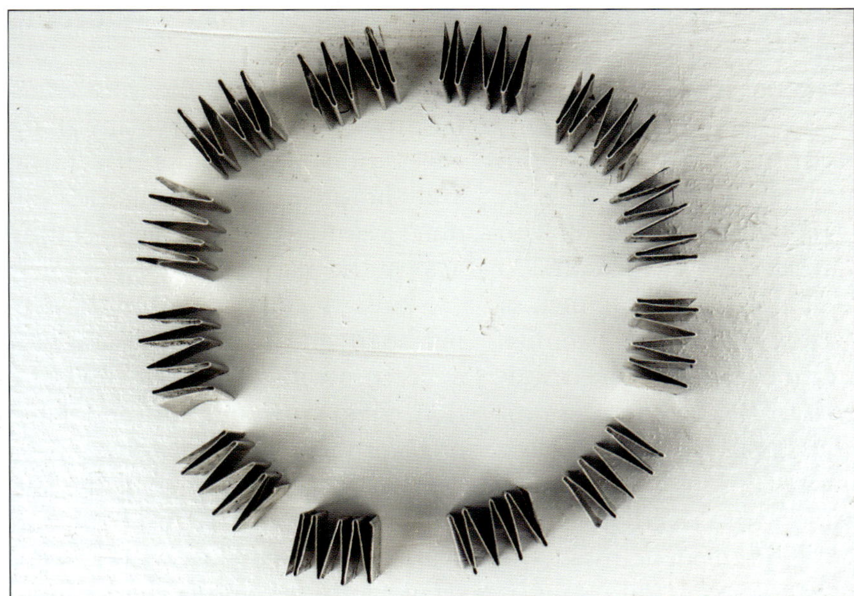

3 *Inspect the springs for damage; they should not be misshapened or crushed. These look fine but will be replaced because the overhaul kit included them.*

4 *A-727 cases have a setscrew that should be checked for tightness.*

5 *Be sure the outer cam is tight in the case, but if not, loosen the setscrew and tap in the cam. Use a blunt chisel to re-stake the case over the original marks, tighten the setscrew, and re-stake it.*

Replacement of the Overrunning Clutch Cam in the A-904

If you find any damage in the overrunning clutch cam or spring retainer, you can correct it by installing a bolt-in replacement cam and spring retainer. Most, if not all, replacements are held in the case using bolts instead of factory-style rivets. If you plan to replace yours, you need a sharp (center) punch, a drill, and correctly sized drill bits.

Remove the bolts that hold the output shaft support to the case and use a soft-faced hammer or a wooden block to tap the support out.

Use a punch and mark the center of the rivet heads. Use a sharp 3/8-inch drill bit to drill through each rivet head while carefully keeping the bit centered to avoid slipping off and drilling the case. Use a small chisel to break off the rivet heads and then knock them out using a suitably sized punch. The cam should be loose and come out with the rivets.

Use a sharp 17/64-inch drill bit and enlarge the holes in the case. Blow or rinse out chips and drilling residue.

Place the new cam and spring retainer into the case so the now-enlarged case holes line up with the threaded holes in the cam. Screw all seven replacement bolts (with washers) into the cam at least a few threads each. If the bolts are equipped with cone-style washers, install them so the inner diameter is coned toward the bolts' head. Tighten the retaining bolts evenly, and after the cam has seated, use an inch-pound torque wrench and tighten each to 100 in-lbs.

Tap in the support using a soft-faced hammer, install the bolts, and torque them to 150 in-lbs.

Replacement of Overrunning Clutch Cam in the A-727

Loosen the setscrew holding the cam in place. If the transmission case is upside down, the setscrew will be on the top.

It should be off, but if it is still on, remove the four bolts that hold the output shaft support on and then tap or pull it off. Using the appropriately sized punch, go through the four bolt holes and knock the cam out of the case, alternating from a bolt hole to the one roughly 180 degrees opposing it.

Before installing the new cam and retainer, lock the spring retainer on the replacement cam by snapping the retainer lugs into the cam's notches.

Position the replacement cam and retainer in the case and verify that the cam's serrations line up with the ones in the case. Using a press, a special tool, a soft-faced hammer, or a long piece of wood and a hammer, drive the cam evenly into the case as far as possible. You will need to hit it in various locations while driving it in. Keep track of the spring retainer's location. After verifying that the cam is bottomed, reinstall the cam-retaining setscrew and snug it tightly. Re-stake the case around the setscrew and also re-stake the case around the cam in the 12 factory locations (using a blunt chisel).

Rinse or blow out any residue and remove any burrs or wooden or plastic particles. Put the output shaft support back on and torque the four bolts that hold it to 150 in-lbs.

Planetary Gear Assembly

The geartrain may have come out in separate pieces and sections, but keep thrust washers in their proper locations so you can identify any planetary or geartrain wear issues. The TorqueFlite is easy on its geartrain; very seldom will you find severe damage unless there was abuse or severe-duty usage.

Teardown

The geartrain was removed and separated in Chapter 4 so it should be ready for verification.

Verification

Inspect all journals on the output shaft for scratches, burn marks, or visible damage. Remove light scratches or small burrs with crocus cloth or a fine stone.

Look closely at the speedometer drive gear and remove any sharp edges from it. Because it's metal and the driven gear is plastic, you don't want any sharp edges rotating against the plastic.

Rinse the oil passages in the output shaft and planetary gears with a clean solvent to remove anything that could cause lubrication-related or governor operational issues.

Inspect the bushings in the sun gear, which is locked into the sun gear shell, to be sure they are not scratched or worn out. These can be changed if needed, but seldom are stock ones worn out.

Inspect all bronze or aluminum thrust washers for wear; they should measure at least .048 to .051 inch thick. Look at the related surfaces that thrust washers rotate against and replace or repair anything that looks damaged, scratched, broken, or cracked. If the washers look damaged, scratched, or are undersized, replace them. Very infrequently are the steel washers worn, but look at them to be sure they are good; replace if not.

Pay close attention to the center splines of the front planet carriers (steel or aluminum) to be sure they are undamaged. Inspect each pinion gear in the carrier for cracks, damage, or broken teeth. If broken teeth are found on the pinion gears, the gears that rotate against them will likely be damaged and need to be replaced.

Overall Planetary Geartrain Endplay on the Output Shaft

The endplay of the entire planetary gear assembly needs to be checked. Place the assemblies back on the output shaft in the opposite order they came off and install the small snap ring. Stand it up so the driveshaft yoke splines are facing up and insert a feeler gauge between the rear annulus gear and the shoulder on the output shaft. The clearance should be between .001 and .047 inch (A-904) and between .009 and .044 inch (A-727). On A-904s or A-727s, the small selective snap ring that holds the entire assembly on will set the endplay. If the clearance cannot be set correctly with the snap ring, you may have to replace the thrust washers and/or related parts. Sonnax makes shims that can be positioned under the thrust washers to reduce excessive endplay.

Geartrain Verification

1 *Inspect all of the output shaft's journals; polish any nicks or scratches.*

2 *The speedometer drive gear is machined on the output shaft so be sure it has no sharp edges to tear up the plastic driven gear.*

3 *The sun gear rides on two bushings on the output shaft journals. Inspect them; these are in great condition.*

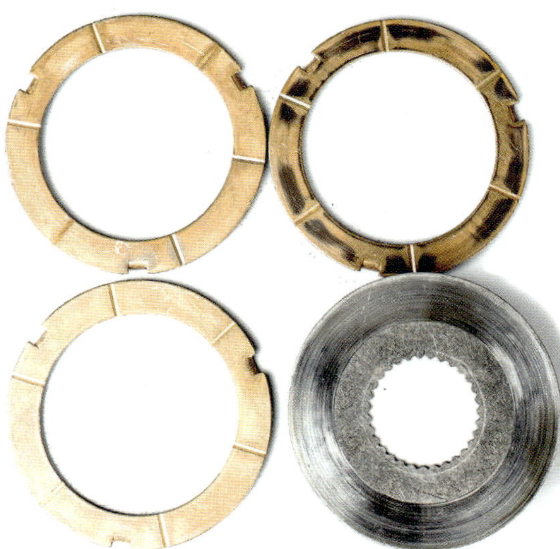

4 *The A-727 has three interchangeable thrust washers depending on the number of pinion gears. Three-tabbed thrust washers (and four-tabbed, not shown) should measure between .059 and .062 inch and should have no deep scratches or burns. One of these has been worn so all will be replaced because the overhaul kit includes them. The steel thrust plate/washer, although lightly marked, measures fine at .035 inch.*

5 *The front planetary gear assembly takes the brunt of the 1–2 shift and, in extreme cases, may have damaged or stripped splines. Some A-904s and aftermarket A-727s use steel carriers; this one is fine.*

6 *Closely inspect the pinion gears in the front and rear planetary to be sure no teeth are cracked, damaged, or chipped. If they are, the corresponding sun gear is also damaged.*

7 *Reassemble the geartrain on the output shaft, stand it up, and insert a feeler gauge between the rear annulus gear assembly and its output shaft journal. The clearance should be between .009 and .044 inch (A-727); with new thrust washers, this one is acceptable with .013 inch of play.*

Reassembly

The planetary geartrain (A-904 and A-727) will be reassembled later.

Kickdown Servo and Band

A controlled-load kickdown servo is found in most 1971 and later A-904 and A-727 transmissions. Many earlier and some later high-performance A-727 transmissions used non-controlled-load servos.

Teardown

Non-controlled-load servos used in many A-904s and heavy-duty A-727s require no disassembly other than removal and replacement of the sealing rings on the piston and servo pin guide.

The controlled-load servo has sealing rings on the piston and guide and an O-ring seal on a smaller internal piston. You access it by removing the snap ring from an internal section of the piston. With the snap ring out, remove the washer, spring, and steel piston/rod from the piston.

Verification: Non-Controlled-Load Servo

Inspect the piston and guide's seal rings and be sure the rings turn freely in the grooves. If the original rings look good, still have tension, spin around, and exhibit no damage, some will reuse them but they come in overhaul kits so you might as well replace them.

Verify that no scratches are in the transmission's kickdown servo bore. If so, you can lightly polish them. Check the fit of the guide on the piston rod and be sure the spring has tension and is not distorted.

Verification: Controlled-Load Servo

If your A-904 or A-727 has a controlled-load servo piston, use the non-controlled load servo verification steps, but also inspect the inside diameter of the servo where the steel piston rides looking for scratches.

Verification: Kickdown Band

The band can be flexible or a cast solid band. Look at the lining for burning or drastic wear and be sure it

Use a snap-ring tool to remove the snap ring, washer, and spring to access the piston.

has no glazing, non-uniform wear, or exposed metal caused by debonding of the friction material. Be sure its anchors are tight and straight. If the lining is damaged or worn, replace the band because a stock band is relatively inexpensive compared to the amount of work spent getting to it.

Kickdown Servo and Band Verification

1 *The O-ring on a controlled-load servo is important for proper function.*

2 *The kickdown servo doesn't suffer much abuse, but you should inspect the rings to make sure that they are not broken or stuck in the groove.*

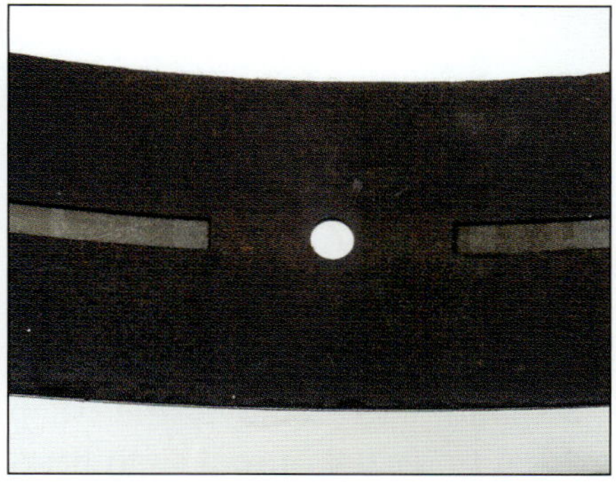

3 *Inspect the kickdown band for burning, tearing, cracking, flaking, or debonding of material. This one looks okay, but the overhaul kit came with one, so it is being replaced.*

4 *Inspect the kickdown band's anchors to be sure that they are tight. Stock TorqueFlites seldom have any kickdown band anchor damage.*

Reassembly: Non-Controlled-Load Servo

There is no reassembly other than installation of new sealing rings on the servo piston and the servo guide.

Reassembly: Controlled-Load Servo

To prepare the controlled-load servo piston for reinstallation, lubricate the new O-ring and roll it in the piston rod assembly's groove. Push the piston rod assembly into the servo piston, rotating it slightly while pushing it. Place the spring over the rod followed by the washer and snap ring. Use pliers to pinch the snap ring slightly to lock it inside the servo piston. Grease the rings lightly before placing them on the servo piston and guide and set the servo assembly aside in a clean, safe area.

Low-Reverse Servo and Band

The low-reverse servo and band are relatively similar between the A-904 and A-727; they will be covered together.

Replace all sealing rings on either style of servo and replace the O-ring on the controlled-load piston.

If you need to pull the piston off the piston plug, compress the spring and remove the small snap ring. A vise works best, but this method works in a pinch.

Remove the rubber lip seal, inspect it for damage, and note its orientation.

Replace the lip seal and put the piston assembly together.

Make sure that the new lip seal faces the correct way before reinstalling it.

Output Shaft, Governor and Parking Gear

Teardown

If it needs to be disassembled, compress the stiff cushion spring by gripping it with pliers or clamp the servo piston in a vise. Remove the small snap-ring.

Pull the rubber lip seal out and roll it off the piston.

Remove the O-ring from the low-reverse band pin that fits in the case.

Verification

Inspect the servo piston and pin, looking for cracks, burrs, pits, or scores in the piston's seal groove. With the spring off, slide the plug/shaft in and out to be sure it is free. Look at the piston bore in the case to be sure it is not damaged; minor scratches can be sanded smooth with fine sandpaper or Scotch-Brite. Inspect the spring for distortion and replace it if needed. If the snap ring has been distorted, replace it.

Look at the lining of the low-reverse band for burning or wear and be sure it has no flaking or debonding of the friction material. It should not be glazed or have unusual wear or cracking of the anchors. If the band is damaged or worn in any way, replace it.

Reassembly

Install a new lip seal on the servo piston.

If the low-reverse servo was disassembled, grease the shaft and insert the piston plug (with the spring on it) into the piston, compress it, and lock it in place with its snap ring.

Install a new O-ring on the pin that holds the anchor link or the band; do not forget this.

The A-904 and A-727 are similar so they will be discussed together.

Teardown

Remove two sealing rings from the governor support/parking gear.

Expand and remove the snap ring that holds the output shaft bearing on and slide the bearing off. If the bearing sticks, tap the shaft with a wooden mallet at the driveshaft end to free the bearing. Remove the other thick snap ring (A-727).

Look inside the smaller bore of the governor assembly and use a small screwdriver or a sharp tool to remove the E-clip from the shaft. Slide the shaft (with the other E-clip still on it) out the opposite side and remove the small valve.

Remove the larger C-clip holding the outer weight in the large end of the governor body and pull the weight

Inspect the rear band for burning, flaking, or debonding. These bands are pretty tough and usually hold up well.

To disassemble the governor, remove one of the small E-clips and pull out the shaft, leaving the clip on it.

Clean the small filter/screen if yours had one. If the rest of the transmission is in good condition, these are usually clean.

The bearing, when lightly lubricated, should roll without any growling, knocking, or binding. When they are damaged, you feel a vibration that becomes worse with speed.

Reassembly

Lubricate all the governor parts with fluid or a special lubricant used for valve bodies.

Install new rings on the governor body assembly.

Place the spring inside the outer weight and follow it with the inner weight and the correct snap ring. Install the assembled weight inside the governor body and lock it in with the larger snap ring. Place the filter/screen (if present) in its cavity and place the locking metal tabs under the bolts that hold the body

out. Remove the smaller C-clip that is holding the inner weight and spring inside the outer weight.

Remove the large thin snap ring that holds the governor parking gear assembly on the output shaft; slide the assembly off.

If present, bend the locking tabs and unscrew the four bolts holding the governor body to the parking gear. Remove the governor body and the screen/filter (if it has one) for cleaning and inspection.

Verification

Before cleaning it, roll the bearing and listen and feel for any growling, whining, or noise that would indicate a rough, brinelled, or damaged ball or race. Replace the bearing if you hear or feel anything. Clean the bearing, but be aware that when it is completely dry, it will be noisier and try to bind until it is lubed.

Inspect the governor parts for any nicks or gouges that could make

them stick. Be sure all valves slide in and out freely. When everything has been cleaned, the valves should slide in their bores, even when dry. Any rough spots can be polished with crocus cloth or Scotch-Brite. Rinse any residue from the governor screen. Be sure that the sealing ring grooves exhibit no abnormal wear.

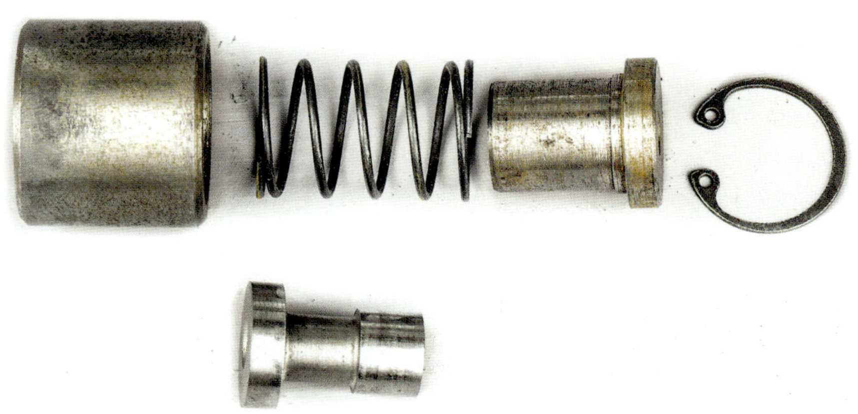

Remove the large governor weight. The inner weight should slide freely in the outer weight even when dry. These are in fine condition, other than light rust from handling.

to the parking gear. Loosely screw the bolts in.

Place the completed assembly on the output shaft in such a way that the hole through the output shaft aligns to the small shaft that fits through it and the governor valves.

Install the thin snap ring that holds the governor parking gear assembly on the output shaft. Torque the four bolts, in a cross pattern, to 100 in-lbs and bend the metal tabs (if used) over the bolt heads to lock them.

Put the remaining small governor valve in the small end, place the shaft through, and install the remaining small E-clip on it.

On the A-727, place one of the large remaining snap rings back on the output shaft and follow it with the lightly lubricated bearing. The large groove on the circumference of the bearing is biased to the front of the transmission.

Reinstall the remaining snap ring and slowly spin the bearing to be sure it is smooth, free, and quiet.

Other than the valve body, the internal subassemblies are now complete, pre-lubricated, and ready to go.

Output Shaft, Governor and Parking Gear Reassembly

1 *When sliding on the almost-completed governor assembly, align the hole in the output shaft with the hole in the governor.*

2 *Install the new sealing rings, slide the pin through, and install the E-clip. Torque the four bolts and re-bend the tabs on the keepers.*

3 *On the A-727, install one large, thick snap ring and slide on the cleaned and lubricated bearing. (A-904 has only one bearing snap ring.) Reinstall the other snap ring making sure the bearing's grove is biased to the front.*

Replacing Damaged Threads

Dealing with aluminum, it's bound to happen: a thread gets stripped, pulled out, or crossed up. No worries. Thread repair kits come from many sources; they all work well and are relatively easy to use. They all involve drilling out the old thread, tapping the larger hole with a special-sized tap, screwing in a new steel thread insert, and then celebrating. ■

1 *Aluminum cases (and some steel parts) can suffer thread damage. Often, pan bolts are screwed in crookedly and ruin the threads. Repair them with a thread insert kit.*

2 *Using the specified drill bit or one contained in the kit, drill out the bad threads. Drill perpendicular to the pan rail.*

3 *Use the supplied tap to re-thread the hole for the new thread insert.*

4 *With the threaded hole cleaned, use a thread-locking compound to hold the insert.*

5 *Using the supplied tool, screw in the new insert to the appropriate depth.*

6 *This Helicoil has a small tab that is to be broken off after installation. Use a punch.*

7 *This is a broken tab; be sure it doesn't get inside the transmission.*

CONTROL VALVE BODY PREPARATION

The control valve body (or simply the "valve body") is covered separately because of its complexity and importance.

The valves in the TorqueFlite are robust and controlled with fairly strong springs. Unlike other manufacturers' valve bodies, it is pretty difficult to overtighten screws and affect its operation. However, always use factory recommendations and torque screws where and when you can.

Pressure Control and Regulation Valves

The main regulator valve controls line pressure.

The governor valve (located in the governor body on the output shaft and rotates at driveshaft speed) creates a "governor pressure signal." Its pressure varies with vehicle speed and it is fed to the valve body to control upshifts, downshifts, and converter lock-up (if equipped).

The throttle valve controls throttle pressure; this pressure varies with the opening of the carburetor or throttle body, and it controls upshifts and downshifts and converter lock-up (if equipped).

Control Valves

The driver controls the manual valve and it changes positions when the shift lever or push buttons are actuated.

The 1–2 shift valve automatically shifts the transmission from Drive Breakaway to Second, and it causes the downshift from Second to Breakaway based on the driver's actions and governor signal.

The 2–3 shift valve automatically shifts the transmission from Second to Direct, and it causes a downshift from Direct to Second depending on the driver's actions and governor signal.

The kickdown valve creates "forced" downshifts from (a) Direct to Second, (b) Second to Breakaway, or (c) Direct to Breakaway. It depends on vehicle speed and the driver's force on the accelerator pedal. If the throttle pressure lever pushes the valve past the detent close to or at wide-open throttle, downshifts happen rapidly.

On one end of the 2–3 shift valve in most TorqueFlites is a throttle pressure plug. Similar to the kickdown valve, it provides a 3–2 downshift, depending upon throttle openings and the speed of the vehicle. This valve is key to the part-throttle downshift module.

The 1–2 shift control valve provides 1–2 shift pressure to the

You can rebuild, clean, and lubricate a valve body with these tools and products.

accumulator piston in preparation for completion and control of the application of the kickdown band during the 1–2 shift and the 3–2 kickdown. The limit valve determines the highest speed at which a 3–2 part throttle kickdown can occur. Some TorqueFlites do not have a Limit Valve and so the max speed for the 3–2 kickdown happens at the "detent" position.

The shuttle valve has two important purposes and performs each independently. First, it provides a quick release of the kickdown band and smooth front clutch engagement when drivers make a "lift-foot" upshift from Second to Direct. Second, the shuttle valve regulates the application of the kickdown servo and band when a kickdown occurs from Direct to Second.

Lock-Up Converter Control Valves

In a lock-up TorqueFlite, the lock-up valve (controlled by the spring tension) applies the converter lock-up clutch if the vehicle is in Direct Drive and is above a predetermined speed. Later TorqueFlite converter clutch lock-ups are controlled by pressure from the lock-up solenoid that is controlled by the engine computer through a feed-through electrical connector in the rear of the case. The computer also controls the torque converter lock-up and unlock at closed throttle, during braking, during engine warm-up, and during part-throttle acceleration.

The fail-safe valve restricts oil flow to the lock-up clutch if front clutch pressure drops off or disappears; by doing so, lock-up can only occur in Direct. The fail-safe valve provides a quick converter clutch un-lock during a kickdown.

The switch valve directs oil to apply the lock-up clutch in one position and releases it in the other, and directs oil to the cooling and lube circuits. In some TorqueFlites, the switch valve is actually a regulator of oil pressure to the torque converter.

Special Requirements

When working on the valve body, never clamp it in anything. Any crushing, bending, or distortion can cause valves to hang up or leaks to occur.

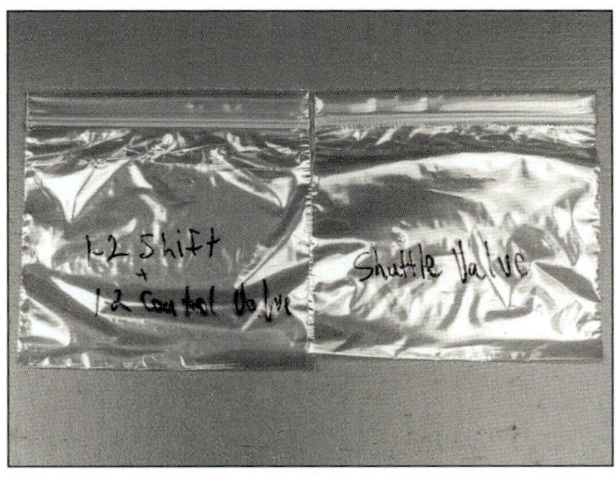

Use plastic sandwich bags and label them to segregate springs and valves.

The valves and plugs have to move freely. Any damage will make them stick rendering the valve body nonfunctional and possibly requiring major rework. When working on a valve body, never force valves as it may cause burrs or damage bores causing valves to stick.

I recommend identifying valves and springs by taking photos of them or putting them in write-on sandwich bags or by tagging them. Whichever method is chosen, keep them separated and identified because several springs may interchange, which causes the valve body to malfunction.

Disassembly

For ease of photography and service, the valve body is mounted on a Miller Tool stand. As long as there is a clean surface and a pan or tray to catch remaining fluid and parts, working on one is straightforward.

Check Balls, Pressure Regulators, Transfer and Separator Plate, Lock-Up Valve Assembly or Stiffener and Filter

It should be off already, but if not, remove the three screws and the oil filter. These screws are longer and have large washers on them.

Remove the top and bottom screws that hold the line-pressure adjusting screw bracket and retainer to the valve body and remove the screw that threads into the side of the valve body (if present). Push/hold the spring retainer while removing the last screw. Ease up on the retainer; pull it off with the line and throttle pressure–adjusting screws. Don't change the settings. Remove the line pressure and torque converter valve regulator springs and segregate/identify them.

Remove the line pressure regulator and torque converter control valves and keep them with their respective springs.

Remove the screws holding the stiffener and separator plate to the transfer plate; keep these separate if different.

If it is a lock-up, remove the lock-up module screws and slowly slide the module away, separating the tube from the valve body. Remove the cover and the lock-up spring and valve. Remove the fail-safe valve and spring and identify or segregate them.

Loosen and remove the 17 (or so) screws that hold the transfer plate assembly to the valve body and lift the assembly off. If it still has one or two small screws holding the separator plate on, remove them, lift the plate off, and remove the 1/4-inch rear clutch check ball from the transfer plate (if present). Remove the pressure regulator valve filter/screen (if present) from the separator plate. In addition, if it has the spring and check valve, remove it.

Note the location and remove the five or more 1/4-inch-diameter check balls and one 11/32-inch-diameter ball from the valve body. If an older model, it may have one 3/8-inch-diameter ball and spring.

Bag or tag springs and valves for identification. Clean and dry all parts.

Check Balls, Pressure Regulators, Transfer and Separator Plate, Lock-Up Valve Assembly or Stiffener and Filter Removal

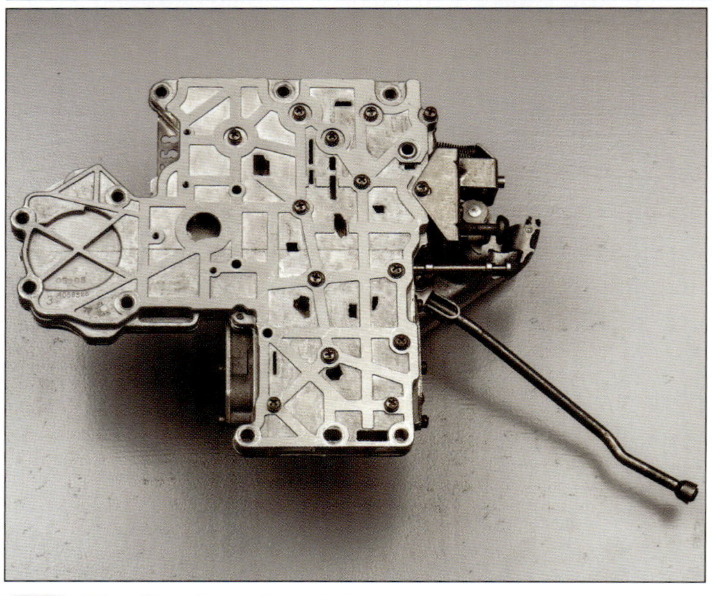

1 *The filter has already been removed; its screws are longer and have larger washers than those holding the valve body together.*

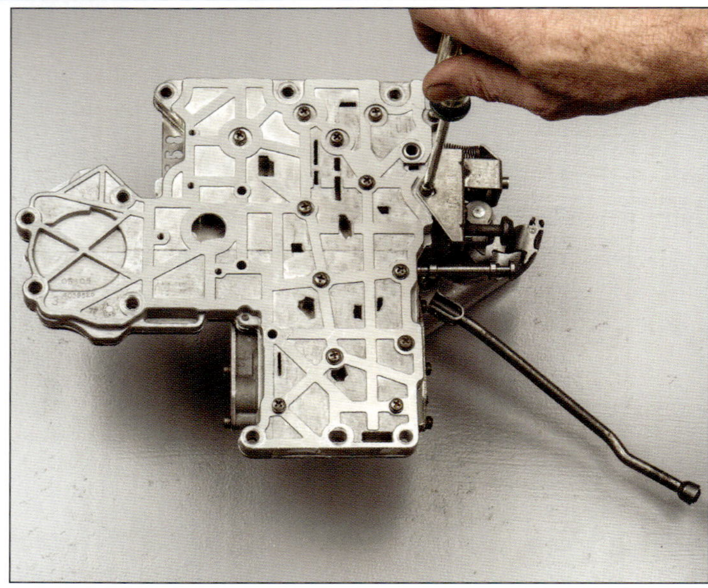

2 *Be careful of the spring tension when removing the line pressure and torque converter valve bracket.*

3 *The top screw is short and may be slotted, Phillips, or Torx depending upon the year.*

4 *Push in on the bracket and, if present, loosen the short screw holding it to the side.*

5 *Identify and segregate the line pressure and torque converter regulator valvesprings.*

6 *Remove the line pressure valve and converter control valve/switch valve and keep them with their respective springs.*

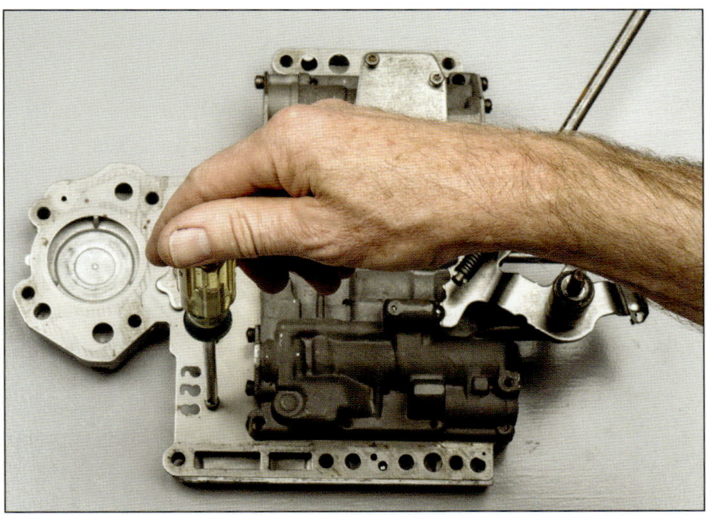

7 *Flip the valve body and remove the accessible screws holding the separator plate to the transfer plate.*

8 *Remove the separator plate stiffener or the lock-up module screws.*

9 *Invert it and remove the 17 (or so) screws holding the transfer plate to the main body.*

10 *Once the screws are out, lift off the plate assembly.*

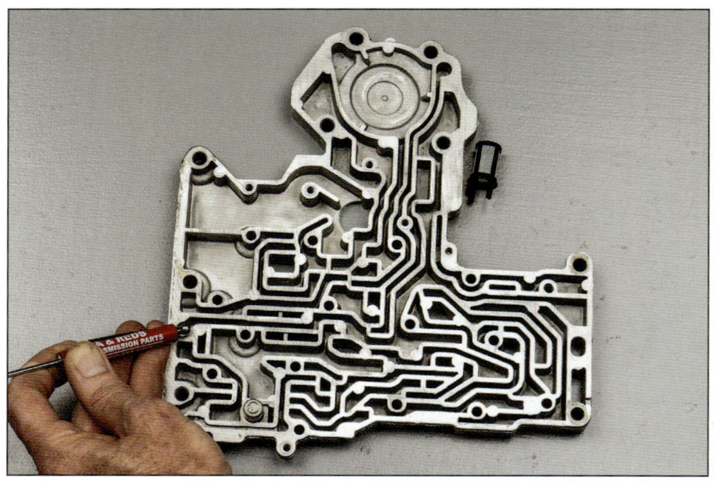

11 *You may find a check ball, spring, filter, and valve under the plate in the transfer plate housing. Keep these springs and valves together.*

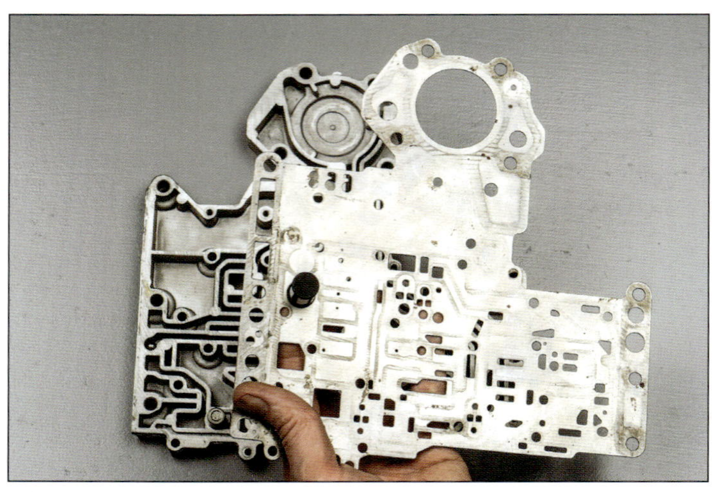

12 *Remove any remaining short screws holding the separator plate.*

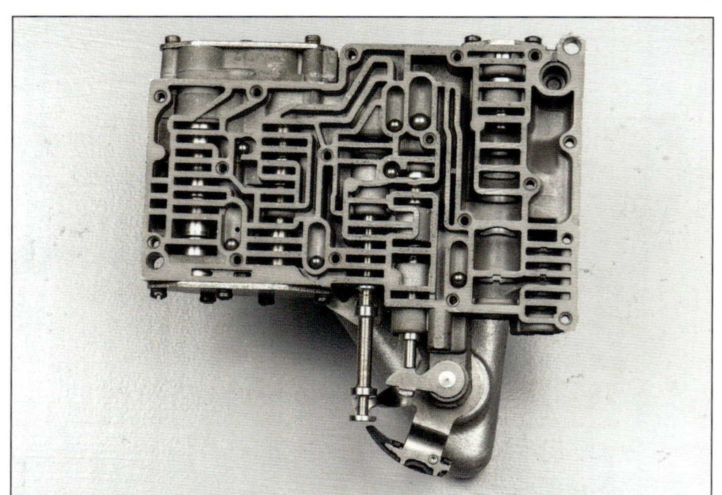

13 *With the transfer plate out of the way, make a note of the location of the 1/4-inch-diameter balls, the 11/32-inch ball in the larger "bathtub" location, and a 3/8-inch ball (if present).*

Shuttle Valve and Governor Plugs

Invert the valve body and remove the shuttle valvecover screws (four or six) and plate.

Remove the governor plug end plate screws and plate. Remove the shuttle valve throttle plug, spring, and 1–2 and 2–3 shift valve governor plugs.

Remove the shuttle valve E-clip, secondary spring, two plastic spring guides, and the shuttle valve.

Shuttle Valve and Governor Plugs Removal

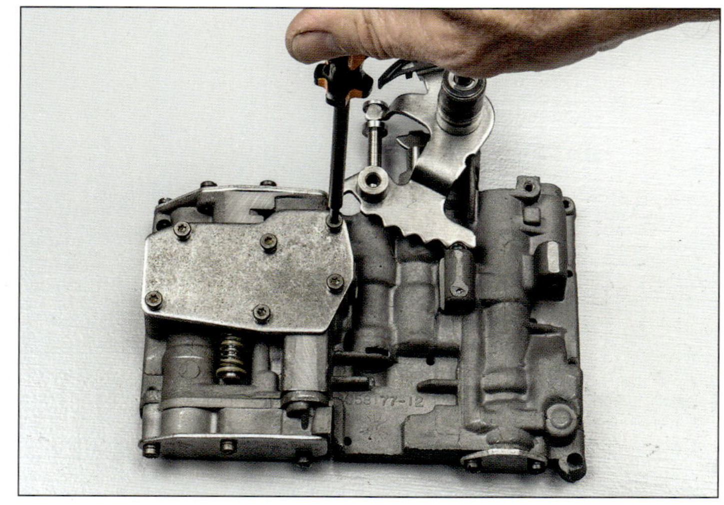

1 *Flip it over and remove the four or six screws holding the shuttle valvecover plate.*

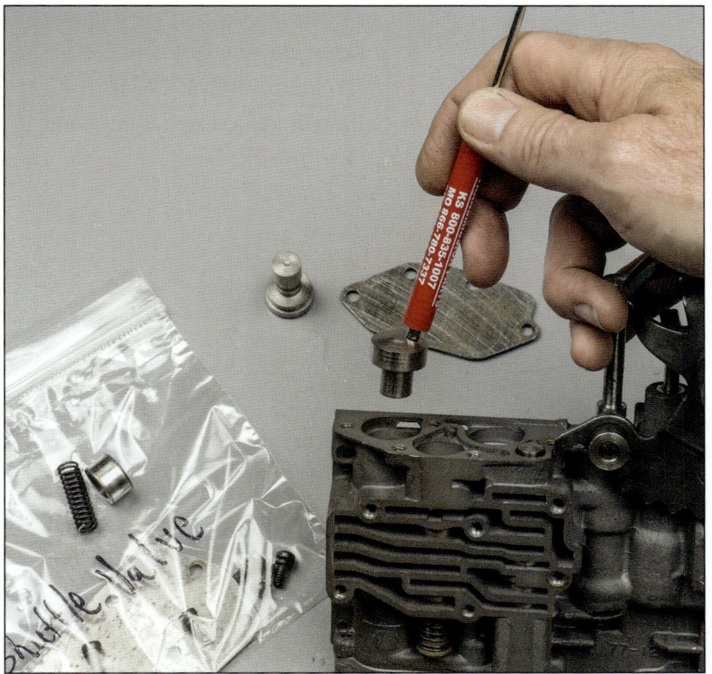

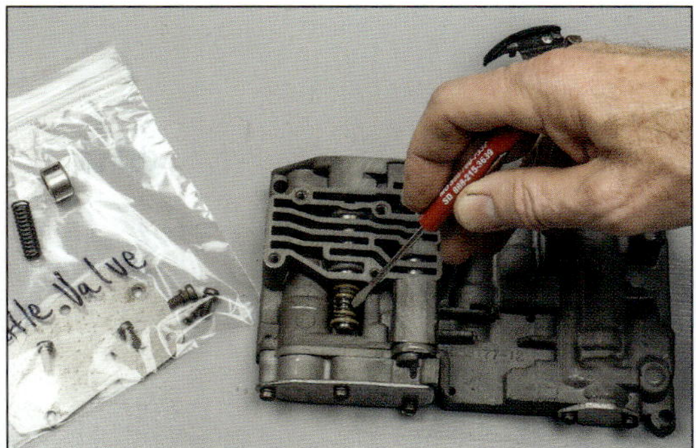

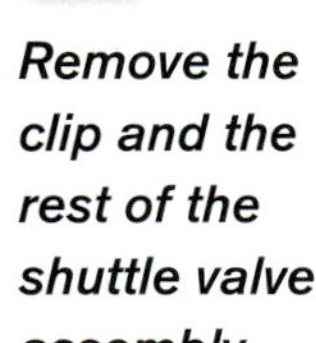

Remove the clip and the rest of the shuttle valve assembly.

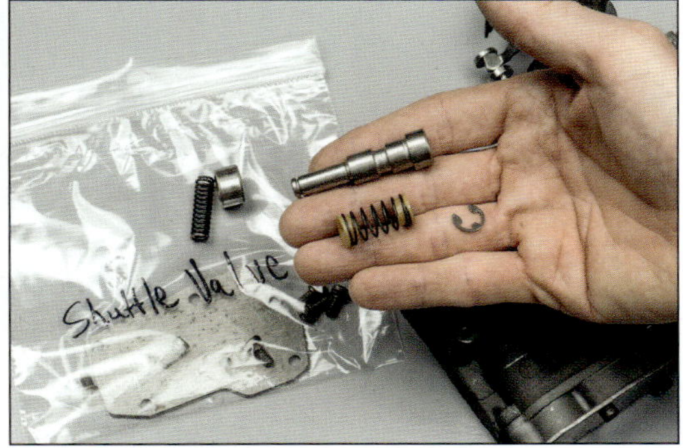

Keep the shuttle valve parts together.

2 *Remove the shuttle valvespring and valve from the main body and keep them together and identified.*

Manual Lever and Throttle Pressure Assembly

If still attached, remove the E-clip holding the park control rod to the manual lever and remove the lever.

File any burrs off the throttle lever shaft where the external throttle lever pinched it. Remove the E-clip, washer, and rubber seal from the throttle valve lever shaft and pull the throttle lever out of the manual lever assembly. Do not raise the manual lever much because the detent ball and spring will fly (it can be reinstalled). I change the seal after everything has been cleaned but for now put the washer and E-clip back on but don't forget to change the seal.

If the manual valve has to be cleaned, remove the E-clip holding the throttle lever in and gently pry the manual lever assembly far enough away from the valve body to let the manual valve slide out from under it. If the detent ball and spring fly out, bag them for later installation.

Rotate the throttle lever out of the way and slide the kickdown detent, kickdown valve, throttle valvespring, and throttle valve out of the valve body; keep them together. Older valve bodies may have a nut and washer on a long Phillips screw holding this assembly in. Measure the bottom of the screw head to the throttle valve before removing it. It should be .180 to .192 inch or so.

Manual Lever and Throttle Pressure Lever Removal

1 *If not removed yet, unclip the park lever.*

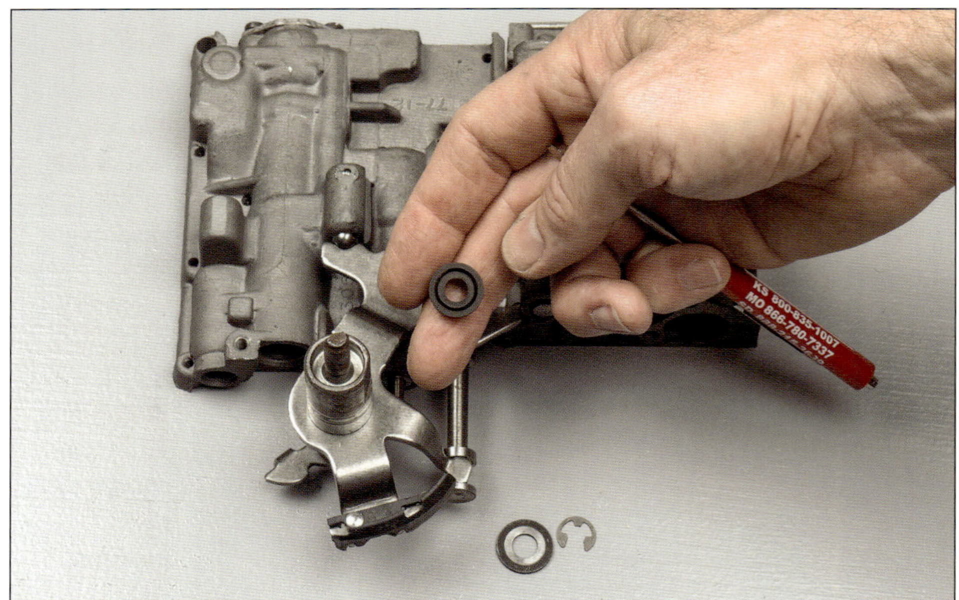

2 *Remove and replace the seal under the washer and E-clip in the throttle lever, but don't let the main control lever come up too far, ejecting spring and ball.*

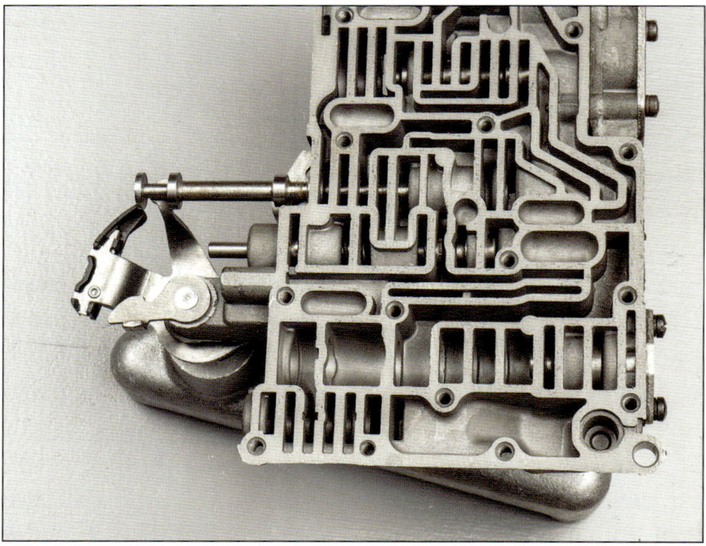

3 *Rotate the throttle lever out of the way, if it is still in place. This valve body has a bracket that contains the throttle lever adjustment screw and it is already out of the way. If yours has the long Phillips screw, measure and record the distance to the bottom side of the screw head and then remove the screw, its jam nut, and spacer keeping the detent valve in.*

4 *The entire detent valve assembly should be kept together and identified.*

Shift Valves and Regulator Valve

Remove two screws holding the line pressure regulator valve end plate on and pull it off.

Remove the line pressure regulator valve sleeve, line pressure regulator valve plug, and throttle pressure regulator valve plug and any spring.

If your valve body has one, remove the 3–2 downshift assembly end plate (three long screws) and the throttle plug, the limit valve, the limit valvespring, and the retainer plate.

Remove the 1–2 shift control valve and spring, the 1–2 shift valve and spring, and the 2–3 shift valve and spring. Bag or tag them.

Shift Valves and Regulator Valve Removal

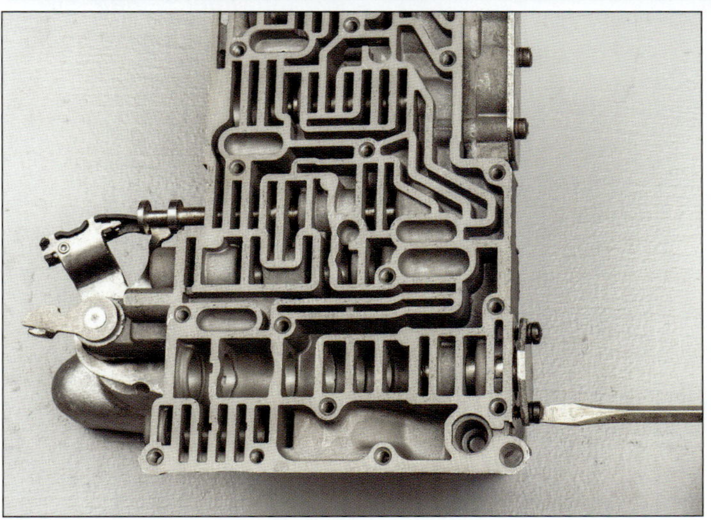

1 *Remove the line pressure regulating valve and spring assembly so that the valve body can be cleaned. The manual valve can be left in place.*

2 *Some valve bodies don't have this spring.*

3 *The part-throttle detent valve assembly is held with three screws. Remove it as an assembly and clean it prior to reassembly.*

4 *Keep the three screws together (shorter heads) and separate them from the screws (larger head, on right) that hold the valve body together.*

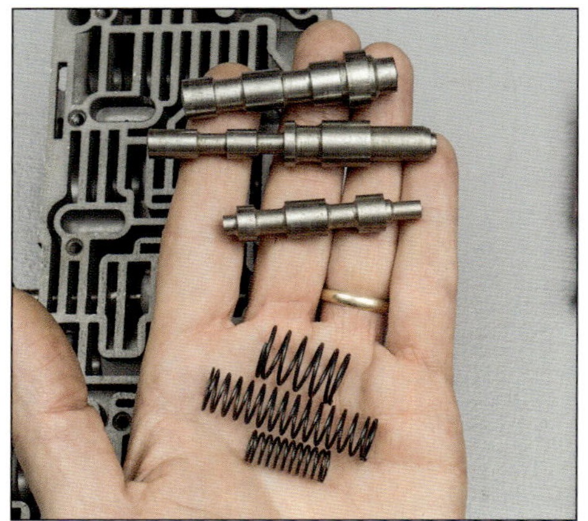

5 *With the part-throttle 3–2 downshift assembly removed,* pull out the 1–2 shift and 2–3 shift valves and springs. Keep them together and identified.

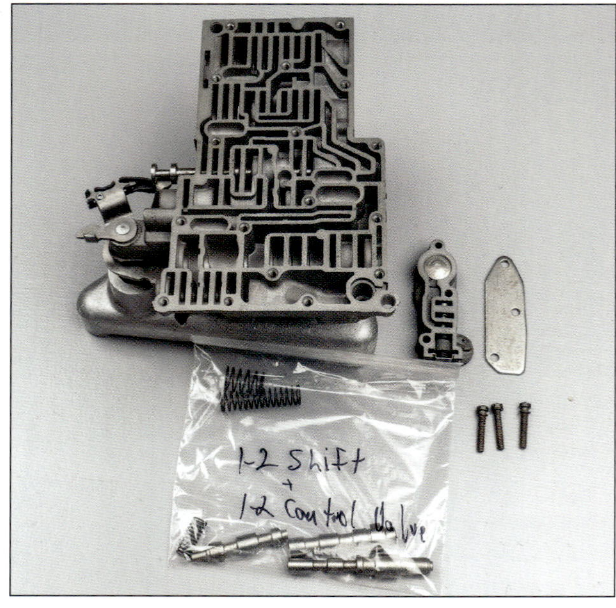

6 *Several of the intermediate-size springs are similar so do not mix them.*

Verification

Look closely at the throttle shaft and remove any burrs, nicks, or gouges using crocus cloth or a fine file.

Use a solvent to clean the springs, valves, screws, and main body parts. Let them air dry or blow them with compressed air.

Be sure all passages, bores, and transfer ports are clean and free from junk.

Clean the regulator filter (if needed).

Inspect the manual and throttle valve levers and shafts for damage. Repair or replace as needed.

If the rooster comb has come loose from the manual lever, it may be repaired by silver soldering it; new or used ones are available. If the plastic insulator is loose or broken off the rooster comb, Sonnax sells replacements and A&A has new manual shaft assemblies with rooster combs.

Inspect mating surfaces of the transfer plate and valve body, and remove irregularities using crocus cloth.

Be sure all holes in the separator plate and valve body are open and not worn out.

Inspect all springs; they should not be bent, distorted, or collapsed.

Do not remove sharp edges from valves or plugs. The valve body depends on the sharp edges to keep material from being caught between the valve and the bore.

After everything is clean, make sure the valves move freely in their bores.

Verification Processes

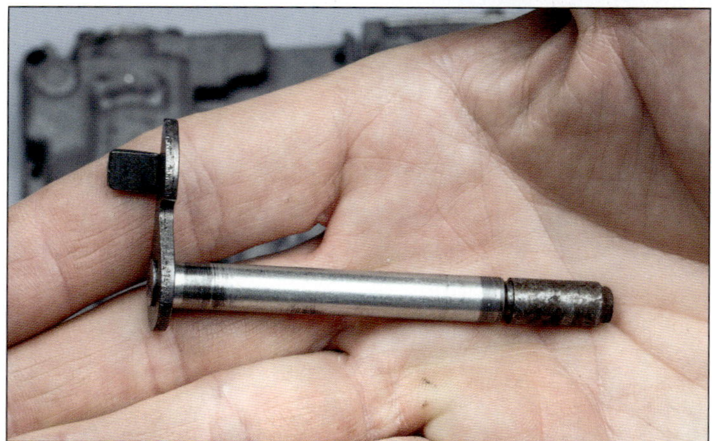

1 *If the throttle valve lever is rough, file off the gouges or grooves where the lever attaches.*

2 *Wiggle the rooster comb to be sure that it is tight on the main control lever assembly. Repair or replace it as needed.*

3 Inspect the separator plate to verify that the steel balls have not pounded their seats open or worn out small paths. This one is acceptable.

4 Use transmission fluid or special lube to pre-lubricate all of the valves and springs during reassembly.

Reassembly

It's very important to lubricate valves and springs and verify everything moves freely before tightening screws. If possible, torque the screws using a small torque wrench with the correct bits.

Shift Valves and Regulator Valve

Install the 1–2 and 2–3 shift valves and springs, along with the 1–2 shift control valve and its spring.

Install the throttle plug, the limit valve, its spring, and retainer in the 3–2 downshift and limit valve assembly. Place the three screws through the end plate and the 3–2 downshift control valve assembly, and thread them in to hold the 1–2 and 2–3 shift and control valves. Torque them to 35 in-lbs or tighten them well.

Shift Valves and Regulator Valve Installation

1 This cleaned valve body awaits components; be sure that all chips and debris are removed and that nothing is cracked, bent, or distorted.

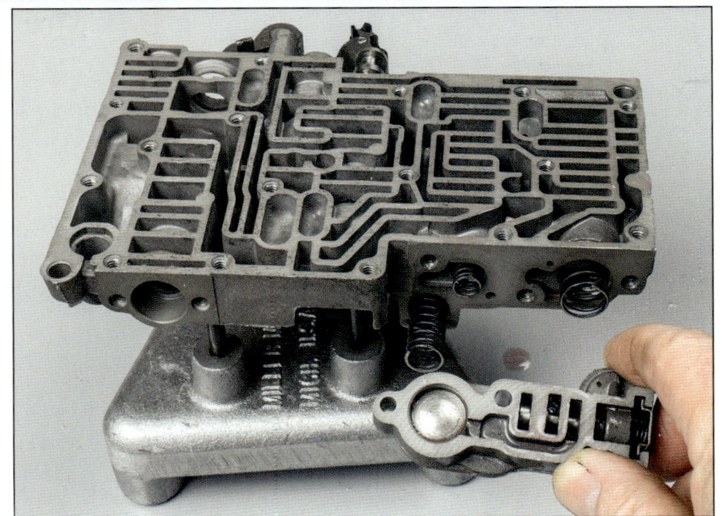

2 Install the 1–2 and 2–3 shift and control valves and springs; lube them before installing the 3–2 part-throttle downshift module. Lubricate everything.

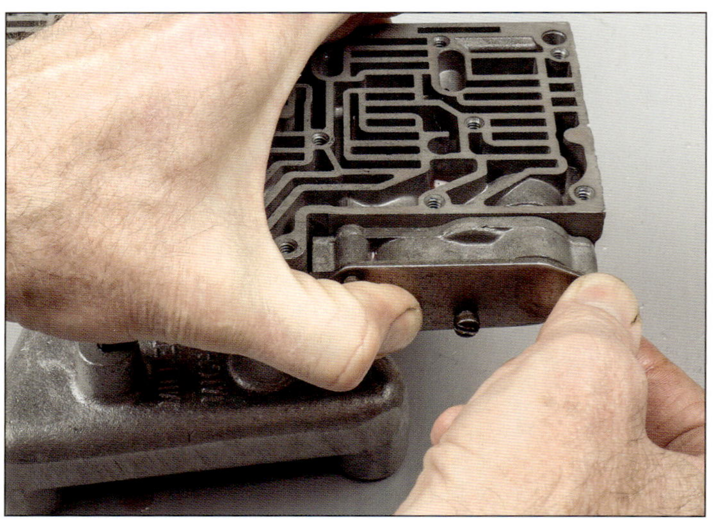

3 As you hold the module, screw the three screws though the plate, the body, and into the side of the valve body.

4 Torque the three screws to 35 in-lbs or tighten them with a screwdriver.

Manual Lever and Throttle Pressure Lever

Install the throttle valve, the throttle valvespring, kickdown valve, and the kickdown detent. The kickdown detent should have its deep bore facing the valve body; if reversed, the downshift function will not work correctly, if at all. If it was present, reinstall the long Phillips screw and locking nut and adjust the cam's distance from the throttle valve.

Remove the E-clip from the throttle lever (again) and carefully pry the manual valve just high enough to allow the manual valve to slide back under the manual level assembly.

After ensuring that the valve correctly moves with the lever, push the manual lever assembly in place, install the new seal, and replace the washer and E-clip. Again, check that the manual valve moves in and out of the valve body as the manual lever is rotated.

Spray lubricant on the moving parts.

Manual Lever and Throttle Pressure Lever Installation

1 Install the detent valve and spring assembly, but do not reverse the outer detent valve (as done in this photograph).

2 This kickdown valve sticks out of the detent valve. This is the correct way to assemble it. If yours had a separate throttle-lever adjustment Phillips screw, install it and its jam nut and adjust the screw to the distance recorded before removal.

3 *If not previously done, remove the E-clip and washer and install the new throttle valve seal.*

4 *Install the washer and the E-clip to hold the main shifter valve/throttle valve assembly together.*

Shuttle Valve and Governor Plugs

Put the 1–2 and 2–3 shift valve governor plugs in their correct bores.

Install the shuttle valve and use a finger or small screwdriver to hold it in so the secondary shuttle valvespring and plastic guides and E-clip can be reinstalled on the "top side" of the valve body.

Install the primary shuttle valvespring and throttle plug.

Install the end plate over the shuttle and governor valves; tighten all screws to 35 in-lbs.

Lubricate the shuttle valve assembly and then install the shuttle valvecover plate. Tighten the screws (4 or 6) to 35 in-lbs.

Shuttle Valve and Governor Plugs Installation

1 *Install and lubricate the plugs and valves.*

2 *Hold in the shuttle valve and push on the plastic cup, the outer spring, and another plastic cup. Install the C-clip.*

3 *Install the main shuttle valve and spring.*

4 *Reinstall the 1–2 and 2–3 governor and shuttle valve and then install and torque (or tighten) the end plate.*

5 *Before reinstalling the cover, apply some lube under it.*

Check Balls, Pressure Regulators, Transfer and Separator Plate, Lock-Up Valve Assembly or Stiffener, and Filter

Install the 1/4-inch-diameter check balls. Be sure the 11/32 ball and 3/8-inch-diameter ball and its spring (if present) are not mixed; reinstall in the correct locations.

Install the rear clutch ball check valve and torque converter pressure relief spring and valve (if present) in the transfer plate and reinstall a clean/new regulator valve screen/filter in the separator plate (if it had one).

Position the separator plate on the transfer plate and install the small screws finger tight. If it had a stiffener, install it and then tighten the screws to 35 in-lbs. If it is a lock-up converter TorqueFlite, install the fail-safe valve and spring, followed by the lock-up spring and valve and plate. Be sure the plates are aligned and tighten the remaining screws to 35 in-lbs.

Position the transfer plate assembly on the valve body. If present, install the lock-up module after sliding the tube into its port on the valve body. Tighten the screws to 35 in-lbs. If the lock-up module seems difficult to install, reverse the tube.

Install the 17 long screws finger tight making sure the pressure regulator filter/screen is properly aligned.

Starting in the center of the transfer plate and working outward, tighten the transfer plate-to-valve body screws to 35 in-lbs. Temporarily leave the one out that holds the line pressure regulator spring retainer to the valve body.

Put the line pressure regulator valve and/or plug and spring, as well as the converter control valve and spring in their proper bores. Attach the cover plate and torque to 35 in-lbs.

Install the line pressure regulator valve adjusting screw assembly in the spring retainer bracket and loosely position it on the valve body.

Attach the bracket to the side of the valve body, being sure to capture the torque converter switch/valve in the tab on the retainer. Place the last of the long screws (that hold the valve body together) through the retainer and into the one hole left open. Snug it to hold the retainer close to its final position. Screw the other small screw in the valve body to hold the retainer into place. Holding it to compress the line pressure and torque converter springs, install the last short screw (if present) that holds the retainer to the side of the valve body; tighten them to 35 in-lbs or tight with a good screw driver or Torx driver.

Be sure all components are properly aligned.

Reinstall the park control rod to the manual lever assembly and install the E-clip.

Install the oil filter and tighten the three screws.

Check and adjust the throttle and line pressure settings if necessary but if the transmission shifted correctly and at the right time before disassembly, do not drastically alter the pressure settings.

Check all containers, boxes, and bags looking for anything not installed. You should have only tools and an old throttle lever seal, the transfer plate filter/screen (possibly), and the main oil filter left.

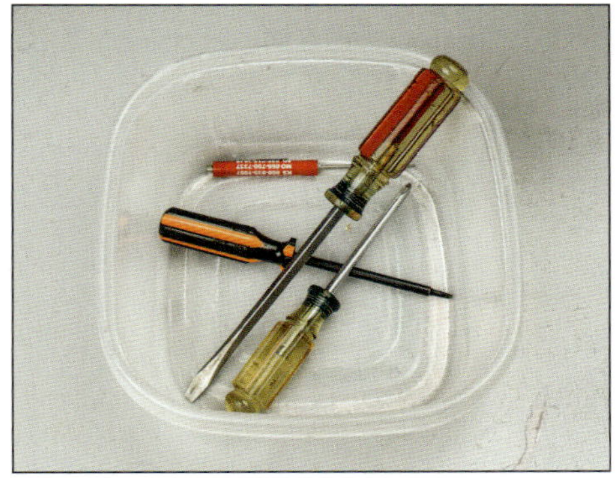

There is nothing left but tools; it's all good.

Pressure Regulators, Check Balls, Transfer and Separator Plate Lock-Up Installation

1 *Install the 1/4-inch-diameter balls in their respective locations (shown) and place the 11/32 ball in its bathtub-shaped location. If yours had the 3/8-inch ball and spring, do not confuse it with the 11/32-inch one. The 3/8-inch ball and spring would go in the top right corner.*

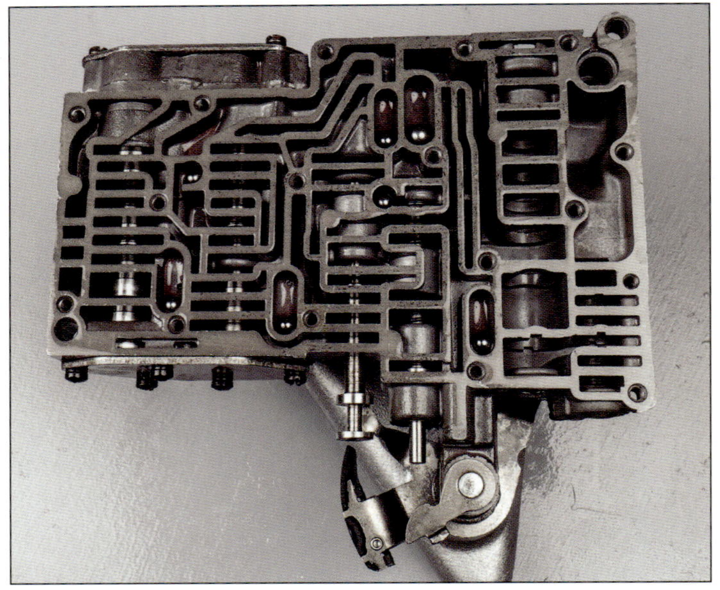

2 *This is where the check balls belong in this valve body.*

3 *Reinstall the 1/4-inch-diameter ball and spring, valve, and filter/screen in the transfer plate (if yours had them).*

4 *Install the short screws and tighten the separator plate to the transfer plate; keep all holes aligned.*

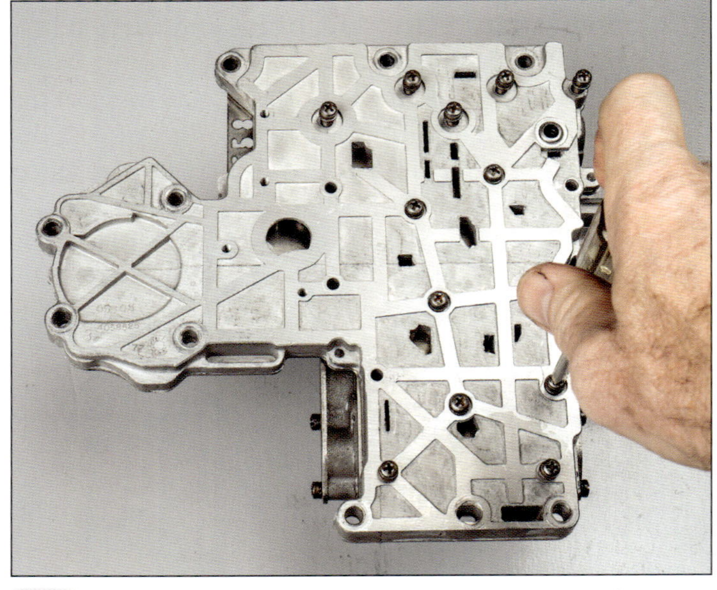

5 *Lubricate the valve body's internal ports and cavities before reattaching the transfer plate assembly. Install the 17 (or so) screws, leaving the three holes open where the filter attaches.*

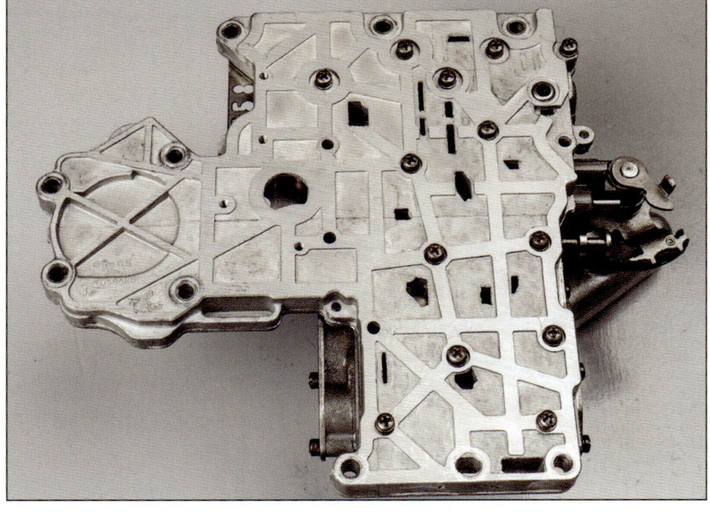

6 *Tighten the screws starting from the center and working outward. Temporarily leave out the screw that holds the line pressure valvespring retainer.*

7 *Reinstall the line pressure regulating valve assembly, springs, and its cover; tighten the screws to 35 in-lbs or tight with a screwdriver.*

8 *With the valve body on its edge, lubricate the main regulating valve and converter/switch valve then place the springs on the valves.*

9 *Use both hands to hold the valve body while you push on the retainer and install the long screw that was temporarily left out. Snug it to hold the retainer in place and then install the top short screw, and, finally, the side screw, if present. Tighten all the screws holding the retainer and transfer plate to the valve body.*

10 *Inspect the retainer to be sure that it is together correctly and that the spring adjustment plate and screw are in their proper positions.*

11 *Reattach the park lever to the shift lever assembly.*

12 *Attach the new filter with the three long screws and tighten them to 35 in-lbs (or tight) with a screwdriver.*

ASSEMBLY

After having stripped the Torque-Flite down to individual parts, taken measurements, and cleaned and prepared subassemblies, it's time to reassemble, check, and adjust it.

Subassembly Installation Tips and Pre-Assembly Tests

Its time to reunite all the individual subassemblies and adjust them. In Appendix B, charts provide specifications for typical A-904s and A-727s. It's a good idea to find a shop manual for the transmission being rebuilt. A chart showing the suggested speedometer pinion (driven) gears for particular axle ratios and tire sizes is also supplied in Appendix B.

Never use extreme force putting subassemblies back together; if the parts don't go together freely, find out why and correct the issue(s). Transmissions will fit together almost easier than they come apart when you work methodically, carefully, and sensibly.

Reminder: Always replace gaskets, internal rubber lip seals, and ALL external seals. Most important, don't forget the O-rings on the pins that hold the low-reverse links or bands in A-904s or A-727s.

All of the subassembly components are ready and waiting.

TECH TIP

Heavy and Sharp

From past experience rebuilding (GM) Turbo 350s, 400s, and TorqueFlites, there are several ways to get hurt when working on them. A fully assembled TorqueFlite weighs more than 100 pounds, has many machined edges, and several ways to pinch/cut fingers. You need to be careful when reaching into case openings because there are sharp areas around the pump passages and the rear of the case. There may be casting flash on other internal and external sections of the case and extension housing. While it is apart, consider breaking the flash off and filing their sharp edges. ■

Use a transmission assembly grease to lubricate lip seals, rotating components, sealing rings, thrust washers, and O-rings. Automatic transmission fluid works, but grease holds better. The special lubricants that are made for lip seal assembly processes melt at low temperature and blend with transmission fluid.

Valve body springs, valves, and bores should already be lubricated with a special assembly lube or transmission fluid.

Air Checking Clutch Assemblies before Installation

It's important to air check the front and rear clutch retainers before installing them. It'll verify that critical internal parts are together correctly and work properly. If there is a leaky seal on a piston and it doesn't move, it's obvious and can be corrected while the transmission is apart. Fortunately, another air check of the transmission assembly will be performed prior to valve body installation. Along with front and rear clutches, servos will be pressurized to test them.

Use a rubber-tipped blowgun and moderate air pressure for testing. With greased reaction shaft support rings and retainer assemblies on the reaction shaft support, 30 to 40 psi of air directed into two passages on the pump will be used. When the air pressure is applied, the pistons move to compress the friction discs and steel plates, usually generating a thump.

Both retainers should be placed on the pump together so the sealing rings are correctly located. When air checking the rear retainer assembly, it may try to drive away from the reaction shaft support so be prepared to hold it. Only the front is shown in photos, but both were tested.

Miscellaneous Component Preparation

In Chapter 5, internal subassemblies were torn down, measured, and reassembled. There are still a few components that need a bit of preparation or installation: the extension housing, shifter shaft seal, and output shaft support.

Extension Housing

The rear seal was removed while the housing was bolted on. If yours was not, use a chisel or an old flat bladed (but relatively sharp) screwdriver and get behind the flange to knock the seal out. These seals are often very snug and may require tapping around them until they pop out.

With the seal out, check the bushing. If your transmission was dripping fluid out the rear, it is often due to the rear bushing being worn, letting the driveshaft yoke wobble around, which exceeds the seal's ability to hold fluid in. If the bushing looks scratched or damaged, it needs replacing. Clean the driveshaft yoke's surface with crocus cloth and polish it to a smooth finish. If it is gouged or grooved, it should

Using pressurized air to check the clutch assemblies is a great way to verify that they are correctly assembled. Notice the waved steel snap ring.

When air is applied, the piston is forced out and clamps the clutch plates; the steel ring flattens.

be replaced. Use the correctly sized bushing driver to get the bushing out or, make a trip to the transmission shop and ask them to drive out the old and install the new. Note that the extension housing has a large groove inside the outlet that corresponds with an opening in the bushing. These need to be aligned.

Apply a thin bead of RTV-type silicone sealant around a new rear seal's flange and tap it in with a hammer and punch or a special tool. If using a booted rear seal, an appropriately sized piece of plastic or metal tubing, a special booted seal installer tool, or a hammer and blunt punch can be used to drive the seal flatly in. The boot may have a small air hole to allow air to escape when the yoke moves in and out; I put it on top.

Extension Housing Preparation

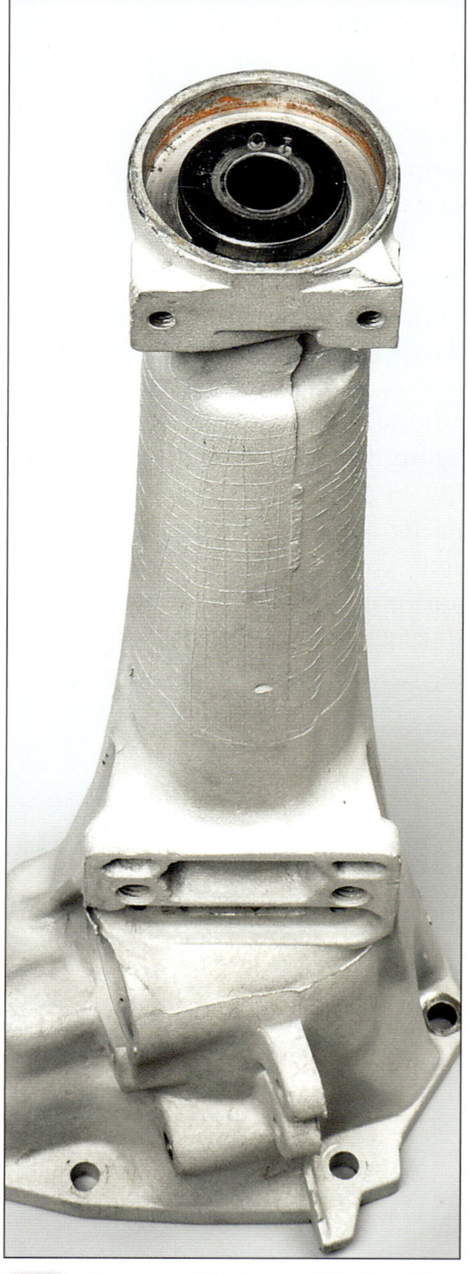

1 *Because it is long, this bushing has a lot of friction, and it takes a heavy hand to drive it out.*

2 *Using a driver is the best way to remove this bushing.*

3 *Note the slots in the top of this extension housing. The bushing has a corresponding opening so fluid can lubricate the yoke.*

4 *The bushing needs to start straight and then be driven in carefully. Fortunately, they are robust.*

5 *Through the seal's opening, you can see that the bushing's lubrication hole is aligned properly. This non-booted seal is typically included in most overhaul kits.*

6 *This is an OEM-like booted rear seal and the Miller tool designed to drive it in. Apply some RTV-type silicone sealer around it before installation. Note the small hole in the boot.*

7 *The seal is driven in flush with the weep hole facing downward.*

Shifter Shaft Seal

A new shifter shaft seal can be driven in easily with the case right side up. Apply a thin bead of RTV-type silicone sealant around the seal and use a bushing driver or a large socket to carefully tap the seal in. A nut and bolt with flat washers also can be put through the seal as it sits in the case. The seal can be pressed in by slowly tightening the nut and bolt. The seal should be flush with the case.

Shifter Shaft Seal Installation

1 *Apply a light coat of RTV-type silicone sealer around the shift shaft seal; you can use this bushing driver handle to install it.*

2 *Tap in the seal carefully; do not deform it. It should end up essentially flush with the case.*

The output shaft support has four 5/16-18 bolts that are torqued to 150 in-lbs to hold it. Tighten them in a cross pattern. Some fit right on; others need to be tapped with a non-damaging hammer or block of wood.

Output Shaft Support

If not in, place the output shaft support in the case aligning its four bolt holes. If needed, use 5/16-inch pilot pins and then push or tap the support in. Install the four bolts and alternately torque them to 150 in-lbs.

Overrunning Clutch

It's common for one side of the overrunning clutch race to "polish." Grease this side and place it inside the cam against the case. Put an overrunning clutch roller between the cam and the race in each pocket. There should be 12 rollers in most A-727s and 10 in most A-904s (except later models of each). Pinch each spring and slide it between the spring retainer tabs and the rollers. It is tricky, but will go more smoothly after installing a couple of them. After half of them are in, rotate the inner race and bias it toward the springs already installed to provide more clearance. I always use new spring and roller kits instead of risking installation of a rough roller or a bad spring. After all springs and rollers are installed, rotate the inner race to be sure it only moves clockwise. You can temporarily put the low-reverse drum in to check it. If it doesn't rotate smoothly, look it over and fix any problem.

Overrunning Clutch Installation

1 *When installing the overrunning clutch inner race, apply assembly grease to the side that rides against the rear of the case.*

2 *Place one roller in each pocket in the outer cam. They should stay fixed, but if they fall over, use a magnet or small screwdriver to remove them and stand them up again.*

3 *To install the springs, pinch and slide them between the roller and the spring retainer tabs. Work around the assembly and they'll go in. Keep all of the springs oriented the same.*

Low-Reverse Servo

Grease the servo piston's lip seal and slowly rotate and push the assembly into the case. Put the spring, retainer, and snap ring on the piston and compress the spring by pushing against the retainer. Hold it and go around the snap ring using a screwdriver to guide/pry it into the slot.

Low-Reverse Servo Installation

1 *Apply assembly grease on the low-reverse servo's seal, rotate it, and drop it in.*

2 *With the servo piston installed, set the return spring and its retainer on top of it. A stock spring is easy to compress.*

3 *Almost any smooth screwdriver and a bit of force enables you to pry and push the snap ring into place.*

4 *When together correctly, the snap ring is seated in its groove like this.*

Low-Reverse Anchor, Band and Drum: A-904

V-8 vehicles with A-904s have a double wrap low-reverse band supported at two points by a "band reaction pin" pressed into the case. If not replaced yet, put a new, greased O-ring on the pin (if grooved), and push it flush in the case. If it is a 6-cylinder A-904, the single wrap band is held with a link and anchor assembly and may not have the grooved reaction pin.

Locate the double wrap low-reverse band so it correctly sits on the band reaction pin; hold it while installing the low-reverse drum. If it is a single wrap band, install the small rectangular band strut between the band anchor and link assembly and snug the band adjustment screw to hold it in place until the low-reverse drum is in.

You'll need to orient the low-reverse drum so its splines align with the overrunning clutch race. Slide it inside the band while rotating it clockwise to seat. When installed, the low-reverse drum will only rotate clockwise (viewed from the front).

Again, be sure to replace/grease O-rings on the pivot pin, press it through the link and anchor (if present), through the band apply lever until the pin is flush with the case. Make sure the anchor assembly is in correctly (if used). If it is incorrect, the low-reverse drum will not fit and the band will not be held properly. Correctly orient the band apply lever and adjust the screw until it touches the band anchor.

Low-Reverse Anchor, Band and Drum: A-727

Remember to install new, greased O-rings on the low-reverse band anchor pin prior to pushing it through the low-reverse servo link and flush into the case. Verify that the low-reverse link is in correctly because the drum will not fit if it is wrong. The A-727 will have a two-piece servo lever; be sure the inner lever is oriented correctly before the anchor pin is pushed through it, the other side of the link, and the case.

If the transmission is upside down, place the low-reverse band with the open end up so it surrounds the overrunning clutch assembly; rotate it slightly until one end can lock into the anchor. Install the short rectangular strut; the narrow sides fit between the band anchor and band apply lever. Pinch the band to fit it in. If needed, use a flat-bladed screwdriver to push and hold against the band anchor while doing this. Tighten the band-adjusting pin enough to hold it all in place.

Install the low-reverse drum inside the low-reverse band and rotate it until its splines interlock with the overrunning clutch race splines. It will slide in place as it rotates clockwise. If it rotates clockwise only, everything up to this point is correct. Snug the band-adjusting screw a bit more to hold the band and strut in position until the final adjustment.

Low-Reverse Anchor, Band and Drum Installation

1 *Be sure to install the new O-rings on this low-reverse servo pivot (or anchor pin). Grease it well.*

2 *The pin should push in flush with the case. The extension housing has a tab that helps hold it in (unless it has been cut off).*

3 *Make sure that the anchor link assembly sits like this so the low-reverse drum fits and the recess clears the case.*

4 *Start with the band positioned like this and roll it clockwise to lock its anchor in the anchor link.*

5 *Place the small rectangular (A-727) strut between the low-reverse servo lever and the band anchor. The short shiny side fits against the anchors. If needed, use a flat-blade screwdriver and push the band closed while putting the strut link in place. When it is together, actuate the lever by hand to verify that it works.*

6 *Slide the low-reverse drum into place inside the band, and rotate it to align and slide into the overunning clutch race splines.*

Planetary Gear Assemblies, Sun Gear and Sun Gear Driving Shell

As with all the rotating parts, the output shaft journals, sun gear bushings, thrust washers, thrust plates, pinion gears, and wear surfaces should be lubricated before installation. Lubricate the pinion gear bearings using automatic transmission fluid or a special assembly lube.

Grease the inside of the output shaft support where the shaft fits in and grease the governor support rings (rotated so the gaps are 180 degrees apart). Push and wiggle the output shaft assembly until the rings compress and the governor body slides into the support. When the output shaft is in correctly, the Park gear is basically flush with the rear of the support.

From the front of an A-904, slide the rear annulus gear support on the output shaft and follow it with a thrust washer (if a steel planetary), the well-lubricated rear planetary gear assembly, and put a thrust washer on the planetary.

With an A-727, slide the rear annulus gear assembly on the shaft; follow it with the steel thrust plate and rear planetary gear assembly. Install the appropriate three- or four-tabbed thrust washer on the assembly.

Rotate the internally greased sun gear driving shell while gently pushing it into the rear planetary gear assembly. It is in when there is no gap between it and the planetary thrust washer.

On the A-727, place the pre-greased three-tabbed thrust washer inside the sun gear shell; it will be held in place by the grease. Carefully slide the well lubricated front planetary assembly (consisting of the front annulus gear assembly, the thrust washer, and front plane-

tary assembly) over the sun gear and against the thrust washer inside the shell.

On the A-904, install the correct thrust washer on the lubricated front planetary gear assembly (consisting of the small, thick thrust washer, the front planetary assembly, the front annulus gear/support and the planetary gear thrust washer) and rotate and lightly push the open part of the assembly over the sun gear.

The planetary geartrain is now in place on the output shaft and the snap ring's slot should be visible on the shaft in front of the planetary gear but if not, recheck the assembly. Install the selective snap ring to provide the correct output shaft endplay you previously measured. If it was set correctly, there will be little play, if any, because the greased thrust washers will take up most of it.

Planetary Gear Assemblies, Sun Gear and Sun Gear Driving Shell Installation

1 Lightly grease and install two governor sealing rings on the support and rotate one of them so its gap is 180 degrees away from the other. Grease the inside of the output shaft support and the output shaft where they fit together.

2 Hold the output shaft and wiggle, wobble, and slowly push to compress the rings in the taper of the support. Be absolutely sure that the sealing rings compress before pushing too hard.

3 When the governor body is installed correctly, it sits almost flush with the support.

4 Place the rear annulus gear over the output shaft and slide it into the low-reverse drum. As the splines engage, it eventually stops.

5 *Grease the steel thrust washer (A-727) and slide it onto the output shaft until its splines align.*

6 *Lubricate the individual pinion gears with transmission fluid or special assembly fluid; grease the gear teeth and the wear surface on the planetary body and "rotate" it into the rear annulus gear. It fits almost even with the low-reverse drum's outer flange.*

7 *To be sure that it stays on, lightly grease both sides of the thrust washer and install in on the rear planetary.*

8 *Lubricate the inner bushings and teeth of the sun gear and grease the steel thrust plate. Rotate and slide it onto the output shaft.*

9 *As with other thrust washers, lightly grease both sides to hold them in place and place the tabs in the three recesses or holes of the sun gear shell.*

10 Lubricate the pinion gears' inner needle bearings. Lubricate the teeth with the assembly grease. Use grease to hold the thrust washer to the planetary and apply some to the wear side.

11 Align the splines, hold the planetary together, and push the entire assembly onto the output shaft until it stops against the thrust washer inside the sun gear shell.

12 The correctly installed geartrain allows room for the snap ring. If this gap is different from what you see here, investigate and correct the problem (it may be an incorrectly positioned thrust washer).

13 Use snapring pliers to install the appropriately thick snap ring that provides the correct endplay.

14 When it is installed correctly, the snap ring should fit tightly in the groove.

Kickdown Servo

On a non-controlled-load servo, grease the sealing rings and lightly tap the piston into the case, or you can use expanding snap-ring pliers to hold, rotate, and push it in. When correct, the piston pushes with minimal effort. Now, place the piston rod and the spring(s) in; grease the center hole and sealing ring of the piston rod guide and set it on the pin/in the case. (Installing a controlled servo is easier because you can grease the rings, hold the rod, and simply push it in. Drop on the spring and the servo guide that has pre-greased rings.

Compressing either type of kickdown servo spring(s) to get the large snap ring in is a little tricky. I push (and tap with a screwdriver handle) against the piston rod guide and drive it straight in and then hold it in, and work the snap ring into its slot. If you need help holding the guide to fit the snap ring, a C-clamp or an engine valvespring compressor will work. If the guide seems to lock up, stop, and remove it to verify that its sealing ring is in and compressing. If you are lucky enough to have the A&A Servo Tool (or similar), attach the tool, push the assembly in, install the snap ring, and remove the tool.

Install and orient the kickdown servo apply lever directly above the kickdown servo. Push the pivot pin through it, apply an RTV-type silicone sealer to the 1/4-inch NPT plug, and torque it to 150 in-lbs.

Kickdown Servo Installation

1 Grease the servo piston's sealing rings. If it is a controlled-load servo assembly, hold the pin and wobble and push it into its bore. If it's a regular servo, you can use expanding pliers to hold its inner bore while wobbling and pushing it into place. Place the pin in the regular servo.

2 Set the spring(s) in place, followed by the servo guide and snap ring. Tap and/or push and hold the servo guide in position; once it is below the groove, pry and guide the snap ring until it drops in.

3 Use of a specialized tool (such as this one from A&A) allows safe compression of the kickdown servo spring(s), making installation of the servo piston guide and snap ring easier.

4 *The servo snap ring should be fully seated.*

5 *Hold the servo apply lever and slide the pivot pin through the case opening and the lever.*

6 *Apply sealer to the pipe plug and tighten it securely to avoid a "mystery leak" in the bellhousing.*

Front and Rear Clutch Retainer

It may be easier to install the front and rear clutch retainers, the band, and the oil pump assembly with the transmission standing up. Often, with it laying horizontally, it may be tough to do because, seemingly, it requires three hands to install flex kickdown bands while holding the retainers. I often stand mine up and drop the parts in.

With the A-904, install the correct selective thrust washer on the end of the output shaft. The input shaft endplay should have been measured before disassembly (between .022 and .091 inch). If the correct selective and other new or correct-thickness washers were installed, the endplay will likely be in range. However, if the endplay was excessive, but the thrust washers in the geartrain, pump, and clutch retainers looked good, figure out how much the endplay was out of range and replace the original selective washer with a thicker one. Be aware that endplay measurements won't be as accurate after the thrust washers and planetary gear assemblies have been greased.

With the A-727, grease and install the steel race (if used) on the input shaft. Install the pre-greased bronze or phenolic thrust washer on the output shaft or the three-tabbed version should be stuck to the rear of the input shaft in the rear clutch assembly.

For either transmission, with the rear clutch assembly sitting on a flat surface with the input shaft up, lightly grease the front thrust washer and input shaft rings and then set the front clutch on the rear clutch hub splines. Hold the front retainer and rotate it back and forth, listening/feeling for friction discs to engage with the rear clutch hub splines. The fluid used to presoak the friction discs adds drag but you can do it.

Once the discs and splines align and the retainer is in place, only a small gap is between them.

This next operation is challenging because the rear friction discs and front retainer driving lugs must all align with their respective parts. Grab the input shaft while keeping the front and rear clutch retainer together, and place the assembly into the transmission so the rear clutch friction discs will engage the splines on the front annulus gear.

If horizontal, hold the front clutch retainer against the rear retainer while twisting the input shaft. This helps align the rear friction discs while they slide on the annulus gear.

The twisting back and forth is mandatory with the transmission laying flat. However, if it is vertical, you can often wobble the input shaft around and around to make the splines align. When the frictions have slid on the splines, the gap between the sun gear shell and the front clutch retainer tabs is minimal. (If horizontal, hold the front clutch retainer in place.)

If it's cold, the assembly may not fit as easily because the drag from the lubricated clutch assembly is higher. Protect the input shaft splines with a cloth or cardboard shim and grab them with a large pair of pliers. Twist the shaft rapidly until the splines engage and the retainers drop into place on the annulus gear assembly.

To make it more visible in these photos, the transmission was stood up and the retainers were twisted to fit them in place. The twisting also helps align the front clutch retainer's driving lugs with the sun gear shell slots. If these assemblies will not line up for you, pull the two retainers out and listen to a good song, take a break, pet your dog or cat, run around the block, or eat something and then come back and try again.

Once all the splines and lugs have been aligned and assembled, you can leave the transmission vertical or hold the retainers in place while moving to the next step.

Front and Rear Clutch Retainer Installation

1 *Some mid- to late-1970s and beyond A-727s used this steel race between the output shaft and the number-3 thrust washer. If you have this steel race, grease both sides and slide it onto the output shaft. Grease the rear side of the three-tab or round thrust washer and stick it into the input shaft assembly.*

2 *Grease the rear clutch retainer thrust washer and then set the front clutch retainer on top of the rear. Twist the front retainer back and forth until you feel it drop as the friction disc splines align.*

4 *If placing the clutch assemblies into a horizontally positioned case, they should be held together. Then twist and push them so that the annulus gear and rear friction disc splines align.*

3 *When correctly installed, the two retainers should be almost touching each other.*

6 *With the case vertical, grab the (protected) splines of the input shaft and twist the two clutch assemblies back and forth so the splines align and the retainers drop into place.*

5 *If putting the clutch assemblies in a vertically positioned case, set them on top of the annulus gear.*

7 *Note the correct fit between the two retainers and the tabs on the front clutch retainer and the slots in the sun gear shell.*

8 *Using one free hand to hold it together while horizontal, this is how it looks when assembled correctly.*

Kickdown Band

Orient the kickdown band; the A-727 and A-904 offset band's anchors are to the rear. Feed the band through the "gap" in the pump opening, and fit it over the front clutch retainer. If it is a cast band, this is easy, but if it is a flex band, it is more difficult because you have to pinch the band ends together to get it through the front of the case while still holding the clutch retainers in place. If the transmission is standing up, this operation is easier.

On the A-904, continue pinching the band together and place an anchor over the partially screwed in band-adjusting pin. Put the strut between the band apply lever and the band while pinching the band together. Screw the adjustment in far enough to hold the band.

On the A-727, continue pinching the band around the front clutch retainer, install the anchor between the band adjusting screw and the band's anchor, and install the long strut between the band adjusting lever and the other band anchor. Screw the adjuster in enough to hold the strut and band in place.

Kickdown Band Installation

1 *Orient the band so its anchors are offset toward the rear of the transmission.*

With the band anchors pinched, it fits into the case opening between the pump bolt holes.

Once the anchors are through the opening, rotate the band to fit the anchor onto the adjustment screw and then pinch it so that the rectangular strut fits. Loosen the adjustment screw as needed and install the strut. After the band is located correctly, snug the adjustment to hold the retainers.

Oil Pump

The A-904 pump should be assembled, greased, and ready to go.

With the A-727, if the correct selective thrust washer is not already on, review the endplay recorded before disassembly and verify that it was between .036 and .082 inch. If you replaced all thrust washers and used the kit-supplied selective thrust washer (which is typically .084- or .102-inch), the endplay is likely in the right range. If endplay was in the correct range and you are reusing thrust washers, proceed. However, if the endplay was approaching or exceeded the larger acceptable limit of .082 inch (such as with the transmission in the photographs) and you reused the internal thrust washers, select a thicker washer to reduce the play.

Screw two pilot studs or headless 5/16-18 x 3-inch-long bolts into the three and nine o-clock positions of the pump bolt holes and orient the pump gasket so its holes match.

Be sure the square-cut rubber O-ring around the pump is correct and greased, the sealing rings are greased and hooked, and the thrust washer and bushings are greased. Carefully slide the pump over the pilot studs and into the case, making sure the bolt holes and fluid passageways align. As the pump slides in, the input shaft, reaction shaft support sealing rings, and the O-ring will offer resistance. When this point is reached, loosen the kickdown band adjusting screw slightly and thread two pump bolts (with new sealing washers) in the six o'clock and twelve o'clock positions. Slowly snug them until the pump is in position. If something binds and you

Keep It in Range

For the A-727, there are four thrust washer thicknesses. As an example, the measured endplay on the photographed transmission was .095 inch and its selective washer was .063 inch thick. We need to increase the thrust washer's thickness to reduce endplay. Let's strive for the center of the range, .059 inch. This is .036 inch less than the .095 inch we started with, so we need to add at least that amount to the existing thrust washer (.063 inch). Therefore, .063 + .036 = .099, and thankfully there is one close to this: .102. The .102-inch washer gets endplay almost in the center of the range but I typically use a washer to put the endplay toward the lower end of the range. ■

hear a "pop," one of the sealing rings likely broke. Don't fret, just remove the broken ring, replace it, correct what caused it, and try again.

Once both bolts snug up correctly and the pump pulls on in, check rotation of the input shaft. If it rotates and you can move the front clutch retainer from the valve body side, its all good. Remove the studs and install the remaining bolts. Torque them in a cross pattern to 175 in-lbs. Check that the input shaft still rotates and that there is some endplay.

Oil Pump Installation

1 *To help with pump installation, screw two 5/16-18 x 3-inch pilot studs in the 3 o'clock and 9 o'clock pump bolt positions. If you have no pilots, you can make some by cutting the heads off 3-inch-long 5/16-18 bolts.*

2 *Orient the gasket's holes correctly and place it over the two pilots.*

3 *Grease the rings on the reaction shaft support, outer O-ring, and inside bushing of the reaction shaft support and carefully slide the pump in place onto the pilots. Push it on slowly; when you feel it hit, loosen the band adjustment screw and push the pump on a bit more.*

4 *Install the bolts into the holes and remove the pilots to install the last two.*

5 *Alternately tighten the bolts at the 3 o'clock and 9 o'clock positions. Tighten each a bit at a time until the pump is flush and the bolts are snug. If it stops or you hear a snap, stop tightening and check for issues because something may be out of alignment.*

6 *Pull and push the input shaft, checking that it has some endplay. Then rotate it. Torque all the bolts in a cross pattern (to 175 in-lbs) and check the rotation of the shaft once again. Apply some grease inside the front seal.*

Low-Reverse Band Adjustment

On the A-904 having a double wrap band, loosen the lock nut and torque the low-reverse band adjustment screw to 72 in-lbs. Back the screw out 2½ to 4 turns (vehicle dependent) before tightening the locking nut. If it uses a single wrap band, some torque to 41 in-lbs and the screw is backed out 7 turns and the nut is locked. Some are torqued to 72 in-lbs and backed out 3¼ turns. I use the factory specifications whenever possible.

On most A-727s, the low-reverse band lock nut is loosened, the screw is torqued to 72 in-lbs and backed out two turns, and then held with a 5/16-inch wrench while the 11/16-inch lock nut is tightened.

Low-Reverse Band Adjustment

1 *Loosen the outer lock nut and torque the low-reverse band adjustment screw to 72 in-lbs (most TorqueFlites).*

2 *Once the band screw is torqued, use the correct open-end wrench to back out the adjustment screw to the specified amount. This one is backed out two complete turns.*

3 *Hold the adjustment screw while tightening the lock nut.*

Kickdown Band Adjustment

With an A-904, the kickdown band screw is torqued to 72 in-lbs and backed out 2 turns before tightening the 3/4-inch lock nut. However, some early 170-ci Slant-6 kickdown bands were backed out 2⅝ turns.

As a general rule, the A-727 kickdown band screw is torqued to 72 in-lbs and backed out 2 turns for all except the Hemi and 440 6-barrel cars, which were backed out 1½ turns. After the adjustment, hold the screw while tightening the 3/4-inch lock nut.

Kickdown Band Adjustment

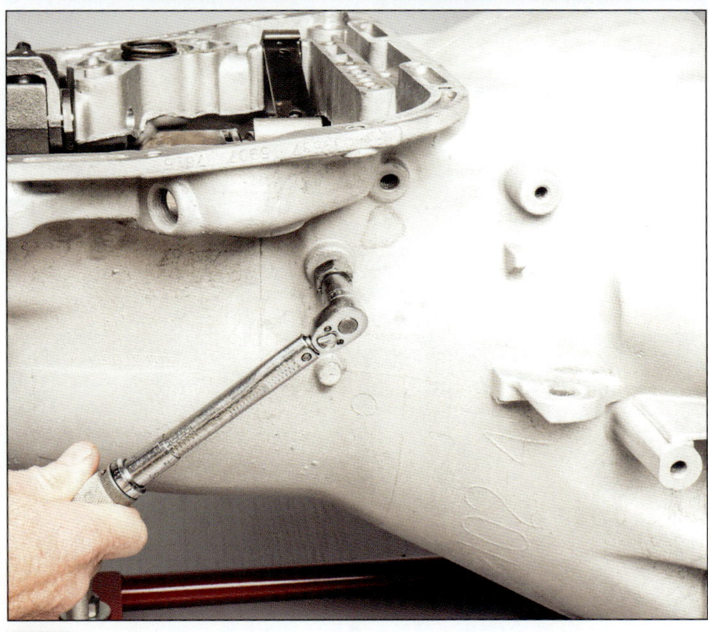

1 *As with the low-reverse band adjustment, loosen the lock nut and torque the kickdown band adjustment screw to 72 in-lbs. Back it out the specified amount.*

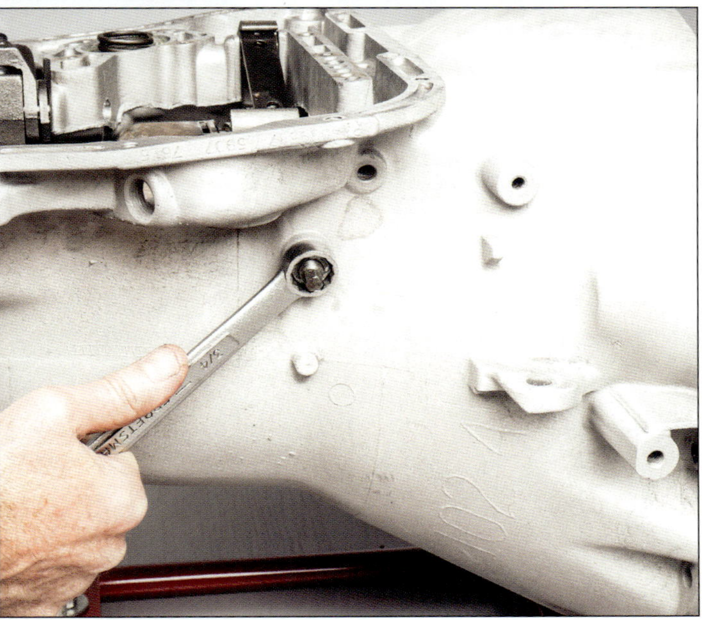

2 *Use a 3/4-inch wrench to snug the lock nut while holding the adjustment screw in place.*

Extension Housing

Put a lightly greased new extension-housing gasket on with its openings lined up.

Be sure the output shaft bearing circumferential groove is biased toward the front of the transmission. Put some grease on the rear seal and bushing, and slide the housing over the shaft. Expand the snap ring while pushing the extension housing over the bearing. Release the snap ring so it falls into the bearing groove. Install six extension housing bolts and brackets or wire clips that were originally under them. Torque the bolts to 24 ft-lbs in a cross pattern. Put a new, lightly greased cork or paper gasket over the snap ring opening, install the plate, install the two screws, and use a good Phillips screwdriver to tighten them.

Remove the old inner seal and outer O-ring, if still on the speedometer adapter. Install the new inner seal, followed by the clip, into the speedometer adapter with the lip facing toward the inside. Roll the outer new O-ring on. Grease the speedometer gear shaft, count the teeth, and put it into the adapter. Install the adapter housing into the extension housing, rotating it so the number of gear teeth correspond to the range of the numbers by the cast-in boss. Install the bolt that holds the clamp and torque it to 100 in-lbs. (A chart is provided in Appendix B showing combinations of speedometer driven gears versus rear axle ratio and tire size.)

Once the extension housing is on and tight, another endplay measurement can be taken to be sure it is in the correct range. After assembly, this transmission had about .056-inch play. If it were completely free of assembly grease, it would be in the .060- to .065-inch range, which is quite acceptable. If the endplay is still too loose on yours, no big deal; tighten the band adjusting screw, pull the pump off, replace the washer with the next thicker size, and reinstall the pump. Readjust the kickdown band.

Extension Housing Assembly Installation

1 Grease the case side of the extension housing gasket and put it in place.

2 Lubricate the rear seal and the rear bushing.

3 Expand the snap ring and slide the extension housing over the rear bearing and into place. Release the snap ring and make sure it drops into the groove.

4 If yours had a wire clip(s), put it (them) into place and torque the six bolts into the case to 24 ft-lbs using a cross pattern.

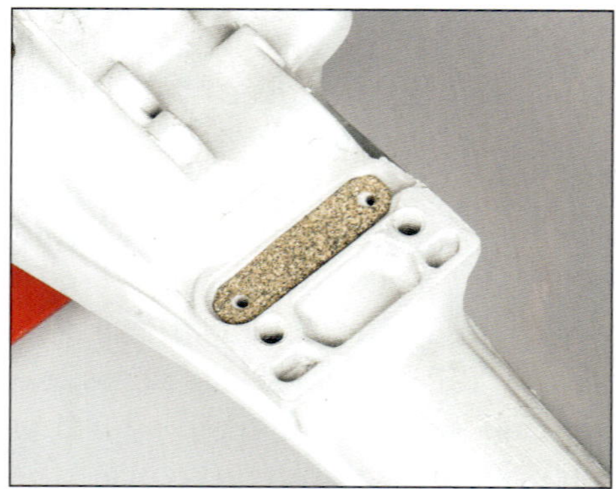

5 Install the lightly greased cork or paper gasket over the bearing snap ring.

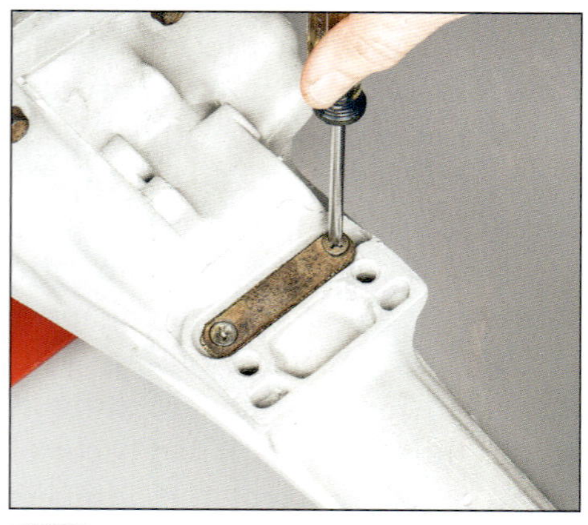

6 Use a Phillips screwdriver and tighten the two plate screws.

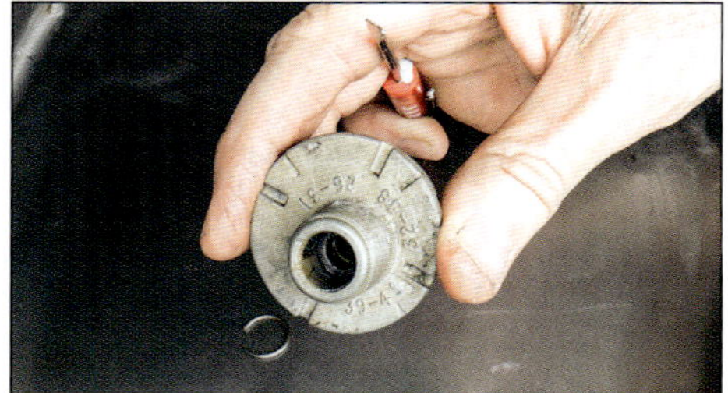

7 If not already switched, use a sharp screwdriver or awl to remove the small wire snap ring from the adapter. Note the direction that the speedometer seal faces and then remove it. Remove the outer O-ring too.

8 *Install the new inner seal and use an appropriate socket to push in the clip and seal. Grease the O-ring and the inner diameter of the adapter before installing the speedometer gear. Note the number of teeth.*

9 *The number of gear teeth corresponds to the range cast into the adapter. Align the correct range with the boss (at 12 o'clock here) on the housing.*

10 *When everything is aligned, install the clamp and snug the bolt. Rotate the output shaft to be sure the speedometer gear turns.*

11 *With the extension housing and pump in place and tight, take another endplay measurement to verify that all is good. This endplay is around .056 inch, which is acceptable. If it were still devoid of grease as it was when the original measurements were made, the measurement would likely be around .065 inch.*

Air Checking Assemblies

With the internal components in and adjusted, 30- to 40-psi pressurized air can be directed into case openings to hear/see everything work.

To test the low-reverse servo, direct air into the round opening between the rear servo and the accumulator. As it is applied, the piston pushes out and clamps the band around the drum. Its movement varies with low-reverse band adjustment.

Apply air to the round kickdown servo apply port located between the accumulator bore and the kickdown servo. The servo pin will push out and clamp the band around the front clutch retainer.

To test the front and rear clutch assemblies, use the valve body openings in the front of the case. To test the front clutch, pressurize the port directly next to a bolt hole beside the smaller of the two rectangular openings. You will hear a thud similar to the noise heard from the front clutch test you made before subassemblies went in. There may be some slight hissing from air leakage, but a little is okay. If you hear or feel no thud and there is a lot of air leaking, there may be an issue; identify and correct it now. Because the assembly tested well before installation, it may be a broken ring or not enough grease on the rings to seal it.

To air test the rear clutch, direct air into the port next to the one used to test the front clutch. When testing this one, the thump may not be as loud. The input shaft can be rotated while applying air; the rear clutches will lock on the splines of the front annulus gear assembly rotating the front planetary assembly. If something feels wrong and/or the air leakage is excessive, take it apart and look for a broken ring. Be sure to correct the issue.

Air Checking Assemblies

1 By putting air in the correct port, the low-reverse servo can be tested. Direct air (at 30 to 40 psi) into this opening using a rubber-tipped blowgun. The piston pushes out against the servo lever, tightening the band around the drum.

2 Do the same to the front servo: Put the gun's tip into the port between the accumulator and the kickdown servo, apply air, and watch the piston push the lever and tighten the band.

3 Even though it was already done with the pump off, you should check the front clutch assembly by putting air into the opening directly next to the bolt hole beside the small rectangular opening in the case. Listen for the thump.

4 The rear clutch assembly can be checked using the hole directly next to the one used for the front clutch. This test does not make as loud a thump, but you should hear and maybe feel some movement. You can also rotate the input shaft with the air applied to be sure that the front planetary turns.

Accumulator, Valve Body, Levers, Filter, Switch and Pan

If the transmission had a spring under the accumulator piston, put it in the bore. Grease the sealing rings and push/tap the accumulator piston in. If it had a spring between the valve body and the piston, place it on now.

Slowly rotate the output shaft and use a finger or a screwdriver to reach in and push the park pawl into the parking gear. Stop rotating when the pawl drops in/engages. The reason for this is the ball on the park rod has to move past this pawl when the valve body is installed; when the pawl drops into the gear, the ball fits. Rotate the valve body manual lever into the Manual Low position. Now, hold the valve body while pushing the parking rod's ball through the parking pawl. Then, slide the shifter shaft through the case bore and the shifter shaft seal. When it is in place, install the 10 valve body bolts by hand.

Screw the reverse light/neutral start switch in and install the shift lever on its shaft. Move the shift lever to Neutral and Park position and verify that the plunger of the neutral start switch touches the valve body rooster comb. Shift the manual lever through all positions to be sure the park rod is correct and everything is aligned. Torque the valve body bolts in a cross pattern to 100 in-lbs.

Install the throttle pressure lever on the shaft and tighten the pinch bolt. Rotate the lever and verify that it is pushed back by the valve body throttle pressure spring.

Install a new filter and tighten the three screws.

Install the pan gasket, the oil pan, and the pan bolts. Snug them several times while working around the perimeter of the pan. Torque them to a final specification of 100 in-lbs.

It's finally time to stand back, relax, and be proud.

Accumulator, Valve Body, Lever, Filter, Switch and Pan Installation

1 *Pre-grease the sealing rings (and if there was a spring under the piston, drop it in) and install the accumulator piston while twisting and pushing.*

2 *Place the big accumulator spring on top of the piston (if it had one).*

3 *Reaching into the park pawl use your finger to feel the park pawl as you rotate the output or input shaft. When it drops into the slot, stop because the parking lever ball will now fit.*

4 *Grease the shifter shaft seal ID.*

5 *Push the park rod into the opening in the case and through the park pawl and then align the shifter shaft and push it through the case opening/seal. Install all 10 valve body bolts and tighten them finger-tight only.*

6 *Screw the neutral starting switch into the case and verify that the rooster comb touches the switch when in Park and Neutral. (Here, the pan is already on.)*

7 *Torque the 10 valve body bolts to 100 in-lbs in a cross pattern.*

8 *If not already in place, install the oil filter and snug the three screws/bolts.*

9 *Be sure that the pan rail is flat (hammer out any dips or recesses) and install the gasket, followed by the pan. Screw in all the bolts by hand.*

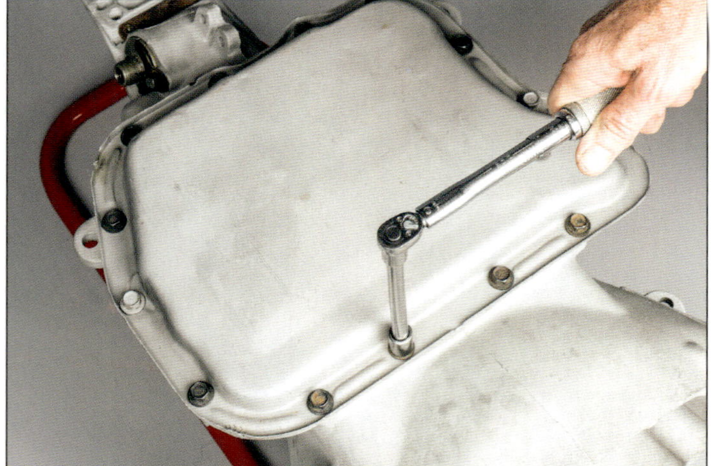

10 *With a torque wrench tighten to 100 in-lbs first, then finish at 150 in-lbs. Be sure that all bolts are tightened an equal amount.*

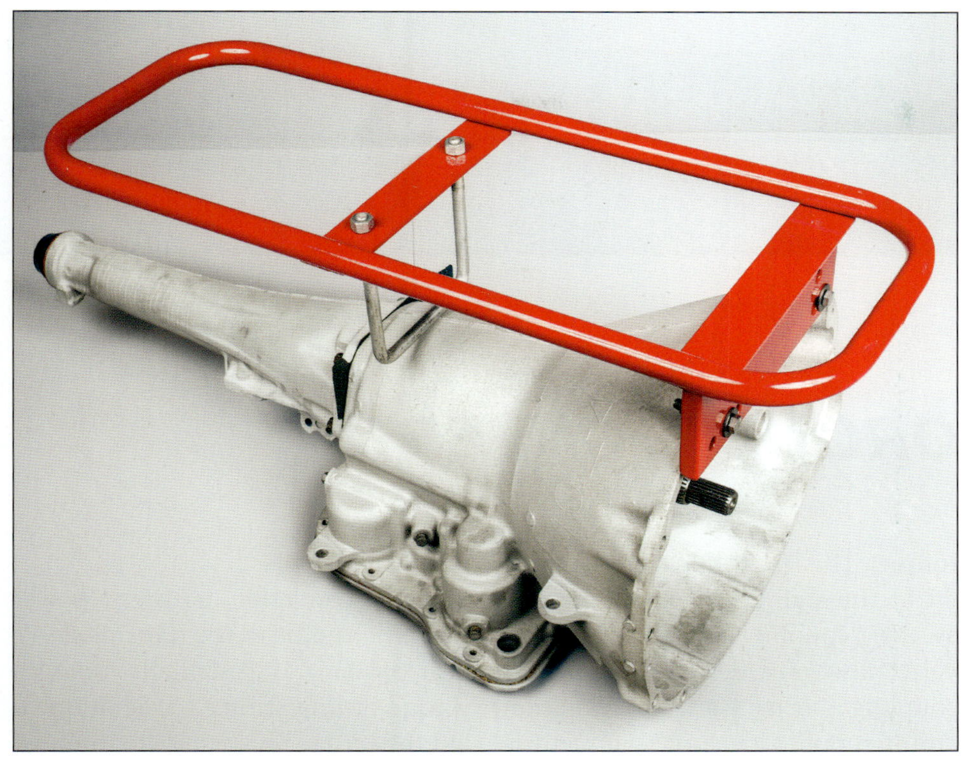

10 *Roll the finished transmission over and remove any support. Be sure to roll it on the side opposite the neutral starting switch to avoid bending pins.*

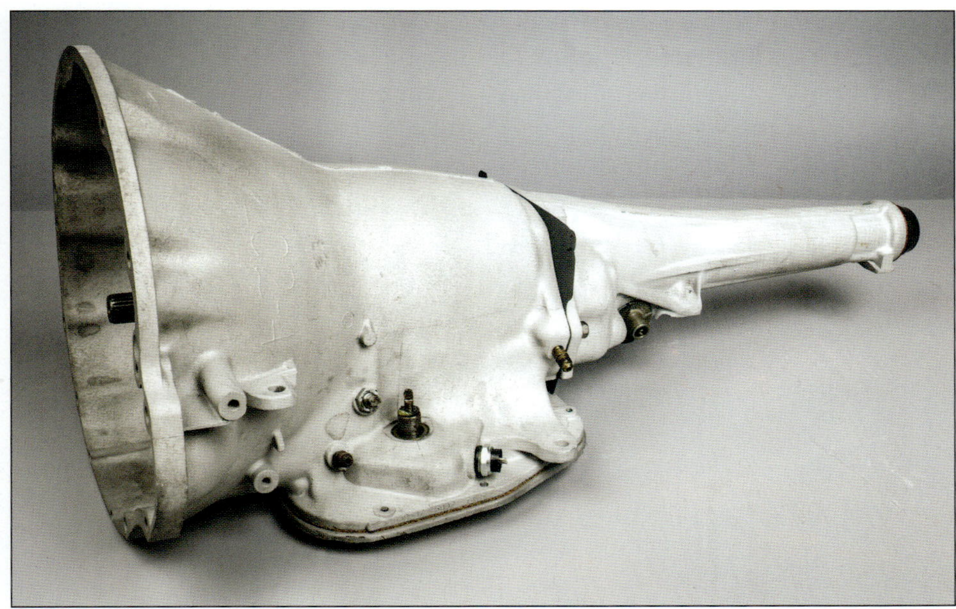

11 *It's done, tested, adjusted, and ready to install. Don't forget to put a new, greased O-ring on the dipstick tube and install your vehicle's shift and throttle levers.*

Post-Install Procedure

Once the transmission is back in the vehicle, lift the rear wheels safely off the ground and, while level, add about 4 quarts of fluid (Dexron, Type 7176, or equivalent), fire the engine, and slowly run through the gears, using the brakes between Forward and Reverse and, finally, Park. Add a couple more quarts and repeat the procedure using brakes between Forward gears and Reverse. Around quart number 6, the wheels will start doing what the shifter says they should be doing. Start checking the level in Neutral with the engine idling. Most A-904s will hold a total of 7¾ to 9 quarts, and A-727s will hold around 9 to 9½ quarts. Verify the throttle pressure and shift linkage is set correctly, be sure everything works, and take a careful test drive.

THE TORQUE CONVERTER

The automatic transmission and torque converter are so reliable and easy to use that drivers, for the most part, pay no attention to them. This is largely due to the advancement and improvement of the stator-equipped torque converter.

Torque Converter Basics

The torque converter performs several key functions; the most important is to multiply engine torque. This multiplication is highest at the stall point but disappears at the "coupling" point. The converter also provides a smooth fluid coupling during initial acceleration and it supplies torsional dampening at all speeds. With a lock-up clutch, when engaged, it transfers virtually 100 percent of the engine's torque. In addition, many converters provide a ring gear that the starter pinion gear engages with when the engine is cranked.

Short and Simple

The converter transfers power from the engine to the transmission's gear system. It essentially doubles torque during strong acceleration to aid the torque characteristics of most internal combustion engines.

Torque converters are "turbo machines" containing multi-bladed elements: the impeller (sometimes called a pump), a turbine, and stator. The fluid flow between them is three-dimensional and in a closed loop. The impeller rotates at engine speed and, in doing so, its blades guide fluid from its inner to outer

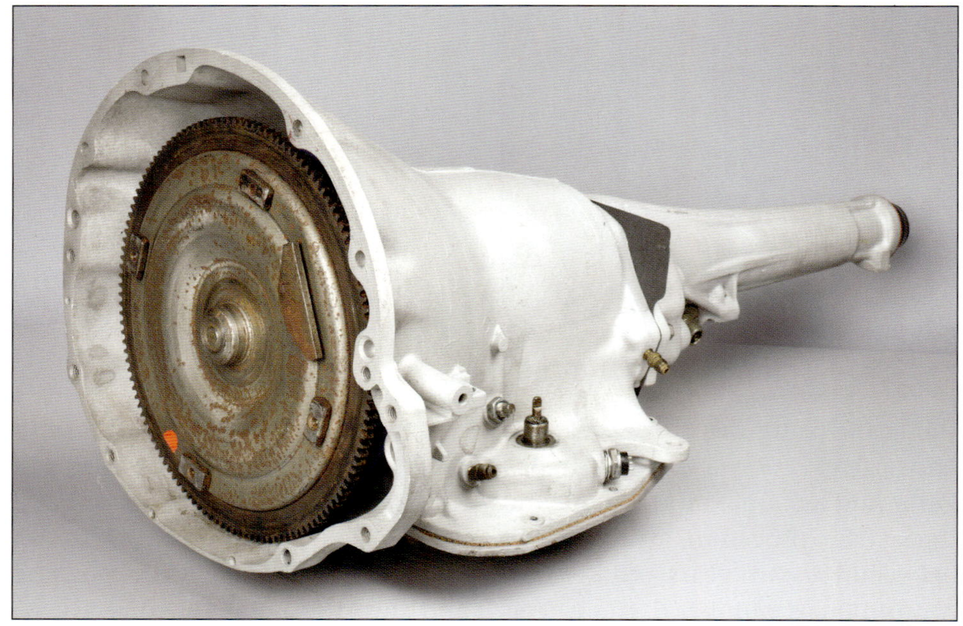

The torque converter is the key to performance, drivability, fuel economy, and even shift feel. With the correct one, you can have a good balance.

Millions of A-904s used a non-lock-up converter; this one has a 122-tooth ring gear, a drain plug, and thick lugs. It fits 1968–1976 318 or Slant-6 225-ci engines.

Converter Components

- Cover: The front half of the converter; it has lugs and centering pilot.

The front half is called the cover; its pilot centers it in the crankshaft and it has four lugs to hold the bolts that attach it to the flexplate.

- Friction material (lock-ups only): A large friction disc bonded to the inside of the cover is on the cover's flat surface, so there's no drain plug. The ring gear or weights can't be replaced or welded without damaging the material.
- Guide Ring (split): A split donut-shaped torus; each half centers between and mounts to the impeller and the turbine.

The turbine's split ring fits very close to the stator and seals similarly to the split ring on the impeller. The amount of clearance between parts affects the converter's stall speed and efficiency.

- Housing: The shell or body of the converter with an integral impeller.

The housing (or shell or body) contains an integral impeller on the inside and a hub that inserts into the pump to rotate the pump gears.

- Hub: It inserts in and drives the oil pump; the input shaft and reaction shaft support fit inside it, and a bushing in the oil pump supports it.
- Impeller: Curved fins/blades that tab and braze into the rear housing of the converter.

Note this impeller's angled blades (or fins), the split ring, and the integral steel washer in the hub area.

Converter Components *CONTINUED*

- Lock-Up Converter Only

The lock-up converter input shaft has a ground journal on its end, which inserts into the lip seal in the turbine clutch assembly. This shaft is not completely engaged.

With the input shaft fully engaged, the lip seal holds tightly around the journal. This is how the fluid coming from the input shaft is sealed to keep the pressure plate away from the friction material during non-lock-up periods.

On the side opposite its blades, you can see this A-727 lock-up converter's pressure plate.

Looking into the turbine's hub, you can see the splines and seal that fit on the input shaft.

The cover on lock-up converters has a bonded-on friction disc against which the pressure plate is forced during lock-up. This is why ring gears, weights, and lugs can't be welded to lock-up converters; the heat can damage the lining.

When the lock-up converter is fully engaged, torsional vibrations (if not minimized) from the engine can be transferred into the vehicle. These are the springs that dampen the vibration; different ones are used with different engines.

- Lock-up piston: Found in front of the turbine and uses two seals to control fluid flow. When unlocked, fluid flows through the input shaft, out and around the piston's unlocked face, through the converter, and back out between the reaction shaft support and the input shaft. When locked, pressure pushes it into the friction material.
- Lug: Four threaded blocks on the cover that accept bolts to hold the converter to the flexplate. Later converters have thin lugs but earlier ones were thicker. Hemi converters had larger holes for stronger bolts.

Most A-727s and A-904s use this double-slot drive method. Other TorqueFlites (in front-wheel-drive cars, for instance) often use converter hubs with two machined flats.

This is a thin lug found on 1977 and later front covers of A-727s and A-904s. There is no gap between it and the cover.

Older converters can be identified by thicker lugs. Here you can see the gap between the lug and the cover. This is a thick lug converter; performance converter companies often prefer these older models to the 1977 and later ones.

- Pilot: Round protrusion in the center of the cover that fits inside the crankshaft and centers the converter.
- Ring Gear: A large diameter (10.75- or 11.75-inch ID) ring with external gear teeth that engages with the starter and is welded to the cover.

A-727s have a 130-tooth ring gear; A-904s have 122 teeth. The gear is welded to the cover and on non-lock-ups, it can be replaced without total disassembly.

- Stator: A "reactive member" that accepts fluid from the inner diameter of the turbine and redirects it back at an advantageous angle toward the impeller.

An A-727 stator's stall characteristics can be determined by looking at the shape of its blades when it's out of the converter. This one's sharply angled orientation confirms that it is a high-stall version.

- Torsional Vibration Dampener: Mounts between the lock-up piston and turbine to absorb engine vibration during lock-up. It has different strength springs for different engines. Around 1978, decals were applied close to the offset lug to define the converter: red: 360/400 engines, white: 318, blue: 225; green and orange: non-lock-up converters. (Decals also indicated High or Low stall.)
- Turbine: Found in the front half of the converter, splined to the input shaft, and is rotated by fluid from the impeller. ■

This side of the turbine is next to and receives fluid from the impeller. Note how drastically curved the inner segments of the blades are that redirect fluid into the stator.

The turbine's inner hub is splined to the input shaft. The torque transfers to it from the hydraulically coupled impeller and turbine.

radius, and into the turbine. The turbine gains momentum from this impeller fluid and then transmits motion to the transmission through its input shaft. The fluid leaves the turbine and enters the stator, where it is redirected favorably into the impeller to provide torque multiplication.

Active Elements

The standard torque converter has three active elements: an impeller driven by the engine via the flexplate and converter housing, a turbine driven by fluid from the impeller and splined to the input shaft of the transmission, and a stator placed between the trailing edges of the turbine vanes and the leading edges of the impeller vanes. It is fixed to the transmission through the oil pump's reaction shaft.

A lock-up style converter contains one more element: an apply piston/clutch assembly.

Details of a Continuous Cycle

The converter's fluid, fed from the oil pump, is centrifugally driven to the outer diameter of the rotating impeller, and then thrown into the turbine. The fluid pushes on the outer diameter of the turbine's curved blades trying to push them and the input shaft splined to the turbine. The fluid being thrown into the turbine is forced to the inner diameter, where it exits into the stator.

The guide ring between the turbine and the impeller eliminates most of the fluid turbulence and guides the now-vortex fluid flow, providing a "constructive path" for fluid transfer between elements.

Torque Converter Terminology

To understand the converter better, let's go over some terms.

Stall Speed

The maximum RPM that an engine reaches at full throttle with the drivetrain locked and no transmission slippage. The engine speed can no longer increase because it has "stalled."

Flash Stall Speed

The RPM that an engine reaches at wide open throttle right at the point the vehicle begins to move (without the brakes being held). It is sometimes described as the RPM at which the converter "flashes" right after the transbrake (or brake) is released. It is difficult to accurately observe and depends on the vehicle weight, tire size, suspension setup, engine power, converter characteristics, etc.

Stall Torque Ratio

The stall torque ratio (STR) is the value of the torque multiplication provided by a converter at stall speed. It is the ratio of engine (input) torque to the converter's (output) torque occurring at stall. A higher STR makes the vehicle drive and feel better.

Efficiency or Coupling Efficiency

The relative amount of coupling between the impeller and turbine. Modern converters are 90- to 96-percent efficient and, with a lock-up clutch, achieve almost 100 percent.

K-Factor

A fixed value based on the converter's physical and functional characteristics; it can be used to calculate the converter's stall speed as it relates to the chosen point for applied input torque (an input torque value of 138 N-m or 100 ft-lbs of torque is commonly used). K factors can be provided in a metric or standard value. The formula is:

$$\text{Stall Speed} = \text{K factor times the square root of the applied input torque.}$$

Here is an example of how it is used to calculate expected stall speed.

A 166K converter is coupled to an engine having high torque:

$$\begin{aligned} \text{Stall speed} &= 166 \times \sqrt{300} \text{ ft-lb input torque} \\ &= 166 \times 17.32 \\ &= 2{,}875 \text{ rpm} \end{aligned}$$

The same 166K converter is used on an engine with less torque:

$$\begin{aligned} \text{Stall speed} &= 166 \times \sqrt{175} \text{ ft-lb input torque} \\ &= 166 \times 13.22 \\ &= 2{,}195 \text{ rpm} \end{aligned}$$

Note how the stall speed of the same converter has changed with less input torque. ■

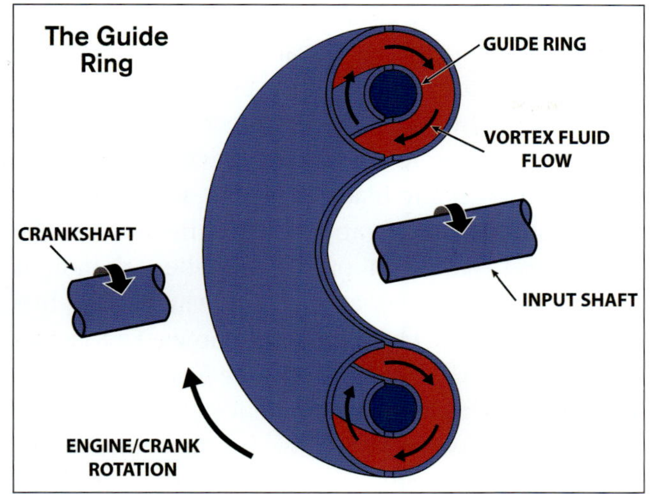

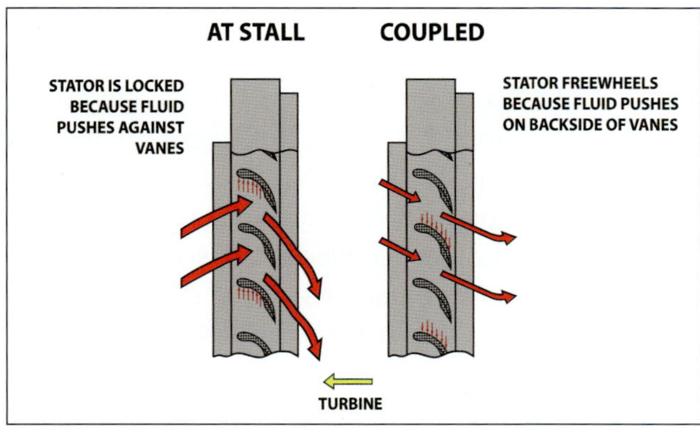

Converters use an internal guide ring to convert violent, turbulent fluid flow into constructive vortex flow.

At stall condition, the turbine's fluid strongly enters the stator and pushes hard against the vanes, locking the overrunning clutch; the fluid is thrown back into the impeller to multiply torque. However, once the turbine and impeller almost equalize in speed (couple), the intensity of the fluid's force has greatly decreased. The overrunning clutch freewheels fluid and now hits the backside of the vane, and torque is no longer multiplied.

The high volume of fluid from the inner diameter of the turbine travels into the front side of the stator's vanes/blades. The overrunning clutch holds the vanes in place, redirecting fluid back to the impeller. This vortex fluid redirection is what creates the torque multiplication.

This fluid transfer and redirection cycle continuously repeats inside a converter but reduces as the impeller and turbine reach the same speed. As a matter of fact, torque multiplication continues any time the turbine is less than about 90 percent of the impeller speed. Once they reach similar speeds, however, there is not a large volume of vortex flow between the impeller, the turbine, and the stator, and without a large flow through them, torque multiplication falls off and eventually ends. In other words, when the vortex flow slows down, torque multiplication reduces when the turbine and impeller "couple."

Because the stator rotates only one way, which is the same direction as the impeller, any fluid coming from the turbine during normal coupling

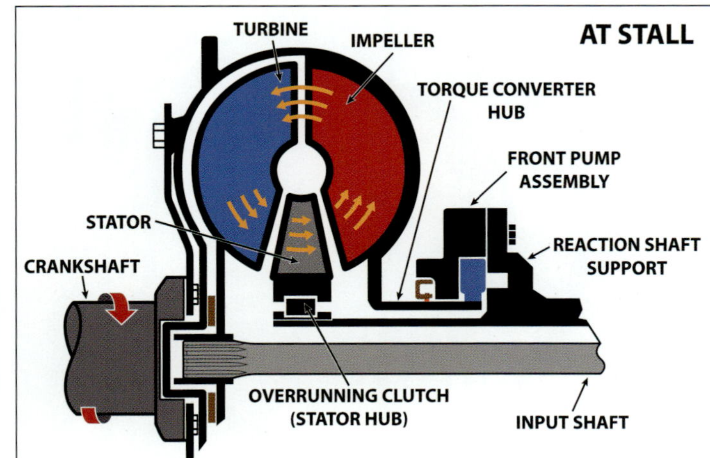

At stall condition, a large volume of fluid transfers between elements. The input shaft is held stationary (indirectly by the brakes) so the turbine is stationary and the converter multiplies the maximum torque.

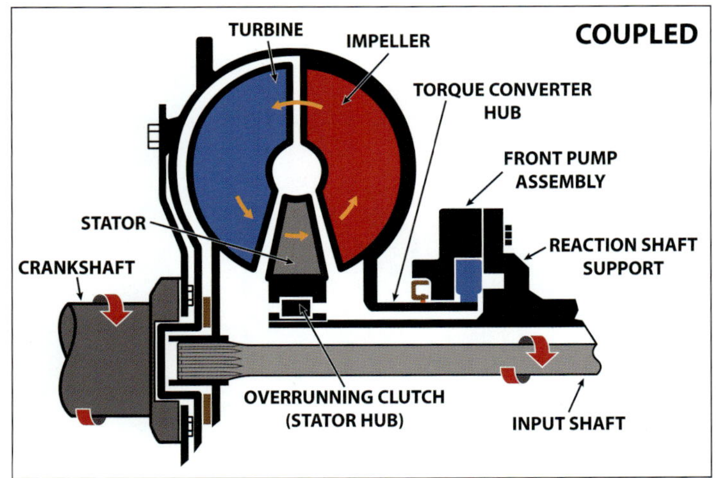

At coupling condition, a smaller volume of fluid transfers between the elements. Because the turbine and impeller are both rotating at almost the same speed, the stator freewheels due to oil hitting its backside. The converter is coupled and vortex flow is essentially zero, so torque is not multiplied.

---

strikes the rear side of the stator's vanes, causing it to "overrun" (freewheel). It basically "just gets out of the way." Again, during this hydraulic "fluid coupling" stage, the converter no longer multiplies torque.

Regarding torque multiplication, some stock TorqueFlite converters are listed as having a Stall Torque Ratio of about 2.2:1, which is another way of saying input torque is multiplied by about 2.2 times at stall. Some front-wheel-drive TorqueFlites had ratios as high as 2.6:1. Regardless of rating, when accelerating in any gear while the converter's impeller and turbine are not coupled, torque multiplication occurs, although at a lower rate than at stall.

Factors That Affect Converter Operation

Let's look at things that affect how a converter works.

Diameter

The diameter of a converter affects its stall speed and efficiency. A larger-diameter converter typically couples better and stalls lower than a smaller one. One of the easiest ways to increase stall speed is to decrease the diameter of the converter, assuming they have similar internal features and components. One source states that each inch of converter diameter reduction increases the stall speed by around 500 rpm. Another states that one inch of diameter changes the stall speed 30 percent.

At the same RPM, a larger converter transfers more fluid faster between the impeller and turbine. The fluid farther from the center travels faster when compared to fluid closer to the center. A larger converter's fluid has higher centrifugal force, putting more fluid into the starter sooner, making it harder for the engine speed to increase; hence giving a lower stall speed.

Impeller and Turbine Blade Angle and Quantity

The blade (fin) angles inside a converter are complex and varied. Changing them can alter the performance characteristic. One way to change the stall speed a few hundred RPM in either direction is to modify the impeller blades' exit angle. If the blades are bent so the angle is sharper and in the direction of the rotation of the impeller, the oil is thrown at a steeper angle and hits the turbine blades harder. This causes the stall speed to be lower and tends to raise the efficiency by lowering the slippage at the coupling point. Conversely, if the blade angle is changed so its exit angle is in the opposite direction of the impeller's rotation, the fluid's force on the turbine blades is lowered, which in turn raises the stall speed. The fluid's exit angle from the impeller is a key factor affecting stall torque ratio. Changing the amount of blades is also used to vary the characteristics of the converter. Making sure the impeller and turbine have different blade quantities eliminates potential torsional vibrations that could be caused when the blade windows exactly correspond.

Depending on application, different converter blade angles and shapes are chosen. These angles affect all characteristics of the converter.

Like a turbine, the impeller has specific blade angles. The number of blades in the turbine and impeller are almost always different to avoid vibration issues. Likewise, the stator has a different number than either of them.

Stator Blade Angle, Shape and Quantity

The stator is very important to the overall converter operation because it redirects fluid from the turbine to the impeller. Its angle and the number of fins control torque multiplication and stall speed. Increasing the stator's fin angle, in other words, making the fluid come out of it and turn sharply, (up to a point) increases the force of the fluid hitting back into the impeller's blades. This increased force on the impeller increases stall speed. To reduce the stall speed, the angle is decreased so fluid exits the stator straighter. Different shapes of blades can also affect converter characteristics and, for this reason, aluminum cast stators are used because the airfoil shape of the blades can be varied and controlled closely. Making sure the stator has a different quantity of blades than either the impeller or turbine can affect the converter: having very few blades is not effective, but too many block the fluid flow paths. Engineering evaluations indicate around 18 to 19 blades worked well with typical 9- to 10-inch-diameter converters.

Blade Clearance

Drastically increasing clearance between the bladed elements in a converter lowers efficiency because larger gaps provide additional fluid leakage paths. Minimizing the clearance is preferred, but if the elements are too close, fluid force and distortion can cause the impeller and turbines to hit, destroying the converter. High-quality converters have roller bearings and carefully controlled turbine and impeller face run-out. Minimizing clearances can slightly lower the stall speed and increase the efficiency; increasing clearance will increase the stall speed but lower the efficiency. Raising the stall speed by increasing clearance is not an efficient way to "loosen" a converter.

Type and Volume of Fluid

The type of transmission fluid can alter the efficiency and stall speed, although incrementally. Synthetic fluids that maintain their viscosity over temperature changes will be more consistent. Colder fluid acts differently because of the way it transfers within the converter. Thinner fluid stalls higher, and if the converter is not fully charged with fluid, it stalls even higher and loses efficiency.

Converter Issues

Like any machines, converters can fail and here are a few ways how.

Stator Failure

If the overrunning clutch in the stator fails by losing its ability to lock, the converter will provide no torque multiplication, making the vehicle feel as if it is starting in High gear. If it fails by locking up completely and not freewheeling during coupling, the vehicle accelerates fine but feels draggy at normal road speeds.

Severe Overheating

Heat damages engineered thermoplastic thrust washers and lock-up converter O-rings and seals, and possibly the friction materials or their bonding agents. Failure of thrust washers will quickly lead to failure of the converter and the transmission, as it ingests damaged turbine, stator, and/or impeller particles.

Blade Damage

Excessive torque input or clearance changes that allow the impeller and turbine to hit will generate metal particles and/or cause complete failure of the converter. Particles that then get into the transmission usually lock the governor first. Blades or fins that break free from their shells and housings can cause extreme damage.

Ballooning

A converter "balloons" when it grows in width from pilot to hub. A lot of torque going into the converter

The stator is a key determining feature of stall speed. Compare the blade angle and shape on the high-stall stator on the left with the low-stall stator on the right. The low-stall versions is almost straight through; the high-stall example drastically angles the fluid.

for extended periods of hard acceleration can cause ballooning. A stock converter used in high-power applications can experience ballooning. Typically, the converter's turbine pushes so hard on the front cover that it transfers the force to the thrust bearing that controls crankshaft for and aft movement. When this happens, the crank tears up the bearing and it then moves front to rear causing belts and pulleys to misalign as engine speed changes. I have seen this in trucks with high-powered 440s and large-diameter stock converters. Because of the way Torque-Flites are designed, it is hard to fit anti-ballooning plates on the impeller side, where they would help.

Hub Damage

TorqueFlite converters with slots sometimes have cracks form in the machined corners. If the cracks propagate, the converter bushing (in the pump) gets damaged, and soon the seal begins to leak. Some remanufactured converters with replacement hubs cracked often if no radius reliefs had been machined in the corners.

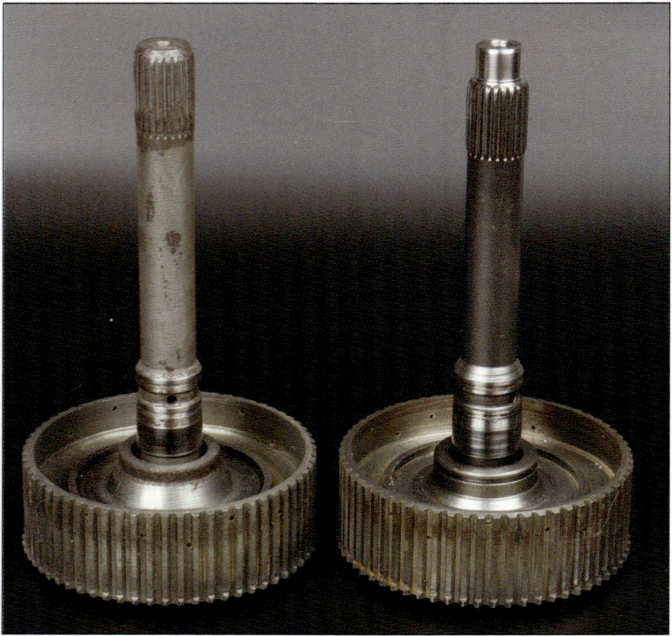

Leakage

Remanufactured converters, if not fully welded, may have pinholes in joints, causing a tough-to-find leak. Over time, the leakage can worsen as loads are applied.

Factory Converters

Very early converters for both the A-904 and A-727 had different stators to fit the smaller diameter input shafts with different amounts of splines. From the mid-1960s forward, non-lock-up converters could physically interchange (between like families) and from 1978 on, lock-up converters interchanged with other lock-ups (between like families). Weighting, balancing, and torsional damping could be different.

The late 1960s A-727 converters used with standard V-8s in cars and trucks were typically 11.75 inches in diameter, and converters for high-performance 340s, 383s, some 440s, and Hemis were 10.75 inches. The smaller-diameter converters are sometimes called "wide ring gear" converters because the ring gear is larger than the one on 11.75-inch converters. The larger diameter converters are referred to as narrow ring gear models. The A-727s have 130-tooth ring gears and A-904s have 122.

Interestingly, 1969 340- and 383-ci converters were the same part number, and they had factory-rated stall speeds of 2,250 to 2,450 rpm

Over time and with miles and wear, the hub can develop cracks on the sharp corners where they engage with the pump gears. A cracked hub can damage bushings and cause leaks.

Aftermarket converter parts suppliers offer new hubs made of stronger material with precise machining to prevent fatigue and cracking.

A-727 converters are often characterized as either "wide ring gear" or "narrow ring gear." This is a Dynamic D-145, wide-ring gear, low-stall stator-equipped converter weighted for 1973–1976 400 and 440 cast-crank engines.

This is a "narrow ring gear" A-727 converter. It is a Dynamic D-839 11.75-inch-diameter, remanufactured converter and is advertised to work with 1962–1972 high-performance cast-crank 440s.

When equipped with cast cranks, the engines were referred to as being externally balanced; the converter and harmonic dampener were typically weighted (shown).

This orange label on the converter indicates that it is a non-lock-up, high-stall converter used behind a 360- or 400-ci engine from about 1978 on.

The orange label on the cover side of this stock converter indicates that it is a high-stall unit. The color indicates that it works with a 360- or 400-ci engine.

The white tag on the cover side of this converter indicates that it has a low-stall stator and is a lock-up unit from a 318-ci engine.

A relatively easy way to identify the type of stator in most A-727 converters is to look for raised casting marks or lines (or the lack thereof) on the aluminum housing's ID. If it has a lot of little teeth or radial lines (shown), it is a high-stall stator. A smooth ID with no teeth or lines indicates a low-stall stator.

and 2,350 to 2,650 rpm, respectively; the Hemi with the same basic converter had a rated stall speed of 2,650 to 2,850 rpm. This again shows how the same converter stalls differently depending upon input torque.

One publication states that the common 11.75-inch converters had a K-factor of 115K and the 10.75-inch converter from 383 4-barrel, 340 4-barrel, and 426 Hemi 2/4-barrel cars was a 135K. The same document shows that the 340, 383, and Hemi had rated stall speeds at around 2,400

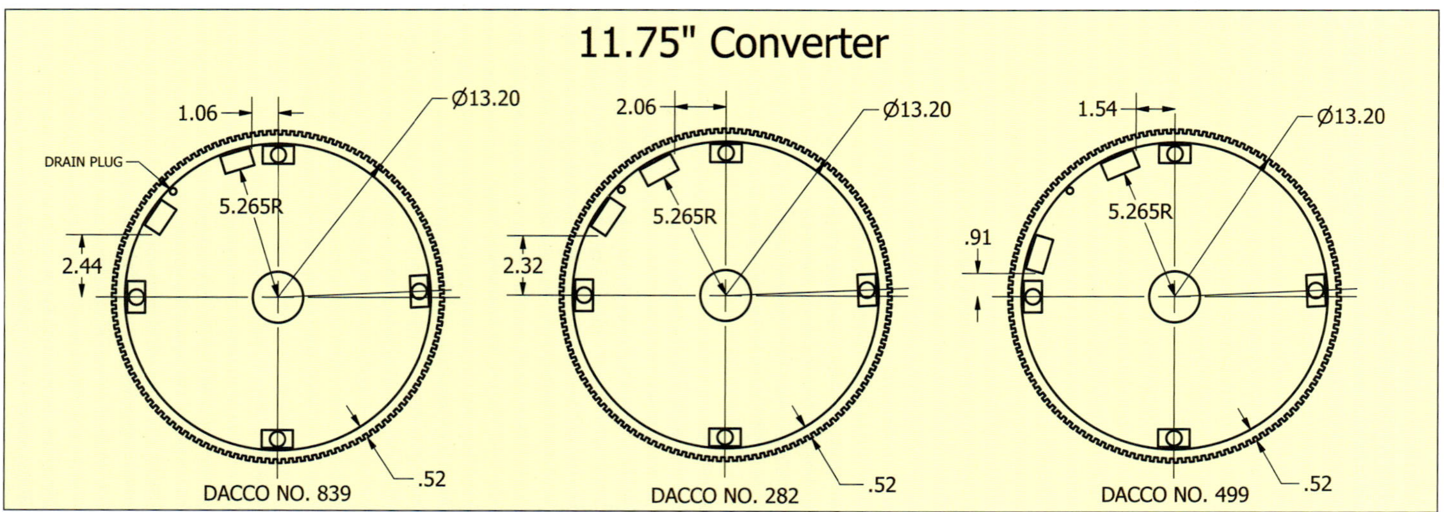

The large-diameter, 11.75-inch, weighted, pre-1977 converters were usually used on 400s and 440s with cast cranks. These are Dacco examples. The 1978 and later converters used only one large weight.

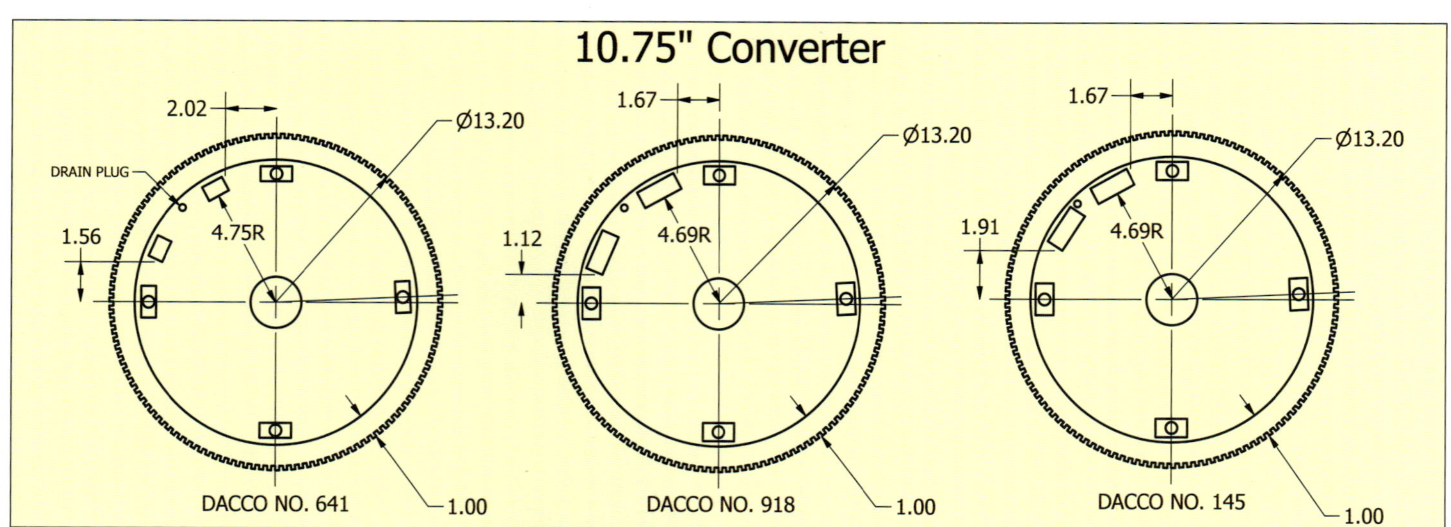

Up until 1977, converters for engines requiring external balancing used multiple weights. These are Dacco 10.75-inch-diameter converters, usually for 360s.

rpm. However, other publications state that a 145K rating relates to a converter with a 1,900- to 2,100-rpm stall speed, a 166K is 2,250 to 2,350 rpm, and a 175K is in the range of a 2,400- to 2,500-rpm rated stall speed. Clearly, you can find a lot of K-factor and stall speed differences. Fortunately, if you have the torque curve for your engine you can compare converters to determine how your vehicle will respond.

From about 1977 on, most A-727 converters were 10.75-inch diameter. The A-904s have used 10.75-inch diameters with just about all Chrysler products. Later model A-727 and A-904 converters have tags on the housing or the covers indicating if they are lock-ups or not and if they are high- or low-stall. If the tags are gone, you can easily determine which stator is in them by checking for multiple ribs or a smooth surface on the surface next to the splines. If the converter is apart, it's easy to tell if it is a high- or low-stall. The low-stall stator has relatively straight vanes with slight curves at the end and the high-stall has very angled vanes.

Depending upon the engine the vehicle has and the type of crankshaft and balancer it uses, there may be different weights welded to the cover. Earlier converters used multiple weights, and later ones typically had a large one.

Aftermarket Converters

Most performance applications require higher-stall torque converters because the performance engines typically have higher power bands with reduced torque at low speeds. A higher-stall converter enables an engine to "flash" up to a point where they develop more usable torque.

These converters let a more radically cammed engine idle better in gear.

In the early days of converters and hot rodding, owners could simply install a smaller converter in place of the stock unit. This allowed the engine to stall at a higher speed, but it also would cause excessive slippage at higher engine speeds. The slippage destroyed speed and gas mileage and generated a large amount of heat. The converter slippage also accelerated the failure rate of many transmissions and converters.

High-stall converters normally require a higher engine speed before they can couple effectively. In a performance situation, this is no big deal; in street applications, it is annoying, wasteful of fuel, and increases heat load.

Stock converters can be modified to increase their stall speed. The blades on the impeller can be bent back to make them flatter and the stator can have the fins on its exit trimmed a bit. Both of these might add a few hundred RPM to the stall speed. The thrust washers can be replaced with bearings and a stronger front cover plate can be added to minimize ballooning. However, modified stock converters can never really substitute for custom-built converters intended specifically for heavy-duty applications.

Today, many high-stall "universal converters" are basically smaller converters with minor changes (stator exit fins cut, impeller fins bent back, additional internal clearance, roller bearings instead of washers, etc.) to raise stall speed and enhance durability. Remember, though, that a specifically stated stall speed on a converter is a misnomer unless you know what torque was applied when the rating was assigned. Unless your engine is exactly the same as the one used for the stated stall-speed rating, the converter may not act the same in your vehicle.

Custom-built converters often provide improved street drivability,

Sonnax supplies ultra-high-performance converter parts to many builders and remanufacturers; this is the 10-inch TorqueFlite Race Kit that can be fabricated in many different variations. The kit comes with a billet steel cover, hardened chrome-moly steel hubs, and a new ring gear. As an option, an almost indestructible sprag and stator assembly can be added.

To the 10-inch TorqueFlite Race Kit from Sonnax, builders add a 245-mm GM impeller and turbine, along with aftermarket roller bearings and special stators. They can produce high-performance converters with rated stall speeds from 3,000 rpm up.

A Hemi converter bolts on with 7/16-inch bolts; all others use 5/16 inchers. This Race Kit converter's cover uses the Hemi-size 7/16-20 bolts and has eight holes to enable it to work with any flexplates made for 10.75-inch converters having offset or straight lugs. The threaded holes are integral to the forged billet cover to add strength.

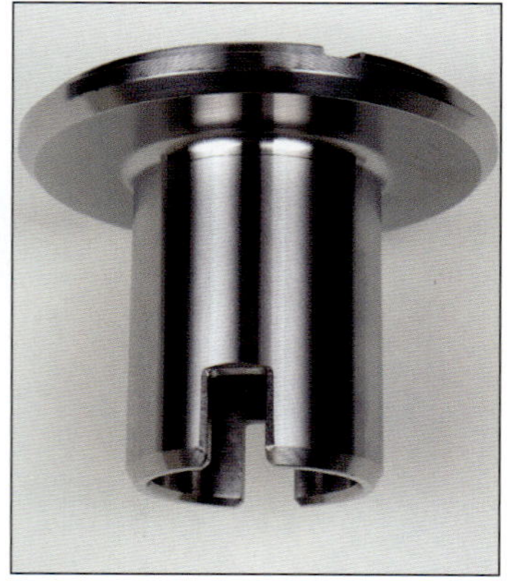

The high-strength hub in the 10-inch Race Kit is "flanged" with enough material that, after welding to the 245-mm converter's impeller body, it can be machined to hold a high-strength needle bearing assembly.

Before the 10-inch Race Kit converter's housing is welded to the cover, it looks like this soon-to-be-built A-727 converter.

The extra-thick one-piece forged and machined cover has the bushing for the turbine already installed. The cover's extra strength prevents ballooning.

Sonnax's turbine hub is welded to the modified 245-mm turbine. It has four channels to let fluid travel into and out of the bushing.

To complement the TorqueFlite 10-inch Race Kit, this is the GM 245-mm-based stator, which is similar to an 8-inch Opel version. It holds a mechanical diode or a sprag cartridge (shown) and is used to create "medium" stall-speed converters with very high-stall torque ratios (STR). The 22-element sprag can withstand more than 800 ft-lbs of torque (more than twice that of stock units).

With one of the stator caps removed, you can see the 22-element sprag. The inner race used with the sprag is hardened steel.

The special stator's 22-element sprag (right) is much more beefy than the 8-element overrunning clutch found inside the stator of stock A-727 converters (left).

easier staging at the strip, more consistency in the 60-foot and the quarter-mile, and higher quarter-mile speed. Moreover, their additional strength eliminates worries about complete transmission destruction caused by internal converter failure. Custom performance converters are typically constructed to handle very high loads. Fins are furnace-brazed, creating a continuous weld between the blades (fins) and the shell they are in. High-strength steels are used for the turbine hub and the stator's internal race. Special high-strength stators are installed, which have stronger overrunning clutches, special sprags, or which use virtually indestructible mechanical diodes.

Aftermarket converter manufacturers employ a host of techniques to improve performance, including the use of smaller diameter and different cores, different shapes and angles of fins on the impeller, turbine, and stator, specifically engineered stators with better one-way clutches, and different clearances between the various components. Many techniques used are generally regarded as company secrets. In addition to performance changes, there are a lot of modifications made to add strength and reliability (billet steel covers to prevent ballooning and the use of specialty steels for hubs).

Selecting a Converter

The overall performance of most stock type cars and trucks having relatively unmodified engines is usually fine using stock converters. The heavier cars and trucks equipped with low numerical rear axle gearing (2.21 to 2.71) typically respond well to slightly looser converters. Changes in camshafts that push the power range higher may require a different converter.

To make any vehicle's launch feel better a torque increase helps. One way to achieve this is to make more power, but this typically comes with increased fuel usage. An often less

GM 245-mm Converter

For many applications, including TorqueFlite converters, a GM 245-mm core is commonly used. These are around 9.7 inches in diameter and have well-designed vanes and many stator configurations. Their impellers are commonly adapted to different billet-steel covers that are manufactured to fit many brands of engines. Extremely strong stators and hubs are available that work with them.

This hardened pump hub is installed in the 245-mm core by machining the proper-size hole and welding it in. Additional machining is performed on the internal flange to use the new stator and roller bearings. Converter builders are well equipped to handle this.

To adapt a GM turbine to the 10-inch TorqueFlite Race Kit, this special hardened turbine hub is welded into a correctly sized and machined opening in the turbine. After all the required machining and use of ultra-high-strength parts, it is easy to understand why custom-built converters are expensive but are worth so much more than modified stock units.

expensive and more effective way to get increased torque is to modify/replace the torque converter with one having a higher-stall torque ratio. In some situations, to lower engine speed for better fuel economy, or to correspond with a high-output (at low speed) engine, a converter with a higher torque capacity (lower K factor) is often desired.

As with most major components, the intended use of the vehicle is key when selecting a converter. A drag race vehicle is usually lighter, has lower numerical rear axle gearing, has no concern for fuel mileage, and normally has a higher-RPM-range engine with less low-end torque. It's obvious that optimum converters for such applications are far removed from dedicated street or street/strip vehicles that are actually driven for normal transportation.

To provide the best combination of acceleration, speed, and drivability, the converter should allow the engine to stall just below or at the beginning of the engine's strong torque range. Any additional increase in stall RPM above this wastes the strong low-RPM torque. Higher stall speeds are normally accompanied by greater slippage and higher uncoupled speed, causing excess heat, less speed or pulling power at the track, and greater fuel consumption on the street.

An important factor related to converter slippage is its effect during gear changes. If the converter is not coupled by the time of a shift, a loss of acceleration may occur. A very loose converter may improve 60-foot and eighth-mile times in a lightweight race car with a high-RPM shifted engine, and it might even help with quarter-mile elapsed times. However, a normal-RPM street car is likely to lose performance in the quarter-mile with a loose converter and that converter may not allow the car to run the full quarter-mile without hitting the redline because it never completely couples.

Keep the following points in mind when choosing a converter.

If your car is driven regularly on the street, it probably is not a racecar, and most race converters won't provide satisfactory overall performance.

Don't install a generic converter without getting comparative data from others who have used one in a situation similar to yours.

Don't install a converter that is too loose.

Do consider variables, such as tire size, gear ratio, expected quarter-mile speed, maximum engine RPM (both physical and where the power begins to drop sharply), engine vacuum at idle, engine torque at low RPM, and expected usage. Reputable suppliers ask about these variables, and many more, before recommending a converter.

Like a stock converter, the correct performance converter still allows some minor creep in Drive at normal idle speeds and will allow normal acceleration in traffic without excessive slippage. When power is needed or the throttle is opened quickly, the correct converter will allow the engine to jump to a higher RPM range.

As with any major component, reliability, warranty, and performance of the converter must be considered along with its initial cost. If a significant change in engine power/RPM characteristics has been made, a custom-built converter is likely required. Contact the major suppliers or manufacturers of converters with your specific vehicle and engine specifications.

With high-quality converters you truly get what you pay for. Good converters are never cheap because they will have state-of-the-art internal vane configurations and extremely strong stators, hubs, and covers. Moreover, if you want to do it right the first time, work with a respected converter manufacturer. More than likely, it will be using many of the parts shown in this chapter.

PERFORMANCE MODIFICATIONS

An automatic transmission definitely makes driving easier. Its push buttons, console shifter, or shift lever is moved to start a vehicle in motion and then most of us leave everything alone until the need to back up or stop arises. The first automatics may have been used for carefree and effortless driving, but they quickly found a place at the dragstrip. In the 1960s, Chrysler products dominated various dragstrip classes in the American Hot Rod Association (AHRA) and the National Hot Rod Association (NHRA).

Prior to the TorqueFlite's debut on the strip, many cars were running manual transmissions because they were faster and quicker. The shock of higher RPM "clutch dumps" on the starting line created enormous loads on tires and various driveline components. If it wasn't for less grippy tires, there would have been an incredible amount of carnage.

Chrysler Corporation was the first to develop better racing automatics because they had already created the most dependable automatic transmission.

The advent of the aluminum TorqueFlite opened many classes that Chrysler could dominate. Because torque converter science was not keeping up with the automatic transmission improvements, B&M Automotive Products developed a new system, the ClutchFlite. It had a regular clutch and flywheel in place of the converter; it was used to launch the car. The automatic's geartrain and clutch assemblies then provide "no-clutch-required" shifting. The "ClutchFlite" was used in funny cars and other full race cars for several years. (Note: I suspect that without a converter to cushion the wide-open throttle shifts, the gear changes were likely tough on internal parts.) Torque converter improvements eventually rendered the ClutchFlite somewhat obsolete, but they were timely and advantageous to many classes.

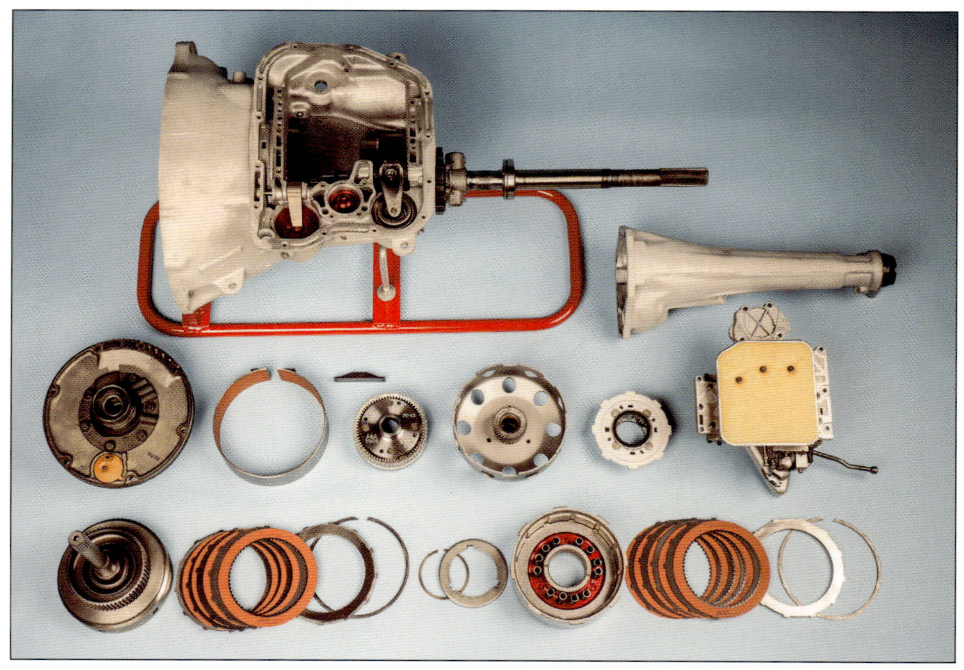

There are many ways to modify TorqueFlites and the correct changes and addition of factory and/or aftermarket parts help them shift quicker and firmer, last longer, and withstand extreme loads.

Why Modify?

Why would you modify a TorqueFlite? Several reasons: make it last longer; help it tolerate more load; or enable it to shift quicker, at higher RPM, firmer, and under driver control. In some cases, if the original TorqueFlite has been removed and the replacement is not set up the same, modifications can get the strength and shift feel desired.

A stock, heavy-duty or high-performance TorqueFlite shifted firmly and quickly. I remember a neighbor's new 1969 440 4-barrel GTX equipped with a 3.23 limited-slip and bias-ply tires as it wailed through Low gear, hit Second, and then grabbed High gear on the street. Later vehicles, such as the 1978 Little Red Express truck with the E-58 360 4-barrel, also had a firm and quick-shifting muscle-car-like TorqueFlite. Making certain changes to the Torque-Flite can provide that same muscle car feel. Modifications to minimize friction disc-to-steel plate or kickdown band-to-front clutch retainer slippage provide longevity and create a more noticeable shift. There are many ways to gain strength and shift feel and we'll look at how the factory did it in the performance TorqueFlites.

TorqueFlite Strengths

Chrysler's engineers designed the two TorqueFlite families to work with all engines and they were classed in three categories. The basic structure stayed the same, but heavy-duty parts were used when the transmission was going into a high-powered or heavy vehicle.

Strong TorqueFlites were used with Hemi and 440 6-barrel engines. These had stronger input shafts, a beveled rear clutch retainer, a higher-shifting governor, a wider kickdown band, a 5.0 servo lever, a different kickdown servo return spring, a wider front clutch retainer, 12 return springs, a special snap ring, and pumps with reliefs to clear the wide retainer. They often used no accumulator spring.

Super Heavy Duty

The 426 Hemi and 440 6-barrel cars had some of the ultimate A-727 TorqueFlites. Like the 340, 383, and 440 4-barrel, the Hemi Torque-Flite used four-pinion planetaries at the front and rear. It had a wider front clutch retainer to hold five higher-coefficient-of-friction discs and it used a wider kickdown band, a uniquely shaped rear clutch retainer, and a modified pump body. To actuate the wider band, it had a 5.0:1 kickdown band apply lever, and a different kickdown servo return spring. The 426 Hemi and 440 6-barrels came with a heavy-duty input shaft, identifiable with the machined groove at the converter end and a yellow stripe or spot. The Hemi Torque-Flite had a higher-shifting governor and some had smooth, slightly wavy, special friction discs in the front clutch retainer, along with 12 return springs. The valve body had a different separator plate and orifice sizes that made shifts "stronger and

quicker." Many Hemi TorqueFlites had no accumulator spring.

Heavy Duty

The A-727 TorqueFlites in 4-barrel muscle cars, the 1978 Little Red Express truck, other heavy-duty trucks, and certain police and taxi applications often had four-pinion planetaries and four friction disc front clutch retainers with 3.8:1-ratio kickdown band-apply levers. Many times, they had higher RPM shifting governors and different valve body orifices for more fluid to pass. Some heavy-duty units from 1978 even had lock-up converters. Certain 401 AMCs used the same heavy-duty input shaft as the Hemi and 440 6-barrel.

The A-904s were originally designed for the lower power, lighter car applications, but starting in 1974, the A-999 was released for 360-ci engines. I call it a small version of the A-727 Hemi TorqueFlite, and it's easy to see why. It had a wider kickdown

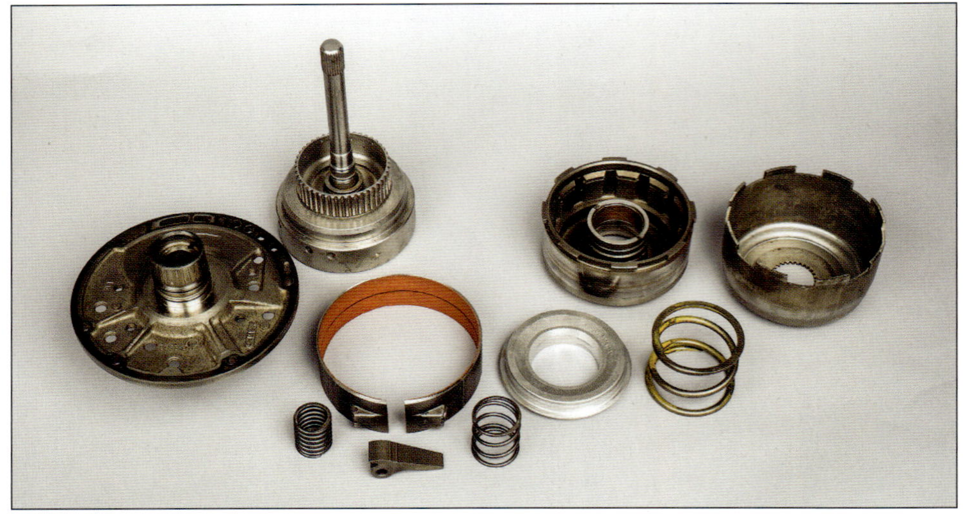

The A-904 was intended for low-powered engines in light cars, but by the mid-1970s, the A-999 identified a mini-Hemi A-904 TorqueFlite. Like the HEMI A-727, the first A-999s had a different reaction shaft support, a wider front clutch retainer and kickdown band, a higher numerical ratio kickdown servo lever (3.8), a stronger return spring in the front clutch retainer, a strong front clutch apply piston, a special kickdown servo return spring, a different rear clutch retainer, and a special sun gear shell.

The A-904 behind V-8s usually had four-friction disc-front clutch retainers, but the A-999 retainer was wider and held five. The retainer has a visible bevel inside.

band, new kickdown servo outer spring, a 3.8 kickdown servo lever, a front clutch retainer to accommodate the wider band, five friction discs, a new front clutch piston, revised accumulator spring, a new rear retainer, different sun gear driving shell, and a modified reaction shaft support.

Standard Duty

These A-727 TorqueFlites were used with 2-barrel engines, non-muscle cars, some trucks, and many later-model vehicles. They generally had three-pinion front and rear planetaries, three friction disc front clutch retainers, a low-rpm-shifting governor, and a lower numerical ratio kickdown band apply lever (2.9 or 3.2). Some were equipped with lock-up converters.

The A-904s were already considered "standard duty" and, as fuel prices went up and efforts to increase fuel economy increased, their use become more prevalent. The A-998s were the versions of A-904s used with 318-ci engines. Some A-904s in 1976 and 1977 even used the A-999 five friction front clutch retainers and the associated required parts but with narrow kickdown bands. Lock-up converters were added in 1978 and wide-ratio gear sets were incorporated in many standard-duty vehicles around 1980.

When placed next to a narrower, four- or three-friction disc retainer, the five-disc version is obviously wider. Later transmissions with this retainer often had a standard-width, flexible kickdown band.

On the reaction shaft support side, the wider A-999 retainer shows an obvious taper.

Fortunately, when comparing the same era of transmissions, many parts are interchangeable between the highest performance and standard performance A-727s and A-904s. They use the same pump pressure regulation system and the same pump configuration. Chrysler didn't add torque capacity by simply cranking up the line pressure; it used more-robust planetary assemblies, a combination of extra clutches, wider bands, matching kickdown servo assemblies, and properly sized orifices in the separator plate, along with stronger input and output shafts, where needed.

Modification Parts

So what parts can be changed and what modifications can be made to TorqueFlites? There are so many parts available that there is not enough space to list them all. Reviewing many suppliers' offerings, I selected a sampling of parts that make TorqueFlites more serviceable, shift crisper and firmer, accelerate quicker, withstand more load and power, be more fun to play with, and last longer. Some "recipes" from experienced mechanics and professional builders are shared in Appendix C.

Transmission Fluid Coolers

If modifications that add additional heat to the transmission and its fluid are made, adding an auxiliary cooler is recommended.

The fluid leaves the pump, charges the converter, and heads for either a cooler inside the radiator and/or an auxiliary cooler that was factory mounted in front of the radiator on certain vehicles. Older transmission fluids had an ideal operating temperature range of between 170

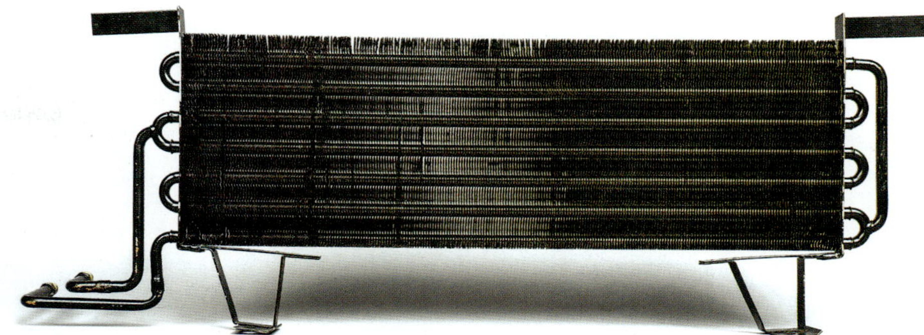

Along with heavy-duty internals, the Hemi TorqueFlite was equipped with an auxiliary cooler. This one came from a 1970 Hemi Cuda; it is similar to a B-body Hemi car in 1970–1971. Police and other heavy-duty vehicles also used auxiliary coolers.

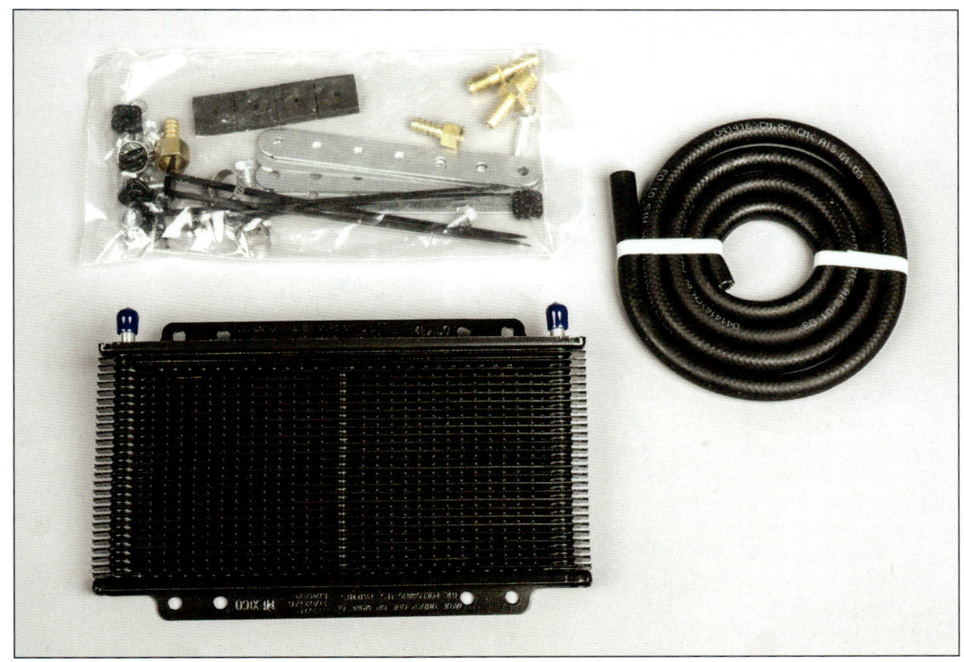

Aftermarket coolers are usually mounted in front of the radiator and/or condenser. Others mount elsewhere and can use a cooling fan. This Dana stacked-plate unit is for vehicles with a 14,500 gross vehicle weight.

and 230 degrees F, but current fluids can withstand a bit more. It's better to keep fluid cool because when it gets too hot, it oxidizes and some additives change chemically. After this occurs, the fluid should be replaced.

Different torque converters that stall at higher RPM add heat more than tighter ones do. For this reason, a converter change should correspond with addition of an auxiliary cooler. Auxiliary coolers should be mounted downstream of the existing radiator cooler. They are rated by gross vehicle weight (GVW), and buying one that matches or exceeds your vehicle's weight is wise.

Pans

Different transmission pans are available for A-904s or A-727s. Chrysler's race engineers suggest

Overdrive A-904s (A-500s) used this type of pan. Although they have no drain plug, they provide extra capacity and are a good addition if used with a filter extension.

Direct Connection/Mopar Performance offers a chrome or non-painted pan for A-904s and A-727s. They come with a filter, gasket, screws, an extension, and a drain plug.

The aftermarket offers deep pans. This finned-aluminum, older Fairbanks pan holds 4 more quarts than the stock A-727 pan.

When using a deep pan, it's best to place the filter close to the bottom. This is a 1.125-inch-tall A&A extension that works with Direct Connection/Mopar Performance steel pans.

This side of the extension fits against the valve body and uses an O–ring to seal.

that a 10-second or quicker vehicle use a deeper pan. Most deep pans hold at least 3 extra quarts, come with an extension that puts the filter close to the bottom of the pan, and (many) have drain plugs to allow fluid changes. There are finned cast-aluminum pans, deeper stock steel pans from A-500 (fit A-904) and A-518 (fit A-727), and stamped steel pans with integral cooling tubes.

An obvious disadvantage to a deep pan is that it is lower and can hit road objects. Most traditional cars and trucks probably don't need a deep pan but its drain plug is nice to have.

Filters

Several types of available filters keep the fluid free of damaging particulate contamination. On early TorqueFlites with rear pumps, a small, metal-screened filter was used in combination with a canister filter in the cooler line. The next generation TorqueFlites had Dacron filters with two holes; one for each pump. After the rear pump went away in 1965, the filter needed only one hole, and in 1973, the filter went square and grew 50 percent.

For higher-performance and race applications, brass or stainless steel screen filters with one or two pump holes are used. These let a higher volume of fluid flow through them, but they also allow larger particulates to pass. More frequent fluid changes when using them are suggested. An inline filter can be added in the cooler line downstream of the converter to catch any wear particles.

Shift Modification Kits or Complete Valve Bodies

Almost every car or truck owner has heard of the term Shift-Kit or Reprogramming-Kit. However, these registered names actually only describe a series of parts and technologies that TransGo sells to modify the shift timing and firmness of automatic transmissions (so I'll use "shift modification kit" to describe all shift improving kits). Gil Younger, one of the early automatic transmission experts, started these two related companies in the late 1950s to early 1960s. Gil was a philosopher who loved automatic transmissions and making customers happier with them.

Some early Torque-Flites (1962) had a small screen filter on the valve body and a canister filter (shown) in the cooler line.

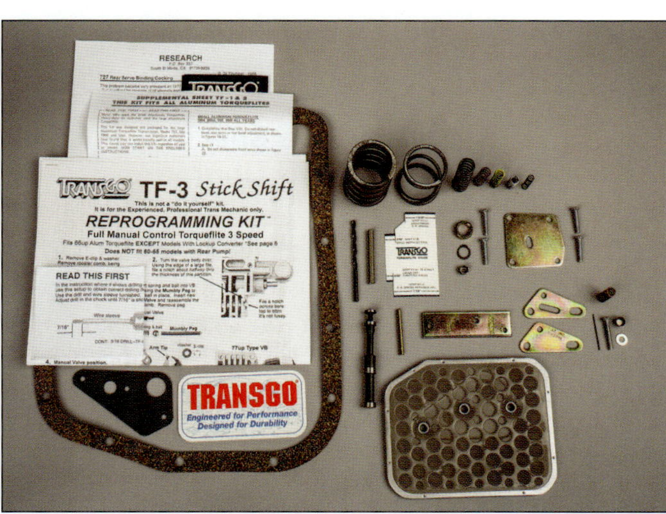

These filters are from more than 40 years of A-904 and A-727 production. There is a rectangular brass or Dacron one and the larger square ones. The early rear-pump TorqueFlites had two-hole filters; later ones had only one. Screen filters are not as effective at capturing small particulates but flow higher volumes of fluid.

TransGo has been in business since before the aluminum Torque-Flite hit the streets. Its large shift kits, TF-1, TF-2, and TF-3 help create a streetable, yet high-performance A-727 or A-904. The TF-3 makes a fully manual valve body that can use throttle pressure to control shift firmness.

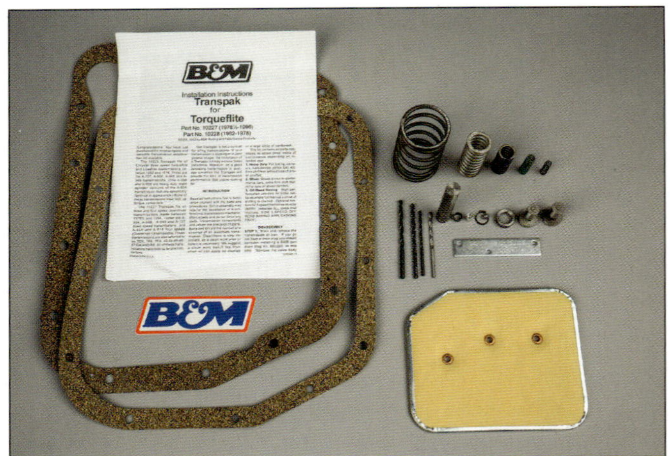

The granddaddy of performance transmissions, B&M Racing and Performance Products, has been in the TorqueFlite business for a long time. Its Transpak turns non-lock-up transmissions into quick- and comfortable-shifting units or into "dash-rattling" monsters.

The Fairbanks Transaction Kit for A-904s and A-727s provides three options: Heavy-Duty, Street & Strip, and Full Competition. Like the TransGo TF-3 and the B&M Transpak, the Fairbanks kit will create a manually controlled TorqueFlite.

Another industry leader in shift modification kits, B&M Automotive Products, was created in 1955 by Bob Spar and Mort Schuman (B and M); Bob's brother Don joined soon after. B&M produced a patented 4-speed Hydramatic racing transmission, played a large part in the Chrysler Turbine Car lock-up TorqueFlite adaptation, and they worked with Chrysler to develop the torque converter for the Hemi Super Stock program in the late 1960s. A Chrysler engineer, George M. Wallace, later joined B&M and was credited with the SuperDrive converter.

Fairbanks was a pioneering transmission product company owned and operated by the Lupo family. In 1995, Fairbanks was merged into Superior Transmission Parts, Inc., founded by Dennis Erickson Sr. in 1987, and joined by his brother Paul. Fairbanks is the name of Superior's Racing and High Performance line of parts. The Fairbanks Transaction is their shift modification kit, which they call an "Automatic Transmission Selective Action Kit."

There are other manufacturers of shift modification kits, but these three are highlighted because of their familiarity. The kits, when installed correctly, generally create quicker shifts with less slippage and provide longer friction life. They address the TorqueFlite's 2–3 overlap and Manual 1–2 binding issues.

Why worry about slippage, overlap, or binding, and why are quicker shifts better? As the friction discs in the clutch retainers are clamped to the steel plates, there is always going to be some slippage because the discs and plates are rotating at different speeds before the shift. A longer, smoother shift has more slippage because it takes longer for both the disc and plate to achieve the same speed. Excessive slippage creates heat that has to be dissipated into the steel plates, friction material, and transmission fluid. A quicker shift has less slippage because the clutches clamp together sooner, but the shifts are more driver-noticeable. A balance is achieved for most street applications, but for racing or heavy-duty use, it has to tilt to the less-comfortable side.

High-performance TorqueFlites with a lot of power running through them at high RPM or while pulling a heavy load can generate a lot of heat if the shifts are not made relatively quickly and with adequate clamping force. The factory engineering teams knew this, and that is why they changed orifice sizes, accumulators, and servo springs, and used front clutch retainers and bands with additional/different friction material. Heavy-duty OEM transmissions typically also have stronger and quicker shifts and shift modification kits advertise similar benefits.

TorqueFlite Specialty Internal Part Upgrades

Because many TorqueFlites have decades of use on them, some parts may be out of tolerance and others may be damaged beyond normal repair. Aftermarket companies now offer better and stronger TorqueFlite parts and it's not unusual to be able to save rare cases and other internal parts.

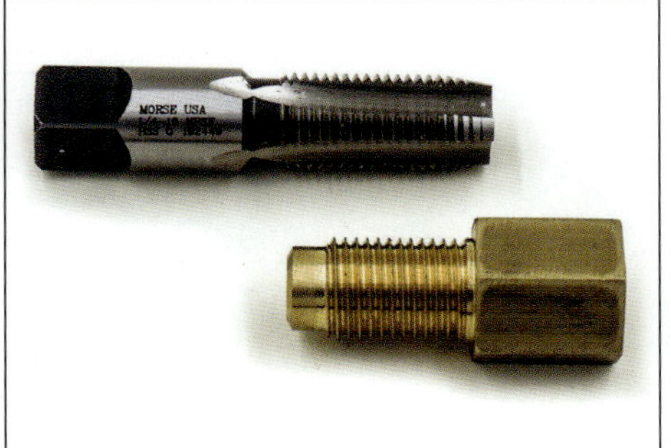

Late-model TorqueFlites have 1/4-inch NPT female-thread cooler line fittings (earlier ones used 1/8-inch NPT). If the threads are damaged, using this tap and the redesigned brass fittings can save the case.

Well-used TorqueFlites can be damaged when the overrunning clutch race rotates against the rear of the case. Rather than trashing a rare or expensive case, a relief can be machined into the case to allow use of this roller bearing.

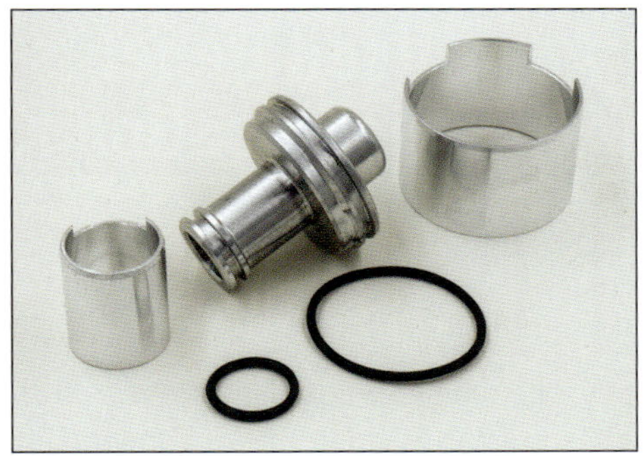

Many miles, a loose accumulator piston, or ring damage in the bore can send a case to the junk pile; this kit can save it. Sleeves are pressed and chemically locked in the bore and a smaller accumulator piston replaces the original.

A well established, high-performance TorqueFlite builder, racer, and component manufacturer, A&A Transmission, has been providing parts since 1980.

Another aftermarket transmission parts company, Sonnax, founded in 1978, manufactures unique things for TorqueFlites. It offers a wide variety of extreme-duty and high-performance parts and it provides innovative components for torque converter remanufacturers and transmission rebuilders. Sonnax's team works closely with transmission specialists, transmission and converter remanufacturers, and transmission rebuilders to create products for specific problems.

There are many other suppliers that have created a multitude of specialty items to improve TorqueFlites. I've highlighted several samples, but there are obviously others that are advantageous to specific applications.

Case-Saving Parts

- Late-model TorqueFlites often use a 1/4-inch NPT cooler line fitting, which may have been broken off or damaged the threads in the case.

- The valve body manual shaft can wear out, wobble, and take out its case bore.
- The overrunning clutch can fail and damage the rear portion of the case.
- In some instances, accumulator pistons wear out their bore.

These four situations normally required case replacement but parts are available to save them.

Valve Body Upgrades

At certain times, some Torque-Flite valve bodies (depending upon year of manufacture and miles) can exhibit lubrication and pump bushing failures, signs of delayed engagements, and odd noises. New pressure regulator valves to correct this are available.

Because A-904 and A-727 Torque-Flites fill the converter in Neutral and not Park, there can be a delay in vehicle movement when shifting from Park to Drive. Redesigned manual valves address this.

Governor-controlled "shift valves" (Governor Bore Plugs) can wear valve body bores and create shuttling 1–2 shifts, cause overly sensitive 2–3 and 3–2 downshifts, and potentially create difficulty setting the throttle pressure linkage. Redesigned Governor Bore Plug kits can correct the problems.

It is common to have the plastic insulator on the TorqueFlite rooster comb crack and break off and it used to require either valve body or rooster comb replacement. A new insulator or complete assembly can now be purchased.

TransGo and others offer a manual valve (on the right) that fills the converter in Park eliminating much of the delay when shifting from Park to Drive or Reverse.

Advertised Benefits Provided by "Full Featured" Shift Modification Kits

Here is how they do it:

1. Elimination/reduction of the 2–3 shift overlap: 2–3 overlap is when the kickdown band stays clamped on the retainer while the front clutch assembly is applied. The transmission is actually in Second and Third gear simultaneously.
2. Increased fluid volume to some hydraulic circuits: Some orifices in the transfer plate and valve body are enlarged to feed more fluid to various circuits.
3. Quicker, firmer positive shifts:

   - Some check balls that direct fluid through restrictions are eliminated.
   - The accumulator spring is often deleted and the piston is blocked close to the valve body transfer plate.
   - Line pressure is increased and/or a slightly stronger line pressure regulator spring is used.
   - Drill bits and a special plate to drill the valve body create a passage to provide more fluid to the front clutch circuit; an orifice control plug to limit the rate at which the extra fluid is applied is included.
   - Stiffer kickdown servo springs that alter the 2–3 shift timing may be supplied.

4. Elimination of Manual 1–2 shift bind-up: When manually shifting from 1–2, a small spacer to eliminate the low-reverse servo's cushion spring minimizes "bind-up" felt with some TorqueFlites. The bind-up is caused by application of the kickdown band before the low-reverse band releases. Some kits also include a higher-rate spring for A-727s to release the servo piston sooner.
5. Manual downshifts at any speed: Special 1–2 shift/governor valves and modifications are often made to enable manual downshifts at any speed.
6. Automatic upshifts at higher speeds: Different throttle pressure springs and modifying the throttle valve raises the maximum wide-open throttle shift points.

Which Kit, If Any, Should Be Used

If a shift modification kit is desired, what type should be selected? The full-featured kits offer more but may be more complex to install. Talking with other owners can help decide what is best for certain applications. There are smaller kits

This shift-modification kit from Superior is good for lock-up and non-lock-up transmissions, providing adjustments for the speed and timing of the converter lock-up, and offering quicker and firmer 1–2 and 2–3 shifts.

The Accumulator

A spring under the accumulator's large diameter "cushions" the application of the rear clutch when shifting from the Park or Neutral to forward positions. Unfortunately, leaving out the spring may sometimes cause a more abrupt engagement. A 2–3 shift does not fully complete until the accumulator piston has moved from the valve body transfer plate up into the case bore and by blocking the accumulator piston in the position closest to the transfer plate, the volume of fluid it would normally have to displace prior to completion of the 2–3 shift is small, therefore, making the shift quicker/firmer.

from the most familiar manufacturers that may be easier to install and are used more often by shops. These smaller kits are good for trailer towing, trucks, and certain street-strip applications. They, too, provide quicker and firmer shifts but may not offer as many manual control features.

Small kits from Mopar Performance/Direct Connection slightly increase the line pressure, sometimes replace the controlled-load kickdown servo piston assembly, and often block the accumulator. These make shifts quicker and firmer; a benefit is that nothing critical is modified in the valve body, making the installation reversible.

If tearing into and modifying valve bodies is not appealing, performance valve bodies are available from suppliers such as A&A, CRT, Turbo Action, TCI, Griner Engineering, and others. These range from basically stock with longevity and wear upgrades to full-manual reverse-pattern units and full-manual valve bodies with built-in brakes.

Issues Some Shift Modification Kits and Special Valve Bodies Create

With many full-featured and small kits, valve body passages and separator plate holes are altered or enlarged, but once this is done, they can't be easily converted back. For numbers-matching cars and components, this might be a real concern.

When a shift modification kit is installed in a heavy vehicle, one with a tighter torque converter, or one with a steeper rear axle ratio (2.20:1, 2.45:1, 2.73:1, etc.) or any combination thereof, the Park-to-Drive or Park-to-Reverse engagements and shifts may be abrupt and more noticeable.

Some kits cause noticeable light-throttle, lift-foot shift "slams or bangs." This is when accelerating from a stop under very light throttle and you lift off the gas to let the throttle pressure drop to provide an early shift.

Some kits create shifts that are just too rough. Fortunately, most of the roughness can be tuned back out, unless the drilled orifices in the separator plate can't be "shrunk." ■

TransGo's small shift kit, the SK-TFSC, provides several benefits. Even though intended for "Experienced Professional Transmission Mechanics," with a basic understanding, it installs easily and fixes several issues.

This small B&M Shift Improver Kit is for non-lock-up TorqueFlites. It is relatively simple to install but does not have the manual control features of the Transpak. It quickens shifts, and with line pressure changes, it offers two level of firmness.

As rare TorqueFlites age, worn-out valve body bores can create major headaches. New governor plugs (valves) that seal using engineered thermoplastic rings correct shifting issues and can save a "numbers matching" valve body.

Cracked or broken-off insulators are frequently found on old TorqueFlites. Valve bodies or rooster combs typically were replaced with used ones, but this part prevents that need. By replacing only the insulator (or using a new A&A rooster comb, not shown), a valve body can be reused.

Some shift-modification kits require changing the springs and physical size of the throttle valve, but wide-open-throttle shifts may occur at the wrong time. Throttle valve kits, such as this one that has different springs and shims, tune the shifts more precisely.

Creating a Super-Heavy-Duty A-727 TorqueFlite

Chrysler did it by adding friction material, but this required heavy (high-rotational mass) parts. Five, thinner, stock, rear clutch frictions can be installed in a stock front retainer, but they don't have quite the heat-absorbing ability or frictional characteristics needed. Fortunately, there are unique parts that can create a Hemi-style TorqueFlite without the mass. Non-LU A-727s can be upgraded with a wider front clutch hub or a complete heavy-duty input shaft/wider front clutch hub assembly, combined with a thinner apply piston for the front clutch retainer. Used together, five or more stock-sized front friction discs can be put in the standard four-friction disc clutch retainer. Alternatively, an Alto PowerPack provides additional, high-strength steels and better frictions. Combine these with a 5- to 8-percent increase in line pressure, a blocking spacer for the low-reverse servo piston, a 10-percent wider kickdown band, and a 16-percent larger apply area kickdown servo to create a high-capacity, heavy-duty TorqueFlite with virtually the same rotational mass as a standard one.

The Hemi TorqueFlite can handle a lot of power because of its additional friction plates, wider band, stronger band application, and four-pinion planet carriers. Unfortunately, the large retainer is heavier and difficult to find. However, using four-pinion planet carriers with several other improved parts can create a very strong TorqueFlite without the weight.

Often, shift modification kits alter the throttle pressure, causing light throttle or wide-open-throttle shifts to occur at the wrong time, no matter how the pressure linkage is set. A Throttle Valve Kit to reduce some of the sensitivity and help in high-torque demand situations (diesel trucks, for example) can correct this.

Since shift modification kits alter the shift points, it may be hard to get them to happen at the same RPM during the 1–2 and 2–3 shift. A "1–2 Split Shift Fix Spring" from A&A can make the shifts happen at the desired engine speed.

To salvage a scored and damaged front clutch retainer, they may need to be machined and polished. Unfortunately, the diameter may be reduced enough that the kickdown band does not clamp the retainer. Longer apply struts are available (.100 or .150 inch longer) or a band reliner (such as Alabama Bands Inc.) can reline a band with thicker material.

Governor Changes

Shift modification kits may create shorter and firmer shifts but may alter when the shift occurs. The pressure regulation and throttle valve springs contained in some shift modification kits alter governor pressure and, therefore, shift timing.

In fact, wide-open throttle shift points may not be controllable. To adjust the shift points, the governor springs and weights can be replaced. Early Max Wedge cars, Hemi cars, and those with 340s had higher shift speeds, but it's been a long time since factory governor parts have been offered. Fortunately, several companies offer reproduction governor kits and 1–2 shift springs to time normal and wide-open throttle shift points.

The governor controls the low-RPM, light- and wide-open-throttle, high-RPM shifts. Without the correct weight and spring combination, it is difficult to achieve 5,200 rpm and higher shifts. Depending on the shift-modification kit, some of the springs may alter shift points but not set them high enough. Complete governor packages can raise low-RPM wide-open-throttle shifts. This one provides a 6,000-rpm shift at wide open throttle with a relatively stock throttle pressure/pressure regulation spring combination.

A-727s have identical steel plates in front and rear clutch assemblies and A-904s also use identical steel plates (although smaller). Different-thickness plates (.068 to .088 inch) can be used to adjust clearance.

Available in the same size and thickness as regular steels, the Kolene-process modified steel plates for A-904s and A-727s can handle much greater loads without wear and heat-related damage.

Steel Plates

There are two types of steel plates available for A-904 and A-727s: the familiar shiny versions and ones having a flat black surface treatment. The original-shiny steel plates work for stock and many performance applications, but for higher-performance transmissions, adaptation of a surface modification treatment (created by the Kolene Corporation) produces the robust black plates. Kolene developed molten salt bath processes to clean and alter surfaces of various materials, and the salt bath nitriding (or ferritic nitrocarburizing) process imparts a stronger and more heat-resistant surface perfect for high-load, heavy-duty applications. It has been reported that this surface treatment enhances wear and fatigue resistance from 200 to 500 percent. (Some brake rotors are being offered with this treatment because of the exceptional surface characteristics it provides.)

To offer adjustment of clutch assembly clearance, both types of steel plates are offered in standard thickness (.068 inch) and a thicker version (.080 to .088 inch). As another option, Alto PowerPacks

---

The Kolene Surface Preparation

The Kolene process conditions the surface of the steel plate a few thousanths of an inch deep. The plates end up with an uneven black surface that is actually a relatively thin scale of loose black oxide.

Accelerating in low gear, a TorqueFlite's front clutch pack is not applied, but because the retainer rotates at such a relatively high RPM, the interaction between the friction discs and steel plates transfers the black oxidation to their corresponding friction discs, making them look burnt. Fortunately, there is nothing wrong with them. Before installing them, many builders remove the black oxide using glass beads or Scotch-Brite pads; I use the general-purpose green ones. ■

Although not TorqueFlite discs, these Turbo 400 BorgWarner intermediate discs have dark rings that reveal signs of slippage and heat damage.

have a thinner pressure plate to allow additional frictions and steels to be used. Some Alto steel plates have "turbulator" holes to allow better fluid transfer.

Friction Upgrades

During any shift, friction discs and steel plates and/or a band clamping around a drum/retainer actually slip before shift completion. During these short periods, heat is generated and the amount depends upon: (a) the difference in disc-plate or band-drum/retainer speed, (b) the time it takes for complete engagement, and (c) the amount of torque transferred during the shift. The heat dissipates in several directions: into friction discs or band, into steel plates or retainers, and into the fluid between and around the surfaces and parts.

Friction discs and bands are often lined with a fiber-friction material tightly bonded to a steel substrate. Research by Raybestos showed that in some applications, the temperature of the friction disc/steel plate interface can actually reach higher than 800 degrees F. Most of this heat has to be carried away by fluid to prevent permanent damage (heat discoloration spots) on steel plates and friction discs.

There are many types of heavy duty friction materials used and shift modification kits create shorter shifts to help lower the amount of heat generated. Adding more friction discs, wider bands, different friction materials, and surface treatments help absorb and/or tolerate heat without impacting the material's life. Remember, a long, slow shift under high loads generates an extreme amount of heat that will damage steel plates and carbonize the (organic) friction materials. OEM-or-better quality friction materials can always be used in stock applications, but when additional power or load is added, upgrading the type and surface area of friction material is recommended.

Friction Material Styles

The TorqueFlite has used a few styles of friction discs. The rear clutch discs are flat with a few grooves; they are .061 to .065 inch thick. Because they are applied in Forward gears only they are not a "shifting clutch." Therefore, no deep grooves or thickness is required to dissipate a lot of heat.

The front clutch discs are sometimes smooth but are usually crosshatched; they are typically .092 to

If there is any doubt as to how much heat is generated in long, slow-slipping shifts, here is the proof. Note that the middle friction still has a hint of tan color, but the other two are black and have material flaking off.

The heat from long shifts has to go somewhere and it's not only into fluid or friction material. It can damage the steel to the point that it becomes heat tinted. Clean steel turns a straw color at around 400 degrees F, but to turn it blue (shown) requires 500 to 590 degrees F.

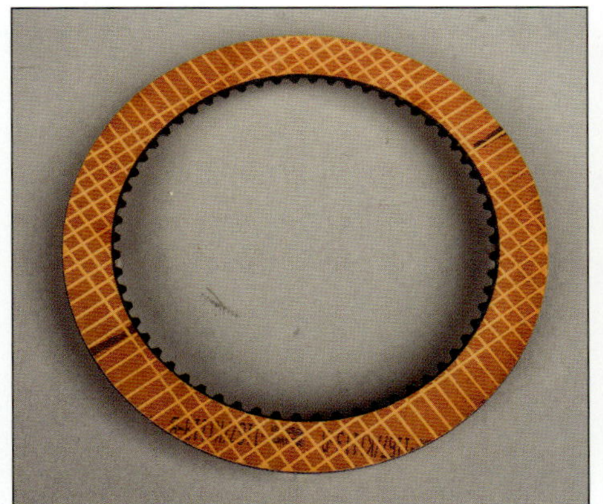

BorgWarner, like Raybestos, is an OEM supplier of friction products. These waffle-cut front clutch frictions (.096 inch thick) are found in many aftermarket overhaul sets.

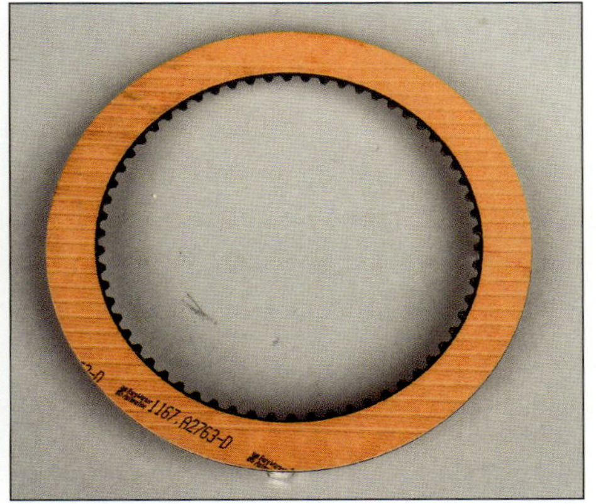

This BorgWarner front clutch friction disc (.0945 inch thick) is an OEM replacement with parallel grooves and is known as a "high-energy" disc.

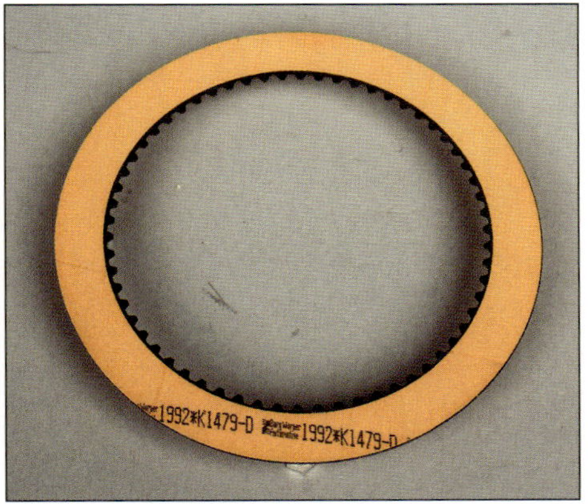

A BorgWarner tan friction plate (.0635 inch thick) is for the rear clutch assembly. These are smooth with eight thin grooves. Not being a shifting clutch, their heat load is less so they can be thinner.

.095 inch thick. Because the front clutch retainer is active during the 2–3 shift, it is a "shifting assembly," and the thicker material with grooves helps with heat dissipation. These grooves provide a path for fluid to escape the friction/steel plate interface during the shift. With available aftermarket discs that handle a higher heat load, more and thinner discs (about .061 to .065 inch) can be combined with heat-tolerant Kolene steel plates increasing the clutch surface area.

Friction Material Brands

BorgWarner, a supplier of OEM frictions for years, offers several friction materials. Some of its tan and green discs are engineered for tougher applications and identified as "high-energy."

Raybestos lists two TorqueFlite performance friction materials:

1. The red Stage 1 Performance versions are for applications requiring friction discs with higher demands than its stock "tan" or "high-energy discs" can provide. These discs have a noticeable but smooth engagement, provide increased holding capacity, and withstand higher temperatures associated with towing heavy loads. They are good for trucks, street rods, and mild street-strip applications.

2. Raybestos' Gen2 Blue Plate Specials are designed for all types of racing and feature friction material made from a blue-colored, high-strength, matrix-bonded

Raybestos, an OEM aftermarket supplier of bands and friction plates for TorqueFlites, produces Generation 2 Blue Plate Specials. These predominantly race and very high-performance frictions can handle extremely quick shifts when high heat and energy loads must be absorbed in a short time.

resin. They provide positive engagement under high-power conditions during very quick shifts when heat and energy absorption is condensed in a very short time. Gen2 Specials are power-absorbing clutches that perform with very low wear, have excellent fatigue strength, high durability, and provide quick shifts with little shock.

Alto Products Corporation has made Red Eagle High Performance clutch discs for the TorqueFlite since the mid-1990s. The Red Eagle clutch is advertised to withstand higher temperatures than other available clutches. The Red Eagle friction material controls "slip" by providing shorter lock-up time to generate less heat. They are made from softer, more resilient friction-based paper saturated with phenolic resin that is cured and saturated a second time in a silicate. The softer paper material causes less wear on the opposing steel plates, and the silicate imparts a higher heat tolerance, preventing steel plate warpage and heat damage.

The PowerPack

Alto offers PowerPack Hi-Performance and Heavy-Duty application-specific modules. They are designed with additional friction discs, a thinner pressure plate for the front, and Kolene steels to enable the engine's power to be spread over more friction and steel surface area. They tolerate higher torque and heat loads. The PowerPack's thinner Red Eagle frictions, Kolene processed steels, and the thinner Alto pressure plate has about the same thickness as four stock frictions, steels, and pressure plate. ∎

This is a standard A-727 four-friction clutch pack and pressure plate. Note the entire clutch pack assembly is approximately .935 inch thick.

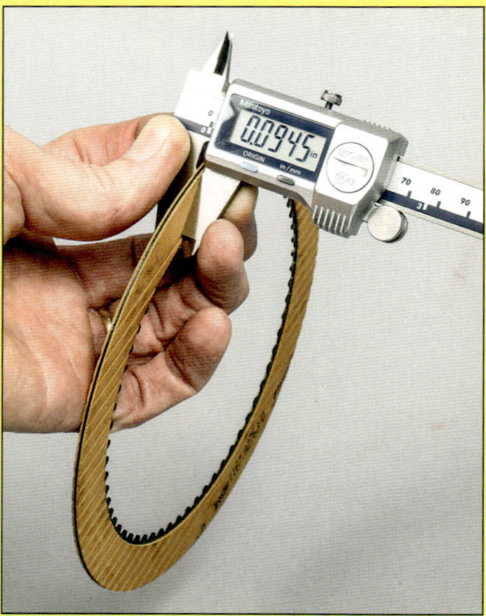

The OEM four-disc setup has stock steels and four of these .0945-inch discs.

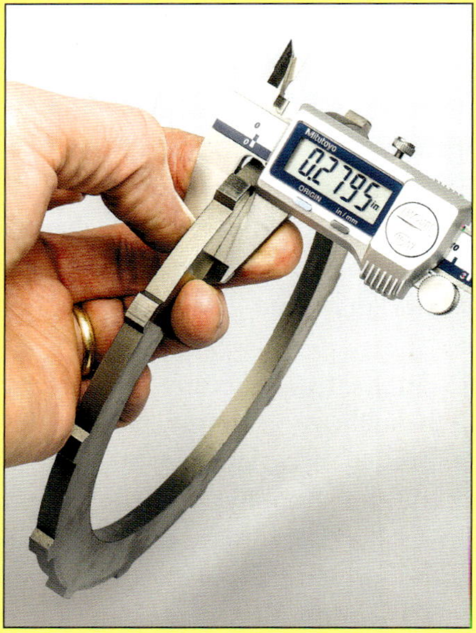

The stock clutch pack assembly has a .280-inch-thick pressure plate.

The Alto PowerPack consists of seven thin friction discs and their associated Kolene steels, along with two extra-thick steels to allow proper clearance adjustment. Note that with six friction and steels, the overall thickness of .951 inch is barely .015 inch more than the stock four-friction setup.

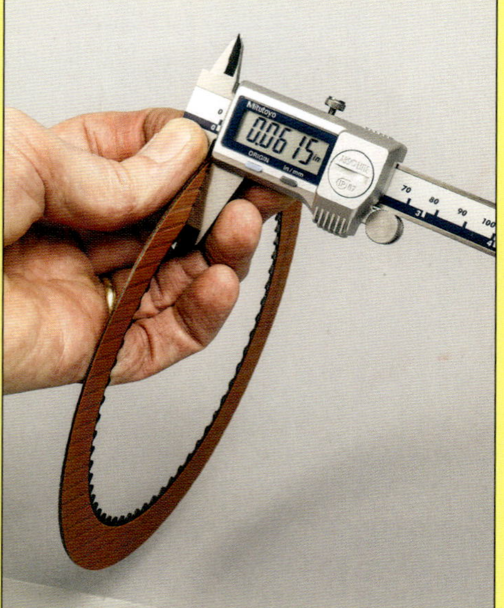

The PowerPack works well because it uses high-heat-capacity Kolene-processed steels and heat-tolerant .061-inch-thick Alto grooved frictions.

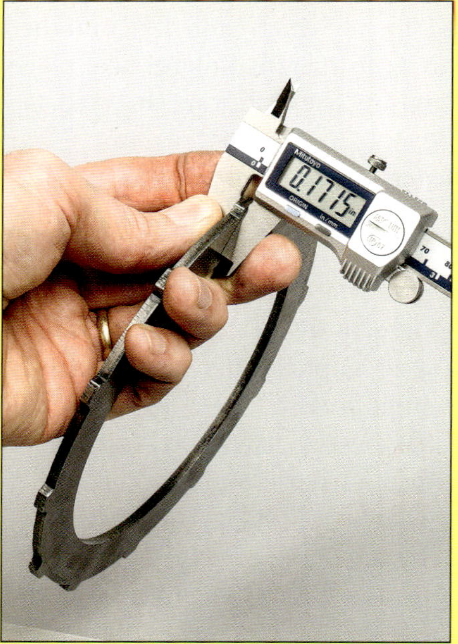

This is part of the magic in a Power-Pack; the pressure plate in the kit is only .171 inch thick.

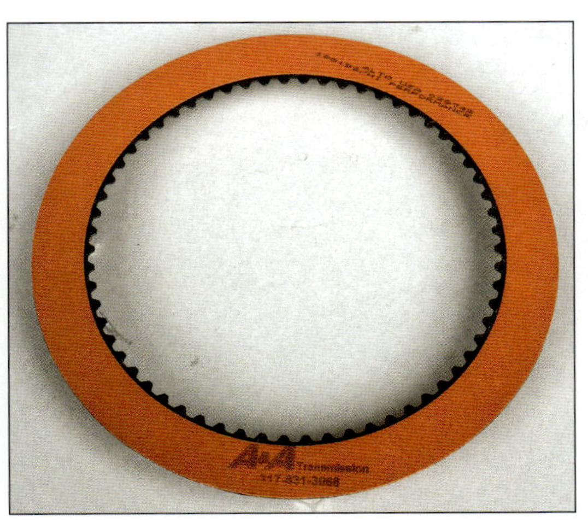

This Alto Red Eagle friction (.0625 or .0865 inch) is smooth for use in the rear or front clutch assembly.

Alto's Red Eagle friction for the front clutch assembly has parallel line grooves to let the fluid exit quicker during rapid clutch applications.

Red Eagle clutches are designed to dissipate oil with or without oil grooves and are available either way.

Bands, Levers and Struts

Like a friction disc, the band's material impacts the shift feel and timing. The low-reverse band is not as critical; it is commonly used "stock." The kickdown band, like front clutch discs, is a critical shifting band and is available with many friction materials. They can have original materials, a Kevlar-based material, or other specialty materials. There are flex bands, solid bands, and wider bands available to fit stock drums.

Various band friction materials can be applied by Alabama Bands, Inc. They have been selling bands and providing band relining services for years. In addition, they offer their own performance materials and material from various suppliers.

Different ratio kickdown servo apply levers can "tune" shifts. Lower-performance transmissions typically use lower numerical ratio levers such as 2.9 and 3.2:1 but higher-performance ones use 3.8 and above. All are available.

If a vehicle is heavy and/or has exceptional power, its kickdown band

Most TorqueFlites (1974 on) use flexible kickdown bands. These can be lined with different friction materials depending on intended use. This example uses OEM BorgWarner tan lining.

This flex band is lined with Raybestos OEM material.

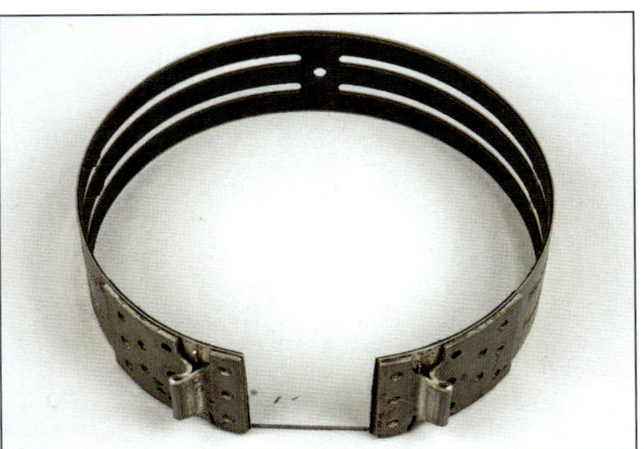

Having the same shape as stock, the Raybestos Pro-Series band is lined with a blue Kevlar fiber blend having a higher coefficient of friction and higher heat resistance. It has heat-treated anchors for heavier load applications.

Built using the older-style rigid core, this Kevlar-lined kickdown band delivers more "positive" shifts suitable for high-performance racing applications. These may be a bit aggressive in certain applications.

This rigid kickdown band features Alabama Band's friction material and is perfect for performance street, heavy-duty, and racing applications because of its outstanding heat tolerance and strong holding ability.

This band's 10-percent extra width and Alabama Band's lining on a rigid core make it one of the best for performance applications. When combined with a standard-width front clutch retainer having five or more frictions, it replicates a Hemi TorqueFlite's torque capacity without the weight.

A standard-width kickdown band (left) is compared to a wider, high-performance band.

A-727s and A-904s, depending on application, came with different ratio kickdown servo levers. From left to right are 2.9, 3.2, 3.8, 4.2, and 5.0 levers.

The 2.9, 3.8, and 4.2 use raised lines as quick identifiers.

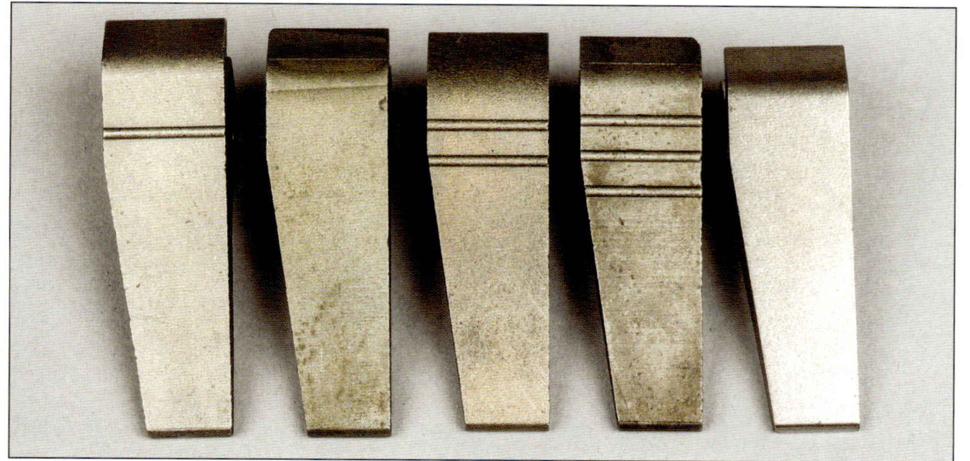

For very heavy-duty or highly loaded A-727s, reinforced and/or exceptionally heavy-duty band-apply struts ensure that the band clamps and stays on.

The A-904, like the A-727, has had four types of bands (narrow flex, rigid, 1.60-inch-wide flex, and 1.75-inch rigid). The narrow flex band (left) contrasts with an Alabama Band–lined wide rigid band. A&A developed and now provides a 1.6-inch-wide, centered-lug, rigid kickdown band for the A-904.

apply strut may be overstressed. Reinforced ones are available from several suppliers for A-904s and A-727s.

The right combination of friction material, the kickdown band apply ratio (lever), a strong enough apply strut, and the proper clearance in the front clutch assembly can provide a nice shift at light throttle, and a quick but firm wide-open-throttle shift that withstands high torque.

Complete Overhaul Sets

There are many variations of overhaul sets with rings, gaskets, seals, frictions, and steels. Master Deluxe Kits also add a filter, overrunning clutch assembly, a neutral start switch, new bushings, bands, overrunning clutch parts, and thrust washers. It's safe to stick with suppliers with known reputations because they provide great parts that are

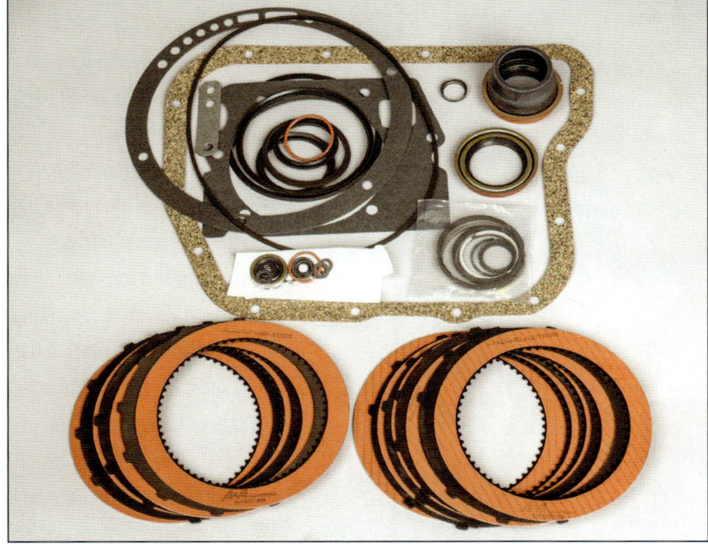

Reputable suppliers offer basic overhaul kits and deluxe kits that include everything that wears. This A-727 basic performance kit (supplied by A&A) has high-quality rings, gaskets, seals, Kolene steels, Alto frictions front and rear, and a booted rear seal.

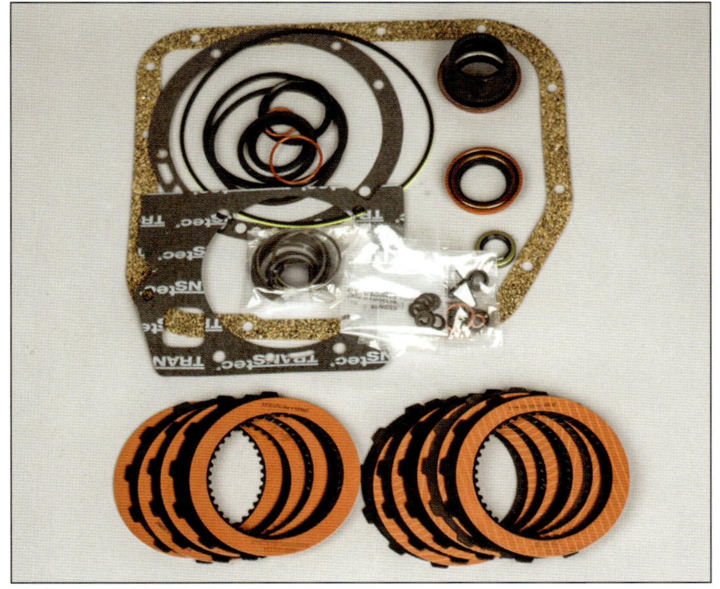

This A&A performance A-904 kit contains high-quality rings, gaskets, and seals along with Kolene steels and Alto Red Eagle frictions front and rear. It also includes a booted rear seal.

often made in the USA. If a kit from an unknown supplier is unbelievably inexpensive, be wary of the quality of the parts contained in it. For example, some lower-quality friction discs in lower cost kits that may not tolerate heavier loads and higher heat.

For high-performance and heavy-duty applications, customized kits are available with upgraded friction discs, kickdown bands, and Kolene surface-treated steel plates. Some have different sealing rings for critical areas and some come with the original booted rear seal.

Alto Products is known for its friction materials and overhaul kits. This A-727 performance kit contains front and rear Kolene steels and Red Eagle frictions (smooth for rear clutch assembly; grooved for front) in standard thicknesses.

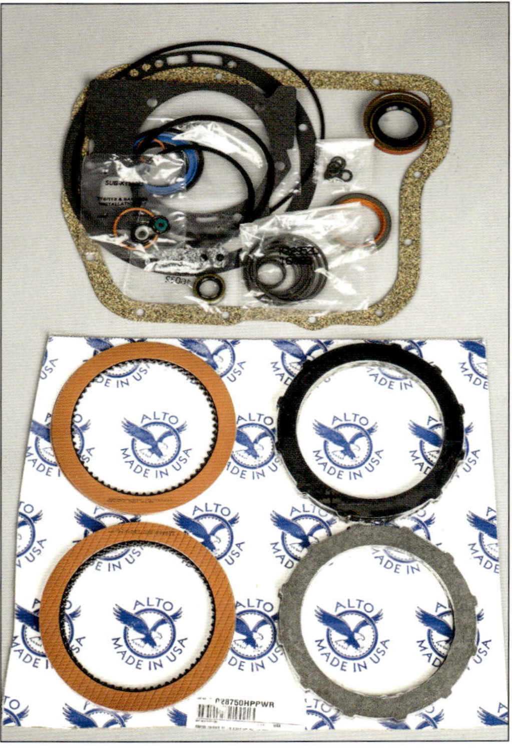

Stepping up in power holding ability, this A-727 overhaul kit includes high-quality rings, gaskets, seals, and a front PowerPack consisting of thin Kolene steels, a set of thin Red Eagle grooved frictions, and a thinner pressure plate, which all fit in a standard front clutch retainer.

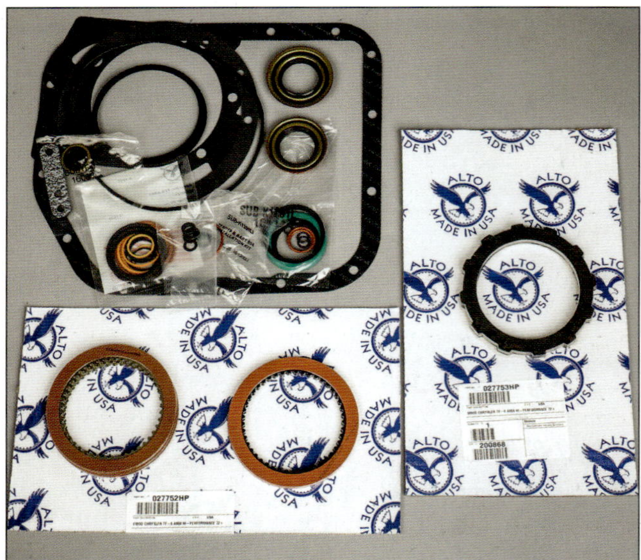

The Alto A-904 high-performance kit includes high-quality gaskets, rings, seals, and standard-thickness smooth Red Eagle frictions front and rear, and Kolene steels for front and rear clutch assemblies.

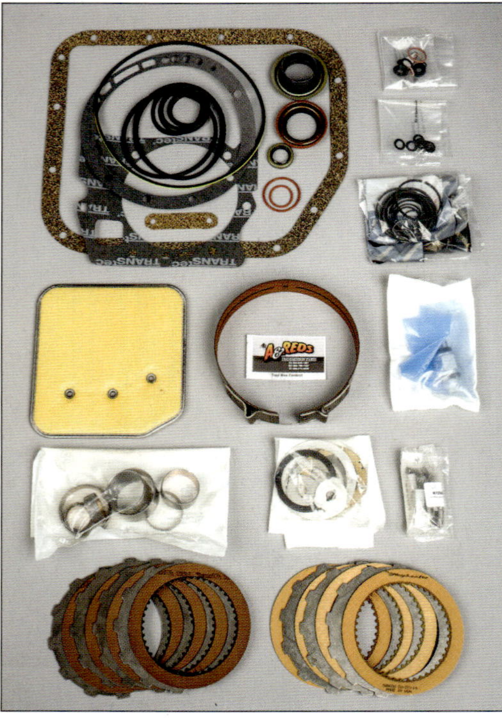

Typical of a deluxe overhaul kit, this is a complete A-904 package from A&Reds. It has high-quality gaskets, seals, rings, a Raybestos or BorgWarner flexible kickdown band and friction discs, standard steel plates, thrust washers, bushings, an overrunning clutch roller and spring kit, a neutral start switch, and a high-quality Dacron filter.

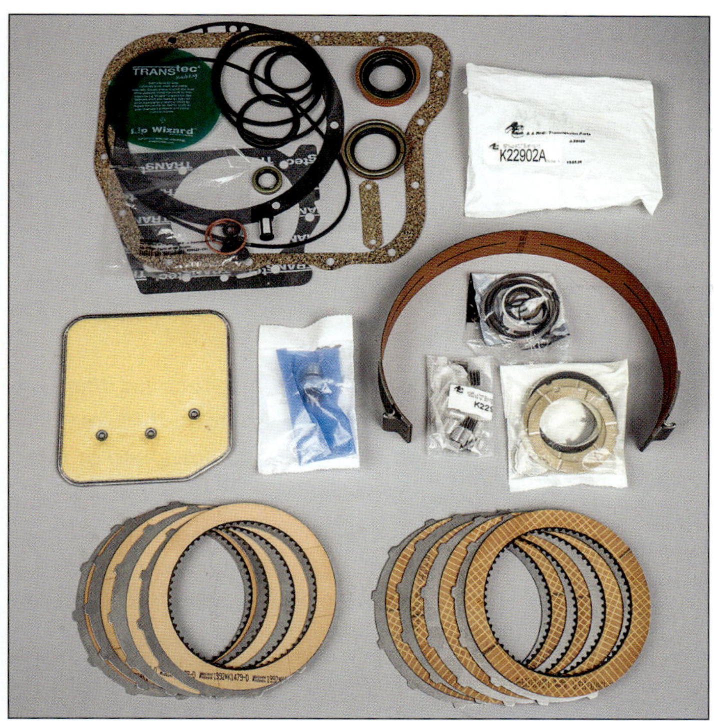

This A&Reds deluxe A-727 kit has great OEM-quality parts and provides all of the things needed for a complete major overhaul. Kits can also be customized.

This is A&A's Ultimate Sprag for the A-727, having 16 rollers and springs (stock has 12) and a cam made of higher-strength material. Its spring cage supports and stabilizes the rollers. This overrunning clutch bolts in, instead of pressing in.

Overrunning Clutch Assembly

One of the most important components in a TorqueFlite is the overrunning clutch assembly (often called "rear sprag"). When it fails (more often in the A-727), it is catastrophic to stock front clutch retainers, cases, and floorpans.

The aftermarket has created almost bulletproof versions with different designs, additional elements, and significantly stronger components. Bolt-in, high-torque versions are sold to replace original riveted A-904s and pressed-in A-727s types. Most A-727s have a 12-element overrunning clutch, but 16-element aftermarket versions withstand a significantly higher torque load.

Installation of some overrunning clutch assemblies requires drilling in areas that previously had no holes but tools are available to help.

Shafts

The TorqueFlite for the 426 Hemi, the 440 6-barrel, and some 401-ci AMC applications had a stronger input shaft and in some cases a

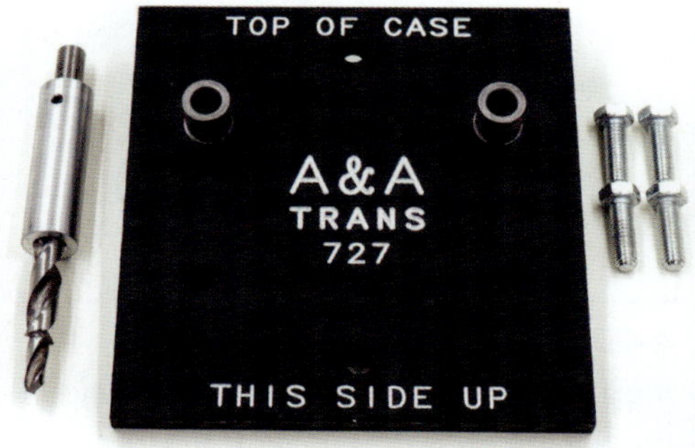

The Ultimate Sprag must be located correctly. This A&A fixture bolts to the rear of the A-727 to enable holes to be drilled accurately.

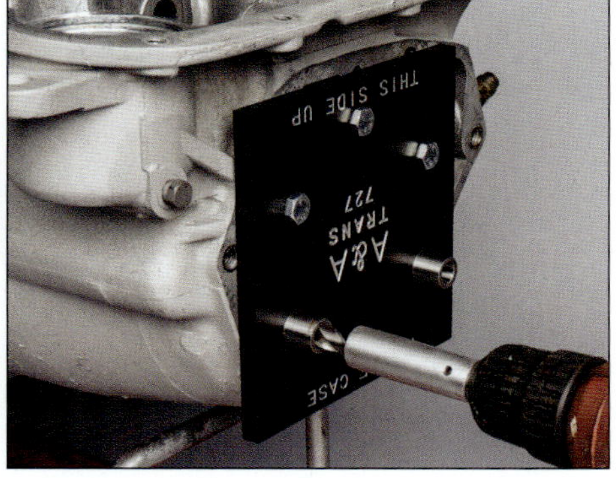

With the fixture on the case (both are upside down), the drill guides locate the two required additional holes.

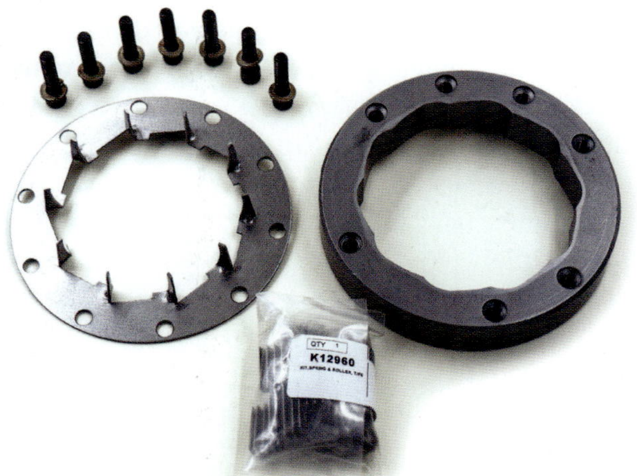

This bolt-in 10-roller version replaces the original riveted A-904 overrunning clutch assembly. Twelve-roller bolt-in units are also available for late-model A-904s.

Hemis, 440 6-barrels, and some 401 AMCs used the strong input shaft, but they are difficult to find. When a strong shaft is needed today, new ones are available to press into a standard or extended (wider) front clutch hub. This Smart-Tech High Capacity Input Shaft and Piston Kit has a one-piece shaft and extended hub made from 300M material. It also comes with a thinner front clutch apply piston and a modified .068-inch steel plate.

The usual A-727 input shaft has splines to fit the turbine in the converter. If you find one with this machined groove, it is the one used with 426 Hemis, 440 6-barrels, and some 401 AMCs. When it's new, it has a yellow spot or stripe to identify it.

Solid Mounts to Destruction

Solid engine mounts eliminate the rocking and rolling from loaded high-performance engines. Solid transmission mounts lock the transmission to the frame, but I'd never use both mounts together. Any frame twist or flex lets the engine rotate relative to the transmission-to-crossmember attaching point. And, guess what? All the twisting will break the extension housing because the twisting force is concentrated where the mount attaches to the housing. I think it is a good idea to let the transmission be somewhat cushioned. ■

stronger output shaft. Now, there are aftermarket shafts made from even stronger (300M or 4340) materials for very high loads, ultra-high horsepower, and extremely heavy-duty applications. The 300M and 4340 is very strong and tough and has great fatigue strength and good ductility.

Clutch-Apply Pistons and Spring Retainers

Front clutch-apply pistons clamp the front discs and plates together and are held back by one large or multiple return springs. The 2–3 shift timing is affected by the strength of the return springs, the friction disc/plate clearance, the type of kickdown band and servo spring assembly, and the band adjustment.

A-904 apply pistons and retainer kits are available with multiple return spring pockets (similar to the

The multi-spring kit eliminates rotation-caused spring tension relaxation. It also allows custom tuning of the return spring pressure to alter 2–3 shift timing.

As part of the Smart-Tech kit, this red anodized, high-strength, thin front clutch apply piston allows use of five standard-thickness steels and frictions or, with Alto's PowerPack, for example, even more performance steels and friction discs fit in standard A-727 front clutch retainers.

A-904 transmissions used in high-RPM shifting applications may have front clutch failures that are related to the winding direction of the stock front clutch return spring. At high RPM, the piston can be forced away from the rear of the retainer, partially applying the clutches and creating drag, heat, and damage. A multi-spring retainer (left) can prevent the problem.

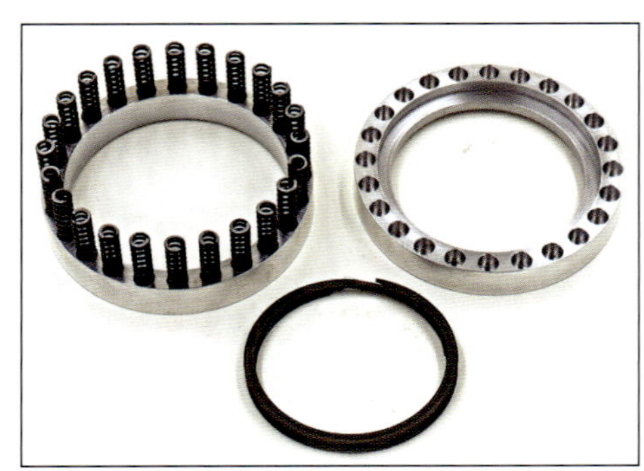

A-727) to allow tuning the 2–3 shift. Also available are thinner A-727 and A-904 apply pistons that give more room for additional steel plates and friction discs.

Servos, Springs and Accumulators

Original servos and pistons were designed for stock pressures and loads but in some cases, stock rear servo pistons may cock sideways, bind in the bore, and possibly crack. Adding additional oil pressure and volume, and higher clamping forces can make stock pistons unacceptable. Various billet-aluminum servo pistons and guides can replace stock ones and certain ones provide higher apply force. Many have internal O-rings or dual seals to minimize leakage.

Some applications require stiffer low-reverse and kickdown servo return springs to alter shift timing and eliminate overlap and bind-up.

Installing stiff springs in the kickdown servo is tough; specialty tools are available to help make it easier.

Leaky accumulator pistons/seals causes various shift feel issues; new pistons with better seals correct them. Some have an integral blocking rod and many are machined from billet aluminum.

A controlled-load servo is used from the early 1970s and beyond. This is a heavy-duty billet-aluminum servo that contains a stronger spring to release the kickdown band quicker during the 2–3 shift.

This servo increases the clamping force on the kickdown band without the need for increased line pressure. It has 16-percent more apply area because of the smaller section that fits into the modified sleeve inserted into the case. It is double-sealed to eliminate leakage around the piston and steel rod. With it, drastically enlarged orifices in the valve body separator plate are not recommended nor are front clutch clearance reductions or the use of fewer return springs.

This kickdown servo guide may look stock, but it's billet aluminum with an internal O-ring to eliminate leakage between the steel rod and guide. Minimizing leakage creates firmer and quicker band applications and releases.

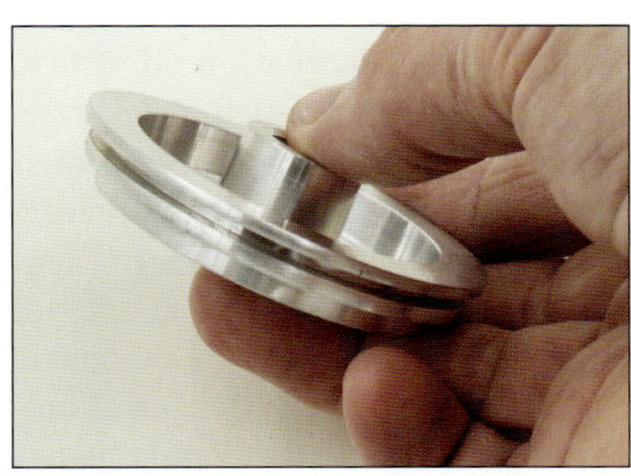

Some A-727 low-reverse servo pistons may roll inside the bore and/or crack under extreme pressure created by race-type valve bodies. This billet-aluminum piston also has an internal O-ring seal to prevent leakage.

Wear or high-pressure race applications can damage the low-reverse servo piston plug. This high-strength, O-ring-sealed steel plug can be modified for use in various TorqueFlite transmissions.

Hemi TorqueFlites used a non-controlled-load kickdown servo with a 20- or 45-pound return spring. The light-duty 20-pound version is about 4.75 inches long with .094-inch-diameter wire; the stiffer one is 3.875 inches long with .121-inch-diameter wire.

Should You Spring for a Good Time?

Common valve body modifications produce higher fluid pressure and volume to provide strong, quick application of servos and clutch packs. A manually shifted TorqueFlite sometimes depends upon application/release of both bands, but when their release is weak, there is binding and overlap during the 1–2 and 2–3 shift. Higher spring tension is a solution: here's why.

A weak low-reverse servo spring will not push the band off before the kickdown band applies. However, a stronger low-reverse servo spring and a "solid" servo piston enable quicker release of the band. A reinforced spring retainer from A&A is recommended.

With the 1–2 shift timing issue corrected, the 2–3 shift needs to be addressed: a weak kickdown servo spring causes the kickdown band to "hang on" too long during front clutch application during the 2–3 causing the transmission to be temporarily in both gears. To correct the timing, a 3.8 or 4.2 lever, combined with a stronger kickdown servo return spring provides the required quicker release. Use of the 5.0 lever is not recommended because the long stroke required for band application also creates a long release.

Adding a full complement of front clutch piston return springs helps delay the front clutch engagement just long enough so that the band release is fully accomplished before complete clutch application. With extra return springs, the front clutch plate clearance can be reduced to avoid flare or spin-up during the 2–3 shift. If it occurs, reducing kickdown band clearance addresses it.

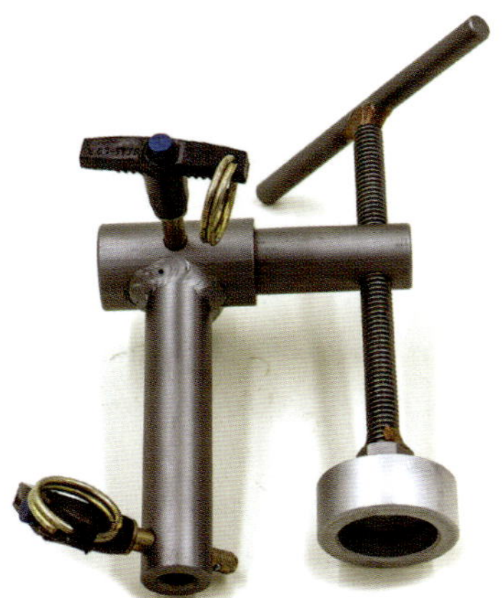

Often, shift-modification kits provide stiffer kickdown servo return springs for A-727s and A-904s that are difficult to install. This tool holds the servo piston guide during removal and installation of the snap ring.

Using a servo piston tool, the piston guide is adjusted downward, eliminating the need to fight the spring tension.

This billet-aluminum accumulator piston is red anodized with dual seals (D-shaped O-rings and scarf-cut Teflon rings) to eliminate leakage.

One of the most common modifications is blocking the accumulator piston close to the valve body transfer plate. This dual-sealed billet-aluminum example has an integral blocking rod.

Front and Rear Clutch Retainers

A-904s and A-727s have front clutch retainers that hold three, four, or five discs. Original retainers are manufactured from powdered metal and they may explode in the event of an overrunning clutch failure. A-727s, due to their retainer diameter, are more prone to damage. Higher-strength billet steel and aluminum drums can better tolerate higher speeds and the over-speed condition during overrunning clutch failure.

Aluminum drums for all locations in the TorqueFlite are usually intended for serious race applications because they are safer and offer

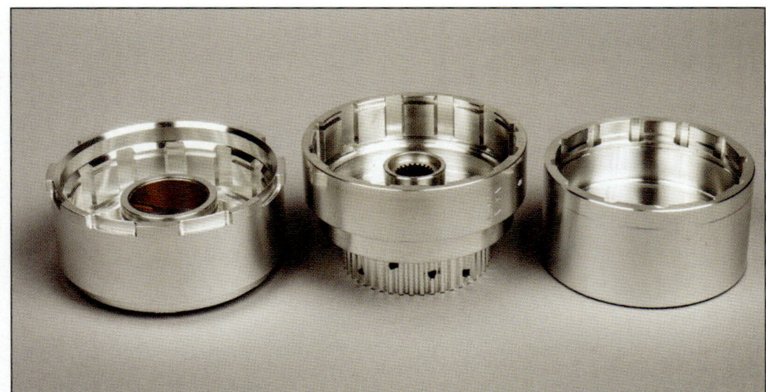

For specialized and racing applications, A&A's aluminum "drums" weigh less than half as much as their steel counterparts.

The standard and aluminum-billet rear clutch retainers look like twins; original parts fit them.

This A-904/A-999 aluminum five-friction-disc front retainer has a multi-return spring piston retainer.

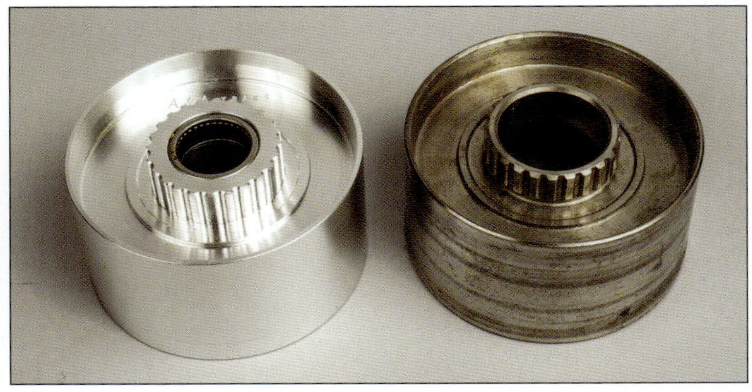

An integral roller bearing aluminum low-reverse drum (left) compares to the original A-904 low-reverse drum (right). Extra machining is required when using this drum.

Reaction shaft supports typically have iron (1962–1970) or tin-plated iron rings to seal the front clutch retainer, but other types may be required depending on the metal used for the retainer. These non-glass-filled Teflon rings work with stock and aluminum retainers to seal well while preventing wear.

Tin-nickel–plated reaction shaft support rings work with A-904 and A-727 steel retainers and aluminum retainers having steel inserts.

quicker acceleration due to their lower rotational mass. For example, three A&A A-904 aluminum drums (together) weigh around 5.3 to 5.5 pounds and the three factory drums weigh about 13 to 13.2 pounds.

Different clutch retainers require different sealing rings and they come in a variety of materials, including Teflon, cast-iron, and tin-nickel–plated cast-iron or steel.

New higher-strength billet-steel Hemi front and rear retainers are available (A&A) for those wanting "original-type" parts.

Geartrain Components

TorqueFlites have had at least four planetary styles. There were aluminum three- and four-pinion planet carriers, and (A-904) steel three- and four-pinion carriers. With harder shifts, more power to the transmission, and heavier loads to carry, some of the aluminum front carriers failed at the output shaft splines, so the spline

Different rear A-904 planetary assemblies were used: aluminum, three- and four-pinion versions (top); steel, three- and four-pinion versions (bottom).

As on the rear, front A-904 planetaries were either aluminum (top) or steel (bottom) with three- and four-pinion configurations. The large-diameter example (bottom right) is from a wide-ratio A-998 or A-999 transmission.

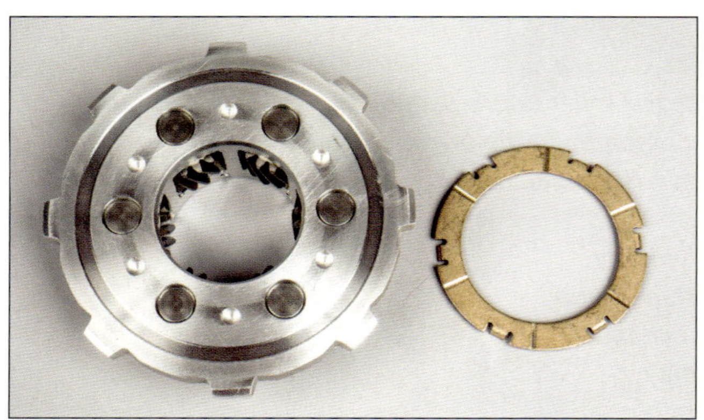

Some of the 4-speed TorqueFlite overdrive transmissions used rear planetary assemblies similar to those on the A-727. This is a six-pinion aluminum version available for heavy-duty applications.

A&A's A-727 five-pinion, extreme-duty, investment-cast steel, standard gear ratio front planetary assembly has Torrington roller bearings and a Delrin ring to keep it centered in the annulus gear.

Here you can see the internal Torrington roller bearings and the bearing race on the external surface of the annulus gear.

angle was changed. Some steel planet carriers were eventually adopted to lower costs and minimize failure.

For racing and heavy-duty usage, there are aftermarket planetary assemblies with significantly more strength and gear ratio options. You can buy complete, investment-cast steel, billet steel, or aluminum four- and five-pinion front carriers having steel hubs that spline to the output shaft.

Some rear planet aluminum carriers have five or six pinions and many contain needle roller bearing(s) to replace highly loaded thrust washers.

For the A-904 family, there are stock and a wide-ratio gear sets.

Different gear ratio planetaries are available for A-727s, and some have straight-cut gears that, although louder, minimize forward and rearward thrust on the geartrain.

For quicker acceleration, different planetary gear sets and lighter and stronger sun gear shells are available for TorqueFlites. Like aluminum drums, these reduce some of the inertia that has to be overcome during acceleration and shifts.

Thrust Washers, Shims and Bearings

It's important to keep output shaft endplay within specification to minimize wear on parts and thrust washers do this. Roller bearings can replace washers, reduce drag, and increase life. They may require machining of existing parts, or use of new ones with more clearance but anything to reduce friction lowers the power absorbed by the transmission to put more of it into acceleration.

Many in the A-904 family had this wide-ratio gear set. It has a low-ratio planetary assembly and a large-diameter sun gear inside the sun gear shell to change the ratio.

A-727s never had wide-ratio planetaries in production, but A&A makes this 2.74:1, 1.54:1, 1:1 (Low, Second, and Direct gear, respectively) version. It is a billet-steel four-pinion unit with roller bearings instead of thrust washers. Wide-ratio gear sets work well in heavier vehicles with lower-power engines or in vehicles that need quicker acceleration on the track or street.

Achieving perfect rear endplay may not be possible with only stock washers, depending on wear. These Sonnax .010-inch shims fit under existing three- or four-tabbed thrust washers for proper endplay.

TorqueFlites have been around for a long time, and with all of the aftermarket offerings and constantly evolving technology they will continue to survive.

Like lighter drums, lightened sun gear shells can reduce rotational mass and increase performance in certain applications.

For A-727s without roller bearings, this Teflon-coated rear thrust washer can reduce wear in four-pinion rear planetary applications.

TORQUEFLITE TRANSMISSION NUMBERS

See the abbreviation key at the end of this Appendix.

Chrysler Passenger Car

1960 Assembly Number	Engine	Type	Notes
2124441	170	904	
2124725	6-Cyl.	904	HD
2125075	6-Cyl.	904	

1961 Assembly Number	Engine	Type	Notes
2204985	6-Cyl.	904	Valiant
2204986	6-Cyl.	904	Plymouth
2204987	225	904	Valiant

1962 Assembly Number	Engine	Type	Notes
2204917	170	904	Valiant, Lancer
2204841	170	904	Plymouth, Dodge
2400154	6-Cyl.	904	Valiant, Lancer
2400155	6-Cyl.	904	Plymouth, Dodge
2204916	225	904	Valiant, Lancer
2400156	225	904	Valiant, Lancer
2400157	318	727	Plymouth, Dodge
2400158	361/383	727	Plymouth, Dodge
2408007	413	727	Plymouth, Dodge
1942275		727	Plymouth, Dodge, Chrysler, Imperial
2205190	413	727	Chrysler, Imperial

Dodge Truck

1962 Assembly Number	Engine	Type	Notes
2230757		727	D-P 100, 200, 300

Chrysler Passenger Car

1963 Assembly Number	Engine	Type	Notes
2408001	6-Cyl.	904	Valiant, Dart
2408002	6-Cyl.	904	HD Valiant, Dart
2408003	225	904	Plymouth, Dodge
2408004	318	727	Plymouth, Dodge
2464099	6-Cyl.	904	Police, Taxi, Plymouth, Dodge
2408005	361	727	2-BBL., Plymouth, Dodge, Chrysler, Imperial
2408006	383/413	727	4-BBL., Plymouth, Dodge, Chrysler, Imperial
2464426	426	727	300J, Plymouth, Dodge, Chrysler, Imperial

Dodge Truck

1963 Assembly Number	Engine	Type	Notes
2232312		727	Convent. & FWD Control

Chrysler Passenger Car

1964 Assembly Number	Engine	Type	Notes
2464427	6-Cyl.	904	Small Car
2466092	225	904	HD, Small Car
2466091	6-Cyl.	904	Small Car
2464979	V-8	727	Small Car
2466093	6-Cyl.	904	Med. Car
2464422	318	727	Police, Taxi
2464425	383/413/426	727	4-BBL., Med. Car, Police
2464423	318	727	Med. Car
2464425	413/426	727	Police
2464426	426	727	Max Wedge Hi-Perf. (Hemi)
2464424	361/383	727	Med. Car, Imperial
2464732	318	727	w/Console
2464734	383/413/426	727	4-BBL., w/Console, Imperial
2464735	413/426	727	Max-Wedge, Console, Imperial
2464735	413	727	300K w/Console
2466121	426	727	Hi Perf. (Hemi)

Dodge Truck

1964 Assembly Number	Engine	Type	Notes
2508475		727	To Ser. 2015000
2508481	6-Cyl.	727	To Ser. 2024206
2508482	V-8	727	Ser. 2015000 to 2024804

Chrysler Passenger Car and Truck

1965 Assembly Number	Engine	Type	Notes
2466111	318	727	Med. Car, Lrg. Car
2466112	361/383/413	727	2- or 4-BBL., Med. Car, Lrg. Car
2466113	383/426	727	4-BBL./Cam, Police
2466118	6-Cyl.	904	Med. Car, Lrg. Car
2466119	225	904	HD Valiant, Dart
2466120	170	904	Std.
2466122	273	904	Med. Car
2466123	273	904	Small Car
2466144	273	904	Hi-Perf.
2466145	273	904	Export
2466152	318	727	Police, Taxi
2466166	318	727	Std.
2466147	361/383/413	727	Std. or 4-BBL., Med. Car
2466148	383/426	727	Hi-Perf., Police
2466149	440	727	Imperial
2466164	426	727	Street Hemi
2512742	318	727	Comp. Truck
2512740	225/318	727	Comp. Truck
2512739	225/318	727	Std. Truck
2538350	273	904	Small Car
2538351	273	904	4-BBL./Cam, Small Car
2538353	273	904	Med. Car
2466134	318	727	Police, Taxi
2466135	273	727	Police, Taxi
2466151	273	727	Police, Taxi

Chrysler Passenger Car and Truck

1966 Assembly Number	Engine	Type	Notes
2538336	170	904	Small Car
2538337	225	904	All Cars
2538385	170	904	Std.
2538386	225	904	Std.
2538338	273	904	Small Car
2538339	273	904	Med. Car

2538340	273	904	Hi-Perf.
2538364	273	904	Export
2538331	225/318	727	Police, Taxi
2538333	318	727	Std.
2538334	383	727	Std.
2538335	383	727	Hi-Perf.
2538380	440	727	Std.
2538389	440	727	Hemi
2514487	440	727	Hi-Perf.
2514483	225/318	727	Comp. Truck
2514480	225/318	727	Std. Truck
2516162	383	727	Std. Truck
2516165	383	727	Comp. Truck

Chrysler Passenger Car and Truck

1967 Assembly Number	Engine	Type	Notes
2801532	170	904	Std.
2801533	225	904	Std.
2801546	225	904	Export
2801534	273	904	Small Car
2801535	273	904	Med. Car
2801536	273	904	Hi-Perf.
2283460	273	904	Export
2801539	225	727	Police, Taxi
2801540	440	727	Std.
2801541	440	727	Hi-Perf.
2801542	318	727	Std.
2801543	383	727	Std.
2801544	426	727	Street Hemi
2829401	383	727	Std. Truck
2829314	225/318	727	Std. Truck
2829404	383	727	Comp. Truck
2829317	170/225/318	727	Comp. Truck

Chrysler Passenger Car and Truck

1968 Assembly Number	Engine	Type	Notes
2892026	170	904	Std.
2892027	225	904	Std.
2892050	225	904	Export
2892028	273	904	Std.
2892029	318	904	Std.
2801539	318	727	Police, Taxi
2801540	440	727	Std.
2801541	440	727	Hi-Perf.
2801542	318	727	Std.
2801543	383	727	Std.
2801544	426	727	Street Hemi
2892031	383	727	Hi-Perf.
2892032	340	727	Hi-Perf.
2892043	225	727	Police, Taxi
2892401	383	727	Std. Truck
2892314	225/318	727	Std. Truck
2832426	170/225	727	Std. Truck
2829404	383	727	Comp. Truck
2892317	170/225/318	727	Comp. Truck
2832424	170/225	727	Comp. Truck

Chrysler Passenger Car and Truck

1969 Assembly Number	Engine	Type	Notes
2892076	170	904	Std.
2892077	225	904	Std.
2892078	225	904	Export

2892079	273	904	Std.
2892080	318	904	Std.
2892086	225	727	Police, Taxi
2892087	318	727	Police, Taxi
2892088	318	727	Std.
2892089	340	727	Hi-Perf.
2892090	383	727	Std.
2892091	383	727	Hi-Perf.
2892092	440	727	Std.
2892093	440	727	Hi-Perf.
2892094	426	727	Street Hemi
2953688	225	727	Std. Truck
2914760	318	727	Std. Truck
2953689	383	727	Std. Truck
2953738	318	727	Comp. Truck
2914754	225	727	Super Comp.
2914755	318	727	Super Comp.
2914756	383	727	Super Comp.

Chrysler Passenger Car and Truck

1970 Assembly Number	Engine	Type	Notes
3410636	225	904	Std.
3410635	225	904	Export
3410637	318	904	Std.
2892086	225	727	Police, Taxi
3410767	318	727	Police, Taxi
3410768	318	727	Std.
3410769	340	727	Hi-Perf.
3410667	383	727	Std.
3410668	383	727	Hi-Perf.
3410669	440	727	Std.
3410670	440	727	Hi-Perf.
3410671	426	727	Street Hemi
3410672	440	727	6-BBL. Hi-Perf.
3410764	426	727	Super Stock
2953688	225	727	Std. Truck
2914760	318	727	Std. Truck
2961919	383	727	Std. Truck
2953738	318	727	Comp. Truck
2914754	225	727	Super Comp.
2914755	318	727	Super Comp.
2961918	383	727	Super Comp.
2961920	413	727	Comp. Truck

Chrysler Passenger Car and Truck

1971 Assembly Number	Engine	Type	Notes
3515803	1.6/1.8	904	Simca
3515804	198/225	904	Std.
3515805	170/225	904	Export
3515806	318	904	Std.
3515809	426	727	Super-Stock
3515811	225	727	Police, Taxi
3515812	318	727	Police, Taxi
3515813	340	727	Hi-Perf.
3515814	360	727	Std.
3515815	383	727	Std.
3515816	383	727	Hi-Perf.
3515817	440	727	Std.
3515818	440	727	Hi-Perf.
3515819	426	727	Street Hemi

Assembly Number	Engine	Type	Notes
3515820	440	727	6-BBL. Hi-Perf.
3515839	340	727	Trans. AM.
3496067	225	727	Std. Truck
3496068	318	727	Std. Truck
3496069	383	727	Std. Truck
3496066	318	727	Med. Truck
3496070	413	727	Med. Truck
3496063	225	727	Short Truck
3496064	318	727	Short Truck
3496065	383	727	Short Truck
P3410417	426	727	Full Race Hemi (1966–1974)

1971 Running changes: long-bushing front clutch 727

A longer bushing was introduced into the 727 front clutch retainer, which necessitated changing the clutch retainers, the reaction shaft support, the cast iron seal rings, the rear clutch piston retainer, and the transmission assembly numbers.

Chrysler Passenger Car and Truck

1971 Assembly Number	Engine	Type	Notes
3515809	426	727	Super-Stock
3515841	225	727	Police, Taxi
3515842	318	727	Police, Taxi
3515843	340	727	Hi-Perf.
3515844	360	727	Std.
3515845	383	727	Std.
3S15846	383	727	Hi-Perf.
3515847	440	727	Std.
3515848	440	727	Hi-Perf.
3515849	426	727	Street Hemi (New Retainer)
3515850	440	727	6-BBL. Hi-Perf. (New Retainer)
3515851	340	727	Trans Am
3496937	225	727	Std. Truck
3496938	318/360	727	Std. Truck
3496939	383	727	Std. Truck
3496936	318	727	Med. Truck
3496940	413	727	Med. Truck
3496941	225	727	Short Truck
3496942	318/360	727	Short Truck
3496935	383	727	Short Truck

Chrysler Passenger Car and Truck

1972 Assembly Number	Engine	Type	Notes
3515874	1.6/1.8	904	Simca
3515871	198/225	904	Std.
3515872	170/225	904	Export
3515873	318	904	Std.
3515809	426	727	Super-Stock
3515841	225	727	Police, Taxi, Lg. Truck
3515843	340	727	Hi-Perf.
3515844	360	727	Std., Police, Taxi, 318
3515845	400	727	Std.
3515846	400	727	Hi-Perf.
3515847	440	727	Std.
3515848	440	727	Hi-Perf.
3515849	426	727	Street Hemi
3515850	440	727	6-BBL. Hi-Perf.
3496937	225	727	Std.Truck, Time Hole
3496938	318/360	727	Std. Truck
3633554	400	727	HD Truck
3496936	318/360	727	Med. Truck
3496940	413	727	Med. Truck
3496941	225	727	Short Truck
3496942	318/360	727	Short Truck
3496935	400	727	Short Truck
3633552	225	727	HD Truck
3633553	318/360	727	HD Truck
3640801	225	727	HD Truck
3640802	318/368	727	HD Truck
3640803	400	727	HD Truck
3497016	318/360	727	Std.Truck, Time Hole

American Motors

1972 AM Assembly Number	Engine	Type	Notes
3213956	232 6-Cyl.	904	
3215484	258 6-Cyl.	904	
3213957	304 V-8	904	
3213958	360 V-8	727	
3215485	401 V-8	727	
3217751	360/258/304 HD	727	
3217752	401/360 HD	727	
3217753	401 HD	727	

International Harvester

1972 IH Assembly Number	Engine	Type	Notes
423976-C91	196 4-Cyl.	727	Scout 4WD
423977-C91	258 6-Cyl.	727	Scout 4WD
423978-C91	258 6-Cyl.	727	Short
423979-C91	304/345	727	Scout 4WD
423980-C91	304/345	727	Short
423981-C91	392	727	Short
426210-C91	392	727	Med.

Chrysler Passenger Car and Truck

1973 Assembly Number	Engine	Type	Notes
3681066	1.6/1.8	904	Simca
3681061	198/225	904	Std.
3681062	225	904	Export
3681063	318	904	Std.
3681051	225	727	Police, Taxi, Truck
3681052	340	727	Hi-Perf.
3681053	360	727	Std. (Police, Taxi 318)
3681054	400	727	Std.
3681055	400	727	Hi-Perf.
3681056	440	727	Std.
3681057	440	727	Hi-Perf.
3640818	400	727	Truck, Short
3460826	318/360	727	Truck, Med.
3640083	225	727	Truck, Long Ext., Time Hole
3640810	400	727	Truck, Long HD Ext.
3640825	413/440	727	Truck, Med.
3640414	318/360	727	Truck, Long, Time Hole
3640082	225	727	Truck, Short
3640817	318/360	727	Truck, Short
3640081	225	727	Truck, Long HD Ext.
3640809	318/360	727	Truck, Long HD Ext.

American Motors

1973 Assembly Number	Engine	Type	Notes
3219184	232	904	Std.
3219185	258	904	Std.

Assembly Number	Engine	Type	Notes
3219186	304	904	Std.
3219187	360 2- & 4-BBL.	727	Std., 258, 304 HD
3219188	401 4-BBL.	727	Std. 360 HD
3219189	401 HD	727	HD

International Harvester

1973 Assembly Number	Engine	Type	Notes
423976C92	196	727	4WD
423977C92	258	727	4WD
423978C92	258	727	Short
423979C92	304/345	727	4WD
423980C92	304/345	727	Short
423981C92	392	727	Short
426210C92	392	727	Med.

Chrysler Passenger Car

1974 Assembly Number	Engine	Type	Notes
3681801	2.0	904	MM-Colt (Alum. Carrier)
3743439	2.0	904	MM-Colt (Steel Carrier)
3681847	1.6/1.8	904	Simca (Alum. Carrier)
3743419	1.6/1.8	904	Simca (Steel Carrier)
3681841	198/225	904	Std. (Alum. Carrier)
3743421	198/225	904	Std. (Steel Carrier)
3681842	225	904	Export (Alum. Carrier)
3743422	225	904	Export (Steel Carrier)
3681843	318	904	Std. (Alum. Carrier)
3743423	318	904	Std. (Steel Carrier)
3681844	360	999	HD
3681861	225	727	Police, Taxi, Truck
3681862	318/360	727	Std.
3681863	360 4-BBL.	727	Hi-Perf.
3681864	400	727	Std.
3681865	400 4-BBL.	727	Std.
3681866	440	727	Std.
3681867	440	727	Hi-Perf.

Dodge Truck

1974 Assembly Number	Engine	Type	Notes
3736627	318/360	727	Long Ext., HD
3736625	440	727	Long Ext., HD
3736139	318/360	727	Med. Ext.
3736140	225	727	Long Ext.
3720902	318/360	727	Long Ext.
3736143	440	727	Med. Ext.
3736144	225	727	Short Ext.
3736145	318/360	727	Short Ext. HD
3736146	225	727	Long Ext. HD
3736147	318/360	727	Long Ext. HD
3736148	440	727	Long Ext.
3736149	440	727	Short Ext.

American Motors

1974 Assembly Number	Engine	Type	Notes
3222774	232	904	Std. (Alum. Carrier)
3222775	258	904	Std. (Alum. Carrier)
3222776	309	904	Std. (Alum. Carrier)
3222777	360 2- & 4-BBL.	727	Std. (304 HD)
3222778	401 (360)	727	Std. (360 HD)
32Z2779	401	727	HD
3223759	232	904	Std. (Steel Carrier)
3223760	258	904	Std. (Steel carrier)
3223761	309	904	Std. (Steel carrier)

International Harvester

1974 Assembly Number	Engine	Type	Notes
451874-C91	258	727	4WD
451875-C91	258	727	Short Ext.
451876-C91	304/345	727	4WD
451877-C91	304/345	727	Short Ext.
444495-C91	304/345	727	Long HD Ext.
451878-C91	392	727	Short Ext.
451879-C91	392	727	Med. Ext.
444496-C91	392	727	Long HD Ext.
451880-C91	400	727	Short Ext.
444498-C91	400	727	Long HD Ext.

Chrysler Passenger Car

1975 Assembly Number	Engine	Type	Notes
3743495	1.6/2.0	904	MM Colt
3743419	1.6/1.8	904	Simca
3743421	198/225	904	Std.
3743476	198/225	904	Std. w/o Console Shift
3743422	225	904	Export
3743423	318	904	Std.
3743479	318	904	Std. w/A-999 Frt. Cl. Ret.
3681861	225	727	Police, Taxi, Truck
3681862	318/360	727	Std.
3681863	360 4-BBL.	727	Hi-Perf.
3681864	400	727	Std.
3681865	400 4-BBL.	727	Hi-Perf.
3681866	440	727	Std.
3681867	440	727	Hi-Perf.

Dodge Truck

1975 Assembly Number	Engine	Type	Notes
3893759	318/360	727	Long Ext., HD, Rr. Time
3893763	440	727	Long Ext., HD, Rr. Time
3893761	318/360	727	Med. Ext., Rr. Time
3893755	318/360	727	Long Ext., Rr. Time
3893765	440	727	Med. Ext., Rr. Time
3736144	225	727	Short Ext.
3736145	318/360	727	Short Ext.
3736146	225	727	Long Ext., HD
3736147	318/360	727	Long Ext., HD
3736149	440	727	Short Ext.
3820696	225	727	4WD
3820697	318/360	727	4WD
3820698	440	727	4WD

American Motors

1975 Assembly Number	Engine	Type	Notes
3223759	232	904	Std.
3223760	258	904	Std.
3223761	304	904	Std.
3222777	360	727	Std. (304 HD)
3222779	401	727	Std. (360 HD)

International Harvester

1975 Assembly Number	Engine	Type	Notes
451876	304/345	727	4WD
451877	304/345	727	Short Ext.
444495	304/345	727	Long Ext., HD
451878	392	727	Short Ext.
451879	392	727	Med. Ext.
444496	392	727	Long Ext., HD

Chrysler Passenger Car

1976 Assembly Number	Engine	Type	Notes
4028427	1.6/2.0	904	MM Colt
4028426	1.6/1.8/2.0	904	Simca
4028462	198/225	904	Std.
4028463	198/225	904	Std. w/o Console Shift
4028466	225	904	Export
4028464	318	904	Std.
4028468	318	904	Std. w/A-999 Frt. Cl. Ret.
4028465	360	999	HD
4028405	225	727	Police, Taxi, Truck
4028406	318/360	727	Std.
4028407	360 4-BBL.	727	Hi-Perf.
4028412	400	727	Std.
4028418	400 4-BBL.	727	Hi-Perf.
4028424	440	727	Std.
4028425	440	727	Hi-Perf.

Dodge Truck

1976 Assembly Number	Engine	Type	Notes
3898855	225	727	4WD
3898863	225	727	Short Ext.
3898857	318/360	727	4WD
3898864	318/360	727	Long HD Ext.
3898865	318/360	727	Long Ext., Rr. Time
3898866	318/360	727	Long Ext.
3898867	318/360	727	Short Ext.
3898868	360	727	Med. Ext., Rr. Time
3897784	400/440	727	Long Ext., Rr. Time
3897785	400/440	727	Short Ext., Rr. Time
3898856	400/440	727	4WD
3898869	400/440	727	Long HD Ext., Rr. Time
3898870	440	727	Med. Ext., Rr. Time

American Motors

1976 Assembly Number	Engine	Type	Notes
3228968	232	904	Std.
3228969	258	904	Std.
3228970	304	904	Std.
3228832	360 2-BBL.	727	Std. (258-304 HD)
3228644	360 4-BBL.	727	Std. (360 HD)
3228645	401	727	Std. (360 4-BBL. HD)

AM General Corporation

1976 Assembly Number	Engine	Type	Notes
5902621	AMG 232	727	Short Ext.

International Harvester

1976 Assembly Number	Engine	Type	Notes
472293	304/345	727	4WD

Chrysler Passenger Car

1977 Assembly Number	Engine	Type	Notes
4028426	1.6/1.8/2.0	904	Simca
4028427	1.6/2.0	904	MM-Colt
4028462	198/225	904	Std.
4028463	198/225	904	Std. w/o Console Shift
4028804	225	904	Export
4028464	318	904	Std.
4028468	318	904	Std. w/A-999 Frt. Cl. Ret.
4028465	360	999	Std.
4028405	225	727	Police, Taxi, Truck
4028406	318/360	727	Std.
4028407	360 4-BBL.	727	Hi-Perf.
4028412	400	727	Std.
4028418	400 4-BBL.	727	Hi-Perf.
4028424	440	727	Std.
4028425	440	727	Hi-Perf.
4028808	360 2-BBL.	727	Std. w/Studs

Dodge Truck

1977 Assembly Number	Engine	Type	Notes
3898855	225	727	4WD
3898863	225	727	Short Ext.
3898857	318/360	727	4WD
3898864	318/360	727	Long HD Ext.
3898865	318/360	727	Long Ext., Rr. Time
3898866	318/360	727	Long Ext.
4036786	318/360	727	Short Ext., Rr. Time
3898868	360	727	Med. Ext., Rr. Time
3899784	400/440	727	Long Ext., Rr. Time
3897785	400/440	727	Short Ext., Rr. Time
3898856	400/440	727	4WD, Rr. Time
3898869	400/440	727	Long HD Ext., Rr. Time
3898870	400	727	Med. Ext., Rr. Time

American Motors

1977 Assembly Number	Engine	Type	Notes
3228968	232	904	Std.
3230823	258	904	Std.
3228970	304	904	Std.
3228832	360 2-BBL.	727	Std. (258-304 HD)
3228644	360 4-BBL.	727	Std. (360 HD)
3228645	401	727	Std. (360 4-BBL. HD)
3229281	2.0	904	Std.

AM General Corporation

1977 Assembly Number	Engine	Type	Notes
5982294	AMG 232	727	Short Ext.

International Harvester

1977 Assembly Number	Engine	Type	Notes
472293	304/345	727	4WD

Colt/Arrow

New transmission assembly P/N 4028841 for with 2.6-liter engine.

Dodge Compact Truck

1977 Assembly Number	Engine	Type	Notes
4039535	225	727	Long Ext.
4039531	318/360	727	Short Ext., Rr. Time
4039537	318/360	727	Long Ext.
4039538	318/360	727	Long Ext., Rr. Time
4039532	400/440	727	Short Ext., Rr. Time
4039540	400/440	727	Long Ext., Rr. Time

1978 transmissions released for building out 1977 compact trucks.

Chrysler Passenger Car

1978 Assembly Number	Engine	Type	Notes
4028851	1.6/2.0	904	MMC Colt-Arrow Non-LU
4028852	2.6	904	MMC Colt-Arrow Non-LU
4028811	225	904	Std., LU, w/Console Shift
4028812	225	904	Std., LU
4028813	225	904	HD, Non-LU
4028876	225	904	Std., Non-LU
4028814	318	904	Std., LU
4028877	318	904	Std., Non-LU
4028815	360	999	Std., LU

Assembly Number	Engine	Type	Notes
4058111	360	999	Std., B-Body Wagon, C-Body LU
4028878	360	999	Std., Non-LU
4028822	318/360	727	Std., Non-LU
4028823	360	727	Hi-Perf., Non-LU, LRE Truck
4028824	400	727	Std., LU
4058114	400	727	Std., Non-LU
4028825	400	727	Hi-Perf., Non-LU
4028826	440	727	Std., Non-LU
4028827	440	727	Hi-Perf., Non-LU

Dodge Truck

1978 Assembly Number	Engine	Type	Notes
4039530	225	727	Short Ext.
4058301	225	727	Long Ext.
4039541	225	727	4WD
4039531	318/360	727	Short Ext., Rr. Time
4058302	318/360	727	Long Ext.
4058303	318/360	727	Long Ext., Rr. Time
4039536	318/360	727	Long, HD Ext.
4039542	318/360	727	4WD
4039533	360	727	Med. Ext., Rr. Time
4039532	400/440	727	Short Ext., Rr. Time
4039540	400/440	727	Long Ext., Rr. Time
4039539	400/440	727	Long HD Ext., Rr Time
4039543	400/440	727	4WD
4039534	440	727	Med. Ext., Rr Time
4089070	MMC	727	Short Ext., Diesel
4089071	MMC	727	Long Ext., Diesel
4089072	MMC	727	4WD, Diesel
4028823	360	727	Hi-Perf., Non-LU, LRE Truck

American Motors

1978 Assembly Number	Engine	Type	Notes
3232864	2.0	904	Std.
3232861	232	904	Std.
3232862	258	904	Std.
3232863	304	998	Std.
3232866	360-2	727	Std. (258-304 HD)
3232865	360-4	727	Std. (360-2 HD)

AM General

1978 Assembly Number	Engine	Type	Notes
5989527	258	727	Short Ext.

International Harvester

1978 Assembly Number	Engine	Type	Notes
492448-C91	304/345	727	Scout
492449-C91	Diesel	727	Scout

Chrysler Passenger Car

1979 Assembly Number	Engine	Type	Notes
4130175	1.4/1.6	904	MMC Colt-Arrow, Non-LU
4130174	2.0	904	MMC Colt-Arrow, Non-LU
4130176	2.6	904	MMC Colt-Arrow, Non-LU
4130411	225	904	Std., LU w/Console Shift
4130413	225	904	Std., LU
4130641	225	904	Std., Non-LU
4130432	225	904	HD, LU
4130721	225	904	HD, Non-LU
4130414	318	998	Std., LU
4130972	318	998	LU
4130415	360	999	Std., LU
4130973	360	999	LU
4130645	360	999	HD, Calif. & EFM, LU
4130971	360	999	LU
4130515	360	999	HD, LU
4130431	318/360	727	Std., LU
4130433	360	727	Hi-Perf., LU
4130705	360	727	Hi-Perf., Non-LU
4130794	1.4/1.6	904	MMC Colt, Arrow, Non-LU
4130795	2.0	904	MMC Colt, Arrow, Non-LU
4130796	2.6	904	MMC Colt, Arrow, Non-LU

Dodge Truck

1979 Assembly Number	Engine	Type	Notes
4058323	225	727	Short Ext., Non-LU
4058311	225	727	Long Ext., LU
4058327	225	727	Long Ext., Non-LU
4058333	225	727	4WD, Non-LU
4058318	318/360	727	Short Ext., Non-LU
4058314	318	727	Long Ext., LU
4058328	318/360	727	Long Ext., Non-LU
4058316	318	727	Long HD Ext., LU
4058332	318/360	727	Long HD Ext., Non-LU
4058334	318/360	727	4WD, Non-LU
4058319	360	727	HD Ext., Non-LU
4130705	360	727	Hi-Perf., Non-LU (LRE Truck)
4058324	440	727	HD Non-LU, Rr. Time
4058326	440	727	Med. Ext., Non-LU, Rr. Time
4058329	440	727	Long Ext., Non-LU, Rr. Time
4058325	Diesel	727	Short Ext., Non-LU
4058331	Diesel	727	Long Ext., Non-LU
4058335	Diesel	727	4WD, Non-LU

American Motors

1979 Assembly Number	Engine	Type	Notes
3234754	2.0	904	Std., Non-LU
3234750	232	904	Std., Non-LU
3234751	258	904	Std., Non-LU
3234752	304	998	Std., Non-LU
3236511	304	904	Std., LU

AM General

1979 Assembly Number	Engine	Type	Notes
5902848	258	727	Short Ext., Non-LU

International Harvester

1979 Assembly Number	Engine	Type	Notes
492448-C9l	304/345	727	Scout, Non-LU

Chrysler Passenger Car

1980 Assembly Number	Engine	Type	Notes
4130951	225	904	Std., LU
4130953	225	904	WR Gear Set, LU
4202095	225	904	WR Gear Set, Non-LU
4130952	225	904	HD, LU
4202094	225	904	HD, Non-LU
4130955	318	998	Std., LU
4130956	318	998	WR Gear Set, LU
4130957	360	999	Std., LU
4202084	1.6	904	MMC Colt-Arrow, Non-LU
4202085	2.0	904	MMC Colt-Arrow, Non-LU
4202086	2.6	904	MMC Colt-Arrow, Non-LU
4202064	318	727	Std., LU
4130976	360	727	Hi-Perf., LU
4058376	360	727	Hi-Perf., Non-LU

Dodge Truck

1980 Assembly Number	Engine	Type	Notes
4058376	360	727	Hi-Perf., Long Ext., Non-LU
4058371	225	727	Long Ext., LU
4058355	225	727	4WD, LU
4058351	318/360	727	Short Ext., LU
4058375	318/360	727	Short Ext., Non-LU
4058373	318/360	727	Long Ext., LU
4058374	318/360	727	Long HD Ext., LU
4058372	318/360	727	Long HD Ext., Non-LU
4058356	318/360	727	4WD, Non-LU
4058358	318/360	727	Med. Ext., Non-LU
4058336	440	727	Med. Ext., Non-LU

Marine and Industrial

1980 Assembly Number	Engine	Type	Notes
4142312	225	727	Short Ext., Non-LU
4142313	225	727	Med. Ext., Non-LU
4142321	318/360	727	Med. Ext., Non-LU
4142362	Diesel	727	Short Ext., Non-LU
4142563	Diesel	727	Med. Ext., Non-LU
4142364	Diesel	727	Long Ext., Non-LU

American Motors

1980 Assembly Number	Engine	Type	Notes
3255770	2.5	904	Std., Non-LU (4-Cyl.)
3237269	258	904	Std., LU
3236581	258	998	4WD, Non-LU
3238455	258	998	Export, Non-LU
3238767	282	998	Med., LU
3235220	258/304	999	Jeep CJ 4WD, Non-LU
5359402	258/360	727	Jeep SR 4WD, Non-LU

AM General

1980 Assembly Number	Engine	Type	Notes
5565798	2.0	904	Std., Non-LU, (4-Cyl.)

International Harvester Corp.

1980 Assembly Number	Engine	Type	Notes
492448-C91	304/343	727	Scout, 4WD, Non-LU

Other

1980 Assembly Number	Engine	Type	Notes
4193341		727	Aston Martin, Non-LU
4193390		727	Aston Martin, LU
4058377	225 Diesel	727	UK, Export, Short Ext.

Chrysler Passenger Car

1981 Assembly Number	Engine	Type	Notes
4202662	225	904	WR Gear Set, Non-LU
4202663	225	904	WR Gear Set, LU
4202664	225	904	HD, WR Gear Set, Non-LU
4058383	225	904	HD, WR Gear Set, LU
4058398	318	999	WR Gear Set, LU
4202675	318	999	WR Gear Set, LU
4202729	318	999	"Imperial", WR Gear Set, LU
4202572	1.6	904	MMC Arrow-Colt, Non-LU
4202573	2.0	904	MMC Arrow-Colt, Non-LU
4202574	2.6	904	MMG Arrow-Colt, Non-LU
4202571	318	727	Hi-Perf., LU
4058393	360	727	Export, Non-LU

Dodge Truck

1981 Assembly Number	Engine	Type	Notes
4058383	225	904	WR Gear Set, LU
4058398	318	999	WR Gear Set, LU
4058384	225	727	Long Ext., LU
4058385	225	727	4WD, LU
4058388	318/360	727	Short Ext., LU
4058389	318/360	727	Short Ext., Non-LU
4058392	318/360	727	Long Ext., LU
4058394	318/360	727	HD Long Ext., LU
4058395	318/360	727	HD Long Ext., Non-LU
4058396	318/360	727	4WD, LU
4058397	318/360	727	4WD, Non-LU

Marine and Industrial

1981 Assembly Number	Engine	Type	Notes
4142312	225	727	Short Ext., Non-LU
4142313	225	727	Med. Ext., Non-LU
4142321	318/360	727	Med. Ext., Non-LU
4142362	Diesel	727	Short Ext., Non-LU
4142363	Diesel	727	Med. Ext., Non-LU
4142364	Diesel	727	Long Ext., Non-LU

American Motors

1981 Assembly Number	Engine	Type	Notes
3238777	2.5	904	WR Gear Set, Non-LU
3238772	2.5	904	4WD, Non-LU
3238778	2.5	904	CJ7 4WD, WR Gear, Non-LU
3240107	258	904	Std., LU
3238771	258	998	4WD, Eagle, LU
3240296	258/282	998	VAM, LU
3238773	258/304	999	CJ7 4WD, LU (2.73 Axle)
3239816	258/304	999	CJ7 4WD, LU (3.31 Axle)
3240219	258	999	CJ7 4WD, Export, Non-LU
3238774	360	727	SR Jeep 4WD, LU (2.73 Axle)
3239817	258/360	727	SR Jeep 4WD, LU (3.31/3.73)
3240255	258/360	727	SR Jeep 4WD, Export, Non-LU

Other

1981 Assembly Number	Engine	Type	Notes
4025739		727	Aston-Martin, LU
4058387	225 Diesel	727	UK Export, Short Ext., Non LU

Chrysler Passenger Car

1982 Assembly Number	Engine	Type	Notes
4202662	225	904	Non LU
4202663	225	904	LU
4202664	225	904	HD, Non-LU
4058383	225	904	HD, LU, Also in Truck
4058398	318	999	LU, Also in Truck
4202675	318	999	LU
4202729	318	999	Imperial, LU
4269051	1.6	904	MMC, Non-LU
4269052	2.0	904	MMC, Non-LU
4269053	2.6	904	MMC, Non-LU
4202571	318	727	Hi-Perf., LU
4058393	360	727	Export, Non-LU

Dodge Truck

1982 Assembly Number	Engine	Type	Notes
4058383	225	904	LU
4058398	318	999	LU
4058384	225	727	Long Ext., LU
4058385	225	727	4WD, LU
4058388	318/360	727	Short Ext., LU
4058389	318/360	727	Short Ext., Non-LU

Assembly Number	Engine	Type	Notes
4058394	318/360	727	HD Long Ext., LU
4058395	318/360	727	HD Long Ext., Non-LU
4058396	318/360	727	4WD, LU
4058397	318/360	727	4WD, Non-LU

Marine and Industrial

1982 Assembly Number	Engine	Type	Notes
4142312	225	727	Short Ext., Non-LU
4142313	225	727	Med. Ext., Non-LU
4142321	318/360	727	Med. Ext., Non-LU
4142362	Diesel	727	Short Ext., Non-LU
4142363	Diesel	727	Med. Ext., Non-LU
4142364	Diesel	727	Long Ext., Non-LU

American Motors

1982 Assembly Number	Engine	Type	Notes
3238772	2.5	904	4WD, Non-LU
3238777	2.5	904	Non-LU
5567640	2.5	904	AM Gen Post Office Truck
3240229	258	904	LU
3241099	258	998	4WD Eagle, LU
3241100	6-Cyl. & V-8	998	VAM, Non-LU
3240231	258	999	CJ7 4WD, LU
3240231	258	999	SR Jeep 4WD, LU (2.73 axle)
3241098	258	999	CJ7 4WD, Export, Non-LU
3238774	360	727	SR Jeep, 4WD, LU, (2.73 axle)
3239817	258/360	727	SR Jeep, 4WD, LU, (3.31/3.73)
3240255	258/360	727	SR Jeep, 4WD, Export, Non-LU

Other

1982 Assembly Number	Engine	Type	Notes
4058387	225 Diesel	727	UK Export, Short, Non-LU
4025739		727	Aston Martin, LU
4202717		727	Roadmaster Rail, Med. Non-LU
3836023		727	Land Rover 4WD, Non-LU
3836024	Diesel	727	IVECO, Med. Ext., Non-LU

Chrysler Passenger Car

1983 Assembly Number	Engine	Type	Notes
4202662	225	904	Non-LU
4202663	225	904	LU
4202664	225	904	HD, Non-LU
4058398	318	999	LU, Also in Truck
4295887	318	999	LU
4202729	318	999	Imperial, LU
4269932	1.6	904	MMC, Non-LU
4269933	2.0	904	MMC, Non-LU
4269934	2.6	904	MMC, Non-LU
4202898	2.6	904	MMC, 4WD, Non-LU
4202571	318	727	Hi-Perf., LU

Dodge Truck

1983 Assembly Number	Engine	Type	Notes
4058383	225	904	LU
4058398	318	999	LU
4058384	225	727	Long Ext., LU
4058389	318/360	727	Short Ext., Non-LU
4058395	318/360	727	HD Long Ext., Non-LU
4058397	318/360	727	4WD, Non-LU
4295941	225	727	Long Ext., Non-LU

Marine and Industrial

1983 Assembly Number	Engine	Type	Notes
4142312	225	727	Short Ext., Non-LU

Assembly Number	Engine	Type	Notes
4142313	225	727	Med. Ext., Non-LU
4142321	318/360	727	Med. Ext., Non-LU
4142362	Diesel	727	Short Ext., Non-LU
4142363	Diesel	727	Med. Ext., Non-LU
4142364	Diesel	727	Long Ext., Non-LU

American Motors

1983 Assembly Number	Engine	Type	Notes
8933000864	2.5	904	4WD, Non-LU
8933000863	2.5	904	Non-LU
5903162	2.5	904	AM Gen. Post Office Truck
3240229	258	904	LU
8933000916	258	998	4WD Eagle, LU
3241100	6-Cyl. & V-8	998	VAM, Non-LU
8933000913	258	999	CJ7-8 and SJ, (2.73) 4WD, LU
8933000917	258	999	CJ 4WD, Export, Non-LU
8933000915	360	727	SJ 4WD, LU (2.73 Axle)
8933000914	258/360	727	SJ 4WD, LU (3.31/3.73 axle)
8933000918	358/360	727	SJ 4WD, Export, Non-LU

Other

1983 Assembly Number	Engine	Type	Notes
4058387	225/Diesel	727	UK Exp., Short, Non-LU
4025739		727	Aston Martin, LU
4202717		727	Roadmaster Rail, Non-LU
3836023		727	Land Rover, 4WD, Non-LU
3836024	Diesel	727	IVECO-Med. Ext., Non-LU
3836040		727	Maserati, LU

Chrysler Passenger Car

1984 Assembly Number	Engine	Type	Notes
4058398	318	999	LU, Also in Truck
4295887	318	999	LU
4329436	318	999	LU, HD Fleet
4329631	318	999	Non-LU, High Altitude
4269932	1.6	904	MMC, Non-LU
4269933	2.0	904	MMC, Non-LU
4269934	2.6	904	MMC, Non-LU
4202898	2.6	904	MMC, 4WD, Non-LU

Dodge Truck

1984 Assembly Number	Engine	Type	Notes
4058383	225	904	LU
4058398	318	999	LU
4058384	225	727	LU, Long Ext.
4295941	225	727	Non-LU, Long Ext.
4329438	318	727	Non-LU, HD, Long Ext.
4329458	318	727	Non-LU, 4WD
4329482	318/360	727	Non-LU, Short Ext.
4329468	360	727	Non-LU, HD Long Ext.
4329488	360	727	Non-LU, 4WD

Marine and Industrial

1984 Assembly Number	Engine	Type	Notes
4142312	225	727	Non-LU, Short Ext.
4142313	225	727	Non-LU, Med. Ext.
4142321	318/360	727	Non-LU, Med. Ext.
4142362	Diesel	727	Non-LU, Short Ext.
4142363	Diesel	727	Non-LU, Med. Ext.
4142364	Diesel	727	Non-LU, Long Ext.

American Motors

1984 Assembly Number	Engine	Type	Notes
8933001416	2.46	904	LU, SX/4, 4WD

Assembly Number	Engine	Type	Notes
8953001141	2.46/2.8	904	LU, "XJ", 4WD
8933000916	258	998	LU, Eagle 4WD
3241100	258/282	998	Non-LU, VAM
8933000913	258	999	LU, CJ7-8, 4WD
8933000917	158	999	Non-LU, CJ, Export 4WD
8933000914	258	727	LU, SJ, 4WD
8933000918	258/360	727	Non-LU, SJ & Export, 4WD

AM General

1984 Assembly Number	Engine	Type	Notes
5995621	2.46	904	Non-LU, Post Office Truck

Other

1984 Assembly Number	Engine	Type	Notes
4058387	225/Diesel	Diesel 727	Non-LU, UK Export, Short
4025739		727	LU, Aston Martin
4202717		727	Non-LU, Roadmaster Med
3836023		727	Non-LU, Land Rover 4WD
3836024		727	Non-LU, IVECO-Short
3836040		727	LU, Maserati

Chrysler Passenger Car

1985 Assembly Number	Engine	Type	Notes
4058398	318	999	LU, Also used in Truck
4295887	318	999	LU
4329436	318	999	LU, Fleet
4269932	1.6	904	MMC, Non-LU
4269933	2.0	904	MMC, Non-LU
4269934	2.6	904	MMC, Non-LU
4202898	2.6	904	MMC, 4WD, Non-LU

Dodge Truck

1985 Assembly Number	Engine	Type	Notes
4958383	225	904	LU
4058398	318	999	LU
4058384	225	727	LU, Long Ext.
4295941	225	727	Non-LU, Long Ext.
4329438	318	727	Non-LU, HD, Long Ext.
4329458	318	727	Non-LU, 4WD
4329482	318/360	727	Non-LU, Short Ext.
4329468	318/360	727	Non-LU, HD Long Ext.
4329488	360	727	Non-LU, 4WD

Marine and Industrial

1985 Assembly Number	Engine	Type	Notes
4142312	225	727	Non-LU, Short Ext.
4142313	225	727	Non-LU, Med. Ext.
4142321	318/360	727	Non-LU, Med. Ext.
4142362	Diesel	727	Non-LU, Short Ext.
4142363	Diesel	727	Non-LU, Med. Ext.
4142364	Diesel	727	Non-LU, Long Ext.

American Motors

1985 Assembly Number	Engine	Type	Notes
8953001334	2.1/Diesel	904	Non-LU, 4WD
8953001141	2.46/2.8	904	LU, XJ, 4WD
8933000916	258	998	LU, Eagle 4WD
8933002366	258	998	Non-LU, Eagle 4WD
8933000913	258	999	LU, CJ, 4WD
8933000917	258	999	Non-LU, Jeep 4WD
8953001836	258/360	727	Non-LU, Jeep 4WD
8993000026	Diesel	727	Non-LU, AM Inter., 4WD

AM General

1985 Assembly Number	Engine	Type	Notes
5995621	2.46	904	Non-LU, 1/4-Ton Postal
5995949	258	999	Non-LU, 1/2-Ton Postal

Other

1985 Assembly Number	Engine	Type	Notes
4205739		727	Aston Martin, LU
3836023		727	Land Rover, Non-LU
3836024	Diesel	727	Iveco, Non-LU
3836040		727	Maserati, LU
3836054	318	727	Stonefield, Non-LU
3836061	Diesel	727	Matbro, Non-LU
3836064	Diesel	727	Boss Motor, Non-LU

Chrysler Passenger Car

1986 Assembly Number	Engine	Type	Notes
4348703	318	999	LU
4412001	318	999	LU
4412002	318	999	LU, Fleet
4348792	1.6	904	MMC, Non-LU
4348793	2.0	904	MMC, Non-LU
4348797	2.6	904	MMC, Non-LU

Dodge Truck

1986 Assembly Number	Engine	Type	Notes
4348798	2.6	904	MMC, 4WD, Non-LU
4329633	225	904	Part Throttle Unlock
4348782	225	904	Non-LU
4348715	318	999	Part Throttle Unlock
4329632	318	999	Part Throttle UL, HD Ext.
4348718	318/360	727	Non-LU, Short Ext.
4377823	318	727	Non-LU, Long Ext.
4348768	318	727	Non-LU, HD Long Ext.
4348783	318	727	Non-LU, 4WD
4348785	318/360	727	Non-LU, HD Long Ext.
4377824	318/360	727	Non-LU, HD Long Ext.
4348786	360	727	Non-LU, 4WD

Marine and Industrial

1986 Assembly Number	Engine	Type	Notes
4142312	225	727	Non-LU, Short Ext.
4142313	225	727	Non-LU, Med. Ext.
4142321	318/360	727	Non-LU, Med. Ext.
4142362	Diesel	727	Non-LU, Short Ext.
4142363	Diesel	727	Non-LU, Med. Ext.
4142364	Diesel	727	Non-LU, Long Ext.
4142901	258/360 AMC	727	Non-LU, Med. Ext.

American Motors

1986 Assembly Number	Engine	Type	Notes
8953001672	2.46/2.8	904	4x2, XJ, LU
8953002097	2.46/2.8	904	4WD, XJ, LU
8933002366	258	998	4WD, Eagle, Non-LU
8933000917	258	999	4WD, Jeep, Non-LU
8953003074	4.2 L	999	4WD, YJ, Non-LU
8953001836	4.2/5.9	727	4WD, SJ, Non-LU
8993000026	Diesel	727	AM International, Non-LU

Other

1986 Assembly Number	Engine	Type	Notes
4025739		727	Aston Martin, LU

4058387		727	Karrier Motors, Non-LU
4348990	Diesel	727	MMC Med., Non-LU
3836023		727	Land Rover, Non-LU
3836024	Diesel	727	Iveco, Short, Non-LU
3836040		727	Maserati, LU
3836054	318	727	Stonefield, Non-LU
3836061	Diesel	727	Matbro, Short, Non-LU
3836063	Diesel	727	Sirmac, Short, Non-LU
3836064	Diesel	727	Boss Motor, Non-LU

Chrysler Passenger Car

1987 Assembly Number	Engine	Type	Notes
4348703	318	999	LU
4412001	318	999	LU
4412560	318	727	LU, Fleet

Dodge Truck

1987 Assembly Number	Engine	Type	Notes
4329633	225	904	PTU
4348782	225	904	Non-LU
4431412	3.9	998	PTU, 4X2
4329628	3.9	998	PTU, 4WD
4329632	318	999	PTU, HD Ext
4348715	318	999	PTU
4348783	318	727	4WD, Non-LU
4348786	360	727	4WD, Non-LU
4377823	318	727	Long, Non-LU
4377824	318/360	727	Long, Non-LU
4412003	318	727	HD Long, Non-LU
4412004	318/360	727	HD Long, Non-LU
4412517	318/360	727	Short, Non-LU

Marine and Industrial

1987 Assembly Number	Engine	Type	Notes
4417114	225	727	Med., Non-LU
4417115	318/360	727	Med., Non-LU
4417116	258/360 (AMC)	727	Med., Non-LU

American Motors

1987 Assembly Number	Engine	Type	Notes
8933004126	258	998	4WD, Eagle, Non-LU
8953005018	4.2	999	4WD, YJ, Non-LU
8953005019	258/360	727	4WD, SJ, Non-LU

Other

1987 Assembly Number	Engine	Type	Notes
3836105		727	Maserati, LU
3836090		727	Renault Truck, Non-LU
3836091	Diesel	727	Iveco Short, Non-LU
3836092	Diesel	727	Matbro Short, Non-LU
3836093	Diesel	727	Sirmac Short, Non-LU
3836094	Diesel	727	Boss Motor, Non-LU
3836095	Diesel	727	USA Canter, Non-LU
3836103	Diesel	727	MMC Canter, Non-LU
3836101	1.6	904	MMC, Non-LU

Chrysler Passenger Car

1988 Assembly Number	Engine	Type	Notes
4471529	318	999	LU (2.94 axle)
4471533	318	999	LU (2.94 axle)
4431572	318	999	LU (2.24 axle)
4446365	318	999	LU (2.24 axle)
4505207	318	999	LU (2.24 axle)

4471537	318	999	LU (2.76 axle)
4471540	318	999	LU (2.76 axle)
4471531	318	999	LU (2.94 axle)
4471535	318	999	LU (2.94 axle)
4505171	318	999	LU (2.94 axle)
4431573	318	999	LU, Police 4-BBL., (2.94 axle)
4446368	318	999	LU, Police 4-BBL., (2.94 axle)
4431574	318	727	LU, Police 2-BBL., (2.94 axle)
4505209	318	727	LU, Police 2-BBL., (2.24 axle)

Chrysler Passenger Car

1989 Assembly Number	Engine	Type	Notes
4471533	5.2	999	LU, 2.94 axle)
4505207	5.2	999	LS, LU (2.24 axle)
4505171	5.2	999	LU (2.94 axle)
4446368	5.2	999	LU Police 4-BBL., (2.94 axle)
4505209	5.2	727	LU Police 2-BBL., (2.24 axle)

Dodge Truck

1988-1989 Assembly Number	Engine	Type	Notes
4471406	3.9	998	HS, ELU, to 11-87
4431425	3.9	998	HS, ELU, aft 11-87
4446367	3.9	998	HS, ELU, to 11-87
4431424	3.9	998	HS, ELU, aft 11-87
4329628	3.9	998	HS, ELU, Long Ext.
4431554	5.2	999	LS, ELU, Long Ext., to 11-87
4431428	5.2	999	LS, ELU, Long Ext., aft 11-87
4431554	5.2	999	LS, ELU, Long Ext., to 11-87
4431427	5.2	999	LS, ELU, Long Ext., aft 11-87
4431563	5.2	727	LS, LU, Long Ext.
4431552	5.2/5.9	727	Lo-Hi Stall, Non-LU, Long Ext.
4412003	5.2	727	LS, Non-LU, Long Ext.
4412004	5.9	727	HS, Non-LU, Long Ext.
4471403	5.2, 5.9	727	Lo-Hi Stall, Non-LU, 4WD
4431561	5.2	727	1988, LS, Non-LU, 4WD
4471464	3.9/5.2	727	1989, Non-LU, 4WD
4431562	5.2/5.9	727	Lo-Hi Stall, Non-LU, 4WD
4428441	5.9	727	Cummins Diesel, Non-LU
4428442	5.9	727	Cummins Diesel, Non-LU

Dodge Truck

1990–1993 Assembly Number	Engine	Type	Notes
4505159	3.9	998	HS, ELU, HD Ext., 1992
53009260	3.9	998	HS, ELU, aft 2-91
53008144	3.9	998	HS, ELU, HD Ext., 1992
52117688	3.9	998	HS, ELU, HD Ext., 1993
4505161	5.2	999	LS, ELU, HD Ext., to 5-91
53009262	5.2	999	LS, ELU, HD Ext., aft 5-91
4505162	5.2	999	LS, ELU, Std. Ext., to 3-91
53009264	5.2	999	LS, ELU, Std. Ext., aft 3-91
52118232	5.2	727	Non-LU, 1992
52117696	5.2	727	Non-LU, 1993
4531012	5.9	727	LS, Non-LU, to 2-91
53007777	5.9	727	LS, Non-LU, aft 2-91
52117522	5.9	727	LS, Non-LU, 1992
52117693	5.9	727	LS, Non-LU, 1993
53008538	5.9	727	Cummins, Non-LU
53008539	5.9	727	Cummins, Non-LU

Dodge Truck			
1994–1996 Assembly Number	**Engine**	**Type**	**Notes**
52118017	3.9	32RH	HS, LU, to 7-93, Rr. Time
52118331	5.2	36RH	Non-LU, to 7-93
52118414	3.9	32RH	
52119176		36RH	Aft. 7-93

Dodge Truck			
1997–1999 Assembly Number	**Engine**	**Type**	**Notes**
52119540		36AH	AB-Van

Dodge Truck			
2000–2003 Assembly Number	**Engine**	**Type**	**Notes**
52119832		32RH	AB-Van 2000
52119750		32RH	AB-Van 2001
52119750		32RH	AB-Van 2002
52119750		32RH	AB-Van 2003

Jeep			
1987–1990 Assembly Number	**Engine**	**Type**	**Notes**
53003074		999	4WD, YJ, LU
53005018		999	4WD, YJ, LU
83505558		999	4WD, YJ, LU
4531005		999	4x2, YJ, LU
53005019		727	4WD, SJ, LU
4531025		727	4WD, SJ, LU

Jeep			
1991–1993 Assembly Number	**Engine**	**Type**	**Notes**
53006925		999	4WD, YJ, LU
53009265		999	4WD, YJ, LU

53008145		32RH (999)	4WD, YJ, LU
52117697		32RH (999)	4x2, YJ, Non-LU
4531025		727	4WD, SJ, LU
53007778		727	4WD, SJ, LU

Jeep			
1994–1996 Assembly Number	**Engine**	**Type**	**Notes**
52119026	2.5	30RH	4WD, XJ, LV
52118412	2.5	30RH	4WD, XJ, LV
52118025	2.5	30RH	4WD, XJ, LV
52119107	2.5	30RH	4x2, YJ, XJ, LV
52119168	2.5	30RH	4WD, YJ, XJ, LV
52116413	2.5	30RH	4WD, XJ, LV
52118024	4.0	31RH	4WD, XJ

Jeep			
1997–1999 Assembly Number	**Engine**	**Type**	**Notes**
52119528	2.5	30RH	4WD, TJ, LV
52119811	2.5	30RH	4WD, TJ, LV
52119520	2.5	30RH	4WD, TJ, LV
52119529	4.0	32RH	4WD, TJ, LV
52119525	4.0	32RH	4WD, TJ, LV
52119813	4.0	32RH	4WD, TJ, LV
52119801	2.5	30RH	4WD, XJ, LV
52119810	2.5	30RH	4WD, XJ, LV

Jeep			
2000–2002 Assembly Number	**Engine**	**Type**	**Notes**
52119830	2.5	30RH	4WD, XJ, LV
52119831	2.5	30RH	4WD, TJ, LV
52119833	4.0	32RH	4WD, TJ, LV

Abbreviation Key	
4x2	Two-Wheel Drive
6-BBL.	6-Barrel Induction
Al. Carrier	Aluminum Planetary Carrier
Calif. & EFM	California and Federal Emissions
Comp. Truck	Compact Truck
Convent.	Conventional
D-P	Dodge-Plymouth
ELU	Electronic Lock-Up Converter
Frt. Cl. Ret.	Front Clutch Retainer
HD	Heavy Duty
Hi-Perf.	High-Performance
HS	High-Stall Converter
Long Ext.	Long Extension
LRE Truck	Little Red Express Truck
LS	Low-Stall Converter
LU	Lock-Up Converter
Max Perf.	Maximum Performance
Med. Car	Medium Car
Med. Ext.	Medium Extension
Med. Truck	Medium Truck
MM or MMC	Mitsubishi Motors
NLU	Non-Lock-Up Converter
PTU	Part-Throttle Unlock
Rr. Time	Rear Timing Hole in Transmission
Std.	Standard
Steel Carrier	Steel Planetary Carrier
Time Hole	Timing Hole in Transmission
To Ser.	To Serial Number
UL	Unlock Converter
WR Gear Set	Wide-Ratio Planetary Gear Set

TROUBLESHOOTING CHARTS, DATA AND SPECIFICATIONS

Problem: Transmission Still in Vehicle	Possible Causes (in order of likelihood) (See Key Below)
Harsh engagement in 1, 2, D, and R	D, B, E, G, Q, N
Slow engagement in 1, 2, D, N, and R	A, C, D, E, M, G, R, Q, N
No upshift; stuck in 1	A, B, C, E, L, N, F, O, R
No low; moves in 2 or Direct	L, N
Abnormal or no kickdown/downshift	A, B, C, F, E, L, N, O, R
Delayed, erratic shifts (harsh or firm)	A, B, C, E, F, L, M, N, O, P
Early, soft upshifts	B, T
Slips in forward ranges	A, B, C, E, F, N, O, P, Q, R
Slips only in Reverse	A, C, E, G, N, P, R
Will not move in forward ranges or Reverse	A, C, E, M, N, R
Reverse is fine; will not move in forward ranges	C, E, N, R
No Reverse	C, E, G, P, R
Creeps or drives in N	C, N
Drags or locks up	E, F, G, I, N, O, P, Q
Growling, grating, or scraping noise	A, I, K, M, G
Knocking noise; changes when in Neutral/Park	U
Buzzing noise	A, L, N, R
Oil blows out of dipstick tube	A, J, M, N
Overheating	A, D, J, F, E, M, G, C
Engine will not crank in N and/or P	C, H, S, N
Sluggish acceleration; heavy throttle needed	A, S, B, T, E
Bearing noise that changes with vehicle speed	K
Starts in 1, skips 2, and shifts to direct	F
Slips in Reverse or manual 1	G
Rear seal leaks; ext. housing bushing worn out	U

Key to Possible Causes

A	Fluid Level and Condition. With engine warm, idling in Neutral, level should be slightly below full; engine hot, at full. Fluid should not be milky, full of bubbles, foamy, dark, or burnt smelling. Fluid should be Dexron or Type 7176 equivalent.
B	Throttle Pressure Linkage. Check for smooth travel, binding, and looseness. Linkage should follow movement of carburetor or throttle body pin. Any variation can affect shift feel and timing.
C	Gearshift Linkage. Shifter should hit Park at one extreme; low at other. Starter should spin in Neutral and Park only; adjust as needed. If linkage is sloppy, replace linkage bushings, pins, and washers. Movement of transmission shift lever and shifter attachment points should be equal.
D	Engine Idle Setting. Idle speed should be correct and throttle pressure linkage set accordingly. High idle can affect the light throttle, lift-foot shift.
E	Hydraulic Pressure. Hydraulic/line pressure should be close to factory specifications. Shift modifications can raise pressures. Line-pressure spring-adjusting plate should be roughly $1\frac{5}{16}$ inches from the valve body (with stock spring). Throttle pressure valve setting at the valve body should be around 3/16 inch between the end of the valve and lever.
F	Kickdown Band. Band should be at correct adjustment; rule of thumb is torque screw to 72 in-lbs or tighten with short wrench and back out two turns.
G	Low Reverse-Band. Band should be at correct adjustment; torque adjusting screw to 72 in-lbs or tighten with a short wrench and back out two turns. A-904 needs accurate adjustment for longevity.
H	Neutral Starting Switch. Starter should spin in Neutral or Park only. Check wires and connecter; test the switch center pin: in Neutral or Park, it should ground. If not, verify that the valve body "rooster comb" is tight. If all is okay, check the starting circuit.
I	Park Lock Mechanism. Shift linkage should be correctly adjusted and the condition of the locking rod/ball should be good.
J	Transmission Oil Cooler. Lines or hoses should not be pinched or bent too tightly. Heat exchanger in radiator should flow fluid freely and have no leaks.
K	Output Shaft Bearing, Bushing, or Seal. Bearing should roll smoothly.
L	Governor Valve. Governor weights, shaft, valves, and bores should have no burrs, nicks, scratches, or binding. Springs should be free of collapsed or distorted coils. Governor body can't have cracks and should be correctly torqued. Governor filter/screen must be open.
M	Oil Filter. Filter must be open and tight on valve body. Excess debris (more than 1 tablespoon in the pan) is cause for alarm. Minor amount on filter or in pan; replace the filter.

N	Valve Body. Valves and springs must not stick and must be assembled correctly; if not, disassemble and clean accordingly. Correct any binding, broken, or damaged parts and then lube, reassemble, and tighten screws correctly.
O	Kickdown Servo and Band Linkage. Servo piston and sealing rings must be crack-free and move easily. Springs should not be bent or damaged and internal O-ring of controlled load servo should not be cut. Band anchors must be tight and all must be correctly assembled. Servo apply lever pivot-pin pipe plug must be sealed.
P	Low-Reverse Servo and Linkage. Servo piston outer and inner diameter and rubber lip seal should be undamaged. Band anchors must be tight and servo apply lever pin O-ring shall be free of leakage.
Q	Accumulator. Piston, rings, and bore should be free of damage or scratches. Consider replacing a plastic accumulator piston.
R	Internal Leakage. Air pressure testing of servos or clutches should show no leakage; excessive air hissing may indicate an internal issue.
S	Engine Performance. Engine must run properly; compression and timing should be close to factory specifications.
T	Converter. Stall-speed values that are too low or high may identify converter issues but can also indicate engine performance problems.
U	Driveshaft Yoke. The driveshaft front yoke condition affects sealing and bushing wear; if rough, grooved, or rusty, the extension housing bushing and rear seal can be damaged.

Problem: Transmission Out of Vehicle	Possible Causes (in order of likelihood) (See Key Below)
Harsh engagement in 1, 2, D, and R	d, e, n
Slow engagement in 1, 2, D, N, and R	b, d, e, j
No upshift, stuck in 1	b, d, j
No low, moves in 2 or Direct	d
Abnormal or no kickdown/downshift	n
Delayed, erratic shifts (harsh or firm)	b, d, n
Slips in forward ranges	b, d, e, g, j, h
Slips only in Reverse	b, d, g, j
Slips in 1 (Drive) but not manual 1	h
Will not move (slips badly) in 1, 2, D and R	a, b, f, j
Reverse is fine, will not move in forward ranges	e, h, f
No Reverse	d, g, j, f
Creeps or drives in N	e, d
Drags or locks up	d, e, f, g, h, b
Growling or scraping noises	a, b, d, f, h, i
Knocking noise, changes when in Neutral/Park	a
Buzzing noise	b, i, h
Oil blows out of dipstick tube	b, c
Overheating	a, d, e
Engine will not crank in N or P positions	m
Sluggish acceleration, heavy throttle needed	e, i
Bearing noise that changes with vehicle speed	l
Hangs in 1, skips 2, and jumps to direct.	k
Slips in R or manual 1	b
Key to Possible Causes	
a	Converter Flex Plate. Plate should be flat and crack-free. Crankshaft and converter bolts must be tight. Cracked flex plate may indicate missing or loose block-alignment dowel pin.
b	Oil Pump. Pump must be free of internal damage (scratches, gouges, grooves, and general wear to gears and pump body). Check convertor hub/pump bushing and front seal: they must have no wear or damage. Clearances must be correct and pump body/reaction shaft support should be flat. Sealing rings/grooves must not be worn or broken.
c	Transmission Vent. Vent must not be blocked internally or externally.
d	Front Clutch Assembly. Clutch plate clearance should be in the proper range and friction discs/steel plates must be free of damage, wear, and hot spots. Retainer assembly and piston and check ball must not be damaged and return spring(s) must be intact and of proper quantity. Reaction shaft sealing rings and grooves should have no excessive wear.
e	Rear Clutch Assembly. Clutch plate clearance should be in the proper range and friction discs/steel plates must be free of damage, wear, and hot spots. Retainer assembly and piston/check ball must not be damaged. Belleville washer/spring must not be collapsed or cracked. Input shaft sealing rings and grooves should have no excessive wear.
f	Planetary Gear Set. Planetary assemblies must have no broken teeth, excessive clearance, excessive pinion gear end clearance, worn out bushings in the sun gear, or damaged thrust washers.
g	Low-Reverse Band. The low-reverse band must not be burnt, have debonded friction material, broken anchors, or uneven wear.
h	Overrunning Clutch Assembly. Inspect the clutch assembly; brinelled or damaged clutch rollers or cam, damaged springs or improperly assembled rollers and/or springs will cause issues. Spring tabs must be straight and not cracked.
i	Torque Converter. Damage or grooves in the hub can cause leaks. Fluid removed from the converter should not indicate foreign material, clutch material, metal particles, or have a nasty, burnt smell.
j	Sealing Rings. The sealing rings on the governor support, reaction shaft support, and input shaft should show no signs of excessive wear or breakage. The inner bore of front clutch retainer and output shaft support must be free of grooves, wear, cracks, and deep scratches. The bearing snap ring grooves must not be too wide.
k	Kickdown Band. Excessive clearance, anchor looseness, friction-lining wear or heat damage can cause/indicate possible slippage.

l	Output Shaft Support Bearing. The output shaft bearing should spin quietly and smoothly and have no binding or roughness.
m	Valve Body. The "roster comb" must not be broken loose from the main shaft.
n	Valve Body Modifications. Valve body changes (non-stock springs, valves, missing check balls, larger orifices, or others) can alter upshift/downshift timing and firmness. Unfortunately, many changes are difficult to undo and may require replacement of assembly.

Problem: With Lock-Up Transmission	Possible Causes (in order of likelihood) (See Key Below)
No lock-up	1, 2, 4, 5, 6, 7, 12, 15
Will not unlock	2, 4, 5, 6, 7
Stays locked up at too low a speed in D	2, 4, 5, 6, 7
Locks up or drags in 1 or 2	1, 4, 5, 7
Sluggish or stalls in Reverse	1, 3, 4, 5, 15
Loud chatter during lock-up engagement when cold	12
Vibration or shutter during lockup engagement	1, 4, 12, 14
Vibration after lock-up engagement	12, 13, 14, 16
Vibration when revved in neutral	12
Overheating: oil blows out of dipstick or pump	3, 5
Shudder after lock-up engagement	1, 3, 4, 12, 13, 14, 16

Key to Possible Causes

1	Oil Pump. Pump must be in good shape; disassemble and check for damage to gear rotors and/or pump body. Measure clearances. Check converter hub bushing for damage or wear. Check sealing ring grooves for wear and rings for cracks, breakage, or wear. Repair or replace as needed.
2	Governor. The weights, shaft, valves, and bores should have no burrs, nicks, scratches, or binding. Springs should be free of collapsed or distorted coils. Governor body should not have cracks and should be correctly torqued. Governor filter/screen must be open. Clean and/or replace as needed.
3	Oil Cooler or Fittings. Lines or hoses should not be pinched or bent too tightly. The heat exchanger in the radiator should flow fluid freely and have no leaks. Remove anything plugging the hoses or the cooler. Flush or replace the cooler, lines, and fittings as needed. Internal cooler leaks create a milky strawberry-color fluid and pumps fluid in the coolant.
4	Valve Body. Valves must move freely in the valve body. Remove, disassemble, and clean everything in the valve body. Look for anything binding, broken, or damaged. After verifying that everything is in good condition, reassemble it and be sure to torque all screws correctly. Replace as needed.
5	Switch Valve. Inspect switch valve for binding and correct anything causing it to stick. Clean, reassemble, and torque screws. Replace if it can't be fixed.
6	Lock-Up Valve. Inspect lock-up module for a stuck valve and free it and correct the issues causing it. Inspect the spring for damage and clean, reassemble, and torque the screws. Replace parts as needed.
7	Fail-Safe Valve. Look for a stuck fail-safe valve and free it; correct the issue that caused it. Clean, reassemble, and torque all screws. Replace as needed.
8	Lock-Up Solenoid.* Test the lock-up solenoid electrically, if good it may have a stuck valve. Replace as needed.
9	Solenoid Wiring.* Test the lock-up solenoid wiring for opens or shorts and verify the connector is good and plugged on. Replace as needed.
10	Lock-Up Solenoid.* Test it electrically; if shorted or open, replace it.
11	Lock-Up Relay.* Test it electrically; if shorted or open, replace it.
12	Torque Converter. Damage or grooves in the hub can cause leaks and must be corrected. Fluid from the converter should not have foreign material, clutch material, metal particles, or a nasty, burnt smell. The lock-up clutch friction disc may be burned or debonded and/or internal seals may create inadequate engagement. Balance weights may come loose; look for evidence of broken welds. Replace with a better or rebuilt unit as required.
13	Exhaust System. Exhaust system interference can act like transmission vibrations; inspect hangers for damage and interfering areas. Align and correct as needed. Weights on the exhaust system or transmission extension housing should be replaced as they help dampen vibrations caused by the lock-up converter.
14	Engine Performance. The engine must run properly; compression and timing should be close to factory specifications.
15	Input Shaft Rings and Grooves. Check the sealing rings for cracks, breakage, or wear and inspect the input shaft ring grooves for wear. Replace as needed.
16	Throttle Pressure Linkage. The linkage must be correct. Check for smooth travel, binding, and looseness. Linkage should follow the movement of the carburetor or the throttle body pin. Any changes can affect shift feel and timing and potentially cause early lock-up along with shudder.
* If equipped with an electronically controlled lock-up torque converter transmission.	

Tightening Specifications: A-904 and A-727, Typical			
Component	Torque	Component	Torque
Cooler Line Fitting	110 in-lbs	Oil Pump Housing to Transmission Case Bolt	175 in-lbs
Cooler Line Nut	85 in-lbs	Output Shaft Support Bolt	150 in-lbs
Converter Drive Plate to Crankshaft Bolt	55 ft-lbs	Overrunning Clutch Cam Set Screw	40 in-lbs
Converter Drive Plate to Torque Converter Bolt	270 in-lbs	Pressure Test Take Off Plug	75-110 in-lbs
Extension Housing to Transmission Case Bolt	24 ft-lbs	Reaction Shaft Support to Oil Pump Bolt	150-160 in-lbs
Extension Housing to Insulator Mounting Bolt	50 ft-lbs	Reverse Band Adjusting Screw Lock Nut	30-35 ft-lbs
Governor Body to Support Bolt	100 in-lbs	Speedometer Drive Clamp Screw	100 in-lbs
Kickdown Band Adjusting Screw Lock Nut	29-35 ft-lbs	Transmission to Engine Bolt	28 ft-lbs
Kickdown Lever Shaft Plug	150 in-lbs	Valve Body Screw	35 in-lbs
Neutral Starter Switch	24 ft-lbs	Valve Body to Transmission Case Bolt	100 in-lbs
Oil Pan Bolt	150 in-lbs		

Tightening Specifications: AMC A-904 Family, Typical

Component	Torque	Component	Torque
Cooler Line Fitting	160 in-lbs	Manual Linkage Control Lever Screw	95 in-lbs
Cooler Line Nut	150 in-lbs	Neutral Starting Switch	24 ft-lbs
Converter Drive Plate to Crankshaft Bolt (4-cyl.)	58 ft-lbs	Oil Pan Bolt	150 in-lbs
Converter Drive Plate to Crankshaft Bolt (6-cyl.)	105 ft-lbs	Oil Pump Housing to Transmission Case Bolt	175 in-lbs
Converter Drive Plate to Torque Converter Bolt (4-cyl.)	40 ft-lbs	Output Shaft Support Bolt	150 in-lbs
Converter Drive Plate to Torque Converter Bolt (6-cyl.)	26 ft-lbs	Overrunning Clutch Cam Set Screw	40 in-lbs
Convertor Housing to Engine Bolts	54 ft-lbs	Pressure Test Take Off Plug	110 in-lbs
Extension Housing to Transmission Case Bolt	24 ft-lbs	Reaction Shaft Support to Oil Pump Bolt	160 in-lbs
Extension Housing to Insulator Mounting Bolt	50 ft-lbs	Speedometer Adapter Clamp Screw	100 in-lbs
Governor Body to Support Bolt	100 in-lbs	Throttle Valve Control Lever Pinch Screw	40 in-lbs
Kickdown Band Adjusting Screw lock Nut	35 ft-lbs	Transmission to Engine Bolt	28 ft-lbs
Kickdown Lever Shaft Plug	150 in-lbs	Valve Body Screw	35 in-lbs
Low-Reverse Band Adjusting Screw Lock Nut	35 ft-lbs	Valve Body to Transmission Case Bolt	100 in-lbs

Thrust Washer Thickness

	A-904 Family (inch)	A-727 (inch)		A-904 Family (inch)	A-727 (inch)
Typical	#1 .061 to .063	#1 .061 to .063	Drive Shell (to Front Annulus)		#5 .060 to .062
	.061 to .063	.061 to .063	Front Carrier (to Drive Shell)	#6 .048 to .050	
	.084 to .086	.102 to .104	Sun Gear Drive Shell Thrust Plate	#7 .050 to .052 (225-318) .034 to .036 (360)	
Rear Clutch Retainer	#2 .061 to .063	#2 .061 to .063		#8 .050 to .052 (225-318) .034 to .036 (360)	
Output Shaft	#3 Selective	#3 .062 to .064			
	.052 to .054		Rear Carrier (to Drive Shell)	#9 .048 to .050	.059 to .062
	.083 to .085		Rear Carrier (to Annulus Thrust Plate)		.034 to .036
Front Annulus	#4 .121 to .125		Rear Carrier (to Annulus)	#10 .048 to .050	
Front Carrier (To Annulus)	#5 .048 to .050	#4 .059 to .062			

Pump Clearances

Pump Clearances	A-904 Family (inch)	A-727 (inch)
Outer Rotor-to-Case Bore	.004 to .008	.004 to .008
Outer-to-Inner Tip	.005 to .010	.005 to .010
End Clearance, Rotors	.001 to .003	.001 to .003
Gear Train Endplay	.001 to .047	.009 to .044
Input Shaft Endplay	.016 to .059	.036 to .084

Snap Rings

Snap Rings	A-904 Family (inch)	A-727 (inch)
Rear/Front Clutch (Selective)	.060 to .062	.060 to .062
	.068 to .070	.074 to .076
	.076 to .078	.088 to .090
		.106 to .108
Output Shaft (Forward End)	.040 to .044	.048 to .052
	.059 to .065	.062 to .066

Clutch Plate Clearance (Typical)

Clutch Plate Clearance (Typical)	A-904 Family (inch)	A-727 (inch)	Clutch Plate Clearance (Typical)	A-904 Family (inch)	A-727 (inch)
Front Retainer	3-Disc, .074 to .125	3-Disc, .070 to .129	Rear Retainer	3-Disc, .032 to .055	
	4-Disc, .067 to .134	4-Disc, .082 to .151		4-Disc, .032 to .055	4-Disc, .025 to .045
	5-Disc, .075 to .152	5-Disc, .022 to .079			

Clutch Assembly Details (Typical)

	A-904 Family (inch)	A-727 (inch)		A-904 Family (inch)	A-727 (inch)
Front Clutch Friction Discs	3 (170, 225 ci)	3 (225, 318 ci)	Rear Clutch Friction Discs	3 (170, 225 ci)	4 (all)
	4 (273, 318, 360 ci)	4 (340, 383, 440 ci)			4 (273, 318 ci)
	5 (360 ci)	5 (426, 440 ci w/6-barrel)			

TorqueFlite Speedometer Pinion Gear Chart: Required Teeth Listed below Axle Ratio

Axle Ratio (:1)	2.45	2.71	2.76	2.94	3.21	3.23	3.55	3.91	Axle Ratio (:1)	2.45	2.71	2.76	2.94	3.21	3.23	3.55	3.91
Tire Size									**Tire Size**								
B78 x 14	27	29	30	32	35	35	38	42	L78 x 15	23	25	25	27	29	29	32	35
C78 x 14	26	29	29	31	34	34	37	41	E70 x 14	26	28	29	31	34	34	37	41
D78 x 14	26	28	29	31	34	34	37	41	F70 x 14	26	28	28	30	33	33	36	39
E78 x 14	25	28	28	30	33	33	36	40	G70 x 14	26	27	28	30	32	32	36	38
F78 x 14	25	27	28	30	32	33	36	40	H70 x 15	24	26	27	28	31	31	34	37
G78 x l4	24	27	27	29	32	32	35	39	E60 x 15	25	28	29	30	33	33	36	40
H78 x 14	24	26	27	28	31	31	34	37	F60 x 15	25	28	28	30	33	36	36	39
F78 x 15	24	27	27	29	31	32	35	39	G60 x 15	24	27	28	29	32	32	35	38
G78 x 15	23	26	27	28	31	31	34	37	6.95 x 14	26	28	29	31	34	34	37	41
H78 x 15	23	26	26	28	30	30	33	36	7.35 x 14	25	27	28	30	33	33	36	39
J78 x 15	23	25	26	27	30	30	33	33									

A-727 Front Clutch Disc/Spring Detail (Typical, 1969)

Engine Size (ci)	Friction Discs	Piston Return Springs	Engine Size (ci)	Friction Discs	Piston Return Springs
225	3	12	383 HP	4	6
318	3	12	440	4	6
340	4	6	440 HP	4	10
383	4	8	426	5	12

A-727 Front Clutch Disc/Spring Detail (Typical, 1974)

Engine Size (ci)	Friction Discs	Piston Return Springs	Engine Size (ci)	Friction Discs	Piston Return Springs
225	3	13	392 IH	4	9
258/304 360 HD AMC	3	9	400	4	9
360-401 HD AMC	4	9	400 HP	4	9
318	3	9	400 IH	4	9
318-360 Truck	4	9	413-440 Truck	4	9
360 HP	3	9			

A-727 Front Clutch Disc/Spring Detail (Typical, 1979)

Engine Size (ci)	Friction Discs	Piston Return Springs	Engine Size (ci)	Friction Discs	Piston Return Springs
225	3	13	318-360 4WD Truck	4	9
318-360 Std.	3	11	440 Truck	4	9
360 HP LU	3	11	Diesel	3	13
360 HP non-LU	3	9	AMG Truck	4	9
318-360 Truck	4	9			

Band Adjustments

Band Adjustments (Typical 1969)

A-904 Engines	Turns from 72 in-lbs	A-727 Engines	Turns from 72 in-lbs
Kickdown			
All except 170	2	All except 426	2
170	2⅝	426	1½
Low-Reverse			
All except 318	3¼	All	2
318	4		

Band Adjustments (Typical 1979)

A-904 Engines	Turns from 72 in-lbs	A-727 Engines	Turns from 72 in-lbs
Kickdown			
All	2	All except 440-4	2½
	Turns from 41 in-lbs	**Engines**	
		440-4	2
Low-Reverse	225	3¼	
Engines	Turns from 72 in-lbs	**Engines**	
All except 225	4	All	2

Torque Converter, Typical									
Engine ci	Year	Transmission	Diameter (Inches)	Stall (RPM)	Engine ci	Year	Transmission	Diameter (Inches)	Stall (RPM)
AMC 153	1981	A-904	9½	2,050–2,350	318	1974	A-727	11¾	1,725–2,025
AMC 258	1981	A-904	10¾	1,850–2,150	360-4 HP	1974	A-727	10¾	2,200–2,500
225	1978	A-904	10¾	1,800–2,100	360-2 and 360-4	1974	A-727	10¾	2,300–2,600
318 Cal Hi Alt.	1978	A-904	10¾	2,125–2,425	400-2 and 400-4	1974	A-727	11¾	1,875–2,175
318 Fed.	1978	A-904	10¾	1,700–2,000	400-4 HP	1974	A-727	10¾	2,400–2,700
225 HD	1978	A-904	10¾	1,800–2,100	440-4	1974	A-727	11¾	1,975–2,275
318 Cal Hi Alt.	1978	A-727	10¾	2,125–2,425	440-4 HP	1974	A-727	10¾	2,600–2,900
318 Fed.	1978	A-727	10¾	1,700–2,000	440-4 HP	1974	A-727	11¾	2,100–2,400
360-4 HD	1978	A-727	10¾	2,150–2,450	170	1969	A-904	10¾	1,500–1,700
360-2	1978	A-904	10¾	1,775–2,075	225	1969	A-904	10¾	1,800–2,000
360-2	1978	A-727	10¾	1,775–2,075	225	1969	A-727	10¾	1,450–1,650
360-4 Cal Hi Alt.		A-904	10¾	2,150–2,450	273	1969	A-904	10¾	1,950–2,150
400-4	1978	A-727	10¾	1,850–2,150	318	1969	A-904	10¾	2,100–2,320
400-4 HD	1978	A-727	10¾	2,300–2,600	318	1969	A-727	10¾	1,750–1,950
440-4	1978	A-727	10¾	1,950–2,250	340-4 HP	1969	A-727	10¾	2,250–2,450
440-4 HP	1978	A-727	10¾	2,500–2,800	383-2	1969	A-727	11¾	1,850–2,100
198	1974	A-904	10¾	1,625–1,925	383-4 HP	1969	A-727	10¾	2,350–2,650
225	1974	A-904	10¾	1,800–2,100	440-4 HP	1969	A-727	11¾	2,000–2,300
318	1974	A-904	10¾	2,125–2,425	426-2-4 HP	1969	A-727	10¾	2,650–2,850
225	1974	A-727	11¾	1,400–1,700					

PERFORMANCE MODIFICATIONS AND SUGGESTIONS

There are unlimited ways to modify TorqueFlites. Below are suggestions for performance and strong street builds from professional transmission mechanics, renowned experts, company owners, enthusiasts, and others who simply love TorqueFlites. Their input is listed alphabetically.

Rick Allison, A-727		
Accumulator: Stock, aluminum only		
Bushings: Standard; babbit for pump		
End Play (Input Shaft and Drum) with transmission standing on output shaft: .010 to .015 inch		
Geartrain Endplay: .010 to .020 inch		
Filter: Name brand Dacron		

Friction Disc
   Street/Restoration: BorgWarner or Raybestos; smooth rear; parallel or waffle grooves front
   Race: Red Eagle. Smooth rear; parallel groove front		

Front Clutch Clearance: .060 to .075 inch, four or five discs, with 12 return springs		
Kickdown Servo Lever Ratio: 3.8 or 4.2, ideal		

Kickdown Band
   Style:
     Name-brand Flex; cast if available
	Lining:
	   Street; BorgWarner or Raybestos
	   Race: Red Eagle, Raybestos Pro-Series High Energy or A&A wide with Alabama Red	

Overrunning Clutch: Stock; bolt-in if higher power potential		
Low-Reverse Band: Stock, or better material as applications require		
Pan: Steel, deep with extension if higher power potential		
Planetary: Three, four, or five pinion; application dependent		
Rear Clutch Clearance: .030 to .035 inch		

Servo Modification
   Front: Non-controlled load and a lot of spring tension to quicken band release
   Rear: Billet with extra spring tension and reinforced retainer		

Shift Modification Kit: A&A modifications to valve body		
Special Components Reinforced Band apply strut	Blast and prep case	Reconditioned pump
Steel Plate Type: Stock; Kolene processed if using Red Eagle or Blue Plate discs		
Thrust Washers: Quality stock replacements		
Valve Body: A&A designed and built		

Rick Allison, A-904 Family

Accumulator: Stock, aluminum only

Bushings: Standard; babbit for pump

End Play (Input Shaft and Drum) with transmission standing on output shaft: .010 to .015 inch

Geartrain End Play: .010 to .020 inch

Filter: Name brand Dacron

Friction Disc
Street/Restoration: BorgWarner or Raybestos; smooth rear; parallel or waffle grooves front
Race: Red Eagle; smooth rear; parallel groove front

Front Clutch Clearance: .060 to .075 inch with a lot of return spring tension

Kickdown Servo Lever Ratio: 3.8, 4.2, and 5.0 per application/servo piston size

Kickdown Band

Style:	*Lining:*
Name brand Flex; cast if available	*Street:* BorgWarner or Raybestos
	Race: Red Eagle, Raybestos Pro-Series or A&A with Alabama Red, or Kevlar

Overrunning Clutch: Stock; bolt-in if higher power potential

Low-Reverse Band: Stock, heavy duty, or Kevlar

Pan: Steel, deep with extension if higher power potential

Planetary: Three or four pinion

Rear Clutch Clearance: .030 to .035 inch

Servo Modification

Front: Non-controlled load with a lot of spring tension	*Rear:* Billet

Shift Modification Kit: A&A modifications to valve body

Special Components

Reinforced Band apply strut	Blast and prep case	Reconditioned pump

Steel Plate Type: Stock; Kolene-processed if using Red Eagle or Blue Plate discs

Thrust Washers: Quality stock replacements

Valve Body: A&A designed and built

Rodney Byrd, A-727

Accumulator: Stock

Bushings: Stock

Overall End Play: Factory spec

Geartrain End Play: Factory spec

Filter: Quality Dacron

Friction Disc

Street: BorgWarner, smooth in rear, parallel grooves in front	*Race:* Red Eagle or Raybestos Blue plates

Front Clutch Clearance: .090 to .100 inch with flat snap ring

Kickdown Servo Lever Ratio: 4.2 but will use 3.8 and 5.0 for special applications

Kickdown Band

Style:	*Lining:*
Rigid	*Street:* Kevlar
	Race: Red Eagle or equivalent (especially with aluminum retainer)

Overrunning Clutch: Stock

Low-Reverse Band: Stock

Pan: Stock

Planetary: Stock

Rear Clutch Clearance: Factory Spec

Servo Modification

Front: Stock	*Rear:* Stock

Shift Modification Kit: TransGo TF-2 or TF-3		
Special Components (use as needed)		
Aluminum billet drums	Roller bearing equipped planetaries	A&A Custom Governors
Steel Plate Type: Stock		
Thrust Washers: Stock		
Valve Body: A&A or Griner for specialized (transbrake/reverse pattern/clean neutral, etc.)		

Rodney Byrd, A-904 Family

Accumulator: Stock aluminum

Bushings: Quality stock replacements

Overall Endplay: .030 inch or less, front endplay of .020 to .025 inch

Geartrain Endplay: .008 inch

Filter: Quality Dacron

Friction Disc
- *Street:* Red Racing or Raybestos Blue plates
- *Race:* Same

Front Clutch Clearance: .012 to .015 inch per friction disc; multi return spring kit, front retainer

Kickdown Servo Lever Ratio: 4.2

Kickdown Band

Style:	*Lining:*
Cast if available	*Street:* Red Racing
	Race: Kevlar

Overrunning Clutch: Stock (to 450 hp); quality aftermarket (above 450 hp)

Low-Reverse Band: Double wrap red racing lined

Pan: Deep with extension

Planetary: Aluminum three-pinion (under 300 hp), steel (above 300 hp)

Rear Clutch Clearance: .030 to .040 inch

Servo Modification
- *Front:* Street, both inner and outer springs
- *Rear:* Aftermarket billet unit

Shift Modification Kit: TransGo TF-1; mild or HD applications; TF-2 for street/strip applications

Special Components: none

Steel Plate Type: Red Racing or Raybestos Blue plates

Thrust Washers: Quality stock replacement

Valve Body: Stock with shift kit, if valves not scored and selector shaft isn't worn. For street, no manual VB unless low band apply

Tom Hand, A-727

Accumulator: Stock, aluminum only

Bushings: Standard; babbit for pump unless OEM converter then bronze

Overall End Play: .035 inch or slightly less with pre-greased parts

Geartrain End Play: .010 to .020 inch

Filter: Name brand Dacron

Friction Disc
- *Street:* BorgWarner or Raybestos; smooth rear; parallel or waffle grooves front
- *Race:* Red Eagle. Smooth rear; parallel groove front

Front Clutch Clearance: .015 inch per friction disc; .022 inch per disc w/TransGo TF-2 kit, flat snap ring

Kickdown Servo Lever Ratio: 3.8

Kickdown Band

Style:	*Lining:*
Name brand Flex; Cast if available	*Street:* BorgWarner or Raybestos
	Race: Red Eagle or Raybestos Pro-Series High Energy or A&A wide with Alabama Red

Overrunning Clutch: Stock; bolt-in if higher power potential
Low-Reverse Band: Stock
Pan: Stock; Deep Steel with extension if higher power potential
Planetary: Four pinion; special bearings or different ratio if required
Rear Clutch Clearance: .030 to .035 inch
Servo Modification
Front: Non-controlled load with special spring if required by shift kit, controlled load if stock
Rear: Stock with disabled inner spring if using TF-2
Shift Modification Kit: Transgo SK TFSC; Superior KTF-SC for mild application; Transgo TF-2: for performance
Special Components (use as needed)
Ultimate Sprag from A&A or similar | Cheetah or A&A Valve body if customer desired
Steel Plate Type: Stock; Kolene processed if using Red Eagle or Blue Plate discs
Thrust Washers: Quality stock replacements
Valve Body: Stock with shift kit

Tom Hand, A-904 Family

Accumulator: Stock, aluminum only
Bushings: Standard; babbit for pump unless OEM converter then bronze
Overall End Play: .025 inch or slightly less with pre-greased parts
Geartrain End Play: .010 to .020 inch
Filter: Name brand Dacron
Friction Disc
Street: BorgWarner or Raybestos; smooth rear; parallel or waffle grooves front | *Race:* Red Eagle. Smooth rear; parallel groove front
Front Clutch Clearance: Stock .015 inch -.020 inch per friction disc; .022 inch per disc with Transgo TF-2 kit
Kickdown Servo Lever Ratio: 3.8 or 4.2
Kickdown Band
Style: Name brand Flex; Cast if available, wide cast for five-friction retainer | *Lining:*   *Street:* BorgWarner or Raybestos   *Race:* Red Eagle, "Wide" A&A Alabama Red Cast for five-friction disc retainer
Overrunning Clutch: Stock; replacement bolt-in if higher power potential
Low-Reverse Band: Stock
Pan: Stock; or Deep Steel with extension if higher power potential
Planetary: Four pinion; wide ratio for higher performance
Rear Clutch Clearance: .030 to .035 inch
Servo Modification
Front: Stock | *Rear:* Stock with disabled inner spring if using TF-2
Shift Modification Kit: TransGo SK TFSC; Superior KTF-SC for mild application; TransGo TF-2: higher performance
Special Components (use as needed)
Heavy-duty bolt-in sprag from A&A or similar
Steel Plate Type: Stock; Kolene if using Red Eagle or Blue Plate discs
Thrust Washers: Quality stock replacements
Valve Body: Stock with shift kit

Lon Kopaska, A-727 Master Rebuild Kit Suggestions

Stock Or Performance Street: 22008 (1962-1970), 22008C (1971-up)
Includes gasket set, sealing rings, metal clad seals, OEM style frictions, steel plates, Dacron style filter, OEM flex style KD band, normal wear bushings and thrust washers, low-roller clutch kit, and forward diaphragm spring.

Race: 22008CFHD (1971-up)
Includes gasket set, sealing rings, metal clad seals, Raybestos high-performance racing frictions, Kolene steel plates, metal screen-type filter, performance-lined flex type KD band, normal wear bushings and thrust washers, low-roller clutch kit and diaphragm-type forward clutch spring.

Normal updated parts for durability or racing

Super servo, S22905H	Reverse band servo piston, S22912	Rear band as needed for specific application
Hardened band strut, S22916-2	Outer roller clutch race (bolt-in type), 22665K	Four pinion planetaries, optional
Band anchor wedge, S22915-3	Billet accumulator piston, S22927	

Lon Kopaska, A-904 Master Rebuild Kit Suggestions

Stock Or Performance Street: 12008A (1960-1971), 12008C (1972-1998), 12008G (1999-2004)
Includes gasket set, metal clad seals, OEM style frictions, steel plates, Dacron filter, OEM style flex KD band, normal wear bushings and thrust washers, low roller clutch kit, forward diaphragm spring.

Race: 12008CFHD (1972- 1998)
Includes gasket set, metal clad seals, Raybestos high-performance frictions, Kolene steel plates, screen-type filter, high-performance lined flex-type KD band, normal-wear bushings and thrust washers, low-roller clutch kit, and forward clutch diaphragm spring.

Normal update parts for durability or racing:

Reverse servo piston, S12912	Hardened band strut, S22916-2

A wide-ratio planetary gear set (found in late style A-904, A500, 44re to 46re units) is available. It provides a gear ratio modification from a stock 2.45 low and 1.45 intermediate to a 2.74 low and 1.54 intermediate. Enables the use of taller rear gears without sacrificing low-end torque.

Lon Kopaska, Basic Rebuild Suggestions: A-904 and A-727

Adjust end clearance

Output shaft: .005 to .048 inch (different thickness snap ring for output shaft)	*Front section:* .022 to .091 inch (different thrust washers)

Adjust clutch clearance

Front clutch assembly (high and reverse): .010 inch per friction plate

    Street; use wave snap ring as is | Race; use flat snap ring (replace waved ring)

Rear clutch assembly with shaft (all forward gears): .010 inch per disc

Thin and oversize steels are available: A-727: .070 and .085 inch, A-904: .068 and .088 inch

Band

A-727 bands; torque both to 72 in-lbs, KD out 2.5 turns, L-R out 2 turns

A-904 bands; torque both to 72 in-lbs, KD out 2 turns, L-R out (dependent on band style): single wrap-out 2 turns, double wrap-out 4 turns

(My preferred method is to set band to 1/4 inch arm travel at servo while pan is off)

Throttle pressure linkage adjustment is critical; do a basic adjustment with case lever all the way back at full throttle position

Fluid: Mopar ATF+4 in all Chrysler units

Valve Body

Valve bodies are one of the biggest topics in performance units; full race bodies and full manual bodies are the most common among racers. Some use reverse pattern shifts (PRN123), some don't apply the low & reverse band in manual low; this can lead to serious explosions if not doing burn outs in second gear.

Superior offers a kit, S22165, preferred for street vehicles; it provides converter fill (and level checking) in park and addresses most of the common issues in TorqueFlite units, from six cylinder to diesel-equipped trucks and it doesn't require modification of valve body castings!

TransGo has well known kits: TF1, TF2, TF3 and each has its own place and type of use

TF1, 22169: Street and HD towing

TF2, 22171: Street and Strip (allows for low gear at any speed)

TF3, 22173: Full Race and manual shift only options (strip use only)

Aftermarket valve bodies are available with manual shift, reverse pattern manual shift, and reverse pattern manual shift with transbrake. They can be expensive but can be a benefit for consistent drag strip elapsed times.

Torque Convertors

By far the biggest topic in performance; most manufactures build good quality products from stock to full-out race versions. Stock convertors are great for normal street driving but just can't allow modified engines to perform at maximum potential. This is the main benefit of an "altered stall" convertor.

"Street stall" convertors are a normally stocked option by most companies and offer advertised stall speeds from 2,500 to 2,800 rpm (for most street use) and are a great option for budget builders and mild street engines.

Any performance build-up requiring a higher stall speed converter should use a custom-ordered converter for specific applications. Only the convertor builders can set the correct stall speed for your vehicle. They will need engine details (including camshaft specs), rear gear ratio, weight of vehicle and what type of use the vehicle is planned for. This is by far the biggest performance option; plan on spending money to get it right the first time!

It is my experience that any performance build requiring a stall speed in excess of 2,800 rpm that will be used on the street must have secondary fluid cooling capacity installed or the excessive heat created by the converter will be the death of the transmission. Install the largest cooler that will fit.

* Most of the referenced part numbers come from Transtar Industries.

Tracy Lambeth, A-727

Accumulator: Stock aluminum

Bushings: Standard and babbit for pump

Overall End Play: .030 inch or less, front end play of .020 to .025 inch

Geartrain End Play: .008 inch

Filter: Quality Dacron; brass screen if raced and serviced

Friction Disc

Street: BorgWarner (stock to 500 hp) Smooth rear; angle-cut grooves front	***Race:*** Red Eagle or Raybestos Blue plates. Smooth rear and front

Front Clutch Clearance: .012 to .015 inch per friction disc; max of .020 inch per disc

Kickdown Servo Lever Ratio: 4.2 unless using aftermarket valve body that requires something different

Kickdown Band

Style:	*Lining:*
Cast if available	***Street:*** BorgWarner or Red Eagle, depends on power level
	Race: Kevlar

Overrunning Clutch: Bolt-in

Low-Reverse Band: BorgWarner (stock to 500 hp). Red Eagle or equivalent (above 500 hp)

Pan: Deep Steel with extension

Planetary: Three pinion (stock to 400 hp) or four pinion (above 400 hp)

Rear Clutch Clearance: .030 to .040 inch

Servo Modification

Front: Non-controlled load, 2 springs. Strictly Race: billet aluminum

Rear: Billet aluminum most; if low HP (stock), use stock piston with disabled inner spring

Shift Modification Kit: TransGo TF-1: mild application; Transgo TF-2: street/high performance

Special Components (use as needed)

Steel or aluminum billet front retainer	Kolene steel plates	Quality valve body like A&A Racing or Cope Racing Transmissions
Billet front and rear servos	Reinforced front band strut	
Rigid front band	Bolt-in Ultimate Sprag from A&A	

Steel Plate Type: Stock to 550 hp, Kolene steel (above 550 hp)

Thrust Washers: Quality stock replacements

Valve Body: Stock with shift kit, if valves not scored and selector shaft isn't worn
For street, no manual VB unless low band apply

Tracy Lambeth, A-904 Family		
Accumulator: Stock aluminum		
Bushings: Quality stock replacements		
Overall End Play: .030 inch or less, Front end play of .020 to .025 inch		
Geartrain End Play: .008 inch		
Filter: Quality Dacron		
Friction Disc		
Street: Red Racing or Raybestos Blue plates		*Race:* Same
Front Clutch Clearance: .012 to .015 inch per friction disc; multi return spring kit, front retainer		
Kickdown Servo Lever Ratio: 4.2		
Kickdown Band		
Style:	*Lining:*	
Cast if available	*Street:* Red Racing	
	Race: Kevlar	
Overrunning Clutch: Stock (to 450 hp). Quality aftermarket (above 450 hp)		
Low-Reverse Band: Double wrap red racing lined		
Pan: Deep with extension		
Planetary: Steel or aluminum three pinion (under 300 hp), steel four pinion (above 300 hp)		
Rear Clutch Clearance: .030 to .040 inch		
Servo Modification		
Front: Street, both inner and outer springs		*Rear:* Aftermarket billet unit
Shift Modification Kit: TransGo TF-1; mild or HD applications; TF-2 for street/strip applications		
Special Components: none		
Steel Plate Type: Stock; Kolene treated as needed		
Thrust Washers: Quality stock replacement		
Valve Body: Stock with shift kit, if valves not scored and selector shaft isn't worn; for street, no manual VB unless low-band apply		

A&A Transmissions
5061 E. N. County Line Rd.
Camby, IN 46113
317-831-3066
aandatrans.com

A&Reds Transmission Parts
3737 W. 29th St. S.
Wichita, KS 67217
1-800-835-1007
areds.com

Alabama Bands
202 Industrial Dr.
Muscle Shoals, AL 35661
800-805-8126
transmissionbands.com

Alto Products
One Alto Way
Atmore, AL 36502
251-368-7777
altousa.com

Automotive Specialty Tools
4883 Witteville Dr.
Poteau, OK 74953
1-866-251-4267
etoolcart.com

B&M Racing & Performance Inc.
100 Stony Point Rd., Ste. 125
Santa Rosa, CA 95401
1-707-544-4761
bmracing.com

BorgWarner
1350 N. Greenbriar Dr., Ste. B
Addison, IL 60101
630-261-9980
ts.aftermarket.borgwarner.com/en/
    products/frictionProducts.aspx

Bouchillon Performance Engineering
937 Commerce Cir.
Hanahan, SC 29410
843-744-6559
bouchillonperformance.com

Cope Racing Transmissions
16768 Wickler Ave.
Lowell, IN 46356
219-374-0100
coperacingtransmissions.com

Dynamic Manufacturing
1930 N. Mannheim Rd.
Melrose Park, IL 60160
708-343-8753
dynamicmanufacturinginc.com

Lokar Performance Products
2545 Quality Ln.
Knoxville, TN 37931
1-877-469-7440
lokar.com

Mancini Racing Enterprises
33524 Kelly Rd.
Clinton Township, MI 48035
1-800-843-2821
manciniracing.com

Pat Blais Transmissions and Parts
P.O. Box 1636
Marysville, WA 98270
206-365-1966
tflitepatty@comcast.net

Raybestos Powertrain
711 Tech Dr.
Crawfordsville, IN 47933
800-729-7763
raybestospowertrain.com

SMR Transmissions and Converters
3030 Concession 8
Bradford, ON Canada L3Z 2A5
888-846-6603
905-775-3801
smrtrans.tripod.com

Sonnax Industries
1 Automatic Dr.
Bellows Falls, VT 05101
800-843-2600
sonnax.com

Superior Transmission Parts
3770 Hartsfield Rd.
Tallahassee, FL 32303
850-575-7155
superiortransmission.com

TCI Automotive
151 Industrial Dr.
Ashland, MS 38603
888-776-9824
tciauto.com

TCS Products
6217 205th St.
Langley, BC, Canada V2Y 1N7
800-960-1177
tcsproducts.com

ToolTopia
125 Freestate Blvd.
Shreveport, LA 71107
800-794-6793
tooltopia.com

TransGo
2621 Merced Ave.
El Monte, CA 91733
626-443-7451
transgo.com

Transtar Industries
7350 Young Dr.
Walton Hills, OH 44146
855-TRANSTAR
transtar1.com

Trans Tool
110 Connelly St.
San Antonio, TX 78203
800-531-5978
atec-trans-tool.com

Turbo Action
1535 Owens Rd.
Jacksonville, FL 32218
904-741-4850
turboaction.com